# PICTURE
# COOK
# BOOK

# PICTURE
# COOK
# BOOK

TIME INCORPORATED • NEW YORK • 1958

TIME INCORPORATED

*Editor-in-Chief*
HENRY R. LUCE

*President*
ROY E. LARSEN

———————————

EDWARD K. THOMPSON, *Managing Editor*
GEORGE P. HUNT, *Assistant Managing Editor*
JOSEPH KASTNER, *Copy Editor*
MARIAN A. MacPHAIL, *Chief of Research*

———————————

"Picture Cook Book" was produced by
the following editorial staff:

*Editor*
MARY HAMMAN

*Art Director*
CHARLES TUDOR
ALBERT KETCHUM, ROBERT YOUNG, *Assistants*

*Copy Editor*
JOHN THORNE

*Head Researcher*
GERRY GRUEN

*Photographs and Illustrations by*
ELIOT ELISOFON, BEN ROSE, TOM YEE, EDGAR DE EVIA,
LESLIE GILL, BRADLEY SMITH, FRED LYON, HANS VAN NES,
ADOLPH E. BROTMAN, RUDOLF FREUND, RENY MARTIN, ANTONIO PETRUCCELLI
(Other photographers and illustrators whose work appears
in this book are named on page 285.)

*Editorial Associates*
ELEANOR PARISH, SARA WELLES, MARGERY BYERS,
JEANNE DEMPSEY, CLARA NICOLAI, LUCY THOMAS

*Copy Readers*
HELEN DEUELL, *Chief*
VIRGINIA SADLER, EDWARD PUCCIA

———————————

*Publisher*
ANDREW HEISKELL

*General Manager*
ROBERT T. ELSON

*Book Manager*
ROBERT L. BLACKMORE

The picture stories that make up most of this book appeared
in LIFE from 1951 to 1958. Working closely on them, with
the above staff, were: Ray Mackland, LIFE Picture Editor;
Irene Saint and Thomas Carmichael, Domestic Newsbureau
Chiefs; George Caturani, Foreign Newsbureau Chief; and the
domestic and foreign correspondents of LIFE.

# TABLE
# OF CONTENTS

# TRADITIONAL DISHES

THE RECIPES FOR ALL DISHES SHOWN
IN THIS SECTION ARE ON PAGES 33-42

# REGIONAL FAVORITES

STRAIGHTFORWARD and plain though they are to the ear, the names of America's oldest traditional dishes still have a romantic ring. Baked beans, fried chicken and crab gumbo conjure up ghosts of Yankee whalers, southern planters, elegant Creoles. Pumpkin pie, chili con carne and salmon steak bring to mind New England Pilgrim harvests, the Southwest's arid plains, the Northwest's tumbling rivers. These dishes and others like them came from a time when the land was tough and the fare was hearty, and their names are so traditional that their places of origin are easy to spot. Though some were invented, and others imported, all were adopted with enthusiasm by the nation. Regional in their beginnings, they are now almost universal in scope. They span the nation's history, and represent America's contribution to the world's cuisine.

Perhaps the oldest and best-known truly American food is corn. This native grain is shown on the opposite page in some of its various forms. Most corn-lovers consider it best when plucked fresh from the field, boiled briefly and served on the cob with butter.

Sir Walter Raleigh's men first tried corn as served up to them by the Indians— they described it as "fair and well-tasted." They undoubtedly ate it roasted in a campfire's ashes or ground between stones and served in cakes like our johnnycakes. Today the coarse meal is still used for corn bread. But the meal, ground fine, is dressed up into fancy cocktail snacks and the grain itself is used for everything from oil and sweet syrup to bourbon whisky.

Most of the regional dishes were conceived by solid common sense. Boston baked beans were a handy Puritan dish because they could be cooked on Saturday and served on Sunday when the Puritan rules forbade work. Philadelphia scrapple was the thrifty Pennsylvania Dutchman's way of using up pig's head and scraps. Farm-style beef stew is a product of the cattle-rich Western plains. These and other regional favorites are shown on the next three pages.

A collection of corn shows variety of its uses. On chest is corn on the cob, a jar of cornstarch, corn snacks. In drawer at top left is caramel corn. Next row from left: corn Fritos, popping corn, Corn Flakes. Bottom drawers hold yellow and white corn meal. On the floor, in back row: spoon bread, corn relish, corn syrup in pitcher. In front row are corn bread, Indian pudding, corn oysters and johnnycakes.

A cigar store Indian, a proud American eagle and three iron stoves make a setting for the 10 American dishes shown at right. Made from time-honored recipes and beginning on back of left stove are beans as Boston housewives cooked them and fried chicken as the South likes it fixed. In foreground at left is the Southwest's chili con carne and beside it Philadelphia scrapple. On right stove tureen holds Creole crab gumbo. Farm-style beef stew simmers in the copper pot and in copper skillet is turkey hash. Sautéed salmon from the Northwest is in left foreground. In center is New England cod chowder and at right is pumpkin pie.

# MAN'S JOB: STEAK

WHENEVER the menu calls for a delicate dish or a fancy pie, most men are more than happy to let their wives take care of the cooking. When it's a matter of steak, this tolerant attitude is replaced by an unassailable belief in masculine know-how. Steak is a man's job.

But steak chefs are a divided clan, full of stubborn preferences. They disagree as to the perfect cut—whether porterhouse, sirloin or filet. They argue about how to cook it. Some, like Quincy Jones, shown on the opposite page, char the steak first, then grill it slowly. Others do it just the other way around. Some connoisseurs go in for spreads and sauces. Others insist on nothing but salt on their steaks. And among the purists, the relative merits of charcoal and wood fires can stir up a storm like the one that brews in Kentucky when the discussion turns to crushing or bruising the mint in a julep.

In the wood-burning faction, many like to use hickory or fruitwoods to give a special taste to the steak. The perfect wood fire should be built just big enough to burn down to a four-inch bed of coals which, when spread evenly, is slightly larger than the steak itself. The fire is ready when the coals are glowing and have a light film of white ash. For the charcoal faction, the small, uniform, top quality briquets will give the best performance. Two dozen should be enough for a medium-size grill. Broiling with charcoal takes less time and fewer briquets than used by most amateur chefs.

The time it takes to cook a steak over an open fire depends not only on the thickness of the steak, but also on four highly variable conditions: the temperature of the steak, how hot the fire is, the temperature of the air and the strength of the drafts or breezes. As a rule of thumb, if a 1½-inch steak is at room temperature and placed about 6 inches from a good bed of coals, it should be rare after 5 minutes on each side, medium rare at 6 minutes, and well done at 10 minutes per side. The surest method is to test the steak just before the allotted time by making a small cut near the center and judging by color. But meat continues to cook for a while after removal from the fire, and the stickler for an exact degree of rareness should stop when the color is still a bit too red.

An outdoor charcoal grill is mounted in the living room of Architect Quincy Jones's Los Angeles home. Here Jones broils individual porterhouse steaks, charring them first, then grilling them slowly.

Individual porterhouse steaks should look like these—not too thick, bright red, fine-grained, firm, marbled with fat. Jones, who sides with the sauce-lovers, will serve these with Western Herb Sauce.

Japanese hibachi charcoal-grills club steaks

# STEAKS CUT THICK, COOKED JUICY

Two things on which all steak chefs agree are that steak for open fire cooking must be cut thick and be of top quality. In the photograph at right five different steaks are spread on grills ready for cooking. A sixth soaks in marinade.

At top left are six 2-inch club steaks, each big enough for two. At top center is softest and most expensive cut of steak, a whole filet, with mushrooms at rim of grill. Behind it are carving board, carving set, red wines. On round center grill is a giant 4-inch porterhouse for eight, less tender than filet. To its right are four 2-inch rib steaks for eight people. This cut tastes something like roast beef, is cheapest per pound. In foreground at right are four 1½-inch T-bones for four.

Marinating in the glass baking dish is a 2-inch sirloin, U.S. open fire favorite. In glass beaker (*center*) is steak sauce. Three bowls hold butter spreads: Roquefort in black bowl, Tabasco in wood, mustard in glass. Jars and bottles hold marinade ingredients, copper pan at bottom right holds melted butter.

How thoroughly steak should be cooked is a matter of taste. Here four steaks are cooked (*top to bottom*) rare, medium rare, medium, well done.

# SEA FOOD

IN the time of Louis XIV there was a chef named Vatel who, when
the *filet de sole* for His Majesty's dinner failed to arrive, fell
on his sword and killed himself. A more famous chef, Escoffier, when asked
200 years later what he would have done in Vatel's place, said
he would not have killed himself. He would have fixed some chicken
up with a sauce so it tasted like fish. To the American housewife, both
French chefs seem like extremists. She usually will not bother
with fish, even if she can get it in time for dinner.
She would rather serve chicken or anything else. This is
culinary ignorance and bad economy.

For people living in a country all but surrounded by water,
Americans are skimpy fish and sea food eaters. The average consumption
is less than 11 pounds per person per year as against more than 150 pounds
of meat. The American housewife is often prejudiced against sea food.
She objects to it because of its bones, or odor, or because
she does not like to handle it or does not know how to cook it.

Actually, these objections make little sense. Women are no longer
obligated to clean or bone fish, or shuck oysters; most markets
will do it for them. And fish that is boiled, baked or broiled
does not smell. Fish fried in hot grease can give off an unpleasant
odor, but so do many fried foods.

Almost all sea food may be cooked in a number of ways—boiled or steamed,
sautéed or deep-fat fried, broiled or baked or used to make a loaf,
cakes or a casserole dish. But in most American households
every fish, regardless of size or succulence, is flung
into a frying pan, which is tiresome for the family, and left there
too long, which is terrible for the fish. There are two rules
that apply to the preparation of all fish. They should
be cooked gently, for overcooking makes fish tough and dry.
And they should be seasoned gently, as the delicate flavor of fish
can easily be overwhelmed. Frozen sea food should be cooked as soon
as it has thawed—or even while frozen.

These four sea food dishes capture the glamor of the sea
in flavor. At top left is lobster *fra diavolo*, of Italian origin;
extra sauce for it is seen in white shell dish at extreme right.
At center left are green peppers stuffed with crab meat
in sauce. Center right is a casserole of oysters and ham with biscuits.
And in right foreground are broiled shrimp in a garlic and butter sauce.

The six common fish shown at left are widely
available across the country, fresh, canned
or frozen. Each has been cooked in a way
that could easily convert a meat-and-potatoes-only
family to fish a couple of times a week.
Starting at the lower left and working around
clockwise, the first dish is
an olive salmon loaf. Other fish, such as tuna,
haddock, red snapper or swordfish,
can be substituted for the salmon. Above it is
baked fillet of flounder with Chablis sauce.
In the center is a party dish:
stuffed broiled haddock with parsley butter.
Above haddock are classic codfish cakes
with tomato sauce. At top right, tuna is used
as a main dinner course, served
with curried almonds and rice. Salmon,
swordfish or crab meat can take the place
of tuna. The casserole at bottom right holds
halibut soufflé, and in the shell to its left
is lobster wine sauce to go with it.

Fresh or frozen oysters may be served raw or cooked, the frozen ones all year round. Here, from lower left clockwise, are skewered oysters in bacon, New Orleans oyster loaf, scalloped oysters, oysters on the half shell with lemon, and oysters Florentine baked in scallop shells. Oysters poulette, made with cream and fresh mushrooms, are in chafing dish in center.

# GREAT SOUPS

SAVORED by epicures, bolted by starving men, served piping hot
or ice-cold, water-thin, fork-thick or stiffly jellied, soup is almost
infinite in its variety. Sometimes it is made with the coarsest
foods, sometimes laced with the finest wines. Once in a while, nowadays,
it even invades the cocktail hour and appears as bouillon and vodka
on the rocks. Its exact origins have disappeared in history. Soup began
with the pot in the fireplace ashes and the kettle on the back
of the stove. They used to be the thrifty receptacles of all leftover foods.
Now soup recipes, tested by the centuries, have become perfected
and accepted by connoisseurs.

Soup can be divided into two general categories. One is the appetizer,
usually a delicate light clear broth or consommé served to stir up
the taste buds and enhance the meal. The other is rich and sometimes thick,
designed to be a meal in itself. On the following six pages,
seven of the latter soups are shown. They come from all over—
Russia, Italy, France, New England — but all have been popped into America's
soup pot and have emerged as national favorites.

There are little tricks in making all of them. For borsch,
the trick is enough lemon juice. In split pea soup it's enough ham
on the hambone. In onion soup it's using plenty of onions. In minestrone,
one should not add the macaroni until 15 minutes before serving.
In bouillabaisse the secret is good saffron—buy it in a pharmacy
if you must. In all these soups consistency can be varied
at will, from soup to solid and in some cases the solid part
can be strained and served with the liquid on the side.

In spite of the fact that these soups are made from honored recipes
(pp. 37, 38), a good deal of leeway is allowed. Other vegetables
can be added, within reason. Frozen fish can replace fresh fish called for
in the bouillabaisse. And soup is always economical to serve. It costs
little extra to double, or even triple, the ingredients in some recipes
and keep a leftover potful in the refrigerator for later meals. Soup
will keep on ice for several weeks if the housewife remembers the soupster's
special secret: the soup must be taken out of the icebox
and brought to a vigorous boil every two days or else it will turn sour.

## THE GREATEST:

Bouillabaisse had its origin on the Mediterranean seacoast when
fishermen's wives made a soup of the unsold portions of the catch.
America has different sea food, but the principle is the same; our bouillabaisse
is made from an assortment of fish (*above, left*) like mackerel, eel and

## BOUILLABAISSE

snapper, as well as lobster and other shellfish. Ludwig Bemelmans,
artist, author and connoisseur of sea food (*above*), calls bouillabaisse the greatest
soup of all. He serves the liquor in a tureen, the fish on a platter.
Then the diner may blend the soup and fish according to his taste.

## BORSCH

Though frequently thought of as a beet soup, borsch is largely made of meat, cabbage and tomatoes and other ingredients shown at top. It may be served hot or cold, with sour cream, preferably with Russian pumpernickel.

## SPLIT PEA

A frugal soup, especially delicious when served with garlic frankfurters, split pea is based on leftover ham and the other ingredients above. It makes a hearty meal in itself when served with cheese and Italian bread.

## ONION SOUP

A classic French dish, onion soup needs a lot of onions, bouillon cubes and condiments like those shown above. It should be served with toasted French bread, Parmesan cheese and a bottle of good Bordeaux.

## MINESTRONE

Based on macaroni and navy beans, zucchini and Parmesan cheese (*above*), minestrone should be served very hot. Its very Italian flavor is accentuated by garlic, can be further enhanced by a bottle of Chianti.

# THE CHOWDER

New England puts milk in its clam chowder.
New York uses water and tomatoes.
New England says it's chowder's birthplace.
So does New York. New Englanders call
New York's Manhattan chowder "vegetable
soup with a clam drawn through it."
New Yorkers say New England chowder is
a stew fit only for infants or invalids.
There is even controversy about the clams.
Manhattan chowder is made of hard-shell
(or quahog) clams which grow in the
Atlantic Ocean. New England chowder
is made of soft-shell (or long-necked)

The rival chowders face each other on these two pages. On the left
is Manhattan clam chowder dished up, as befits its elegance, in a formal
silver tureen and surrounded by its host of ingredients including green pepper,

# CONTROVERSY

clams which are indigenous to the Atlantic
but are now available in the Pacific too,
where they were planted accidentally
in the 1860s along with some oysters.
Manhattan clam chowder is sophisticated.
New England clam chowder is hearty.
This war of the chowders has been going on
for two or three centuries. The owner
of an unprejudiced palate might like
to sample both before taking sides.
If by chance he likes them equally well,
he had better keep it quiet or both camps
will drum him out of culinary society.

catsup *(second row, fourth from left)* and tomato. On the right, in an
ironstone tureen that goes well with its own stern integrity, is
New England clam chowder with its few simple ingredients arranged on a platter.

# DOMESTIC FOWL

THE most important birds in history, from a trencherman's point of view, should be the red jungle fowl that once strutted in Asia's forests, the graylag goose of Europe, the original mallard duck and some turkeys that once belonged to an Aztec Indian. These four are the forebears of almost all the world's common domestic fowl and the offspring of most have simmered in pots ever since pots were invented. All but the turkey, a relative newcomer to the list, which was brought to Europe from Mexico by the Spaniards in about 1519. It got a belated welcome from the great French gourmet Brillat-Savarin in 1825 when he wrote, "The turkey is certainly one of the most beautiful presents that the New World has made to the Old."

While all these birds have spread and multiplied, man has been working to adapt them to his tastes. The early Romans discovered the extra plumpness of the capon, or gelded rooster. In the 1870s an American crossed the mallard with the Peking duck of China, and the fat, delicious Long Island duckling was produced. Since then the discovery that vitamins could be substituted for sunshine has made mass indoor breeding possible. Now frozen fowl are commonplace. Scientists, particularly at the government research center at Beltsville, Md., have developed chickens that are almost all white meat and turkeys small enough to be practical for a small family or an apartment oven. Nowadays, for the family where everyone howls for the drumstick, chicken and turkey, fresh or frozen, can be bought in parts.

All this has turned the spring chicken and the autumn turkey into year-round phenomena. It has also had a profound effect on American eating habits—Americans eat a billion more chickens a year than they did 10 years ago and three times as many turkeys. Ducks are more popular than ever. Even the goose, once a holiday chore to prepare, is now available frozen.

Fowl is a versatile food. It can be broiled, sautéed, fried, roasted or stewed, served in casseroles or with sauces, flavored with sweet or sour, spicy or subtle seasonings. As a rule sharp spices and dry stuffings are best for ducks and geese, bland stuffings like oysters or bread for the less fatty chicken or turkey.

Displayed with an old bull's-eye lantern and a decorative duck are five duck dishes. In center foreground is a platter of broiled duck with celery hearts and lemon wedges. Reading clockwise from platter, other dishes are braised duck with black cherries, ragout of duck in casserole, roast duck with orange and pineapple and duck Spanish style. Two small bowls hold sauces.

Some favorite dishes of domestic fowl are grouped behind symbolic chicken wire. In top row in left half of picture are, left to right, jellied goose with wine, chicken Tetrazzini and chicken cerise. The two dishes in next row are goose with garlic sauce and chicken asparagus casserole. In third row are sesame fried chicken and a roast turkey with a choice of stuffings, in four cups: mushroom, rice, corn bread and oyster. The turkey itself

is filled with a basic bread stuffing. At top of the right half of picture
is chicken Cumberland. The two dishes below it are breasts of chicken
with ham on toast and Brunswick stew. Next two dishes are chicken Mexican and
breasts of chicken with wild rice and below them is chicken Vendange
with green grapes. In the foreground, the round platter
holds three rotisserie chickens and the oblong platter chicken in white wine.

# VEGETABLE VARIETY

**I**N France, where they are usually served as a separate course
demanding as much respect as a meat dish, vegetables are chosen
for the table with the greatest of care. The only people really
considered fit to buy them are those who have grown their own, have had
the pleasure of picking them young and tender in the garden
and can expertly spot a carrot, pea or pepper at its best.

Certainly making good vegetable dishes begins with the selection
of fresh vegetables in the market—beans that crackle when snapped,
Brussels sprouts that are tiny, squash that is firm. Frozen vegetables,
always picked and packaged at the peak, are far better than fresh ones
past their prime. A second important step is to cook
these vegetables quickly and with a minimum of water. In the U.S.
vegetables are too often drowned in water and boiled until flavor and texture
are gone. The natural color is often lost too unless, even worse, it has
been preserved and brightened to an unnatural shade with soda.

Vegetables can be boiled (in small amounts of water) or steamed
(as are the six shown opposite), grilled, baked or braised.
Large vegetables can be stuffed. The Japanese, Chinese and French,
who eat vegetables because they taste good and not because they are
supposed to be good for them, traditionally cook them quickly with plenty
of seasoning and ingenuity. Steamed peas, for example, can be served
with shallots, bits of ham and mint leaves. Lima beans gain new flavor
with dill in a sauce of olive oil and lime juice. Broiled tomatoes
can be served with ripe olives and minced ham. Cauliflower is excellent
with almonds and garlic. Onions improve the flavor of spinach
and Brussels sprouts. Sour cream is a good companion to any fresh vegetable
whether cooked with the vegetable or served as a dressing.

None of the dishes shown here represents the daintified tearoom type
of cooking that comedians love to mock. Instead they are
hearty and sometimes even historic, like the cabbage
pictured on pages 30, 31. It was handed down from the Roman days,
when it was first eaten by soldiers and road builders.

Framed by the glass cylinder in which they were originally steamed
to preserve color and tenderness are six dishes: left to right, bottom row, peas
with shallots and ham, cauliflower with almonds. Middle row,
broccoli with herb butter, lima beans with dill; top row, Brussels sprouts
in onion cream, piquant green beans. When cooked in steam
these vegetables were not allowed to touch water, and steamer was covered.

Fresh combinations give
vegetables new flavors.
On vegetable crates are shown,
front row, left to right:
broiled mushrooms in wine,
acorn squash baked with pineapple;
fried celery with chicken livers,
baked green peppers.
In middle row: zucchini
with walnuts, slowly sautéed
onion slices, asparagus Parmesan
in a copper pan. In back row:
eggplant stuffed with oysters,
broiled tomatoes with ripe olives,
stuffed cabbage leaves,
deviled carrots, baked spinach
with bacon. Still life
photograph in background shows
vegetables uncooked.
The four crates hold,
from left, cabbage, spinach,
carrots, asparagus.

# RECIPES FOR
# TRADITIONAL DISHES

REGIONAL FAVORITES

MAN'S JOB: STEAK

SEA FOOD

GREAT SOUPS

DOMESTIC FOWL

VEGETABLE VARIETY

# REGIONAL FAVORITES

### SPOON BREAD

| | |
|---|---|
| 1 cup white corn meal | 4 eggs, well beaten |
| 1 quart milk | ¼ teaspoon salt |
| 2 tablespoons butter | |

Scald milk in the top of a double boiler. Place over hot water, stir in corn meal, butter and salt. Cook for 15 minutes or until thickened, stirring frequently. Pour over eggs. Bake in a greased casserole in a hot oven (400°) for 45 minutes. Serves 6.

### CORN RELISH

| | |
|---|---|
| 5 cups cooked corn, cut from cob | 1 tablespoon mustard seed |
| ½ cup chopped green pepper | 2 teaspoons celery seed |
| ½ cup chopped red pepper | ½ teaspoon ground turmeric |
| ¾ cup chopped onion | ¾ cup sugar |
| ½ cup chopped celery | 1 pint vinegar |
| 1 tablespoon prepared mustard | 2 teaspoons salt |

Combine ingredients with ½ cup water, simmer for 30 minutes. Pack in hot sterilized jars to within ½ inch of top. Seal at once. Makes 3½ pints.

### CORN BREAD

| | |
|---|---|
| ¾ cup yellow corn meal | 1 cup milk |
| 1⅔ cups sifted flour | 4 tablespoons melted butter |
| 1 tablespoon baking powder | ½ teaspoon salt |
| 1 egg, well beaten | |

Mix dry ingredients. Mix egg, milk and butter. Stir all together until lightly mixed. Bake in greased pan (8x8x2) in hot oven (425°) for 30 minutes. Serves 6.

### INDIAN PUDDING

| | |
|---|---|
| ¼ cup yellow corn meal | ½ teaspoon ground ginger |
| 1 quart milk | ½ teaspoon ground cinnamon |
| 1 cup molasses | 1 teaspoon salt |

Scald milk in the top of a double boiler. Place over hot water, stir in corn meal and cook for 15 minutes or until thickened, stirring frequently. Mix in the rest of the ingredients. Pour into a greased casserole, set the casserole in a pan of hot water. Bake in a slow oven (325°) for 2 hours. Stir the pudding once after 1 hour of baking. Serves 6.

### CORN OYSTERS

| | |
|---|---|
| 1 cup whole kernel corn | 1 teaspoon baking powder |
| 2 eggs, well beaten | ½ teaspoon salt |
| 1 cup flour | Oil or vegetable shortening |

Mix ingredients. Drop batter by teaspoonfuls into ¼ inch of hot fat. Fry until brown. Makes 12.

### RHODE ISLAND JOHNNYCAKES

| | |
|---|---|
| 1 cup white corn meal | 1 teaspoon salt |
| ½ cup milk | |

Stir corn meal and salt into 1 cup of boiling water. Simmer for 10 minutes or until thickened, stirring frequently. Remove from heat and add milk gradually, stirring until thickened. Drop by tablespoonfuls on hot greased griddle. Fry. Serves 6.

### BOSTON BAKED BEANS

| | |
|---|---|
| 2 cups dried navy beans | 2 teaspoons grated onion |
| ½ pound salt pork, halved | ½ teaspoon dry mustard |
| ½ cup dark molasses | |

Soak beans overnight in water to cover. Bring to a boil in the same water, reduce heat, cover and simmer for 1 hour. Drain, save water. Put half of pork in 6-cup bean pot. Add beans, molasses, onion, mustard and ½ cup bean water. Put other pork half on top. Cover and bake in a slow oven (300°) for 5 hours, adding bean water if needed. Uncover, bake for 1 hour. Serves 6.

### SOUTHERN FRIED CHICKEN

| | |
|---|---|
| 3 two-pound chickens, cut up | Vegetable shortening |
| ¼ cup flour | 1 teaspoon salt |
| Butter | Freshly ground black pepper |

Mix flour, salt and pepper in a paper bag; put chicken in bag and shake. Melt enough butter and vegetable shortening to cover the bottom 2 inches of a large skillet. Add chicken, cover skillet, cook slowly for 30 minutes. Uncover, drain fat, add enough water to cover bottom of skillet. Cover skillet again, simmer for 30 minutes. Serves 6.

### CHILI CON CARNE

| | |
|---|---|
| 4 cups canned red kidney beans | 2½ cups canned tomatoes |
| 2 pounds ground beef | 4 tablespoons chili powder |
| 2 cups sliced onion | ½ teaspoon crushed red pepper |
| 3 garlic cloves, minced | ¾ teaspoon oregano |
| ¼ cup oil | 1 teaspoon salt |

Sauté onion and garlic in oil for 10 minutes. Add beef, brown. Add other ingredients, cover, simmer for 30 minutes. Serves 6.

### SCRAPPLE

| | |
|---|---|
| 1½ pounds pork shoulder | ¼ teaspoon ground thyme |
| ¼ pound pork liver | 1 teaspoon ground sage |
| 1 cup yellow corn meal | 1 teaspoon ground marjoram |
| ¼ cup finely chopped onion | 2 teaspoons salt |
| ⅛ teaspoon ground cloves | Freshly ground black pepper |

Simmer meats in saucepan with 4 cups of water for 1 hour. Drain and save broth. Bone pork shoulder and chop shoulder and liver. Combine corn meal, salt, 1 cup cold water and 2 cups broth in saucepan. Cook, stirring until thickened. Add meat, onion and spices. Cover and simmer for 1 hour. Pour scrapple into loaf pan (9x5x3). Chill for 4 hours. To serve, slice, dip in flour and fry.

### CREOLE CRAB GUMBO

| | |
|---|---|
| 1 pound cooked crab meat | 1 cup diced green pepper |
| 1 pound okra, cut up | 2 garlic cloves, crushed |
| ½ cup sliced onion | 1 teaspoon ground nutmeg |
| 4 tablespoons butter | 2 teaspoons salt |
| 4 tablespoons flour | Freshly ground black pepper |
| 5 cups canned tomatoes | |

Sauté onion in butter 10 minutes. Stir in flour and brown. Add crab meat and other ingredients plus 2 cups of water. Bring to a boil, reduce heat, cover, simmer for 1 hour. Serves 6.

## FARM-STYLE BEEF STEW

| | |
|---|---|
| 3 pounds stewing beef, cubed | ½ teaspoon thyme |
| 2 tablespoons fat | 1 cup peas |
| 2 large onions, sliced | 12 small carrots |
| 2 garlic cloves, minced | 12 small onions |
| 1 cup chopped celery | 6 potatoes, quartered |
| ¼ cup chopped parsley | ½ cup flour |
| 2½ cups canned tomatoes | 1 tablespoon salt |
| 1 bay leaf, crumbled | Freshly ground black pepper |

Melt fat in saucepan and brown meat. Add sliced onions, garlic, celery, parsley, tomatoes, bay leaf, thyme, salt, pepper and 2½ cups water. Bring to a boil, reduce heat, cover and simmer for 2 hours. Add remaining vegetables and simmer for 1 hour. Blend flour with ¾ cup cold water and stir into stew. Simmer for 5 minutes. Serves 6.

## TURKEY HASH

| | |
|---|---|
| 3 cups diced cooked turkey | ½ cup chopped onion |
| 4 tablespoons butter | 2 tablespoons |
| 2 tablespoons flour | chopped parsley |
| ½ cup heavy cream | ½ teaspoon ground sage |
| ½ cup soft bread crumbs | ½ teaspoon salt |
| ½ cup chopped green pepper | Freshly ground black pepper |

Melt 2 tablespoons of the butter in saucepan, blend in flour and cream and stir until thickened. Add turkey and all the other ingredients except the remaining butter. Melt these 2 tablespoons butter in a large skillet and add the turkey mixture. Sauté uncovered for 25 minutes. If desired, brown the top of the hash under the broiler before serving. Serves 6.

## SAUTEED SALMON STEAK

| | |
|---|---|
| 6 salmon steaks | ¼ cup butter |
| 2 tablespoons | ¼ cup cider |
| prepared mustard | |

Spread salmon steaks with mustard. Melt butter in skillet, add cider. Sauté steaks for 10 minutes on each side. Serves 6.

## COD CHOWDER

| | |
|---|---|
| 2 pounds cod | 1 bay leaf, crumbled |
| 2 ounces salt pork, diced | 1 quart milk |
| 2 onions, sliced | 2 tablespoons butter |
| 4 large potatoes, diced | 1 teaspoon salt |
| 1 cup chopped celery | Freshly ground black pepper |

Simmer cod in 2 cups water for 15 minutes. Drain. Reserve broth. Remove bones from cod. Sauté diced pork until crisp, remove and set aside. Sauté onions in pork fat until golden brown. Add cod, potatoes, celery, bay leaf, salt and pepper. Pour in cod broth plus enough boiling water to make 3 cups of liquid. Simmer for 30 minutes. Add milk and butter and simmer for 5 minutes. Serve chowder sprinkled with pork dice. Serves 6.

## PUMPKIN PIE

| | |
|---|---|
| 2 cups strained | 1 teaspoon ground cinnamon |
| cooked pumpkin | ½ teaspoon ground ginger |
| 2 eggs, lightly beaten | ¼ teaspoon ground cloves |
| 1⅔ cups evaporated milk | ½ teaspoon salt |
| ⅔ cup sugar | 1 nine-inch unbaked pie shell |

Mix ingredients. Pour into pie shell. Bake in hot oven (425°) for 40 minutes.

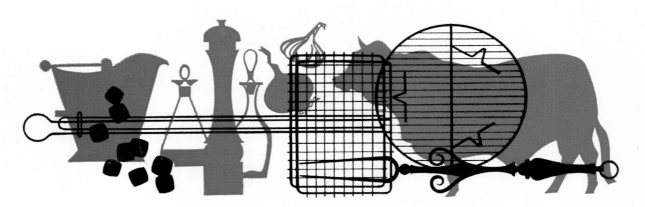

# MAN'S JOB: STEAK

## TARRAGON MARINADE

| | |
|---|---|
| 3 tablespoons | ½ teaspoon dry mustard |
| tarragon vinegar | ½ cup dry red wine |
| 2 large onions, sliced | 1 cup olive oil |
| 1 lemon | 1 teaspoon salt |
| 5 garlic cloves, split | Freshly ground black pepper |
| 1 bay leaf | |

Line a shallow glass baking dish or a wooden trough with some onion slices. Squeeze lemon juice over the onion, toss in the lemon rinds. Add garlic, spices, salt, pepper. Pour in vinegar, wine and oil. Lay a steak in the marinade and spread the rest of the onion slices on the steak. Marinate for 3 hours, basting frequently. This amount is enough for 2 pounds of 2-inch sirloin. Serve the marinated onions raw with the cooked steak.

## BASTING SAUCE

| | |
|---|---|
| ¾ cup olive oil | 1 teaspoon oregano |
| ¾ cup dry red wine | ½ teaspoon thyme |
| 1 tablespoon lime juice | 1 teaspoon sugar |
| 1 garlic clove, mashed | 1 teaspoon salt |
| ⅓ cup finely chopped onion | Freshly ground black pepper |

Combine ingredients and beat or shake until well blended. Spread liberally over steak while cooking, both before and after turning.

## STEAK SPREADS

**ROQUEFORT SPREAD:** Cream 2 ounces of Roquefort cheese with 4 tablespoons butter.
**TABASCO SPREAD:** Cream ¼ teaspoon Tabasco sauce and 1 tablespoon Worcestershire sauce with ½ cup butter.
**MUSTARD SPREAD:** Cream 4 tablespoons of prepared mustard with ½ cup butter.
These may be spread on hot steak before serving.

## WESTERN HERB SAUCE

| | |
|---|---|
| 2 tablespoons | 3 tablespoons |
| chopped scallions | chopped parsley |
| ½ pound mushrooms, sliced | ½ cup chopped |
| ¼ cup olive oil | pickled walnuts |
| ¼ cup butter | 3 tablespoons bottled |
| 2 tablespoons chopped chives | Escoffier Sauce Diable |
| 2 tablespoons | ½ teaspoon salt |
| chopped tarragon | Freshly ground black pepper |

Sauté scallions and mushrooms in combined olive oil and butter for 5 minutes. Add remaining ingredients and simmer for 5 minutes. Makes about 3 cups of sauce. Serve hot with broiled steak. This makes a thick sauce which may be thinned by adding ½ cup beef bouillon and simmering the sauce an additional 5 minutes.

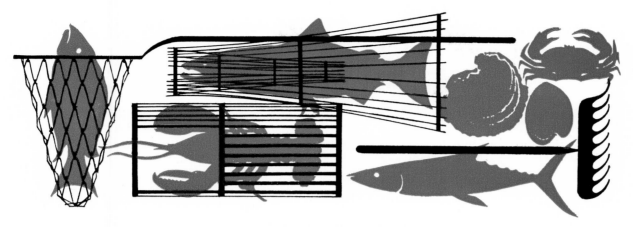

# SEA FOOD

### LOBSTER FRA DIAVOLO

| | |
|---|---|
| 6 one-pound lobsters, split | 3 tablespoons minced garlic |
| ¾ cup olive oil | ¾ teaspoon oregano |
| 3 cups tomato sauce | 1 teaspoon salt |
| 6 tablespoons finely | Freshly ground black pepper |
| chopped parsley | |

Sauté lobsters, cut side down, in oil for 5 minutes. Arrange lobsters cut side up in large roasting pans. Spoon mixture of sauce and seasonings over them. Add ¼ inch water, cover pans tightly and cook over low heat for 30 minutes. Serves 6.

### GREEN PEPPERS WITH CRAB MEAT

| | |
|---|---|
| 6 green peppers | ¼ cup dry white wine |
| 2 cups cooked crab meat | 1 teaspoon lemon juice |
| 1 cup light cream | 1 cup cooked rice |
| 4 tablespoons butter | Paprika |
| ¼ teaspoon ground nutmeg | 1 teaspoon salt |
| 2 tablespoons cornstarch | |

Cut tops off peppers, remove seeds. Parboil peppers 5 minutes. Drain. Scald cream, add butter and nutmeg. Mix cornstarch, wine, lemon juice and salt. Add to cream. Cook until thickened, stirring constantly. Combine with crab meat and rice, and spoon into peppers. Sprinkle with paprika. Bake in a greased baking dish in a moderate oven (350°) for 20 minutes. Serves 6.

### ITALIAN BROILED SHRIMP

| | |
|---|---|
| 2 pounds jumbo shrimp | 2 tablespoons minced garlic |
| ¼ cup flour | 4 tablespoons |
| ¼ cup olive oil | minced parsley |
| ¼ cup melted butter | 1 cup drawn butter sauce |

Shell shrimp, leaving tails on. Dry, dust with flour. Stir oil and butter into flat baking dish. Put shrimp in dish, broil at medium heat for 8 minutes. Add garlic and parsley to drawn butter sauce. Pour over shrimp, stir until shrimp are coated. Broil for 2 minutes. Serve immediately. Serves 6.

### DRAWN BUTTER SAUCE

| | |
|---|---|
| 4 tablespoons butter | 1 teaspoon lemon juice |
| 2 tablespoons flour | Freshly ground black pepper |

Melt 2 tablespoons of the butter, add flour, lemon juice and pepper and stir until smooth. Add 1 cup hot water; bring to a boil, stirring constantly, reduce heat and cook for 5 minutes. Add remaining 2 tablespoons butter and stir until melted.

### OYSTER AND HAM PIE

| | |
|---|---|
| 1 pint oysters | ½ cup milk |
| 2 cups diced cooked ham | 2 cups peas |
| 2 tablespoons butter | Freshly ground black pepper |
| 2 tablespoons flour | 12 unbaked baking powder |
| ½ cup dry white wine | biscuits with chives |

Drain oysters and keep the liquor. Melt butter and stir in flour. Add ½ cup oyster liquor, wine and milk. Cook until thickened, stirring constantly. Add oysters, ham, peas and pepper. Pour into casserole, arrange biscuits on top. Bake in a hot oven (425°) for 15 minutes. Serves 6.

### BAKING POWDER BISCUITS WITH CHIVES

| | |
|---|---|
| 2 cups sifted flour | ½ cup shortening |
| 1 tablespoon double-acting | ⅔ cup milk |
| baking powder | 1 teaspoon salt |
| ¼ cup chopped chives | |

Sift flour with baking powder and salt. Cut in shortening with a pastry blender until the mixture resembles coarse meal. Add milk and chives, stirring until a soft dough is formed. Knead gently on a lightly floured board for 30 seconds. Roll or pat dough ½ inch thick. Cut into 12 biscuits. Bake on a baking sheet in a hot oven (425°) for 15 minutes.

### OLIVE SALMON LOAF

| | |
|---|---|
| 3 cups flaked salmon | 2 tablespoons grated onion |
| ¼ cup sliced ripe olives | ½ cup minced parsley |
| 3 cups bread cubes | ¼ cup lemon juice |
| ¾ cup milk | 1 teaspoon salt |
| 3 eggs, lightly beaten | Freshly ground black pepper |

Combine all ingredients. Mix well. Pour into greased loaf pan or fancy mold. Bake in moderate oven (375°) for 40 minutes. Serves 6.

### FLOUNDER WITH CHABLIS SAUCE

| | |
|---|---|
| 6 flounder fillets | 1 tablespoon butter |
| ½ cup Chablis wine | 1 tablespoon flour |
| 6 small onion rings | 2 egg yolks |
| 2 tablespoons lemon juice | ¼ teaspoon salt |
| ½ bay leaf | 6 peppercorns |

Place flounder fillets on onion rings in greased, shallow baking dish. Add Chablis, lemon juice, bay leaf, salt and peppercorns. Cover with a sheet of buttered wax paper. Bake in a moderate oven (350°) for 15 minutes. Remove fillets from baking dish and keep warm. Strain sauce, add water if needed to make 1 cup. Melt butter, add flour and strained sauce. Cook, stirring constantly, until thickened. Beat egg yolks with 1 tablespoon of water and add to sauce. Cook for 1 minute, stirring vigorously. Place fillets in shallow baking dish, pour sauce over them. Set in pan of boiling water in hot oven (400°) for 3 minutes. Serve immediately. Serves 6.

### BROILED STUFFED HADDOCK

| | |
|---|---|
| 1 five-pound haddock | ½ cup melted butter |
| 2 cups bread stuffing | Parsley butter |
| ¼ cup flour | |

Wash whole fish and dry well. Stuff fish with bread stuffing. Dust with flour and brush with half of melted butter. Broil under low heat for 15 minutes. Turn fish, brush with butter and broil for 20 minutes. Serve with parsley butter. Serves 6.

### PARSLEY BUTTER

| | |
|---|---|
| 1 cup butter | 2 tablespoons lemon juice |
| 2 tablespoons | Freshly ground black pepper |
| chopped parsley | |

Cream butter, add remaining ingredients and mix thoroughly. Makes about 1¼ cups.

## CODFISH CAKES

| | |
|---|---|
| 1 pound salt codfish | Cayenne pepper |
| 6 medium potatoes, boiled | 1 cup dry bread crumbs |
| 1 large onion | ½ cup butter |
| 2 eggs, lightly beaten | Tomato sauce |
| ½ teaspoon curry powder | |

Wash cod in warm running water for 5 minutes. Soak in 4 cups of water overnight to remove salt. Drain, discard water. Put cod, potatoes and raw onion through food grinder. Stir in eggs, curry powder and few grains of cayenne pepper. Shape into 12 cakes. Dip cakes in crumbs and sauté in butter until brown. Heat tomato sauce and serve it with codfish cakes.

## TUNA WITH CURRIED ALMOND RICE

| | |
|---|---|
| 2 seven-ounce cans tuna fish, drained | 1 garlic clove, minced |
| 3 cups hot cooked rice | 1 teaspoon Worcestershire sauce |
| 1 cup blanched almonds, slivered or coarsely chopped | Tabasco sauce |
| ½ teaspoon curry powder | 6 tablespoons flour |
| 8 tablespoons butter | 3 cups milk |
| 2 medium tomatoes, peeled and chopped | Paprika |
| | 1 teaspoon salt |
| | 4 peppercorns, crushed |

Melt 6 tablespoons butter in saucepan. Add tomatoes, garlic, Worcestershire, 4 drops of Tabasco, ½ teaspoon paprika, salt and peppercorns. Cover and simmer for 5 minutes. Add flour and stir until blended. Add milk and simmer until thickened, stirring constantly. Add tuna fish, cover and simmer for 10 minutes. Meanwhile melt remaining 2 tablespoons butter in another saucepan. Add almonds and curry powder and sauté until almonds are golden, stirring constantly. Add almonds to cooked rice and toss lightly together. Serve tuna over the curried almond rice. Sprinkle with additional paprika. Serves 6.

## HALIBUT SOUFFLE

| | |
|---|---|
| 1 pound halibut fillets | 4 egg yolks, lightly beaten |
| 2 cups light cream | 4 egg whites, stiffly beaten |
| 4 slices soft bread, cubed | 1 teaspoon salt |
| 2 tablespoons butter | Freshly ground black pepper |
| ¼ teaspoon celery salt | Lobster wine sauce |

Wash halibut, pat dry. Put through food grinder using coarse blade. Scald cream in top of a double boiler. Place over boiling water. Add halibut, bread cubes, butter, celery salt, salt and pepper, and cook for 5 minutes, stirring occasionally. Reduce heat and beat in egg yolks. Cook over hot (not boiling) water for 5 minutes, stirring constantly. Remove from heat and cool slightly. Fold halibut mixture slowly into beaten egg whites. Pour into a 3-quart casserole. Set the casserole in a pan of hot water and bake in a moderate oven (350°) for 1 hour or until puffy and well browned. Serve immediately with lobster wine sauce. Serves 6.

## LOBSTER WINE SAUCE

| | |
|---|---|
| 1 cup diced cooked lobster | 1¾ cups milk |
| ¼ cup dry white wine | 1 teaspoon salt |
| 4 tablespoons butter | Freshly ground black pepper |
| 4 tablespoons flour | |

Melt butter. Add flour and stir until smooth. Add milk and simmer for 5 minutes or until thickened, stirring constantly. Add lobster and wine, salt and pepper, and simmer for 5 minutes. Makes about 3 cups sauce.

## SKEWERED OYSTERS

| | |
|---|---|
| 2 dozen oysters, shucked | Lemon juice |
| 24 strips bacon | Freshly ground black pepper |

Drain oysters and discard liquor. Season with lemon juice and pepper. Wrap each oyster in a strip of bacon and thread on skewer, leaving some space between wrapped oysters. Broil under moderate heat, turning frequently, for 15 minutes or until bacon is crisp and thoroughly cooked, or rest skewers on rim of baking pan and bake in a hot oven (425°) for 15 minutes.

## NEW ORLEANS OYSTER LOAF

| | |
|---|---|
| 3 dozen oysters, shucked | 4 tablespoons melted butter |
| 3 small loaves French bread | Milk |
| 1 garlic clove | |

Split the loaves of bread lengthwise, leaving a hinge along one side. Scoop out the soft centers, leaving a 1-inch shell, and tear into coarse crumbs. Set crumbs aside. Rub the inside of the loaves with cut garlic, then brush inside and crust with 2 tablespoons of the butter. Drain oysters and save liquor. Sauté the oysters in the remaining 2 tablespoons of butter for 5 minutes or until the edges curl. Stuff the oysters into the hollow loaves. If additional filling is needed use ½ cup oyster liquor mixed with crumbs. Close the loaves and wrap each one in cheesecloth dipped in milk. Twist the ends of the cheesecloth tightly and tuck them under the loaves. Bake on a baking sheet in a moderate oven (350°) for 30 minutes. To serve, unwrap loaves and cut them in half. Serves 6.

## SCALLOPED OYSTERS

| | |
|---|---|
| 3 dozen oysters, shucked | Paprika |
| 3 cups dry bread crumbs | 1 teaspoon salt |
| 3 tablespoons butter | Freshly ground black pepper |
| Chicken bouillon | |

Drain oysters and keep the liquor. Season bread crumbs with paprika, salt and pepper. Arrange alternate layers of oysters and crumbs in a greased baking dish, saving ½ cup of crumbs for the top. Dot each layer of crumbs with some of the butter. Pour in oyster liquor plus enough chicken bouillon to make 1½ cups of liquid. Sprinkle the top with remaining bread crumbs and dot with the rest of the butter. Bake in a hot oven (450°) for 15 minutes or until top is browned. Serves 6.

## OYSTERS FLORENTINE

| | |
|---|---|
| 2 dozen oysters, shucked | 2 tablespoons heavy cream |
| ½ cup finely chopped cooked spinach | 1 egg |
| 2 tablespoons finely chopped onion | 1 egg yolk |
| | 6 tablespoons dry bread crumbs |
| 1 garlic clove, mashed | 1 teaspoon salt |
| 3 tablespoons butter | Freshly ground black pepper |

Drain oysters and save liquor. Chop 12 of the oysters. Set all oysters aside. Sauté onion and garlic in 1 tablespoon butter for 5 minutes. Add chopped oysters, spinach, cream, salt and pepper. Cook over low heat for 5 minutes, stirring constantly. Remove from heat and add to combined egg and egg yolk, stirring briskly. Simmer the whole oysters in 1 cup oyster liquor until edges curl. Drain oysters and put two each in 6 scallop shells, cover with oyster-spinach mixture, sprinkle with bread crumbs and dot with remaining 2 tablespoons butter. Bake in a hot oven (450°) for 15 minutes. Serves 6.

## OYSTERS POULETTE

| | |
|---|---|
| 2 dozen oysters, shucked | ½ cup heavy cream |
| ¼ pound mushrooms | ½ teaspoon salt |
| 3 tablespoons butter | Freshly ground black pepper |
| 1 tablespoon lemon juice | 6 slices toast |
| 2 tablespoons flour | 2 tablespoons minced parsley |
| Dash of nutmeg | |
| 2 egg yolks | |

Remove mushroom caps. Slice and save them. Cook mushroom stems in ¾ cup water for 20 minutes. Strain and save mushroom liquor. Discard stems. Meanwhile drain oysters and save liquor. Simmer oysters in 1 tablespoon butter, lemon juice, salt and pepper until edges curl. Remove from heat and set aside. Melt remaining 2 tablespoons butter in top part of double boiler. Add flour and stir until smooth. Add ½ cup mushroom liquor and ½ cup oyster liquor and cook, stirring constantly, until thickened. Add oysters and their sauce, mushrooms and nutmeg. Simmer for 5 minutes, stirring occasionally. Place over hot (not boiling) water and stir in egg yolks beaten with cream. Cook over hot water for 10 minutes, stirring occasionally. Serve over toast and sprinkle with parsley. Serves 6.

# GREAT SOUPS

## CLASSIC BOUILLABAISSE

| | |
|---|---|
| 2 two-pound lobsters | 4 cups canned tomatoes |
| 1 pound eel | 3 garlic cloves |
| 1½ pounds striped bass or | 2 tablespoons |
| sea bass | chopped parsley |
| 3 pounds red snapper or | 2 tablespoons chopped |
| mackerel | fennel (optional) |
| 2 dozen shrimp, shelled | ½ teaspoon saffron |
| 2 dozen mussels | 1 bay leaf, crumbled |
| 2 dozen clams | ½ teaspoon thyme |
| ½ cup chopped carrot | 1 tablespoon salt |
| 3 leeks, chopped | Freshly ground black pepper |
| ¾ cup chopped onion | ½ cup butter, melted |
| ½ cup olive oil | 12 thick slices French bread |

Cut up lobster, leaving shell on. Cut eel, bass and snapper in 1-inch slices. Scrub mussels and clams thoroughly to remove all outside sand and grit. Sauté carrot, leeks and onion in olive oil for 10 minutes in a large pot. Add tomatoes, 2 minced garlic cloves and other seasonings. Add lobster, eel and 2 quarts of water and bring soup to a boil. Reduce heat and simmer for 15 minutes. Add bass and snapper and cook for 10 minutes. Add shrimp, mussels and clams and cook for 20 minutes or until shells open. Mix butter and 1 crushed garlic clove. Spread some on one side of French bread slices and toast, buttered side up, in the broiler under moderate heat until brown. Turn slices, spread with rest of butter and toast the other side. Serve the toast with the bouillabaisse. This elaborate recipe by Louis Diat, for 40 years executive chef of the old Ritz-Carlton Hotel in New York City, serves 12 generously.

## SIMPLE BOUILLABAISSE

| | |
|---|---|
| 6 frozen lobster tails | 2½ cups canned tomatoes |
| 3 pounds frozen fish fillets | 1 bay leaf, crumbled |
| 1 cup frozen or canned | 1 cup dry white wine |
| shrimp or crab meat | 1 tablespoon lemon juice |
| 1 can whole clams or mussels | ¼ cup chopped parsley |
| ¼ cup chopped carrot | ½ cup diced pimento |
| 1 cup chopped onion | ½ teaspoon saffron |
| 1 garlic clove, minced | 1 tablespoon salt |
| ½ cup olive oil | Freshly ground black pepper |

Sauté carrot, onion and garlic in olive oil for 10 minutes. Add fish cut into 3-inch pieces, tomatoes, bay leaf and 2 quarts of water. Bring to a boil, reduce heat and simmer for 20 minutes. Add lobster tails with shells split down middle, shrimp, clams and remaining ingredients and simmer for 30 minutes. Serves 6.

## BORSCH

| | |
|---|---|
| 2 cups diced beets | 6 garlic cloves, minced |
| 4 cups shredded cabbage | ¼ cup chopped parsley |
| 3 pounds beef shinbone | 1 small bay leaf, crumbled |
| 2 pounds beef brisket, | 1 teaspoon paprika |
| cut into 1-inch pieces | 3 tablespoons sugar |
| 2 large onions, chopped | 1 teaspoon salt |
| 3½ cups canned tomatoes | Freshly ground black pepper |
| ¾ cup lemon juice | Sour cream |

Cover shinbone and brisket with 2 quarts of water. Bring to boil, reduce heat, cover pan and simmer for 1 hour. Add vegetables, lemon juice and seasonings and simmer for 2 hours. Remove shinbone, trim off meat and discard bone. Cut meat into 1-inch pieces. Return meat to soup and simmer for 10 minutes. Serve with sour cream. Serves 6.

## SPLIT PEA SOUP

| | |
|---|---|
| 2 cups green split peas | 1 cup milk |
| 1 ham bone with some meat | 2 cups beef bouillon |
| on it | 6 kosher-style garlic |
| ½ cup chopped onion | frankfurters, sliced |
| 2 cups chopped celery | Salt |
| with leaves | 10 peppercorns, cracked |
| 2 carrots, sliced | |

Soak peas in 2 quarts water overnight. Bring to a boil in the same water, reduce heat, add ham bone and peppercorns, cover and simmer for 1 hour. Add vegetables and simmer for 1 hour. Remove ham bone, cut meat from it, discard bone and chop meat fine. Press the rest of the soup through coarse sieve or food mill. Add chopped ham, milk, bouillon and sliced frankfurters, and simmer for 20 minutes. Add salt if necessary. Serves 6.

## ONION SOUP

| | |
|---|---|
| 12 onions, thinly sliced | 6 one-inch slices |
| 14 cups beef bouillon | French bread |
| 4 tablespoons butter | 6 tablespoons grated |
| 1 teaspoon Worcestershire | Parmesan cheese |
| sauce | Salt |
| ¼ teaspoon Tabasco sauce | Freshly ground black pepper |
| 1 teaspoon Kitchen Bouquet | |

Sauté onions in butter in a large saucepan for 15 minutes or until golden brown. Add bouillon, Worcestershire, Tabasco, Kitchen Bouquet, pepper, and salt if needed. Bring to a boil, reduce heat, cover and simmer for 4 hours. Toast French bread in a moderate oven (350°) until brown on both sides. Sprinkle each slice with 1 tablespoon cheese. Broil under low heat until cheese is browned. Serve toast with the soup. Serves 6.

## MINESTRONE

| | |
|---|---|
| 2 cups dried navy beans | ¼ cup chopped parsley |
| 1 cup chopped celery | 2 cups shredded cabbage |
| with leaves | 1 zucchini, thinly sliced |
| 1 cup finely chopped onion | 2 cups cut macaroni |
| 1 garlic clove, minced | 1 tablespoon salt |
| ½ cup olive oil | 4 peppercorns |
| 2½ cups canned tomatoes | Grated Parmesan cheese |

Soak beans in 10 cups of water overnight. Bring to a boil in the same water, reduce heat, add salt and peppercorns, cover and simmer for 1 hour. Sauté celery, onion and garlic in olive oil for 10 minutes or until onion is lightly browned. Add to beans with tomatoes and parsley. Bring to a boil, reduce heat, cover and simmer for 1 hour. Add cabbage, zucchini and macaroni and simmer uncovered for 15 minutes, stirring occasionally. Serve with grated Parmesan cheese. Serves 6.

## MANHATTAN CLAM CHOWDER

| | |
|---|---|
| 2 dozen hard-shell clams, shucked | 3 cups diced potato |
| 2 ounces salt pork, diced | 1 cup canned tomatoes |
| ½ cup thinly sliced leeks | ¼ cup catsup |
| ½ cup chopped onion | ¼ cup chopped parsley |
| 1 garlic clove, minced | 1½ teaspoons thyme |
| ½ cup chopped green pepper | 1 bay leaf, crumbled |
| ½ cup diced carrot | 4 whole cloves |
| ¼ cup chopped celery | 2 teaspoons salt |
| | Freshly ground black pepper |

Strain clams, keep liquor. Mince hard part of clams, chop soft part coarsely. Sauté salt pork until golden brown. Add leeks, onion and garlic and sauté for 5 minutes. Add minced clams, green pepper, carrot, celery, potato, salt and 6 cups of water. Bring to a boil, reduce heat, cover and simmer for 10 minutes. Add chopped clams and clam liquor plus enough water to make 3 cups. Add tomatoes, catsup, parsley, thyme, bay leaf, cloves and pepper. Simmer for 20 minutes. Serves 6.

## NEW ENGLAND CLAM CHOWDER

| | |
|---|---|
| 3 dozen soft-shell clams, shucked | 4 cups milk, scalded |
| 2 ounces salt pork, diced | 2 cups light cream, scalded |
| 1½ cups sliced onion | 3 tablespoons butter |
| 6 cups diced potato | 2 tablespoons flour |
| 2 small bay leaves, crumbled | 1 tablespoon salt |
| | Freshly ground black pepper |

Strain clams, keep liquor. Mince hard part of clams, chop soft part coarsely. Sauté salt pork until golden brown. Add minced clams, onion, potato, bay leaves, salt and pepper, and 3 cups of water. Bring to a boil, reduce heat, cover and simmer for 15 minutes. Add clam liquor plus enough water to make 3 cups. Add chopped clams, milk, cream, and butter blended with flour. Simmer for 20 minutes. Serves 6.

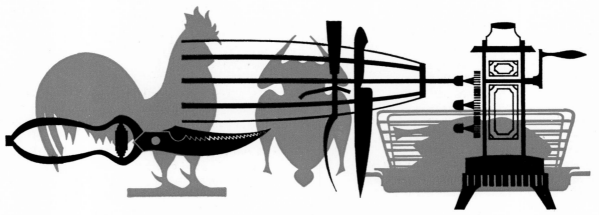

# DOMESTIC FOWL

## BROILED DUCK QUARTERS

| | |
|---|---|
| 2 five-pound ducks, quartered | ¼ cup olive oil |
| ½ cup dry white wine | ½ teaspoon ground ginger |
| ¼ cup lemon juice | 1 teaspoon salt |

Trim excess fat from ducks. Place skin side down on broiler rack and broil at medium heat for 15 minutes, baste once with combined wine, lemon juice, oil, ginger and salt. Turn duck. Broil for 30 minutes, basting every 10 minutes. Serves 6.

## BRAISED DUCK WITH BLACK CHERRIES

| | |
|---|---|
| 2 five-pound ducks, quartered | 1½ cups chicken bouillon |
| 2½ cups canned black cherries | 1 bay leaf, crumbled |
| 4 tablespoons butter | 3 tablespoons cornstarch |
| 2 tablespoons minced onion | 1 teaspoon salt |
| ¾ cup dry Marsala wine | Freshly ground black pepper |

Brown duck quarters in butter. Place duck in shallow pan and roast in slow oven (325°) for 1 hour. Meanwhile pour off all but 2 tablespoons fat from skillet in which duck was browned. Sauté onion in skillet fat for 5 minutes. Add wine, bouillon, bay leaf. Drain cherries and mix ¾ cup juice with cornstarch, salt and pepper. Stir into sauce and simmer until thickened. Add cherries and simmer for 5 minutes. Serve with duck. Serves 6.

## RAGOUT OF DUCK

| | |
|---|---|
| 2 five-pound ducks, cut up | ½ teaspoon ground nutmeg |
| ½ cup brandy | 4 tablespoons butter |
| 3 cups dry red wine | 1 cup chopped celery |
| 1 cup chopped onion | ½ pound mushrooms, sliced |
| 1 garlic clove, minced | 1 teaspoon salt |
| ¼ cup chopped parsley | Freshly ground black pepper |

Marinate duck for 2 hours in mixture of brandy, wine, onion, garlic, parsley, nutmeg, salt, pepper and 1 cup water. Remove duck and dry, sauté in butter until golden brown. Place duck in heavy saucepan and pour unstrained marinade over it. Bring to a boil, reduce heat and simmer for 30 minutes. Add celery and mushrooms and continue cooking for 30 minutes. Serves 6.

## ROAST DUCK WITH ORANGE AND PINEAPPLE

| | |
|---|---|
| 2 five-pound oven-ready ducks | 1 cup dry Marsala wine |
| 2 oranges | 2 cups chicken bouillon |
| 4 slices canned pineapple | 1 teaspoon tomato paste |
| 1 teaspoon tarragon | ½ cup currant jelly |
| 3 garlic cloves | 3 tablespoons potato flour |
| 2 tablespoons butter | 1 teaspoon salt |
| ½ cup brandy | Freshly ground black pepper |

Shred rind of oranges and save shredded rind. Quarter the oranges and mix with pineapple, tarragon and 2 chopped garlic cloves. Use mixture to stuff both ducks. Place ducks on rack in shallow baking pan and roast in slow oven (325°) for 2½ hours or until done. Meanwhile sauté duck livers in butter for 10 minutes. Heat brandy, light it and pour over livers. When flame dies, remove livers, chop and keep warm. To sauce remaining in skillet add shredded orange rind and 1 minced garlic clove and cook for 5 minutes. Combine Marsala and bouillon with tomato paste, jelly, potato flour, salt and pepper. Add to sauce and cook, stirring constantly, until smooth. Add livers and simmer for 15 minutes. Pour into sauceboat, serve with duck. Serves 6.

## DUCK SPANISH STYLE

| | |
|---|---|
| 2 five-pound oven-ready ducks | 4 tablespoons flour |
| ½ cup butter | 1 cup tomato sauce |
| ½ cup minced onion | 1 tablespoon paprika |
| ½ pound mushrooms, sliced | 1 teaspoon salt |
| ½ cup dry sherry | Freshly ground black pepper |
| 1 teaspoon tomato paste | |

Place ducks on rack in shallow baking pan. Roast in a slow oven (325°) for 2½ hours or until done. Meanwhile sauté duck livers in butter for 10 minutes. Remove, cool, chop and set aside. To butter remaining in skillet add onion and sauté for 5 minutes. Add mushrooms and sauté for 5 minutes. Add remaining ingredients and ½ cup water and cook, stirring constantly, until thickened. Add liver and simmer for 5 minutes. Pour into sauceboat and serve with duck. Serves 6.

## JELLIED GOOSE WITH WINE

| | |
|---|---|
| 1 twelve-pound goose, quartered | 3 carrots |
| 2 large onions, sliced | 1 lemon, sliced |
| 8 tablespoons chopped parsley | 1 cup dry white wine |
| 2 bay leaves | 3 envelopes unflavored gelatine |
| 1 teaspoon thyme | Chives |
| 1 whole clove | 1 tablespoon salt |
| 2 garlic cloves | 10 peppercorns, crushed |

Place goose, onions, 6 tablespoons parsley, bay leaves, thyme, clove, garlic, carrots, lemon, salt and peppercorns in large pot with water to cover. Bring to a boil, cover, reduce heat and simmer for 1 hour, or until goose is done. After first 30 minutes remove carrots, slice and save them. When goose is done, remove it, let it cool, then skin and slice it thin. Strain hot broth through fine sieve or cheesecloth. Skim off fat. Add 3 cups broth to wine in which gelatine has been softened. Stir until gelatine is dissolved, chill until syrupy. Pour a thin layer of gelatine mixture into bottom of 2-quart mold. Decorate with 3 scored lemon slices, 3 carrot slices and chives to form flower spray. Chill gelatine layer until firm, then fill mold with alternate layers of goose and carrots. Combine the 2 tablespoons parsley with remaining gelatine mixture and pour into mold. Chill 4 hours. Serves 6.

## CHICKEN TETRAZZINI

| | |
|---|---|
| 3 two-pound chickens, cut up | 2 tablespoons dry sherry |
| 1 cup chopped celery tops | 8 ounces fine noodles, boiled and drained |
| ¼ cup chopped parsley | ½ cup dry bread crumbs |
| 1 small onion, sliced | |
| ½ pound mushrooms, sliced | 4 tablespoons grated Parmesan cheese |
| 4 tablespoons butter | |
| 4 tablespoons flour | 2½ teaspoons salt |
| 1 cup heavy cream | Freshly ground black pepper |

Place chicken in saucepan with celery, parsley, onion and 2 teaspoons salt. Add 3 cups water. Bring to a boil, cover, reduce heat and simmer for 30 minutes. Remove chicken and bone it. Strain broth and keep it. Sauté mushrooms in butter. Stir in flour, ½ teaspoon salt, and pepper. Add 2 cups broth and cream slowly and cook, stirring constantly, until thickened. Add chicken and sherry to sauce. Place noodles in greased, shallow baking dish. Top with chicken mixture. Sprinkle with bread crumbs and cheese. Brown in broiler. Serves 6.

## CHICKEN CERISE

| | |
|---|---|
| 3 two-pound chickens, halved or split | ⅛ teaspoon dry mustard |
| | 1 cup canned crushed pineapple |
| 2 cups canned red sour pitted cherries (water pack) | 2 tablespoons dark rum |
| 6 tablespoons butter | 1 chicken bouillon cube |
| 1 tablespoon flour | ¼ teaspoon red food coloring |
| 1 teaspoon sugar | Paprika |
| ⅛ teaspoon ground allspice | 1 teaspoon salt |
| ⅛ teaspoon ground cinnamon | 3 cups hot cooked rice |

Season chicken with paprika and ½ teaspoon salt. Sauté chicken in butter until brown. Remove chicken. Blend flour, sugar, spices and ½ teaspoon salt in butter remaining in skillet. Drain cherries and pour the liquid into the skillet. Return chicken to skillet. Add pineapple, rum, bouillon cube and food coloring. Cover, simmer for 30 minutes. Add cherries and simmer for 10 minutes. To serve, arrange chicken on a bed of rice; spoon some sauce over chicken and serve the remaining sauce separately. Serves 6.

## GOOSE WITH GARLIC SAUCE

| | |
|---|---|
| 1 twelve-pound goose, cut up | ½ teaspoon tarragon |
| 3 onions, sliced | 4 cups milk |
| 1 carrot, sliced | 12 garlic cloves |
| 1 cup chopped celery | 4 egg yolks |
| ½ cup chopped parsley | 4 teaspoons salt |
| ½ teaspoon thyme | 8 peppercorns, crushed |

Place goose in saucepan with onions, carrot, celery, parsley, thyme, tarragon, 2 teaspoons salt, peppercorns and water to cover. Bring to a boil, cover, reduce heat and simmer for 1 hour or until done. Remove goose and keep hot. Scald 3 cups of milk with garlic in top of double boiler. Beat egg yolks with remaining milk and stir into scalded milk. Add remaining 2 teaspoons salt. Place over hot water and cook, stirring constantly, until thickened. Pour sauce over goose. Serves 6.

## CHICKEN ASPARAGUS CASSEROLE

| | |
|---|---|
| 12 slices cooked chicken | Tabasco sauce |
| 1 pound cooked asparagus | 4 tablespoons chopped pimento |
| 3 cups canned condensed cream of mushroom soup | |
| 1 cup heavy cream | 4 tablespoons grated Parmesan cheese |
| 1 teaspoon curry powder | Paprika |

Place asparagus in greased, shallow baking dish. Arrange chicken over it. Combine soup, cream, curry powder and 4 drops of Tabasco. Heat, stirring constantly, until smooth. Add pimento. Pour over chicken and asparagus and sprinkle with cheese and paprika. Bake in a hot oven (400°) for 15 minutes. Serves 6.

## SESAME FRIED CHICKEN

| | |
|---|---|
| 2 three-pound chickens, quartered | ½ cup butter |
| | ½ cup oil |
| 4 tablespoons sesame seeds | ½ teaspoon paprika |
| 1¼ cups flour | 1½ teaspoons salt |
| 1 teaspoon poultry seasoning | Freshly ground black pepper |
| ⅔ cup evaporated milk | |

Combine sesame seeds, flour, poultry seasoning, paprika, salt and pepper. Dip chicken quarters into milk, then roll them in the sesame seed mixture. Sauté chicken in combined butter and oil for 30 minutes or until golden brown and tender, turning frequently. Serves 6.

## ROAST TURKEY IN FOIL

| | |
|---|---|
| 1 twelve-pound oven-ready turkey | 1 teaspoon thyme |
| | 1 teaspoon basil |
| Butter | Salt |
| ¼ cup dry white wine | Freshly ground black pepper |
| ¼ cup brandy | 1 recipe of stuffing |

Rub inside of turkey's cavity with salt and pepper and rub the skin with butter. Fill the turkey loosely with stuffing and wrap it in foil, pouring wine, brandy and herbs over the turkey before closing the foil tight. Roast the turkey in a hot oven (400°) for 3½ hours. Fold the foil back, and roast for 30 minutes or until the turkey is brown.

## BASIC BREAD STUFFING

| | |
|---|---|
| 8 cups bread crumbs or cubes | ½ teaspoon poultry seasoning |
| ½ cup butter | 2 tablespoons chopped parsley |
| 1 cup chopped onion | |
| 1 cup diced celery with leaves | ¼ cup chicken bouillon |
| ½ teaspoon Tabasco sauce | 1½ teaspoons salt |

Melt butter. Add onion, celery, Tabasco, poultry seasoning and salt. Cook until onion is tender but not brown. Combine with bread crumbs and parsley. Add bouillon, toss lightly with a fork until well mixed. Yields enough for one 12-pound turkey or two 6-pound turkeys, using ¾ cup stuffing per pound dressed weight.

If desired, stuffing may be baked separately to serve with chicken, veal or beef. Place stuffing in foil; seal edges tightly. Bake in a moderate oven (350°-375°) for 35 minutes, or in a slow oven (325°) for 45 minutes.

**MUSHROOM STUFFING:** Add ½ cup canned sliced mushrooms to basic recipe and omit bouillon.
**RICE STUFFING:** Substitute 3 cups cooked rice and 5 cups bread crumbs for bread in basic recipe.
**CORN BREAD STUFFING:** Substitute 4 cups corn bread crumbs and 4 cups bread crumbs for bread in basic recipe.
**OYSTER STUFFING:** Add a pint of oysters, drained and coarsely chopped, to basic recipe.

## CHICKEN CUMBERLAND

| | |
|---|---|
| 3 two-pound chickens, halved | 1 teaspoon dry mustard |
| 4 tablespoons butter, melted | ⅛ teaspoon ground ginger |
| 3 tablespoons lime juice | ¼ teaspoon Tabasco sauce |
| 1 cup red currant jelly | 1 tablespoon Ac'cent |
| 1 six-ounce can frozen | 1 teaspoon salt |
| concentrated orange juice | Freshly ground black pepper |
| 4 tablespoons dry sherry | |

Season chicken with Ac'cent, salt and pepper. Line broiler pan with foil, place chicken on broiler rack. Broil chicken under medium heat for 1 hour, turning once, basting frequently with combined butter and lime juice. Meanwhile combine jelly, orange juice, sherry, mustard, ginger and Tabasco sauce. Simmer until smooth and hot, stirring constantly. Serve sauce with the chicken. Serves 6.

## BREASTS OF CHICKEN WITH HAM

| | |
|---|---|
| Breasts of 3 three-pound chickens | ¼ teaspoon thyme |
| | ½ cup dry sherry |
| 6 slices cooked ham | ¼ cup dry white wine |
| 6 tablespoons butter | 1 tablespoon cornstarch |
| 1 cup canned sliced mushrooms | 1 cup heavy cream |
| | 1 teaspoon salt |
| ¼ teaspoon savory | Freshly ground black pepper |
| ¼ teaspoon rosemary | 6 slices toast |

Bone and skin chicken breasts and cut them in half. Season with salt and pepper. Sauté breasts in 4 tablespoons butter for 10 minutes or until golden brown. Drain mushrooms and add ½ cup mushroom liquid to chicken. Set mushrooms aside. Add herbs to chicken, cover and simmer for 20 minutes. Add sherry and wine and simmer for 10 minutes. Add mushrooms and cornstarch dissolved in cream and simmer for 5 minutes or until sauce is thickened, stirring constantly. Sauté ham in remaining 2 tablespoons of butter. Place ham on toast, top with chicken, and spoon sauce over. Serves 6.

## BRUNSWICK STEW

| | |
|---|---|
| 1 three-pound chicken, cut up | ¼ teaspoon basil |
| 4 tablespoons butter | ¼ teaspoon Tabasco sauce |
| 2 medium onions, sliced | 1 package frozen cut corn |
| 5 cups canned tomatoes | 1 package frozen lima beans |
| 1 cup chopped celery with leaves | 1 tablespoon cornstarch |
| | 1 tablespoon salt |
| ¼ teaspoon marjoram | Freshly ground black pepper |
| ¼ teaspoon thyme | |

Season chicken with salt and pepper. Sauté chicken in butter in deep saucepan for 10 minutes or until brown. Remove chicken, keep hot. Sauté onions in butter remaining in saucepan for 10 minutes or until lightly browned. Return chicken to pan, add tomatoes, celery, herbs, Tabasco and 1 cup of water. Bring to a boil, reduce heat, cover and simmer for 45 minutes. Add corn and lima beans and simmer for 20 minutes, stirring occasionally. Combine cornstarch with ¼ cup cold water, add a small amount of hot liquid from stew and stir until smooth. Stir into stew and simmer for 5 minutes, stirring constantly. Serves 6.

## CHICKEN MEXICAN

| | |
|---|---|
| 1 six-pound oven-ready chicken | ¾ cup dry red wine |
| | 2 cups chicken bouillon |
| 4 tablespoons oil | 1 cup blanched almonds |
| 3 large onions, chopped | ½ cup sliced, stuffed olives |
| 3 garlic cloves, minced | 1 tablespoon chili powder |
| 1 tablespoon sesame seeds | 1 teaspoon salt |
| ¼ teaspoon marjoram | Freshly ground black pepper |

Season chicken with salt and pepper. Sauté chicken in oil for 15 minutes or until brown on all sides. Remove chicken, keep hot. Add onions and garlic to oil remaining in skillet and sauté for 10 minutes or until lightly browned. Add sesame seeds, marjoram and wine and simmer for 5 minutes. Put chicken, onion mixture and bouillon in a deep casserole. Add almonds, olives and chili powder. Cover and bake in a moderate oven (350°) for 30 minutes. Uncover and bake 15 minutes. Serves 6.

## BREASTS OF CHICKEN WITH WILD RICE

| | |
|---|---|
| Breasts of 3 three-pound chickens | 4 tablespoons brandy |
| | 4 tablespoons dry sherry |
| 1 pound mushrooms, sliced | ½ teaspoon salt |
| ½ cup butter | Freshly ground black pepper |
| 1 tablespoon grated onion | 8 ounces wild rice, cooked |
| 2 cups heavy cream | |

Bone and skin chicken breasts. Season with salt and pepper. Sauté in butter over low heat for 20 minutes or until rich brown. Remove chicken and keep hot. Add mushrooms and onion to butter remaining in pan and cook for 5 minutes, stirring constantly. Reduce heat and add cream slowly, stirring constantly. Simmer for 5 minutes. Add brandy and sherry and simmer for 5 minutes. Arrange chicken on wild rice, pour sauce over it. Serves 6.

## WILD RICE

| | |
|---|---|
| 8 ounces wild rice | 1 teaspoon salt |

One of the best ways to cook wild rice is to cover the rice three times with boiling water. This method takes 1½ hours. First wash the wild rice thoroughly in cold water. Put rice in a saucepan. Cover rice with 4 cups of rapidly boiling water, put lid on pan and let the rice stand 30 minutes. Drain. Repeat this twice, adding salt to the last 4 cups of water. Serves 6.

## CHICKEN VENDANGE

| | |
|---|---|
| 3 two-pound chickens, cut up | 1 teaspoon grated onion |
| ½ cup butter | Cayenne pepper |
| ¾ cup dry white wine | Paprika |
| Chicken bouillon | 1 teaspoon salt |
| 1 tablespoon lemon juice | 1 pound green grapes |

Season chicken with paprika and salt. Sauté in butter for 10 minutes or until golden brown. Add wine, ½ cup chicken bouillon, lemon juice, onion and a few grains of cayenne pepper. Cover, reduce heat and simmer for 20 minutes. Turn chicken and add another ¼ cup of bouillon if the pan juices have cooked away. Simmer for 10 minutes. Serve with chilled grape clusters. Serves 6.

## ROTISSERIE CHICKEN WITH BRAZIL NUTS

| | |
|---|---|
| 2 three-pound oven-ready chickens | 1 eight-ounce package stuffing mix |
| 1 cup chopped Brazil nuts | ½ teaspoon thyme |
| ¾ cup butter | 1 cup chicken bouillon |
| ½ cup chopped onion | Salt |
| 1 cup chopped celery with leaves | Freshly ground black pepper |

Sauté livers of the chickens in ½ cup butter for 5 minutes or until lightly browned. Remove livers and chop. Sauté Brazil nuts, onion and celery in butter remaining in pan for 10 minutes or until onion is tender. Stir into stuffing mix. Add livers, thyme and bouillon and toss lightly together. Rub inside of chicken cavities with salt and pepper. Fill chickens loosely with the stuffing. Melt the remaining ¼ cup dutter. Place chickens on revolving spit of rotisserie, brush with melted butter and cook on medium heat for 1½ hours. Serves 6.

## CHICKEN IN WHITE WINE

| | |
|---|---|
| 3 two-pound chickens, cut up | 1 cup sour cream |
| ½ cup plus 2 tablespoons dry white wine | ¼ teaspoon Tabasco sauce |
| | 2 teaspoons Ac'cent |
| 4 tablespoons olive oil | 1½ teaspoons salt |
| ¼ pound mushrooms, sliced | Freshly ground black pepper |

Season chicken with Ac'cent, 1 teaspoon salt and pepper. Sauté in olive oil for 10 minutes or until golden brown. Add ½ cup wine, cover, and simmer for 30 minutes. Remove chicken and keep hot. Add mushrooms and remaining 2 tablespoons of wine to sauce remaining in skillet and simmer for 5 minutes, stirring frequently. Remove from heat, stir in sour cream, Tabasco and ½ teaspoon salt. Return to heat and simmer gently for 2 minutes or until thoroughly blended, stirring constantly. To serve, pour sauce over chicken. Serves 6.

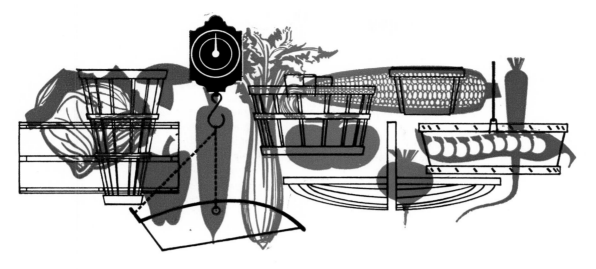

# VEGETABLE VARIETY

### PEAS WITH SHALLOTS AND HAM

3 cups peas
4 tablespoons
  minced shallots
1 cup julienne strips
  of cooked ham
4 tablespoons butter
1 tablespoon sugar
1 teaspoon chopped fresh
  mint leaves
1 teaspoon salt
Freshly ground black pepper

Steam peas on a perforated rack over boiling water in a tightly closed pan for 15 minutes or until tender. Peas should not touch the water. Sauté shallots in butter until golden. Add ham, sugar, salt and pepper and sauté for 5 minutes, stirring frequently. Add mint leaves and stir in peas. Serves 6.

### CAULIFLOWER WITH ALMONDS

1 large cauliflower
½ cup slivered almonds
1 cup soft bread crumbs
1 garlic clove, minced
4 tablespoons butter

Steam cauliflower for 20 minutes or until tender. Sauté remaining ingredients in butter until the almonds are golden and crumbs crisp. Serve over cauliflower. Serves 6.

### BROCCOLI WITH HERB BUTTER

3 pounds broccoli
½ cup butter
4 tablespoons lemon juice
1 garlic clove, minced
¼ teaspoon oregano
¼ teaspoon salt
Freshly ground black pepper

Trim heavy, coarse stalks from broccoli. Steam broccoli spears for 20 minutes or until tender. Combine and heat remaining ingredients and pour over broccoli. Serves 6.

### LIMA BEANS WITH DILL

2 pounds lima beans
4 tablespoons olive oil
1 tablespoon lime juice
2 tablespoons chopped fresh
  dill or 2 teaspoons dill
  seeds, crushed

Steam lima beans for 20 minutes or until tender. Heat remaining ingredients and pour over lima beans. Mix well. Serves 6.

### BRUSSELS SPROUTS IN ONION CREAM

1½ pounds Brussels sprouts
½ cup chopped onion
1 pint sour cream
2 tablespoons butter

Steam Brussels sprouts for 15 minutes or until tender. Sauté onion in butter until rich brown. Stir in sour cream and heat, stirring constantly. Add Brussels sprouts and mix well. Serves 6.

### PIQUANT GREEN BEANS

1½ pounds string beans
4 strips bacon
2 tablespoons diced pimento
2 tablespoons
  red wine vinegar
¼ teaspoon sugar
1 tablespoon Worcestershire
  sauce
¼ teaspoon dry mustard
Tabasco sauce

Steam whole beans for 15 minutes or until tender. Cut bacon into ½-inch strips. Sauté until crisp, remove bacon from fat and add to beans. To bacon fat in skillet, add pimento, vinegar, sugar, Worcestershire, mustard and 2 drops of Tabasco. Bring to a boil, stirring constantly. Pour over beans, mix well. Serves 6.

### BROILED MUSHROOMS

1½ pounds mushrooms
1 cup olive oil
1 cup dry red wine
1 garlic clove, minced

Remove mushroom stems. (Save stems for soup or sauce.) Score caps and marinate in remaining ingredients for 2 hours. Drain and keep marinade. Broil caps under medium heat for 5 minutes or until tender. Heat marinade and serve with broiled mushrooms. Serves 6.

### ACORN SQUASH BAKED WITH PINEAPPLE

3 acorn squashes, halved
½ cup crushed pineapple,
  drained
2 tablespoons dry sherry
2 tablespoons brown sugar
6 tablespoons butter
¼ teaspoon ground nutmeg
1 teaspoon salt

Scoop out squash seeds and fibers. Place in greased baking dish and put 1 teaspoon each of sherry, brown sugar and butter in each half. Cover and bake in a hot oven (400°) for 30 minutes or until tender. Scoop cooked squash out of shells, leaving wall about ¼ inch thick. Mash squash and combine with 4 tablespoons butter and remaining ingredients, beating until well blended. Spoon back into shells and return to hot oven (425°) for 15 minutes. Serves 6.

### FRIED CELERY WITH CHICKEN LIVERS

6 whole celery hearts
  with leaves
½ cup butter
1 pound chicken livers,
  cut up
1 cup sliced mushrooms
½ cup dry sherry
½ cup heavy cream
1 teaspoon salt

Sauté celery in butter for 15 minutes. Remove from skillet and keep warm. Sauté chicken livers and mushrooms for 10 minutes in butter remaining in skillet. Add sherry, cream and salt. Simmer, stirring frequently, until hot (do not allow to boil). Return celery to sauce to heat thoroughly. Serves 6.

### BAKED GREEN PEPPERS

6 green peppers
½ cup olive oil
2 garlic cloves, minced

Cut each pepper into quarters, remove seeds and fibrous portions. Put into baking pan with oil and garlic and bake in moderate oven (350°) for 15 minutes, stirring frequently. Serves 6.

### ZUCCHINI WITH WALNUTS

1½ pounds zucchini
1 cup walnuts,
  coarsely chopped
½ cup sliced scallions
½ cup olive oil
¼ cup dry red wine
2 tablespoons lemon juice

Cut zucchini in ½-inch slices. Sauté zucchini and scallions in oil for 5 minutes, stirring frequently. Add wine, lemon juice and ¼ cup water. Simmer for 5 minutes. Add walnuts. Serves 6.

### SAUTEED ONION SLICES

6 large onions
½ cup butter

Peel onions and cut into ½-inch slices. Sauté very slowly in butter for 10 minutes or until tender, turning once. Serves 6.

## ASPARAGUS PARMESAN

| | |
|---|---|
| 3 pounds asparagus | 1 cup dry bread crumbs |
| 1 tablespoon grated | ¼ teaspoon garlic powder |
| Parmesan cheese | ½ cup olive oil |
| ½ cup flour | 1 teaspoon salt |
| 1 egg | Freshly ground black pepper |
| 2 tablespoons dry white wine | |

Break off tough ends of asparagus stalks. Dip stalks first in flour, then in egg beaten with wine and then into crumbs combined with cheese, garlic powder, salt and pepper. Sauté in olive oil for 10 minutes or until tender. Serves 6.

## EGGPLANT STUFFED WITH OYSTERS

| | |
|---|---|
| 1 two-pound eggplant, | 2 tablespoons minced celery |
| halved lengthwise | ½ cup butter |
| 1 pint oysters, drained | 1 cup soft bread crumbs |
| and chopped | ¼ cup minced parsley |
| ¼ cup minced onion | ½ teaspoon thyme |
| 1 garlic clove, minced | |

Scoop out center of eggplant, leaving wall about ½ inch thick, and chop. Sauté chopped eggplant, onion, garlic and celery in butter, until onion is golden. Combine oysters and the remaining ingredients and add to hot eggplant mixture. Spoon into eggplant shells and place in buttered baking dish. Bake in a moderate oven (375°) for 30 minutes. Serves 6.

## BROILED TOMATOES WITH OLIVES

| | |
|---|---|
| 6 large tomatoes | 4 tablespoons chopped parsley |
| 4 tablespoons chopped | ½ teaspoon basil |
| ripe olives | ½ cup mayonnaise |
| 1 cup minced cooked ham | |

Cut tomatoes in half crosswise and place cut side up in greased baking dish. Bake in a moderate oven (350°) for 10 minutes. Combine remaining ingredients and spoon on top of each tomato. Broil at moderate heat until lightly browned. Serves 6.

## STUFFED CABBAGE LEAVES

| | |
|---|---|
| 12 large cabbage leaves | 2 tablespoons |
| ¾ pound ground veal | chopped fresh dill |
| ¾ pound ground beef | 1 teaspoon thyme |
| 4 tablespoons grated onion | 3 cups canned tomato sauce |
| ½ cup butter | 1 teaspoon salt |
| 1½ cups cooked rice | Freshly ground black pepper |

Combine meats and sauté with onion in butter until lightly browned. Add rice, dill, thyme, salt and pepper, and mix well. Place cabbage leaves in boiling water for 1 minute. Drain and pat dry. Spoon meat mixture on center of leaves, fold over, envelope fashion, and secure with toothpicks. Place in greased, shallow baking dish, pour tomato sauce over, cover and bake in a slow oven (325°) for 45 minutes. Serves 6.

## DEVILED CARROTS

| | |
|---|---|
| 6 large carrots, | 2 teaspoons dry mustard |
| quartered lengthwise | Tabasco sauce |
| ½ cup butter | ½ teaspoon salt |
| 2 tablespoons brown sugar | Freshly ground black pepper |

Sauté carrots in butter for 5 minutes. Add brown sugar, mustard, 2 drops of Tabasco sauce, salt and pepper, and cook for 10 minutes or until tender. Serves 6.

## BAKED SPINACH

| | |
|---|---|
| 3 pounds spinach | 2 tablespoons red |
| 6 slices bacon | wine vinegar |
| ½ cup chopped onion | 1 teaspoon salt |
| ½ teaspoon ground cinnamon | Freshly ground black pepper |

Wash spinach. Cut leaves crosswise into ½-inch strips. Cut bacon into 1-inch pieces. Sauté bacon with onion until onion is lightly browned. Remove from heat, add cinnamon, vinegar, salt and pepper. Combine with spinach, place in greased baking dish, cover and bake in a moderate oven (350°) for 30 minutes or until spinach is tender. Serves 6.

# INTERNATIONAL FOOD

THE RECIPES FOR ALL DISHES SHOWN
IN THIS SECTION ARE ON PAGES 67-76

# EXOTIC CURRY

**T**HERE is no prettier meal to serve than curry, nor any that leaves
more latitude for experiment. Basically, curry is
a highly spiced Indian stew, sometimes, but not always, made
with curry powder. It is not so much cooked in the kitchen as it is
concocted in the imagination, for any kind of food—fish, fowl,
meat or vegetable—can be used in it. The ingredients pictured on the
opposite page give an idea of the scope of the curry.

Curry is exotic but also very practical. It may be made
from leftovers and actually tastes better when warmed up a day or two
after cooking. Because a busy housewife can prepare it
at her leisure, store it in the refrigerator and reheat it for her family
and guests, the dish is being served with increasing regularity
in the U.S. An added reason for its new popularity is the discovery
by experimenting cooks that curry does not need to be hair-raisingly hot
but can be made as bland as taste demands.
Fresh fruits make the best desserts to serve with a curry.

There are over 200 varieties of curry powders available in the U.S.
and the experimental cook will try mild, hot and medium powders.
In addition to full-scale curry dishes, curry powder may be used to give
added flavor to broiled tomatoes, eggs, soups, sandwich spreads,
cheese dips, rice and baked beans. It may also add an exotic touch
to mayonnaise, cream sauce, French dressing and butter.

Almost as important as the ingredients that go into a curry are
the condiments that are served with it. These can be as simple as potato chips
or as fancy as crystallized violets, and the range of their color
and flavor is almost unlimited. Many curry condiments are shown on the
next three pages. The traditional ones are chutney, chopped pickle
and shredded coconut. But the array of condiments presented
may number as many as 30—savory, sharp, dulcet, pungent, sweet,
salty, tart foods in small dishes or Chinese divided trays.
The curry connoisseur combines sweet with sour, salty with savory, mixing
a little of each with mouthfuls of curried chicken or sea food and rice.

Lobsters, crabs, lentils, round steak, fish, eggs and leftover turkey
all are good foods to curry. This picture shows them surrounded by ingredients
that can go with them. Copper pan of lentils is surrounded clockwise
by black pepper, curry powder, salt, brown sugar, cayenne pepper
and whole ginger. At top is basket of curry powders and Worcestershire sauce.
Wooden scoop in center foreground holds broken walnuts.

Thirty condiments surround the three curry
and two rice dishes shown here. At lower left,
in round bowl, is Indian chicken curry.
Circling it, from bottom left, are white raisins,
dark raisins, chopped chives, chopped baked ham,
shredded Bombay duck, mustard pickle,
pickled walnuts, crumbled potato chips.
At bottom left, in pink bowl,
are crystallized rose petals. Above curry
are kumquats, and above them, fresh chutney
and rice pilau. Big pink bowl holds boiled rice
served with chopped parsley. Center foreground
is chutney, behind which are peanuts
and shredded coconut. To left behind big bell
are chopped lemon peel, orange marmalade,
fresh scallions and radishes, a bowl of pickles.
In right foreground is shrimp curry,
circled from left by watermelon pickles,
crystallized violets, chopped lime peel,
chopped egg yolk, sweet pickled onions and
salted coconut flakes. Brass bowl above shrimp
holds curried lamb, is circled
by guava jelly, chopped egg white,
crystallized ginger, chopped green olives,
chopped bacon. Behind lamb curry is spicy
lemon pickle, and at top right, preserved ginger.

# CHINESE
# COOKING

**A**N ancient Chinese gourmet said, "Every eating material can be
made palatable," and his countrymen have always taken him at his word.
Among the eating materials that the Chinese use are snakes, shark fins,
fermented eggs and birds' nests. Such out-of-the-way ingredients
as these have given many housewives the impression that Chinese cooking
is too strange and difficult to undertake. But actually it is the
Chinese genius for giving flavor and spirit to commonplace vegetables,
meat and fish that has earned them their great culinary fame.

Most Chinese dishes call for familiar foods, such as chicken, shrimp,
pork, eggs, mushrooms, duck, cabbage and cucumbers, all of which,
as well as the other needed ingredients, are usually available
at any corner market. Many Chinese dishes have Western near-counterparts.
Egg foo yung, made with meat or sea food, is really much like
an omelet. Won ton soup is a clear chicken stock with pork-filled won tons,
a kind of Chinese ravioli. Some of the dishes allow an imaginative cook
a lot of leeway. "Chop suey" simply means mixture. And "sub gum,"
though it translates as "10 different varieties of beauty," means a mixture
of 10 different things, usually vegetables.

For all their elaborate look and interesting flavors, most Chinese dishes
are economical to make. Chinese cooking requires a strong arm
for chopping and a wary eye for timing. The meat is usually cut
in very thin slices across the grain. The vegetables are sliced thin,
cross grain, and diced finely or cut carefully into equal lengths. Thus
Chinese dishes often take longer to prepare than American ones. But all those
shown here can be fixed in advance and, except for pineapple duckling,
they take much less time to cook. Chinese use only the youngest,
tenderest vegetables and cook them two or three minutes—just enough
to preserve their freshness. Even meat and fish are mildly cooked.

Chinese and American meals differ widely in manner of serving. The
American meal builds up to an important main course, while the Chinese
is based on four or five important courses, all served at once. Rice
accompanies all dishes. On the next pages are some Chinese dishes
modified to American taste. For still more Chinese dishes which
go well as a midday meal, see Party Brunches on pages 103 through 108.

Rice, the staple of all Chinese meals, is shown in two versions: boiled rice,
in individual dishes, and shrimp fried rice in an antique Chinese bowl.
The table is decorated with festive dragons; caddy at upper right holds tea.

48

Displayed against a gay background,
these Chinese dishes are, beginning at top left,
won ton soup in an ironstone tureen,
and Chinese fried shrimp curls at its right.
Next right in the pedestal bowl
is beef chop suey, and below that is
sub gum chow mein. Farthest right
in top row are sweet and sour meat balls.
Egg foo yung is in second row at left,
stirred cabbage in pedestal bowl
to the right. In front of the cabbage,
in round tureen, is cucumber and meat slice soup.
To the right are egg rolls and, next right,
sweet and pungent pork in low dish.
At bottom right is pineapple duckling—
the Chinese cook duck better than anybody else.
At far left are the standard tea and rice.
In center foreground are almonds,
mustard and plum sauce, sweet and tart
Chinese condiments. Behind the egg rolls
is a dish of soy sauce, which accompanies
most Chinese dishes. The cups
at left and right are Chinese covered teacups.

# DISHES
# OF INDIA

IN India, as in other countries where people are poor, food is prepared
with a high degree of ingenuity. Connoisseurs rate Indian cooking
with the French and Chinese as one of the world's great cuisines. The secret
of Indian cooking lies in the seasoning, which is not pepper-hot
as most people imagine. Prepared curry powder is not used in India.
Instead, spices are added in various combinations to suit individual taste.
Thus dishes range from bland to hot over the whole scale of taste.

The Indians' experience with herbs and spices goes back to the beginnings
of civilized history. There are traces of spice boxes
as far back as 4000 B.C., and it was the lure of Indian spices
that set Columbus on his way. In India today, the imaginative use
of spices is a highly developed art. But the beginner can quickly learn
its basic rules. Generally, the stronger spices like cloves,
ginger and turmeric go best with meats. Care should be taken not to use
the gentler, aromatic herbs like basil, chervil and tarragon together,
as each tends to cancel the other's flavor. Like Chinese dishes,
Indian food can be prepared in advance and refrigerated until needed.
If this is done, spices and herbs should be used more sparingly
because refrigeration tends to strengthen them.

Rice is almost as important as spices in Indian cooking. Rice is
believed to have originated in India and thousands of different kinds
are grown there today. The best rice is selected
by experts, and sometimes aged as much as 15 years. Most Indian cooks
boil it, but they also fry it, cook it with meat or with gravy
or serve it with syrup as dessert.

Indian cooking is very precise. But it is not complicated and,
with a little care and imagination, anyone can prepare authentic dishes
as they are done in India. There housewives rival
the great chefs, and some of the finest cooking is done in the homes.
The recipes for the regional foods shown on the opposite page
were collected from Indian housewives. Most of India's regions have
their own famous delicacies. Punjab, which is considered
a gourmet's paradise, is widely known for its lamb. Bengal is celebrated
for its fish dishes, Malabar and Chamba for their sea food and rice.

Seven regional dishes of India cover map. Clockwise from top of map are: sweet rice from Chamba, a dessert; roast chicken from Uttar Pradesh; poached haddock from Bengal; broiled shrimp from Malabar in a marinade of olive oil, mint leaves and spices; stuffed squash from the Deccan; cubed lamb with spinach from Punjab; skewered pork from Rajasthan with sliced eggs, onions, beets.

# FRENCH LESSON IN INNARDS

**T**HE French say that it takes either a great gourmet or a simple peasant to prepare hearts, kidneys, tripe and other innards (American butchers call them variety meats) so they are fit to eat. In the U.S. these meats, though served in the best and most expensive restaurants, are hardly ever eaten at home. This is partly because most Americans have an unthinking prejudice against them, but also because they are tricky meats which, though not hard to cook, have to be handled carefully.

The very delicacy of these variety meats is what makes their handling critical. They must be absolutely fresh, since they deteriorate quickly, so it is a good idea to order them from the butcher a couple of days in advance. Most of them require preliminary preparation. Brains and sweetbreads (calves' are the sweetest and tenderest) should be precooked the minute one gets them home, then refrigerated. Veal and beef kidneys should be parboiled and rinsed before cooking to remove their alkaline flavor (lamb kidneys do not require this). Lamb and pork (but not beef and calf) liver should be scalded. And sweetbreads and hearts have tissues that must be removed.

Once these simple chores are done, innards are no harder to handle than other meats. Tripe should be cooked slowly; it gets tough unless cooked over a low heat for a long time. Liver and kidneys, on the other hand, get tough unless cooked quickly over high heat. Liver is best cut very thin and served slightly rare in the center— if overdone, it gets rock-hard. Liver is not a good leftover dish so it should be ordered carefully, about one-half pound to a person.

As cooked by the French, with wine and herbs and special seasonings, variety meats are more than worth the trouble. All of them are highly nutritive and are economical because there is practically no waste. Arranged in casseroles and chafing dishes as shown on the next three pages, they are suitable for the fanciest occasions. But they are just as suitable for the day-to-day family table where they can provide a refreshing change from run-of-the-mill meat dishes. And those who cook them well and taste them with interest will have the additional pleasure of deciding for themselves which kind of culinary snobs they are—great gourmets or simple peasants.

Tripe and sweetbreads cooked in traditional French style
load a cellar table. Clockwise from the left foreground they are:
sautéed tripe; a platter of sweetbreads en brochette with mushrooms
and bacon, and a bowl of château sauce behind it; a chafing dish
of sweetbreads and ham in sherry to be served on toast;
a casserole of tripe à la mode de Caen; and sweetbreads baked with herbs.

Great dishes made from variety meats
are fine party fare. On the left-hand table,
clockwise from left, are: brains
with black olives; brains au beurre noir
in a chafing dish; cold beef tongue
with a small casserole
of horseradish cream sauce in front of it;
lamb tongues with raisin sauce.
On table in back, clockwise from left,
are: baked liver and onions;
roasted calf liver, in front of the
bread sticks, with bowl of béarnaise sauce;
veal heart and red wine stew in
white casserole; and deviled pigs' feet.
On the table in right foreground,
clockwise from left, are:
beef kidney pie to serve with the
waffles in holder to its right; basket
of bread; veal kidneys Ardennaise
on rice; casserole
of veal kidney and brandy stew.

# ANCIENT FARE

LIKE Amos 'n' Andy or pepper and salt, meat and potatoes
are commonly thought of together, and cooks nowadays feel they
are showing considerable ingenuity when they serve up the meat with rice
or some noodles instead. But there are foods that make just as good
potato substitutes and a pleasant change in the menu as well. They are
the dried beans, cereals, lentils and chick peas which have been enjoyed
with meat, fowl and fish since the days of the early Egyptians.

Lentils are probably the first food ever cultivated by man.
Wheat and barley were considered by the Egyptians to be a gift
from the goddess Isis, and the Greeks believed they came from Demeter.
In the New World dozens of varieties of beans were grown
long ago by the Indians. These foods have a comparatively bland flavor
which permits many different seasonings and has made them
perennial favorites in many parts of the world.

In the U.S. cereals have been used almost entirely as a breakfast food,
mainly for small children. Only three bean dishes
are commonly served: baked beans, bean soup and chili con carne.
Dried beans exist in almost every color of the rainbow,
spotted, speckled, big and small, and although the varieties
can be used interchangeably in most recipes, each has
its own subtle flavor. There are many different ways of cooking them
and tedious overnight soaking is no longer needed. Boiling the beans
for two minutes cuts soaking time to one hour.

All of these foods are at their best in simple recipes. Their flavor
is brought out by straightforward butter and herb sauces,
but it can also be enhanced by the addition of mushrooms, sour cream,
almonds or pungent sweet and sour sauce. Cracked wheat, buckwheat groats
and pearl barley are coarser than the usual breakfast cereals
and consequently have more flavor and texture. The nutty taste
of wheat and buckwheat makes them excellent side dishes with hearty
beef roasts, and delicately flavored barley goes particularly well
with ham. These foods are often as good cold as they are hot.
On the following pages these ancient ingredients are shown cooked in ways
that should be welcome additions to the menus of most modern cooks.

Five versatile and widely grown Mexican and South American beans are shown here raw and in dishes prepared from them. In foreground, left to right, are dried pink, black, large lima, red kidney and pinto beans. In next row are prepared dishes: pink beans with herb sauce and kidney beans in red wine. Above them are puréed limas and pinto bean cakes. At top are black beans in garlic sauce.

Some of man's oldest foods are shown in dishes prepared for modern menus. The ingredients are shown in five small containers at bottom right. They are chick peas, which were cultivated by the Egyptians and Jews; barley, grown by the Egyptians about the time of the invention of writing; wheat, originally found in Asia; lentils; and buckwheat, which spread to Europe from Asia. The cooked dishes in front of Greek figurines (left) are,

in foreground, cracked wheat with sour cream, next to it wheat
with mushrooms. Behind these are a pearl barley casserole and barley
with green butter. At top left in tureen are puréed chick peas and, beside it,
marinated chick peas. In right half of picture, dishes in back row
near ancient Chinese burial figures are boiled lentils and buckwheat puffs.
In front of them are sweet and sour lentils and buckwheat groats.

# PERFECT PASTA

**I**F you tried to eat your way through all the different kinds of pasta you could taste a new one every Sunday night for the next four years. The pasta family ranges from the familiar spaghetti, macaroni and lasagne to delicate little butterflies (*farfalle*), skeins (*matasse*) and sea shells (*maruzze*). It is the basis of the most widely popular Italian dishes in the U.S., the staple item of Italian restaurants, spaghetti joints and many American dinner tables. Pasta provides an inexpensive, easy, filling meal, but it can also be fixed with a party look and served to an elastic number of hungry guests.

Pasta is basically a mixture of durum wheat, which has been ground to the coarseness of sugar, and water. The paste is pressed into plain or fancy shapes, which determine the name, and then dried. The high gluten content of this amber-colored wheat, grown in the north central states, gives the adhesiveness necessary for shaping.

There are three fundamental rules which apply in cooking all pasta. The first is to use plenty of water. Using too little is the most common error. For one pound of spaghetti (enough for six) use six quarts of water. Four quarts of water is a minimum for even a handful of spaghetti—if less, it will be sticky and taste pasty. The second rule is that the water must be brought to a furious boil before the pasta is put in. Place it in the water gently and stir it immediately. Different kinds of pasta take different lengths of time to cook, and a timetable may be found on page 75. The third rule is to drain the pasta into a colander the instant it is done. Put it back in the hot pot, add a little butter and put on the lid.

Pasta can be served in countless ways by varying the sauces. They range from the popular tomato sauce to less usual ones of clams, chicken livers, anchovies or mushrooms. These should be put on each individual serving, and grated Parmesan or Romano cheese should be kept handy to sprinkle on top. Then it is up to the eater. If the pasta is spaghetti he has several techniques to pick from. The shovel-and-slurp school is best for speed, but hard on vest and tablecloth. The chop-and-balance school is neatest, but hard on the temper. The wind-on-fork school is most efficient, but it requires skill and a nimble wrist.

Behind an array of spices, meats and sea foods for his spaghetti sauces, Gene Leone, master chef and owner of a New York City restaurant, stirs a pot of pasta. In collection on table are the ingredients common to most spaghetti sauces: olive oil, tomatoes, garlic, onions. When spaghetti is almost done, he will test a strand with his teeth to make sure it is *al dente*—firm, not limp and soft.

Five popular Italian dishes
include, from left: manicotti,
a pasta form stuffed with mozzarella
and ricotta cheese; elbow macaroni
and cheese topped with tomato slices.
In the chafing dish, center, is
chicken cacciatore, cooked with tomatoes,
red wine, onions, peppers, served
with noodles. Next dish is lasagne,
made of pasta strips baked
in layers with meat, Parmesan cheese
and tomato sauce. Copper pan
at right holds peas and pasta shells.
While most pasta dishes are best served
immediately, this one may be prepared
ahead, refrigerated until dinnertime.
Behind the cooked dishes are
fresh fruits, vegetables, bread and
cheese and the Italian wines that line
the cellar of Leone's restaurant.

# RECIPES FOR INTERNATIONAL FOOD

# EXOTIC CURRY

### CHICKEN CURRY

| | |
|---|---|
| 3 two-pound chickens, cut up | 4 medium-sized apples, |
| 1 cup oil | pared and chopped |
| 1 cup finely chopped celery | ⅛ teaspoon cayenne pepper |
| 1 cup finely chopped onion | 2 teaspoons salt |
| 3 tablespoons curry powder | Freshly ground black pepper |

Sauté chicken in oil for 10 minutes or until brown. Remove chicken and keep hot. Add celery and onion to oil remaining in skillet and sauté for 5 minutes. Add all other ingredients. Cover and simmer for 30 minutes. Add chicken and 2 cups of boiling water, cover and simmer for 30 minutes. Serves 6. Turkey, duck or capon can be substituted for chicken but may take longer to cook. If leftover chicken is used, prepare the sauce separately and add the chicken 15 minutes before serving.

### SHRIMP CURRY

| | |
|---|---|
| 3 pounds shrimp | 2 cups milk |
| 3 coconuts | 2 tablespoons finely chopped |
| ¼ cup finely chopped onion | ginger root or 1 teaspoon |
| ¾ cup butter | ground ginger |
| ¾ cup flour | 3 tablespoons lemon juice |
| 2 tablespoons curry powder | 1 tablespoon salt |

Shell and wash shrimp. Pierce eyes of 3 coconuts, drain coconut liquid. If yield is less than 3 cups of liquid, add enough water to make 3 cups. Crack coconuts and grate their meat. Heat coconut liquid and pour over grated coconut. Let stand for 20 minutes and drain, saving coconut milk. (Keep grated coconut to serve with curry.) Sauté onion in butter in large saucepan for 5 minutes. Stir in flour and curry powder. Add coconut milk and fresh milk and cook over low heat until thickened, stirring constantly. Add shrimp, ginger, lemon juice and salt. Simmer, uncovered, for 30 minutes, stirring frequently. Serves 6. Any lean fish or shellfish cut in small pieces can be substituted for shrimp. Hard-cooked eggs can be used instead of sea food; in this case sauce should be prepared separately and quartered hard-cooked eggs added 10 to 15 minutes before serving. If fresh coconut is not obtainable, combine 3 cups shredded coconut with 3 cups fresh milk in a saucepan and let them stand at room temperature for 20 minutes. Bring to a boil, reduce heat and simmer for 10 minutes. Strain milk and substitute it for fresh coconut milk. Discard the coconut. Before chopping whole ginger root, soak it in cold water to cover for 1 hour. Drain the ginger root and squeeze out all of the water.

### CURRIED LAMB

| | |
|---|---|
| 3 pounds lamb shoulder | 4 tablespoons raisins |
| or neck | 2 tablespoons Worcestershire |
| ¼ cup flour | sauce |
| 2 garlic cloves, minced | 2 lemons, sliced |
| 4 large onions, sliced | 4 tablespoons shredded |
| ¾ cup butter | coconut |
| 4 small apples, pared | ¾ cup chopped walnuts |
| and chopped | ½ teaspoon grated lime peel |
| 4 tablespoons curry powder | 1 tablespoon salt |
| 4 tablespoons brown sugar | |

Cut meat into 2-inch cubes. Roll it in flour. Sauté garlic and onions in butter in large skillet for 5 minutes or until lightly browned. Add meat and sauté for 10 minutes, stirring constantly. Add apples and curry powder. Simmer for 5 minutes, stirring occasionally. Add the remaining ingredients and 2 cups of water. Bring to a boil, reduce heat, cover and simmer for 1 hour. Serves 6. Beef, veal or pork can be used instead of lamb. Fresh or leftover peas, string or wax beans, carrot slices, mushrooms or quarters of green pepper may be added to curry during the last 10 minutes of cooking.

### CURRIED LENTILS

| | |
|---|---|
| 1 cup dried lentils | 1 tablespoon flour |
| 2 tablespoons butter | ¼ cup dry white wine |
| 1 onion, sliced | 1 teaspoon salt |
| ¼ cup diced celery | Freshly ground black pepper |
| 1 tablespoon curry powder | |

Cook lentils in water to cover, with salt, for 30 minutes. Drain. Melt butter in skillet. Add onion, celery and curry powder and ¼ cup water. Cover and simmer for 10 minutes. Stir in flour mixed with wine and blend well. Add lentils and pepper. Simmer for 15 minutes. Serves 6.

### RICE PILAU

| | |
|---|---|
| 2 cups rice | Whole allspice |
| 1 cup butter | 1-inch piece stick cinnamon |
| 1 onion, finely chopped | ½ teaspoon ground turmeric |
| 1 garlic clove, chopped | ¼ cup blanched almonds |
| 12 cloves | ½ cup raisins |
| 12 cardamom seeds | 2 teaspoons salt |

Wash rice thoroughly in cold water. Drain. Sauté onion and garlic in ½ cup butter in large saucepan for 5 minutes. Add rice and continue cooking for 5 minutes, stirring constantly. Add 4 cups of boiling water and all the spices. Cover and simmer 30 minutes or until all water is absorbed. Melt remaining ½ cup butter in a skillet, add almonds and cook, stirring constantly, until golden brown. Stir almonds and raisins into the cooked rice. Serves 6.

### FRESH CHUTNEY

| | |
|---|---|
| ¼ cup chopped onion | ¼ cup chopped sweet |
| ½ cup chopped green pepper | red pepper |
| 2 tomatoes, peeled | ½ cup lemon juice |
| and chopped | |

Combine all ingredients. Let stand at room temperature for 1 hour, stirring frequently. Chill 1 hour. Makes about 2 cups.

### SPICY LEMON PICKLE

| | |
|---|---|
| 1 pound lemons, quartered | 1 teaspoon paprika |
| 4 tablespoons crushed | 3 cups oil |
| red pepper | 3 tablespoons salt |
| ¼ teaspoon garlic powder | |

Roll each lemon quarter in salt. Place them in a bowl. Cover and let stand at room temperature 4 days. Add red pepper, garlic powder and paprika. Heat oil. Pour over lemons. Cool. Cover and let stand at room temperature 4 days. Makes 1 quart.

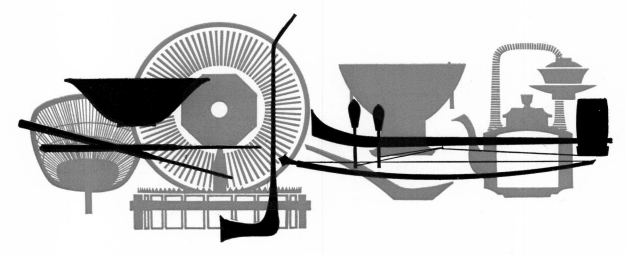

# CHINESE COOKING

### CHINESE STYLE BOILED RICE

Boiled in the Chinese manner, rice is very light and fluffy. Allow 3 cups long grain rice for 6 servings. Rinse rice in cold water until water runs clear. Put rice in deep, heavy saucepan. Add water, measuring proper amount by placing hand lightly on rice and adding enough to cover back of hand. Add salt to taste. Fit lid tightly on pot. Bring to boil over high heat. Cook for 3 minutes after steam shows around lid. Then cook over medium heat for 5 minutes. Turn to lowest heat and cook for 12 minutes. Remove from heat and let stand at least 10 minutes before serving.

### SHRIMP FRIED RICE

| | |
|---|---|
| 2 cups chopped cooked shrimp | 2 tablespoons soy sauce |
| 4 cups boiled rice | 1 teaspoon salt |
| ¼ cup oil | Freshly ground black pepper |
| 2 eggs, lightly beaten | 3 scallions, chopped |

Fry shrimp in oil in deep frying pan for 1 minute, stirring constantly. Add eggs, salt and pepper and fry over medium heat for 5 minutes, stirring constantly. Add rice and soy sauce and fry for 5 minutes, stirring frequently. Garnish with chopped scallions. Serves 6. Diced cooked chicken, pork or ham may be used instead of shrimp.

### WON TON SOUP

Won ton soup is a chicken broth with meat-filled pastries, called won tons, in it. Make the soup in three steps: first the meat filling, then the pastry "skins," finally the soup. This recipe serves 6.

#### WON TON FILLING

| | |
|---|---|
| 1 pound finely ground pork | 1 tablespoon soy sauce |
| 1 egg, beaten | Freshly ground black pepper |

Combine pork with other ingredients and mix thoroughly.

#### WON TON SKIN

| | |
|---|---|
| 2 cups flour | 1 teaspoon salt |
| 1 egg, lightly beaten | |

Sift flour and salt into a mixing bowl. Stir in egg. Add about ⅓ cup of water, a few drops at a time, mixing well after each addition until dough is right for rolling. Turn dough out onto a lightly floured board and knead it until it is smooth. Cover it with a towel and let stand for 20 minutes. Roll dough paper-thin and cut into 2-inch squares. There should be about 18. Place a spoonful of the won ton filling in the center of each square skin. Fold each skin around its filling, using a little water or egg white to stick the edges together.

#### COOKING THE SOUP

| | |
|---|---|
| Filled won tons | 2 tablespoons |
| 8 cups chicken bouillon | chopped scallions |
| Soy sauce | |

Bring bouillon to a boil in a large saucepan. Add a few won tons and cook them for about 5 minutes or until they float to the surface of the bouillon. Remove, drain, and keep them hot. Repeat until all won tons are cooked. Return cooked won tons to the soup before serving. Serve with soy sauce and garnish with chopped scallions.

### FRIED SHRIMP CURLS

| | |
|---|---|
| 3 pounds shrimp | 3 one-inch pieces ginger root, |
| ½ cup hoy sien jeung sauce | minced |
| 2 tablespoons sugar | 3 garlic cloves, minced |
| 6 tablespoons vinegar | 1 tablespoon cornstarch |
| ½ cup oil | 2 teaspoons soy sauce |
| 12 scallions, cut in | 2 teaspoons salt |
| 1-inch pieces | Freshly ground black pepper |

Wash shrimp. Pull off legs but not shells and tails. Make sauce of hoy sien jeung, sugar, vinegar, salt and pepper. Fry shrimp in oil for 1 minute on each side. Add sauce, scallions, ginger and garlic. Fry for 5 minutes, stirring constantly. Add cornstarch mixed with soy sauce and 1 tablespoon water. Fry for 2 minutes. Serves 6. This is based on an ancient Chinese recipe from Doreen Feng's *The Joy of Chinese Cooking*. One-half teaspoon garlic salt mixed with 2 tablespoons bouillon may be used instead of the Chinese flavoring hoy sien jeung.

### BEEF CHOP SUEY

| | |
|---|---|
| 1½ pounds beef, diced | 2 cups beef bouillon |
| ¼ cup oil | 2 cups canned bean sprouts, |
| 2 tablespoons soy sauce | drained |
| 3 cups celery, cut in | 3 tablespoons cornstarch |
| 1-inch pieces | 2 teaspoons salt |
| 2 large onions, chopped | Freshly ground black pepper |
| 1 tablespoon molasses | 6 cups hot boiled rice |

Fry beef in oil over high heat for 3 minutes, stirring constantly. Stir in soy sauce, salt and pepper. Remove meat and keep hot. To oil remaining in saucepan add celery, onion, molasses and bouillon. Bring to a boil and cook for 10 minutes, stirring frequently. Add bean sprouts and cook for 3 minutes. Replace beef. Mix cornstarch and ¼ cup water, and add. Cook until thickened, stirring constantly. Serve with rice. Serves 6. This is a recipe used at House of Chan, New York restaurant, and is included in *The House of Chan Cookbook*.

### SUB GUM CHOW MEIN

| | |
|---|---|
| 3 cups finely shredded | ¾ cup thinly sliced |
| cooked chicken | green beans |
| ½ cup oil | 9 scallions, chopped |
| 1½ cups diced canned | 2 garlic cloves, minced |
| water chestnuts | 1 tablespoon sugar |
| 1½ cups diced canned | 3 cups chicken bouillon |
| bamboo shoots | 3 tablespoons cornstarch |
| 3 cups diced celery | ¼ cup soy sauce |
| 2 cups sliced | 1 tablespoon salt |
| Chinese cabbage | Freshly ground black pepper |
| ¾ cup diced mushrooms | Chow mein noodles |
| 1 large green pepper, diced | ¾ cup toasted almonds |

Fry vegetables, sugar, salt and pepper in oil for 1 minute, stirring briskly. Add bouillon, bring to a boil, reduce heat, cover and simmer for 10 minutes. Combine cornstarch, soy sauce and 4 tablespoons water. Add to vegetable mixture and cook until thickened, stirring constantly. Add chicken and cook for 5 minutes. Serve with noodles, garnish with almonds. Serves 6.

## SWEET AND SOUR MEAT BALLS

| | |
|---|---|
| 1½ pounds ground beef | 2 tablespoons cornstarch |
| 2 eggs | 2 tablespoons soy sauce |
| 3 tablespoons flour | 1 teaspoon Ac'cent |
| ¾ cup oil | ¾ cup vinegar |
| 1½ cups chicken bouillon | ¾ cup pineapple juice |
| 3 large green peppers, diced | ¾ cup sugar |
| 6 slices canned pineapple, diced | ½ teaspoon salt |
| | Freshly ground black pepper |

Shape ground beef into 18 balls. Combine eggs, flour, salt and pepper. Dip meat balls in batter and fry in oil until brown. Remove meat balls and keep hot. Pour out all but 1 tablespoon oil from skillet. Add ½ cup bouillon, green pepper and pineapple. Cover and cook over medium heat for 10 minutes. Mix remaining ingredients and add. Cook, stirring constantly, until mixture comes to a boil and thickens. Add meat balls and simmer for 15 minutes. Serves 6.

## EGG FOO YUNG

| | |
|---|---|
| 6 eggs, lightly beaten | ½ cup canned bean sprouts, drained |
| 3 cups chopped cooked chicken | 6 tablespoons oil |
| 8 dried black Chinese mushrooms | Salt |
| 2 scallions, chopped | Freshly ground black pepper |
| ½ cup chopped celery | Chinese brown sauce |

Each serving of egg foo yung is usually cooked separately. First soak the mushrooms in 1 cup of water for 2 hours. Drain and chop. Combine eggs, chicken, vegetables, salt and pepper, stirring lightly. For each serving, heat 1 tablespoon of the oil in a 6-inch skillet. Pour in about 1 cup of the egg mixture and cook it over low heat until brown on one side. Turn carefully and cook until brown on the other side. Serve with Chinese brown sauce. Serves 6. This recipe is from Shanghai Low's in San Francisco. Shrimp, pork, turkey or crab meat may be substituted for the chicken. One cup canned water chestnuts or canned mushrooms, drained and chopped, may be substituted for Chinese mushrooms.

## CHINESE BROWN SAUCE

| | |
|---|---|
| 3 cups chicken bouillon | ½ teaspoon sugar |
| 2 tablespoons cornstarch | Freshly ground black pepper |
| 2 teaspoons soy sauce | |

Mix cornstarch with ½ cup cold bouillon. Combine with remaining bouillon, soy sauce, sugar and pepper. Bring to a boil, reduce heat and simmer until thickened, stirring constantly. Serve hot. Makes about 3 cups.

## STIRRED CABBAGE

| | |
|---|---|
| 1 two-pound Chinese cabbage | 1 teaspoon salt |
| ¼ cup oil | |

Cut cabbage in half lengthwise and remove stem. Slice cabbage crosswise into ½-inch strips. Chop stem. Fry stem in oil for 1 minute. Add salt and ½ cup water. Cover and cook for 3 minutes. Add the sliced cabbage leaves, cover and cook over medium heat for exactly 3 minutes. Serve cabbage with any juice that remains. Serves 6. New American cabbage may be substituted for the Chinese. Quarter cabbage. Discard center stalk, then cut cabbage crosswise into ½-inch strips. Heat oil in skillet, add cabbage, cook for 1 minute. Add salt and water. Cook covered for 3 minutes.

## CUCUMBER AND MEAT SLICE SOUP

| | |
|---|---|
| 2 medium cucumbers, sliced | ½ teaspoon sugar |
| ½ pound flank steak, sliced paper-thin | 1 tablespoon oil |
| 1 tablespoon sherry | 3 pounds beef marrow bones |
| 2-inch piece ginger root | Salt |
| | Freshly ground black pepper |

Marinate beef in sherry, ginger root, sugar, oil, salt and pepper for 1 hour. Put cucumber and marrow bones into 2 quarts of boiling water. Bring to a boil, reduce heat, cover and simmer for 45 minutes. Add beef and marinade to the soup and simmer for 10 minutes. Skim off any fat. Serves 6. This recipe is from Lum Fong's Chinese restaurant in New York.

## EGG ROLLS

Egg rolls are made in three steps. A vegetable, shrimp and meat filling is wrapped in pancake-like skins and then fried in oil. This recipe makes 12.

### EGG ROLL FILLING

| | |
|---|---|
| ½ cup finely chopped celery | 4 scallions, finely chopped |
| ¾ cup shredded cabbage | ½ cup water chestnuts, drained and finely chopped |
| 3 tablespoons oil | |
| ½ cup diced cooked shrimp | 1 garlic clove, minced |
| ½ cup diced cooked pork | ¼ cup soy sauce |

Put celery and cabbage in ½ cup water. Bring to a boil. Drain. Heat oil in skillet, add shrimp and pork. Fry for 3 minutes, stirring constantly. Add remaining ingredients and fry for 5 minutes, stirring constantly. Ham, beef, veal or chicken may be used instead of pork.

### EGG ROLL SKINS

| | |
|---|---|
| ¾ cup sifted flour | Sugar |
| 1 tablespoon cornstarch | ¼ cup oil |
| 2 eggs, beaten | 1 teaspoon salt |

Sift flour, cornstarch and salt into a bowl. Beat in eggs and a pinch of sugar. Add 1½ cups of water slowly, beating constantly, until batter is smooth. To make each egg roll skin, grease a hot 6-inch skillet with about 1 teaspoonful of oil. Pour about 3 tablespoons of batter into skillet, tipping skillet to spread batter over bottom. Fry over medium heat until batter shrinks from the sides of the skillet. Turn skin and fry for 1 minute on the other side. Remove and cool. Batter is sufficient to make about 12 skins.

### COOKING THE EGG ROLLS

| | |
|---|---|
| 12 egg roll skins | 1 tablespoon flour |
| 1 recipe of egg roll filling | ½ cup oil |

Place 4 tablespoons filling on center of each egg roll skin, fold two sides over edges of filling and roll up the skin. Seal with paste made from flour and 2 tablespoons water. Fry in oil until golden brown. Serves 6.

## SWEET AND PUNGENT PORK

| | |
|---|---|
| 1½ pounds pork shoulder, cubed | ¾ cup brown sugar |
| 2 eggs, beaten | 1 cup vinegar |
| 1 cup flour | 3 tablespoons molasses |
| Peanut oil | 3 tomatoes, peeled and diced |
| 3 green peppers, cut in strips | 2 tablespoons cornstarch |
| 2 cups drained canned pineapple chunks | 1 teaspoon salt |
| | Freshly ground black pepper |

Combine eggs, flour, salt and ¼ cup water. Add pork cubes and stir until coated. Fry pork in 2 inches of hot oil (375°) for 3 minutes or until golden brown. Drain pork, keep it hot. Combine green pepper, pineapple, brown sugar, vinegar, molasses, black pepper and 1½ cups of water. Bring to a boil, stirring constantly. Add tomatoes and simmer for 5 minutes, stirring occasionally. Combine cornstarch with ¼ cup cold water, and stir into green pepper mixture. Cook until thickened, stirring constantly. Add pork and simmer for 15 minutes. Serves 6.

## PINEAPPLE DUCKLING

| | |
|---|---|
| 2 five-pound ducks, quartered | ½ teaspoon ground ginger |
| ¼ cup oil | 2 tablespoons cornstarch |
| 3 cups canned pineapple chunks, drained | 2 tablespoons soy sauce |
| ¾ cup pineapple juice | 1 tablespoon salt |
| 1 cup diced green pepper | Freshly ground black pepper |
| | 6 cups hot boiled rice |

Put duck in a large saucepan with salt and 6 cups of water. Bring to a boil, reduce heat, cover and simmer for 45 minutes. Remove and dry duck. Strain and save broth. Sauté duck in oil for 15 minutes or until golden brown. Add 2½ cups of broth, pineapple chunks, green pepper and ginger. Cover and simmer for 15 minutes. Remove duck and keep it hot. Combine pineapple juice, cornstarch, soy sauce and black pepper and stir into broth mixture. Cook until thickened, stirring constantly. Return duck to broth, cover and simmer for 10 minutes. Serve with rice. Serves 6.

# DISHES OF INDIA

### SWEET RICE FROM CHAMBA

1½ cups rice
¼ teaspoon whole saffron
  or ⅛ teaspoon
  ground saffron
1 cup sugar
¾ cup butter
Seeds of 2 cardamom pods
2 cloves
2 tablespoons raisins

2 tablespoons unsalted
  pistachio nuts
2 tablespoons cashews,
  Brazil nuts or filberts
2 tablespoons
  blanched almonds
1 tablespoon lemon juice
½ teaspoon salt

Boil rice in 3 cups of water with saffron and salt for 10 minutes. Drain. Boil sugar in 2 cups of water for 1 minute, stirring constantly. Set aside. Melt butter in heavy saucepan, add cardamom seeds and cloves. Simmer for 10 minutes. Add rice and 1½ cups sugar syrup. Mix well. Simmer for 10 minutes, stirring frequently. Add remaining ingredients and simmer for 15 minutes or until rice is done, stirring once or twice. If mixture becomes too dry add remaining syrup. Remove from heat, cover and let stand for 15 minutes. Serve warm or cold. If desired, serve with whipped cream. Serves 6.

### ROAST CHICKEN FROM UTTAR PRADESH

3 two-pound chickens
8 tablespoons
  coriander seed
1½ teaspoons ground ginger
6 onions
1 cup yoghurt

1 cup heavy cream
½ cup butter
1 tablespoon ground turmeric
Seeds of 4 cardamom pods
1 teaspoon salt
Freshly ground black pepper

Wash and dry chickens. Prick them all over with a fork. Crush coriander and mix with ginger and pepper. Rub into chickens. Grate 4 onions and mix with yoghurt, cream, butter, turmeric, cardamom seeds and salt. Roast chickens in moderate oven (350°) for 45 minutes, basting frequently with onion and cream mixture. Slice the 2 remaining onions and place on the chickens. Roast for 15 minutes. Serves 6.

### POACHED HADDOCK FROM BENGAL

3 pounds haddock
1½ teaspoons ground turmeric
6 cups buttermilk
1 tablespoon lemon juice
1 tablespoon cumin seed

3 tablespoons chopped
  green pepper
5 tablespoons butter
1 teaspoon salt
Freshly ground black pepper

Wash and dry fish. Rub with turmeric and pepper. Poach in buttermilk for 5 minutes. Remove fish and keep warm. Add lemon juice and salt to liquid remaining in pan and simmer until liquid reduces to one half. Replace the fish and add cumin and green pepper. Simmer for 10 minutes. Brown the butter and pour over the fish. Serves 6.

### BROILED SHRIMP FROM MALABAR

3 pounds shrimp
1½ cups oil
5 garlic cloves, crushed
2 tablespoons chopped mint
2½ teaspoons chili powder

1 tablespoon ground turmeric
1 tablespoon basil
2 tablespoons vinegar
1 teaspoon salt
Freshly ground black pepper

Shell and wash shrimp. Marinate in remaining ingredients for at least 6 hours. Pour shrimp and marinade into shallow pan and broil under high heat 6 to 10 minutes, turning once. Serve with the marinade. Serves 6.

### STUFFED SQUASH FROM THE DECCAN

3 medium-sized squash,
  yellow or zucchini
1 onion, minced
Whole saffron
½ cup butter
¼ cup yoghurt
Seeds of 1 cardamom pod,
  crushed

1 cup cream
⅓ cup almonds, blanched
  and ground
2 teaspoons lemon juice
1½ teaspoons
  coriander seed
½ teaspoon salt
Freshly ground black pepper

Split squash lengthwise and scoop out center, leaving wall ½ inch thick, and chop. Add onion and a pinch of saffron. Sauté in ¼ cup butter for 5 minutes. Add yoghurt and cardamom and simmer for 10 minutes. Add cream mixed with ground almonds, lemon juice and salt. Simmer for 5 minutes. Place the mixture in squash shells, dot with remaining ¼ cup butter and sprinkle with coriander and pepper. Bake in a moderate oven (350°) for 20 minutes. Serves 6.

### LAMB WITH SPINACH FROM PUNJAB

3 pounds lean lamb, cut in
  2½-inch cubes
1½ pounds spinach, cut in
  ¼-inch strips
3 onions, thinly sliced
6 tablespoons butter
1½ teaspoons ground turmeric

1 tablespoon coriander seed
4 teaspoons ground ginger
¾ teaspoon chili powder
3 tablespoons yoghurt
¼ teaspoon thyme
4 teaspoons mustard seed
1 teaspoon salt

Sauté onions in butter. Add meat, turmeric, coriander, ginger and chili powder and simmer for 10 minutes. Stir in spinach, yoghurt, thyme, mustard seeds and salt. Cover and simmer for 15 minutes, stirring occasionally. Add ¼ cup water and simmer for 15 minutes. Serves 6.

### SKEWERED PORK FROM RAJASTHAN

3 pounds pork, cut in
  1-inch cubes
6 onions
3 cups yoghurt
3 tablespoons
  coriander seed
1 teaspoon ground ginger
¾ cup butter

2 teaspoons ground cinnamon
1 tablespoon
  cardamom seed
1 tablespoon whole cloves
3 eggs
3 beets, sliced thin
¾ teaspoon ground turmeric
1½ teaspoons salt

Simmer meat, 3 sliced onions, yoghurt, coriander, ginger, ½ cup butter and ½ cup of water for 30 minutes, stirring occasionally. Add cinnamon, cardamom, cloves and salt. Stir, cover and simmer for 5 minutes. Meanwhile boil eggs, 3 whole onions and beets together for 15 minutes. Shell eggs and slice eggs and onions thin. Remove meat and put alternate pieces of meat, eggs, onions and beets on small skewers. Sprinkle with turmeric, sauté in skillet with remaining ¼ cup butter for 10 minutes or until brown. If desired, strain the sauce that meat cooked in and serve with skewered pork. Serves 6.

# FRENCH LESSON IN INNARDS

### TRIPE

The inner lining of the stomach of beef, tripe, is always parboiled before it is sold. In parboiling some butchers use more salt than others. Add salt cautiously when preparing tripe.

#### SAUTEED TRIPE

| | |
|---|---|
| 3 pounds tripe | 1 cup butter, melted |
| 2 stalks celery with leaves, cut up | 1 cup dry bread crumbs |
| ½ cup chopped parsley | 1 tablespoon salt |
| ½ teaspoon thyme | 12 peppercorns, cracked |
| 1 large onion, sliced | 2 tablespoons chopped chives |
| 1 garlic clove | |

Cut tripe into 2-by-3-inch pieces. Cover with cold water. Add celery, parsley, thyme, onion, garlic, salt and peppercorns. Bring to a boil, reduce heat, cover pan and simmer for 4 hours. Remove from heat and let stand in broth until cold. Drain thoroughly, dip tripe in melted butter and then into crumbs Sauté in remaining butter for 10 minutes or until golden brown. Sprinkle with chives. Serves 6.

#### TRIPE A LA MODE DE CAEN

| | |
|---|---|
| 6 pounds tripe | 3 garlic cloves, minced |
| 2 pounds marrow bone | 10 shallots, minced |
| 1 calf's foot, cut up | 1 bay leaf, crumbled |
| 1 cup apple brandy | ¼ cup chopped parsley |
| 2 cups dry white wine | ½ cup chopped celery leaves |
| 4 cups beef bouillon | 1 tablespoon salt |
| 2 cups diced carrot | Freshly ground black pepper |
| 2 cups chopped onion | |

Cut tripe into 2-inch squares. Combine with remaining ingredients in a deep casserole or Dutch oven with a tightly fitting lid. Wrap covered casserole in foil. Cook in a slow oven (300°) for 12 hours. Remove bones before serving. This is a classic recipe and serves 12 generously.

### SWEETBREADS

Only lamb, beef and calf sweetbreads are used in cooking. Calf's heart sweetbreads are the sweetest and tenderest. Sweetbreads should be precooked the second one gets them home. Plunge them into fresh cold water to cover. Add 1 tablespoon vinegar, 1 teaspoon salt for each quart of water. Bring the water to a boil and simmer gently for 15 minutes. Drain the sweetbreads and plunge into cold water. When they are cold, cut away and discard the tough tissue that connects them. Put sweetbreads back in refrigerator with a plate on top of them to flatten them if desired. Serve them within 24 hours.

#### SWEETBREADS EN BROCHETTE

| | |
|---|---|
| 3 pairs sweetbreads | 3 medium green peppers, cut in 1-inch squares |
| 1 egg, beaten | |
| 1 tablespoon dry white wine | ½ cup butter, melted |
| ½ cup bread crumbs | ½ teaspoon salt |
| 6 slices bacon, cut in pieces | Freshly ground black pepper |
| 24 mushroom caps | Château sauce |

Cut each parboiled sweetbread into 4 pieces, dip into egg beaten with wine, salt and pepper. Then dip into bread crumbs. Thread on skewers, alternating sweetbreads with bacon, mushrooms and peppers. Broil under low heat, basting with melted butter, until golden brown. Serve with château sauce. Serves 6.

#### CHATEAU SAUCE

| | |
|---|---|
| ½ cup chopped onion | 3 cups strong beef bouillon |
| 2 tablespoons chopped shallots | 2 tablespoons bottled meat extract |
| ¾ cup butter | ¼ cup chopped mushrooms |
| 4 tablespoons flour | ¼ cup dry white wine |
| ⅓ cup canned tomato purée | |

Sauté onion and shallots in 4 tablespoons butter until golden. Add flour and cook until deep brown, stirring constantly. Add tomato purée, bouillon and meat extract and cook until thickened, stirring constantly. Combine mushrooms with wine and cook over high heat for 5 minutes. Stir into thickened sauce. Melt the remaining ½ cup of butter and beat it into the sauce with a wire whisk or rotary beater until thoroughly blended. Makes about 4 cups.

#### SWEETBREADS AND HAM IN SHERRY

| | |
|---|---|
| 2 pairs sweetbreads | ½ pound mushrooms, sliced |
| ½ pound boiled ham, cubed | 1 cup heavy cream |
| ½ cup dry sherry | ½ teaspoon salt |
| 4 tablespoons butter | Freshly ground black pepper |
| 1 green pepper, cut in strips | Toast |

Cut parboiled sweetbreads into cubes. Melt butter, add sweetbreads, ham and green pepper and sauté for 10 minutes, stirring frequently. Add mushrooms and cook for 5 minutes. Add sherry and the remaining ingredients and simmer for 5 minutes. Do not boil or sauce will curdle. Serve on toast. Serves 6.

#### SWEETBREADS BAKED WITH HERBS

| | |
|---|---|
| 3 pairs sweetbreads | 1 bay leaf, crumbled |
| 4 tablespoons butter, melted | ½ teaspoon thyme |
| ½ cup chopped onion | 2 tablespoons dry sherry |
| 1 garlic clove, minced | 1 cup beef bouillon |
| ½ cup diced carrot | 1 teaspoon salt |
| ¼ cup chopped parsley | |

Pour butter into casserole; add onion, garlic, carrot, parsley, bay leaf and thyme. Bake in a very hot oven (450°) for 15 minutes. Put sweetbreads on top of mixture. Add sherry, bouillon and salt. Reduce heat to 350° and bake for 45 minutes, basting occasionally. Serves 6.

### BRAINS

Calf's brains have the most delicate flavor but beef, pork or lamb's brains may be used. Allow one pound for 3 or 4 people. Brains should be precooked as soon as one gets them home. To precook, put brains in saucepan with enough cold water to cover, add 2 tablespoons vinegar, 1 teaspoon salt, 5 peppercorns, ½ onion sliced, 1 small carrot sliced, pinch of thyme, a bay leaf. Bring to a boil and let simmer for 30 minutes. Store in refrigerator in this liquid until ready for final cooking.

## BRAINS WITH BLACK OLIVES

| | |
|---|---|
| 3 pairs calf brains | 2 tablespoons finely chopped |
| ½ cup sliced black olives | green pepper |
| 4 tablespoons butter | 1 tomato, peeled and diced |
| ¼ cup grated onion | 1 tablespoon capers |
| 2 tablespoons flour | 2 tablespoons lemon juice |
| 2 cups beef bouillon | 1 teaspoon salt |
| 2 egg yolks, beaten | |

Remove brains from liquid in which they were stored. Cut into cubes. Melt butter, add onion and flour and stir until well blended. Add bouillon and cook until thickened, stirring constantly. Stir 2 tablespoons of this hot mixture into the beaten egg yolks. Gradually add egg mixture to hot sauce, stirring constantly. Simmer for 5 minutes (do not boil). Add brains and remaining ingredients and simmer for 15 minutes. Serves 6.

## BRAINS AU BEURRE NOIR

| | |
|---|---|
| 6 pairs calf brains | 2 tablespoons lemon juice |
| 4 tablespoons flour | ¼ cup chopped parsley |
| ¾ cup butter | 2 tablespoons capers |

Remove brains from liquid in which they were stored and dry them. Dust with flour. Sauté in butter until golden brown. Put brains on a platter and keep them hot. Continue cooking butter until it turns dark brown. Remove from heat and add lemon juice, mixing well. Pour over brains. Sprinkle with chopped parsley and capers. Serves 6.

## LIVER

Beef and calf livers do not require scalding but lamb or pork livers do. To scald, drop into boiling water for 1 minute. Drain immediately. Lamb or pork liver may be substituted for calf's liver in any recipe and prepared in the same way.

## BAKED LIVER AND ONIONS

| | |
|---|---|
| 6 slices beef liver | 1 bay leaf, crumbled |
| 2 large onions | 1 teaspoon thyme |
| ½ cup butter | ½ cup flour |
| ½ cup dry red wine | 1 teaspoon salt |
| ¼ cup chopped parsley | Freshly ground black pepper |

Cut onions into ½-inch slices. Arrange in baking dish. Dot with butter. Add wine, parsley, bay leaf, thyme, salt, pepper and ½ cup of water. Cover and bake in a moderate oven (350°) for 30 minutes. Coat liver with flour. Place on top of onion slices, cover and bake 30 minutes, basting two or three times. Remove cover, bake for 10 minutes. Serves 6.

## ROAST CALF LIVER

| | |
|---|---|
| 1 three-pound calf liver | ½ teaspoon salt |
| 12 slices bacon | Freshly ground black pepper |
| 1 tablespoon grated onion | Béarnaise sauce |

Put 6 slices of bacon on bottom of baking dish and place liver on top of it. Spread liver with grated onion, sprinkle with salt and pepper. Put 6 remaining bacon slices on top of liver. Bake in a moderate oven (325°) for 1 hour. Serve with béarnaise sauce. Serves 6.

## BEARNAISE SAUCE

| | |
|---|---|
| 1 cup dry white wine | 1 teaspoon tarragon |
| 3 egg yolks, beaten | 1 teaspoon chervil |
| 2 tablespoons | 1 cup butter, melted |
| tarragon vinegar | ½ teaspoon salt |
| 1 tablespoon chopped parsley | Freshly ground black pepper |
| 1 tablespoon minced shallots | |

Beat 2 tablespoons of the wine into egg yolks. Set aside. Combine the remaining wine with vinegar, parsley, shallots, ½ teaspoon tarragon, ½ teaspoon chervil, salt and pepper and cook for 15 minutes, stirring occasionally. Remove from heat and add egg yolk mixture slowly, stirring briskly. Add butter 2 tablespoons at a time, beating thoroughly after each addition. Strain through a fine sieve. Add the remaining tarragon and chervil and stir well. Makes about 2 cups.

## KIDNEYS

Veal or beef kidneys should be parboiled for 15 minutes in salted water, drained and rinsed at once to remove all alkaline odors. Lamb kidneys do not need this. All these kidneys may be used in any kidney recipe.

## BEEF KIDNEY PIE

| | |
|---|---|
| 2 beef kidneys | 4 tablespoons butter |
| 6 large onions, chopped | 1 teaspoon salt |
| 1 garlic clove, minced | Freshly ground black pepper |
| ¾ cup flour | 6 waffles |
| 2 tablespoons dry sherry | |

Cover parboiled kidneys with 2 quarts water, add onion, garlic, salt and pepper. Bring to a boil, reduce heat, cover and simmer for 1 hour. Remove kidneys from broth, cool, trim and dice. Mix flour with 1 cup water, add to broth and cook until thickened, stirring constantly. Add sherry. Sauté diced kidneys in butter for 5 minutes and add to thickened broth. Serve on waffles. Serves 6.

## VEAL KIDNEYS ARDENNAISE

| | |
|---|---|
| 12 veal kidneys | 1 cup chicken bouillon |
| 2 tablespoons | 3 tablespoons flour |
| minced shallots | ½ teaspoon salt |
| 1 cup sliced mushrooms | Freshly ground black pepper |
| ¼ cup diced green pepper | 3 cups hot cooked rice |
| ½ cup butter | ½ cup chopped parsley |
| ½ cup brandy | |

Split kidneys and cut into ½-inch slices. Sauté shallots, mushrooms and green pepper in butter for 5 minutes. Add kidneys and simmer for 5 minutes, stirring once or twice. Heat brandy, light it and pour over kidney mixture. When flame dies, stir in bouillon. Cover, simmer for 10 minutes. Stir in flour mixed with salt, pepper and ¼ cup water, and cook until thickened, stirring constantly. Serve over rice mixed with parsley. Serves 6.

## VEAL KIDNEY AND BRANDY STEW

| | |
|---|---|
| 6 veal kidneys | ¼ cup dry white wine |
| 2 tablespoons brandy | 1 cup beef bouillon |
| 1 onion, minced | 1 tablespoon |
| 4 tablespoons butter | chopped parsley |
| 1 cup sliced mushrooms | 1 teaspoon salt |
| 3 tablespoons flour | Freshly ground black pepper |

Dice kidneys. Sauté onion in butter until golden brown. Add kidneys and mushrooms and simmer for 10 minutes, stirring frequently. Add flour and mix well. Add wine and beef bouillon and cook until thickened, stirring constantly. Add brandy and remaining ingredients, simmer for 5 minutes. Serves 6.

## TONGUE, HEART, PIGS' FEET

Lamb's tongue is bought fresh. Beef tongue comes fresh or smoked. In the heart recipe, beef, lamb or pork heart may be used. Veal heart is most flavorful and tender. Heart should be rinsed in cold water and the coarse fibers at the top and inside removed before cooking. Pigs' feet may be bought whole or split. For the deviled pigs' feet recipe, ask the butcher to split them.

## LAMB TONGUES WITH RAISIN SAUCE

| | |
|---|---|
| 12 lamb tongues | ½ cup brown sugar |
| ½ cup raisins | ½ cup dry white wine |
| 1 large onion | 2 tablespoons cornstarch |
| 1 garlic clove | 1½ teaspoons salt |
| 1 bay leaf | Freshly ground black pepper |

Cover tongues with cold water. Add onion, garlic, bay leaf and 1 teaspoon salt. Bring to a boil, cover, reduce heat and simmer for 2 hours. Remove from heat and let cool for 30 minutes in stock. Remove tongues and skin them. Strain stock. Add raisins and brown sugar to 2 cups of strained stock. Bring to a boil and stir in wine mixed with cornstarch, remaining ½ teaspoon salt, and pepper. Reduce heat and simmer until thickened, stirring constantly. Add tongues and simmer 20 minutes. Serves 6.

## COLD BEEF TONGUE

| | |
|---|---|
| 1 three-pound smoked beef tongue | 1 bay leaf |
| 2 onions | 4 tablespoons butter |
| 1 garlic clove | 1 cup dry white wine |
| 1 stalk celery with leaves, cut up | 1 tablespoon salt |
| 1 clove | 6 peppercorns, crushed |
| | Horseradish cream sauce |

Cover tongue with cold water. Add onions, garlic, celery, clove, bay leaf, salt and peppercorns. Bring to a boil, reduce heat, cover and simmer for 3 hours. Drain, discard stock and cool tongue. Peel tongue and remove bones and gristle from thick end. Sauté in butter in a deep pot until brown. Add wine and 1 cup of water. Bring to a boil, reduce heat, cover and simmer for 2 hours, turning after 1 hour. Remove from heat and allow tongue to cool in the broth. Drain and chill. Serve with horseradish cream sauce. Serves 6.

## HORSERADISH CREAM SAUCE

| | |
|---|---|
| ¼ cup horseradish | 1 teaspoon salt |
| 1 cup heavy cream | |

Add salt to cream and whip until stiff. Fold in horseradish. Chill. Makes about 2 cups.

## VEAL HEART AND RED WINE STEW

| | |
|---|---|
| 1 pound veal heart, diced | ½ cup chopped parsley |
| 1 pound veal kidney, diced | 1 garlic clove, minced |
| ½ pound pork liver, diced | 2 cloves |
| 2 cups dry red wine | 1 bay leaf, crumbled |
| ½ cup flour | ½ teaspoon thyme |
| 4 tablespoons butter | ½ pound mushrooms, sliced |
| ½ cup chopped celery leaves | 1 teaspoon salt |
| 1 tablespoon chopped chives | Freshly ground black pepper |

Roll diced heart, kidney and liver in flour. Sauté in butter in large saucepan for 10 minutes or until lightly browned, stirring constantly. Add celery, chives, parsley, garlic, cloves, bay leaf, thyme, salt and pepper plus enough water to cover. Bring to a boil, reduce heat, cover pan and simmer for 3 hours, stirring occasionally. Add wine and mushrooms and simmer for 15 minutes, stirring occasionally. Serves 6. If desired, the stew may be thickened with cornstarch. Mix 1 tablespoonful with ¼ cup cold water, add a little hot broth from the stew, and stir cornstarch mixture into the stew.

## DEVILED PIGS' FEET

| | |
|---|---|
| 6 pigs' feet, split | 2 eggs, beaten |
| 1 large onion | 2 tablespoons dry white wine |
| 2 garlic cloves | 1 tablespoon A-1 sauce |
| ½ cup chopped celery with leaves | ¼ teaspoon Tabasco sauce |
| 6 tablespoons chopped parsley | 1 cup dry bread crumbs |
| 1 teaspoon thyme | ¼ teaspoon dry mustard |
| 1 teaspoon sage | ½ cup butter |
| 1 bay leaf | 1½ teaspoons salt |
| ½ cup flour | Freshly ground black pepper |
| | Applesauce |

Scrub pigs' feet thoroughly. Put them in heavy saucepan and add onion, garlic, celery, 4 tablespoons parsley, thyme, sage, bay leaf and 1 teaspoon salt, plus enough water to cover. Bring to a boil, reduce heat, cover pan and simmer for 2 hours or until pigs' feet are tender. Drain and discard stock. Cool pigs' feet. To devil the pigs' feet roll them in flour and dip into egg mixed with wine, A-1 sauce, Tabasco sauce, remaining ½ teaspoon salt, and pepper. Then dip into bread crumbs seasoned with mustard and remaining 2 tablespoons parsley. Sauté in butter for 10 minutes or until golden brown. Serve with cold applesauce. Serves 6.

# ANCIENT FARE

## PINK BEANS WITH HERBS

| | |
|---|---|
| 2 cups dried pink beans | ½ cup chopped chives |
| ½ cup olive oil | 1 teaspoon oregano |
| ½ cup butter | 1 teaspoon rosemary |
| 2 tablespoons lemon juice | 1 teaspoon salt |

Soak beans overnight in water to cover. Simmer them in the soaking water with salt for 2 hours. Drain beans and keep them hot. Combine remaining ingredients and simmer for 10 minutes. Add to beans and mix well. Serves 6. Dried lima, pinto or navy beans may be substituted for pink beans.

## KIDNEY BEANS IN RED WINE

| | |
|---|---|
| 2 cups dried red kidney beans | 2 tablespoons butter |
| 1 cup dry red wine | 2 tablespoons flour |
| 4 slices bacon, cut up | 1 teaspoon salt |
| 1 tablespoon grated onion | Freshly ground black pepper |

Soak beans overnight in water to cover. Simmer them in the soaking water with bacon and salt for 2 hours. Drain beans and keep them hot. Sauté onion in butter for 5 minutes. Add flour and pepper and stir until smooth. Add wine and cook until thickened, stirring constantly. Add to beans and mix well. Serves 6. Black beans may be substituted for red kidney beans. Four cups of canned kidney beans, heated and drained, may be used instead of 2 cups of dried beans, soaked and cooked.

## PUREED LIMA BEANS

| | |
|---|---|
| 2 cups dried lima beans | 4 tablespoons chopped parsley |
| 1 cup chopped onion | |
| 4 tablespoons butter | 1 teaspoon salt |

Soak beans overnight in water to cover. Simmer them in the soaking water with salt for 1 hour. Drain. Sauté onion in butter for 10 minutes. Press beans through coarse sieve or food mill. Add all but 4 tablespoons of the sautéed onion and 2 tablespoons parsley. Beat well and put in casserole. Sprinkle remaining onion on top and bake in a moderate oven (350°) for 20 minutes. Sprinkle with remaining parsley before serving. Serves 6. Pinto, navy or Great Northern beans may be substituted for lima beans. Four cups of canned lima beans, heated and drained, may be used instead of 2 cups of dried limas, soaked and cooked.

## PINTO BEAN CAKES

2 cups dried pinto beans
¼ teaspoon crushed red
   pepper or 1 chili pepper,
   minced
2 garlic cloves, chopped
½ cup butter
1 teaspoon salt

Soak beans overnight in water to cover. Simmer them in the soaking water with salt for 2 hours. Drain beans and chop them coarsely or put them through a food grinder using coarse blade. Add red pepper and garlic. Shape into 12 cakes and sauté in butter for 10 minutes or until golden brown. Lima, navy or Great Northern beans may be substituted for pinto beans. Four cups of canned pinto or lima beans, heated and drained, may be substituted for 2 cups of dried beans, soaked and cooked.

## BLACK BEANS IN GARLIC SAUCE

2 cups dried black beans
2 ounces salt pork, diced
2 garlic cloves, sliced
1 teaspoon cumin seed
1 teaspoon salt

Soak beans overnight in water to cover. Simmer them in the soaking water with salt for 2 hours. Drain and keep hot. Sauté diced pork for 5 minutes. Add garlic and sauté for 5 minutes or until pork dice are crisp and garlic slices are golden brown. Stir in cumin seeds and beans. Serves 6. Four cups of canned limas, heated and drained, may be used instead of 2 cups of dried beans, soaked and cooked.

## CRACKED WHEAT WITH SOUR CREAM

2 cups cracked wheat
1 cup sour cream
½ cup butter
½ cup olive oil
3 cups chicken bouillon

Sauté cracked wheat in butter and olive oil until golden brown, stirring constantly. Add bouillon and simmer for 30 minutes, stirring occasionally. Stir in sour cream, serve hot or cold. Serves 6.

## CRACKED WHEAT WITH MUSHROOMS

1½ cups cracked wheat
1 cup sliced mushrooms
½ cup chopped onion
¼ cup butter
3½ cups chicken bouillon
1 teaspoon salt
Freshly ground black pepper

Sauté mushrooms and onion in butter for 5 minutes or until lightly browned, stirring occasionally. Add cracked wheat and cook for 5 minutes, stirring constantly. Add bouillon, salt and pepper. Bring to a boil, reduce heat, cover and simmer for 30 minutes, stirring occasionally. Serves 6.

## PEARL BARLEY CASSEROLE

1 cup pearl barley
½ cup pine nuts
½ cup butter
1 cup finely chopped onion
1 cup finely chopped parsley
½ cup finely chopped chives
6 cups beef bouillon
1 teaspoon salt
Freshly ground black pepper

Sauté pine nuts in butter for 5 minutes or until golden brown. Remove nuts and sauté onion in butter remaining in skillet for 5 minutes. Add barley and brown lightly, stirring constantly. Add parsley, chives, bouillon, salt and pepper and half of the pine nuts and pour into casserole. Bake in a moderate oven (350°) for 1 hour, stirring once after 30 minutes. Sprinkle the rest of the sautéed pine nuts over the top and bake for 20 minutes more. Serves 6.

## BARLEY WITH GREEN BUTTER

1 cup pearl barley
½ cup butter
1 tablespoon grated onion
4 tablespoons chopped parsley
2 teaspoons
   poultry seasoning
1 teaspoon salt

Combine barley with salt and 4 cups of water. Bring to a boil, reduce heat, cover and simmer for 1 hour or until barley is tender. Drain barley and rinse with hot water to remove excess starch. Return to pan, cover and keep hot. Sauté onion in butter for 5 minutes or until lightly browned. Add parsley and poultry seasoning to onion and stir into barley. Serves 6.

## PUREED CHICK PEAS

2 cups dried chick peas
¼ cup heavy cream, scalded
¼ cup butter, melted
Nutmeg
1 teaspoon salt

Soak peas overnight in water to cover. Simmer them in the soaking water with salt for 30 minutes. Drain. Press through coarse sieve or food mill. Add cream and butter slowly, beating constantly. Sprinkle with nutmeg. Serves 6. Four cups of canned chick peas, heated and drained, may be used instead of 2 cups of dried peas, soaked and cooked.

## MARINATED CHICK PEAS

2 cups dried chick peas
1 cup vinegar
¼ cup olive oil
½ cup minced onion
1 garlic clove, minced
1 teaspoon sugar
¼ teaspoon Tabasco sauce
2 teaspoons salt
Freshly ground black pepper

Soak peas overnight in water to cover. Simmer them in the soaking water with 1 teaspoon salt for 30 minutes. Drain. Combine remaining ingredients and pour over hot peas. Let stand at room temperature for 3 hours. Chill for 1 hour or more. Serves 6. Four cups of canned chick peas, heated and drained, may be used instead of the dried peas, soaked and cooked.

## BOILED LENTILS

2 cups dried lentils
6 medium onions, sliced
2 tablespoons chopped parsley
2 ounces salt pork, sliced
1 small bay leaf, crumbled
¼ teaspoon ground cloves
½ cup butter
Freshly ground black pepper

Combine all ingredients except butter and simmer in water to cover for 30 minutes. Drain. Add butter and mix well. Serves 6.

## BUCKWHEAT PUFFS

½ cup buckwheat groats
4 tablespoons butter
¼ teaspoon Tabasco sauce
½ cup flour
2 eggs
4 tablespoons minced onion
2 teaspoons salt
Oil or vegetable shortening

Bring butter, Tabasco, salt and ½ cup water to a boil. Add flour all at once and cook over low heat, stirring constantly, until mixture leaves sides of pan and forms compact ball. Remove from heat and add eggs, one at a time, beating well after each addition. Continue beating until the mixture has a satiny sheen. Beat in the groats and onion. Drop by teaspoonfuls into hot oil (375°) 2 inches deep. Cook for 5 minutes or until golden brown. Makes 12 puffs.

## SWEET AND SOUR LENTILS

2 cups dried lentils
2 slices bacon
4 tablespoons chopped onion
1 garlic clove, minced
2 tablespoons wine vinegar
1 tablespoon cornstarch
2 tablespoons sugar
¼ teaspoon ground nutmeg
1 teaspoon salt
Freshly ground black pepper

Simmer lentils in water to cover, with salt, for 30 minutes. Drain lentils and keep them hot. Keep broth. Sauté bacon until crisp. Remove bacon, cool, crumble and save it. Add onion and garlic to bacon fat and sauté until golden brown. Combine 1 cup of lentil broth with remaining ingredients. Add to onion mixture and cook until thickened, stirring constantly. Add lentils and mix well. Sprinkle with crumbled bacon. Serves 6.

## BUCKWHEAT GROATS WITH ALMONDS

2 cups buckwheat groats
1 cup blanched almonds,
   slivered
½ cup olive oil
1 garlic clove, minced
4 tablespoons
   chopped onion
4 tablespoons chopped
   green pepper
4 cups chicken bouillon

Sauté almonds in olive oil until golden brown. Remove and save almonds. Add garlic, onion and green pepper to oil remaining in saucepan and sauté until onion is golden brown, stirring frequently. Add groats and bouillon and mix well. Pour into casserole and bake in a slow oven (325°) for 30 minutes. Stir in almonds. Bake for 15 minutes. Serves 6.

# PERFECT PASTA

## HOW TO COOK PASTA

| MACARONI | COOKING TIME |
|---|---|
| Elbow macaroni | 7-10 minutes |
| Long macaroni | 9-12 minutes |
| Cut macaroni | 9-12 minutes |
| **SPAGHETTI** | |
| Thin spaghetti | 6 minutes |
| Regular spaghetti | 8-10 minutes |
| **EGG NOODLES** | |
| Fine egg noodles | 6-8 minutes |
| Regular egg noodles | 8-10 minutes |
| Wide egg noodles | 10-12 minutes |
| **VARIETY SHAPES** | |
| Alphabets | 6-8 minutes |
| Farfalle (butterflies) | 9-12 minutes |
| Mostaccioli (quills) | 7-12 minutes |
| Pastina | 5-7 minutes |
| Rigatoni | 9-12 minutes |
| Maruzze (sea shells) | 7-10 minutes |
| Lasagne | 6-10 minutes |
| Manicotti | 6-10 minutes |

### TOMATO MEAT SAUCE

2 medium tomatoes, peeled and diced
4 cups tomato purée
1 pound ground beef
4 ounces Italian salami, finely chopped
1 beef marrow bone
1 cup chopped onion
½ cup olive oil
½ cup butter
2 garlic cloves, minced
6 bay leaves, crumbled
½ cup chopped parsley
2 teaspoons oregano
½ teaspoon ground allspice
Crushed red pepper
1 teaspoon salt
Freshly ground black pepper

Sauté onion in olive oil and butter for 10 minutes, add garlic and bay leaves, cover and simmer for 10 minutes. Add beef and salami and sauté for 10 minutes, stirring frequently. Add tomatoes and all the other ingredients. Bring to a boil, reduce heat, cover and simmer for 1 hour, stirring occasionally. Remove marrow bone before serving. Makes about 6 cups.

### CHICKEN LIVER SAUCE

½ pound chicken livers, cut up
2 cups finely chopped onion
2 garlic cloves, minced
¾ cup olive oil
¼ cup butter
6 slices bacon, minced
½ cup minced parsley
2 green peppers, finely chopped
Crushed red pepper
3 cups canned Italian tomatoes
¼ cup dry red wine
2 teaspoons salt
Freshly ground black pepper

Sauté onion and garlic in combined olive oil and butter for 10 minutes or until onion is golden brown. Add chicken livers and sauté for 5 minutes. Add bacon, parsley, green peppers, a pinch of red pepper, salt and black pepper. Cover and simmer for 10 minutes. Add tomatoes and wine and bring to a boil. Reduce heat, cover and simmer for 20 minutes, stirring occasionally. Makes about 6 cups.

### ANCHOVY SAUCE

2 two-ounce cans anchovy fillets
2 garlic cloves, minced
1 cup olive oil
½ cup butter
1 cup finely chopped parsley
½ teaspoon basil
Freshly ground black pepper

Sauté garlic in combined olive oil and butter for 5 minutes. Add anchovies and their oil, parsley, basil and pepper; simmer for 15 minutes, stirring occasionally. Makes about 3 cups.

### MUSHROOM SAUCE

1½ pounds mushrooms, sliced thin
2 garlic cloves, minced
½ cup olive oil
¼ cup butter
2½ cups canned Italian tomatoes
½ teaspoon oregano
1 teaspoon salt
Freshly ground black pepper

Simmer mushrooms, garlic, salt and pepper in combined olive oil and butter for 10 minutes, stirring frequently. Add tomatoes and oregano and simmer for 30 minutes. Makes about 6 cups.

### CLAM SAUCE

2 dozen cherrystone clams, shucked
3 garlic cloves, finely chopped
¾ cup olive oil
1 cup butter
½ cup finely chopped parsley
1 teaspoon basil
½ teaspoon oregano
Crushed red pepper
Freshly ground black pepper

Drain clams and save their liquor. Chop clams coarsely. Sauté garlic in combined olive oil and butter for 5 minutes. Add the clams and clam liquor, parsley, basil, oregano, a dash of red pepper and black pepper. Simmer for 20 minutes, stirring occasionally. Makes about 6 cups. To make a red clam sauce, add 2 cups canned tomato purée when adding the clams.

### TOMATO SAUCE

2½ cups canned Italian tomatoes
2 six-ounce cans tomato paste
½ cup chopped onion
2 garlic cloves, minced
¼ cup olive oil
2 tablespoons butter
2 tablespoons chopped parsley
¼ teaspoon oregano
¼ teaspoon basil
1 teaspoon salt
Freshly ground black pepper

Sauté onion and garlic in combined olive oil and butter for 10 minutes. Stir in tomatoes, tomato paste, parsley, oregano, basil, salt and pepper. Bring to a boil, reduce heat, cover and simmer for 40 minutes, stirring occasionally. Makes about 6 cups.

### GARLIC SAUCE

6 garlic cloves, sliced
1 cup olive oil
1 cup butter
1 tablespoon fresh chopped parsley
1 teaspoon basil
½ teaspoon oregano
1 teaspoon salt
Freshly ground black pepper

Sauté garlic in combined olive oil and butter for 5 minutes. Add parsley, basil, oregano, salt and pepper and simmer for 5 minutes, stirring constantly. Makes about 2 cups.

## MANICOTTI

12 ounces manicotti, boiled
and drained
12 ounces mozzarella cheese,
diced
¾ cup ricotta
or cottage cheese
3 eggs, lightly beaten

6 tablespoons grated
Parmesan cheese
2 tablespoons butter
2 cups tomato sauce
½ teaspoon salt
Freshly ground black pepper

Combine mozzarella, ricotta and 2 tablespoons Parmesan cheese, eggs, butter, salt and pepper. Stuff each manicotti with cheese mixture. Pour a thin layer of tomato sauce in a shallow baking dish and put manicotti on top of it. Spoon the rest of the tomato sauce over the manicotti and sprinkle with remaining Parmesan cheese. Bake in a moderate oven (375°) for 20 minutes. Serves 6.

## MACARONI AND CHEESE

8 ounces elbow macaroni,
boiled and drained
1 cup diced mozzarella cheese
½ cup grated
Parmesan cheese
½ cup grated Cheddar cheese
4 tablespoons butter
2 tablespoons flour

3 cups milk
1 teaspoon grated onion
1 tablespoon A-1 sauce
4 medium tomatoes, peeled
and sliced
1 teaspoon salt
Freshly ground black pepper

Melt butter, add flour and blend until smooth. Add milk and cook until thickened, stirring constantly. Add cheeses, onion, A-1 sauce, salt and pepper. Cook until cheese melts, stirring constantly. Remove from heat and combine with macaroni. Put half of this mixture into a greased casserole and arrange half of the tomato slices on top. Repeat. Bake in moderate oven (350°) for 20 minutes. Broil under medium heat for about 10 minutes or until cheese sauce bubbles and begins to brown. Serves 6.

## CHICKEN CACCIATORE AND NOODLES

2 three-pound chickens,
cut up
8 ounces noodles, boiled
and drained
½ cup olive oil
½ cup butter
2 cups finely chopped onion

1 green pepper, chopped
4 garlic cloves, mashed
½ teaspoon basil
1 cup canned tomatoes
¼ cup dry red wine
1 teaspoon salt
Freshly ground black pepper

Sauté chicken in combined olive oil and butter for 10 minutes or until golden brown. Add onion, green pepper, garlic, basil, salt and black pepper and simmer for 5 minutes. Add tomatoes. Bring to a boil, reduce heat, cover and simmer for 20 minutes, stirring occasionally. Add wine and simmer for 10 minutes. Put noodles into warm casserole or serving dish. Serve chicken and sauce over the noodles. Serves 6.

## LASAGNE

8 ounces lasagne, boiled
and drained
1 cup chopped onion
½ cup olive oil
2 tablespoons butter
2 garlic cloves, finely chopped
2 pounds ground beef
½ pound salami, chopped
1 teaspoon ground nutmeg

½ teaspoon ground allspice
¼ teaspoon crushed
red pepper
3 cups tomato sauce
½ cup grated
Parmesan cheese
½ teaspoon salt
Freshly ground black pepper

Sauté onion in combined olive oil and butter for 10 minutes. Add garlic and sauté for 5 minutes. Add beef and salami and sauté for 15 minutes, stirring frequently. Add spices, cover and simmer for 15 minutes, stirring frequently. This lasagne is made with four layers of the lasagne noodles, three of meat. Pour about ¼ inch of tomato sauce in the bottom of a baking dish. Put one layer of lasagne on top of the sauce, add a third of the meat mixture and sprinkle lightly with Parmesan. Repeat, ending with a layer of lasagne. Pour about 1 cup of tomato sauce over the lasagne. Bake in a moderate oven (375°) for 30 minutes. Heat the rest of the tomato sauce and serve it with the lasagne. Serves 6.

## PEAS AND PASTA SHELLS

8 ounces pasta shells,
boiled and drained
2½ cups cooked fresh, frozen
or small canned peas
1 cup finely chopped onion
2 garlic cloves, minced

¼ cup olive oil
¼ cup butter
1 cup finely chopped parsley
½ teaspoon salt
Freshly ground black pepper

Sauté onion and garlic in combined olive oil and butter for 10 minutes. Add pasta shells, peas, parsley, salt and pepper and mix well. Put in a casserole. Cover and bake in a moderate oven (350°) for 15 minutes. Serves 6.

# ENTERTAINING

THE RECIPES FOR ALL DISHES SHOWN
IN THIS SECTION ARE ON PAGES 121-138

# FLAMING FOOD

**O**NE of the most festive ways to entertain formally is to cook, or finish cooking, the food right on the table, before the guests' eyes. It is also one of the most practical. Quick, hot, on-the-scene preparation improves the flavor of many good dishes and whets the appetite of the diners while adding drama to the occasion.

The most spectacular method, of course, is to flame the food itself, in a chafing dish or in a platter or on a skewer that can be as fancy as the dagger shown on the opposite page. The real purpose of serving food *flambe* is to add a final fillip to a dish which has already been cooked in a chafing dish or prepared in the kitchen. To flame the food use distilled spirits like brandy, whisky, gin, rum or kirsch—a good domestic brandy will do as well as a fine cognac. First warm a spoon over a match or candle. Pour in the liquor, light it and pour it on the food. The warm spoon makes the liquor light readily and does away with those fizzled-out matchsticks sometimes found floating in the platter. By the time the flame has gone out the food will have absorbed the taste of the liquor, as well as some of its zip.

A commoner method is to use a chafing dish for on-the-table cooking. Back in the '20s these dishes were mainly used for such niceties as fudge or Welsh rarebit, but today they are being put to work in many maidless households to make or warm more solid fare. Because it can keep food warm as well as cook it, the chafing dish is ideal to use at teen-age parties, after football games or at any meal where guests are apt to drift in late. Basically the chafing dish is a pan on a stand over a heater. The pan can be copper, brass, silver, pottery or aluminum, as plain or fancy, cheap or expensive as you like. Some chafing dishes, primarily used to warm food for serving, are heated by candles or alcohol lamps. Others, which do more actual cooking, use canned heat or electricity.

Some of the dishes shown on the next three pages, like the Swiss fondue and sukiyaki, are best when actually cooked at the table. Others, like the chipped beef in mushroom sauce and Mexican corn casserole, can be kept warm for hours on end. And the rest, like the flaming duck or kippers, are eye-catching when served *flambé*.

With a ball of brandy-soaked cotton flaming at its tip, a handsome dagger pierces a tomato and beef collops interspersed with mushrooms and pieces of green pepper. Before they were flamed on the dagger, collops and vegetables were cooked on a skewer over hot coals in the brazier at upper right. At lower left peach halves flame in brandy in a copper pan over an alcohol stove.

Nine main course dishes, three desserts and two winter drinks are shown
flaming, cooking or keeping hot on the table. Starting in left half
of picture, counterclockwise from lower left, are: sukiyaki ingredients,
sukiyaki cooking in pan, chicken with broccoli, flaming crepes Suzette,
flaming fruitcake. Left center on red starred warmer is Mexican corn casserole.
In center foreground in chafing dish is shrimp Newburg. Flaming cabbage

with meat balls, center, has at its left its accompanying barbecue sauce.
Behind cabbage are Swiss fondue in casserole and flaming kippers
in oval copper dish; behind the kippers, a casserole for warming rolls.
In front of kippers is chipped beef in mushroom sauce and in right foreground,
flaming duck in copper pan beside its sauce. At far right are
farmer's punch in big bowl, four flaming sundaes, café diable and cups.

# FULL-SUPPER SANDWICHES

JOHN MONTAGU, fourth Earl of Sandwich, once spent 24 hours at the gaming table sustained only by slices of cold beef clapped between slabs of bread. This refreshment was promptly named after him and became popular in England with persons who were busy— whether at the gaming table or elsewhere. It also captured the fancy of tea-sipping ladies who cut off the crusts of the bread and trapped a damp cucumber between the slices.

The two major sandwich schools—the businesslike and the ladylike— persist to this day. In the U.S. drugstores and lunch counters everywhere dispense the former and the latter is as much in evidence as gossip at any bridge party. But currently an even more interesting kind of sandwich is gaining popularity. It is the full-supper sandwich served to family or to guests as a meal in itself.

This sandwich marks a sharp break with the old English tradition. It is neither an effete snack nor a neatly stacked store concoction. It is more like the Swedish, Danish and Italian sandwiches which use several fillings and many different kinds of bread. Actually it is a couth relative of the Dagwood sandwich brought out of the kitchen into the dining room or patio.

The best way to serve the full-supper sandwich is to set out the various fillings and the bread and let the diners help themselves, varying the proportions as they please to satisfy both their appetites and creative urges. How varied the ingredients of these meal-in-the-hand sandwiches may be and how many kinds of crusty bread may be used is shown opposite and on the following pages.

Some of these sandwiches have a stylish past, as does the Riviera on page 85, a favorite of the Côte d'Azur. Others, like the New Orleans poor boy, a hearty, hero-type sandwich, have plebeian origins and have long been known to laborers' lunch boxes. These sandwiches may be served for lunch or supper and even the hot ones will not spoil if guests are late. After the meal the cook has few plates, knives or forks to wash, and even the inveterate three-course-dinner man will have had enough to eat.

Pink onion and Liederkranz supper sandwich is concocted from marinated Italian
onions (in pink bowl above), slices of softened Liederkranz cheese
(on cheese board) and sour rye bread (on bread board). Sandwich can also
be made with pumpernickel, Kommissbrot or other breads of strong character.
The cook merely soaks the onion slices for one hour (allotting one onion
per person), sets out the creamy cheese. Diners do the rest.
Liederkranz connoisseurs say that the cheese is best at almost runny consistency.
For this, take it out of the refrigerator two hours before serving.

**POOR BOY SANDWICH**

**PIZZA SANDWICH**

**FISH FRY SANDWICH**

**CHICKEN ROLL SANDWICH**

**RIVIERA SANDWICH**

Proving that the whole is even tastier than the sum of its parts is the cheese and chili-burger combination above, which is simply the traditional hamburger patty made with red wine and dressed with chili and/or cheese sauce (kept hot in the casseroles over candle flame). Cheese sauce can be thinned by adding beer or milk. Burgers should be served with raw onion rings, hot buttered rolls.

# GAME BIRDS

**N**ORTH AMERICA was once a vast game preserve whose skies darkened
with immense flocks of wild birds. Then the white man came
with his taste for game, his guns and dogs that killed it
and his plows that tore up the natural breeding grounds. By 1900
whole species of birds had all but vanished. Since then an intelligent
conservation policy and the adaptability of the birds themselves
have restocked the sky. Now, in any normal season, hunters can expect
to bring home some 70 million assorted fowl. On the next four pages
seven of the best known of these birds appear in photographic still lifes,
accompanied by the guns that killed them and by the condiments,
side dishes and wine that will accompany them on a well-dressed table.

All game birds have a very special flavor, something over and above
the taste or consistency of their flesh. To a hunter each bite
of a bird he has shot will re-create moments he has loved—the sudden burst
of a grouse from cover, the silky whistle of ducks coming in,
the skittering flight of a woodcock. Even nonhunters, as they first savor
the unaccustomed gaminess, are for an instant transported
to the woods, fields and marshes and the days when man hunted to live.

In actual taste the game bird varies much more than the domestic fowl.
On the gamier side are birds like rail and woodcock, whose flesh
has a strong, wild flavor. On the milder side are pheasant, quail and grouse,
which are basically white-meat birds. Ducks vary with place
and time of the year. Their taste depends on what they have been eating,
and the delicious mallard shot in the Midwest, where it has been
eating grain, may be almost inedible in the deep South,
where it has been feeding in swamps. An important variable in taste
is the length of time the birds are hung. Quail need little or no hanging
and may be eaten the day they are shot. Other birds, like pheasant,
improve in flavor if they are hung for a while in a cool, airy place. Depending
on the weather, a pheasant may be hung from two days to two weeks.

In cooking the birds shown on the following pages there are two basic rules.
An old bird should never be roasted but cut up and stewed or served
in a casserole. Pheasant and partridge are drier birds than goose
and duck; they should be covered with strips of bacon before roasting.

Pheasant, the gourmet's favorite bird, was successfully
introduced to U.S. only in 1881. It is especially good roasted
with brandy and cream, served with wild rice.

Canada goose flies at a 2,000-foot altitude
from Alaska and Canada to winter in the U.S. It can be
a tricky target, makes a flavorsome meal.

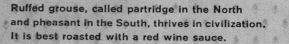

Ruffed grouse, called partridge in the North
and pheasant in the South, thrives in civilization.
It is best roasted with a red wine sauce.

Mourning dove, found in all 48 states, is regarded
as a songbird in some but a game bird
in 30 of them. It is cooked stuffed with onion.

Mallard duck, most plentiful North American waterfowl, is a fast, far-ranging flier. A famous delicacy, it is excellent with apricot sauce.

Quail, of which six species (these are bobwhite) inhabit open spaces from Manitoba to Texas, are adaptable, fast breeding, wary when much hunted.

Wild turkey, once native to 39 states, is still found in 22. Roasted with peanut stuffing, served with white wine, it makes a memorable dinner.

# EGG DISHES

IN its form alone, artists like to say, the egg approaches perfection.
In content, the nutritionists say, it is a nearly perfect food.
But the average American, who eats an egg a day, tends to take his privilege
lightly. To him the egg is the commonest thing in the kitchen.
And when he is asked about his own culinary skill he is pretty certain
to come up with the coy disclaimer, "Well, I can boil an egg."

As a matter of fact, an egg should never be boiled.
High temperatures or prolonged exposure to heat makes the egg white,
which is almost pure protein, shrink, lose its moisture and
turn into something like leather. And, all in all, there is a great deal
more to simple egg cooking than most people think.

The way not to boil an egg is to pluck it out of a chilly icebox
and toss it into fast-boiling water. To soft-cook an egg properly, put it
in a saucepan and cover it with cold water. Place the saucepan
over high heat and bring the water to a boil. Then turn off the heat,
cover the pan and let the egg stand from two to four minutes,
according to taste. If the egg is to be hard-cooked, let it stay in the water
15 minutes. Then take it out and cool it immediately under cold
running water. Fast cooling makes the shell easier to remove and helps
avoid a greenish tinge around the edge of the yolk. There are lots
of little tricks to poaching, frying and scrambling eggs. When poaching
an egg, to make it round and wrapped in its white, stir a whirlpool
in the water and drop the egg in the middle. When frying,
to make the egg look its best, break it first in a saucer and slide it
into the hot pan. And when scrambling, instead of stirring the egg, lift it
gently with a fork or spatula from the bottom of the pan.

Properly prepared, the most ordinary forms of eggs, like those shown opposite,
become real delicacies for any table. In their more elaborate states,
as in the special LIFE omelet shown on page 94, they are treats
for special occasions. To get the very best out of these dishes, fresh eggs
are required. Normally they come in five sizes, from extra large
to peewee. But size makes no difference to the taste.
Neither does color, even though many people think so—New Yorkers
like their eggs white, New Englanders like them best brown.

Seen through the opening of a confectioned Easter egg are five egg dishes that are familiar to all cooks. At top is the most common of all, bacon and eggs, sunny side up. Below this are hard-cooked eggs in a basket, poached eggs decorated with parsley sprigs, soft-cooked eggs in individual silver eggcups, and scrambled eggs and sausage, decorated with water cress.

On the egg-shaped table at left are eight fancy and famous egg dishes, accompanied by decorative 19th Century Easter eggs made of mother-of-pearl, Bristol glass and opaline glass. Starting left across the top of the table are Huevos Rancheros, eggs Florentine (good with a Mornay sauce), sausage and egg pie and a fluffy baked omelet. At the bottom from left are the LIFE special omelet, eggs Benedict, shirred eggs Duchesse (with a Madeira sauce to its right) and French fried deviled eggs. Tomato celery sauce for these is just above them. The success of these egg specialties depends on following recipes carefully and being accurate about timing. In the Victorian china hand at upper left are the seven herbs that team best with eggs: parsley, oregano, basil, chervil, chives, tarragon and marjoram.

# DESSERTS

OF all the dishes on the menu, dessert is one that ought to be an unalloyed delight. Instead it is becoming something of a culinary problem. Americans have not lost their taste for sweets, but they now hold back from eating them for fear of gaining weight. And a good many cooks hold back from concocting desserts because they think it is too much work. On the following pages this book attacks the dessert problem on both fronts—overweight on the waistline and overtime in the kitchen.

The overtime problem can be settled out of hand. The desserts on pages 98, 99 leave housewives no further excuse. Any one of them can be whipped up in less than 10 minutes. To be sure, most of them have to be chilled or frozen, but this is more work for the refrigerator than for the cook. The secret of most of them is the use of the new instant mixes which enable a housewife to turn out such relatively complicated dishes as a rum and butterscotch pie or shortcake in less time than it takes to make a pot of coffee.

The overweight problem is not quite so easy. Something about the word "nonfattening" connotes a pale and tasteless object that will just barely fool the dieter into thinking he is eating dessert. Just to escape such dishes many dieters conscientiously munch on fruit. Fruit, however, is not always the solution; its calorie count ranges from cantaloupe, at 37 calories for half a melon, to richer things like apples which can chalk up a healthy 120. But there is an answer. With the low-calorie foods and noncaloric sweeteners now on the market, "nonfattening" desserts can be made as rich and luscious-looking as anyone could want. As the pictures on pages 100, 101 show, they even include such hitherto forbidden delicacies as creamy zabaglione, strawberry whip and *petits fours*. Not one of them counts more than 90 calories a serving, about as much as is found in half a grapefruit.

Not only do these new desserts look tempting but they have lost that "nonfattening" taste. Proof is the boom in the low-calorie industry, which has 100 processors serving the hordes of U.S. dieters. No longer does a hostess have to torment weight-conscious guests with forbidden dishes. Today, when she notices that nervous, craving look, she can tot up the calories and set their minds at peace.

From the wire basket, fresh eggs spill out around five cooked egg dishes. Clockwise from top left are eggs in aspic, Scotch woodcock, eggs Castellane made with mushroom sauce, baked eggs with chicken livers, and eggs in sour cream.

Time-saving desserts are, starting at back row left, peppermint chocolate ice cream, cranberry sherbet, rum and butterscotch pie, baked Alaska. In the foreground, from left, are icebox cake, sour cream and cherry jam

in scalloped bowl, strawberry-bordered *coeur à la crème*, ice cream cup
topped with peppermint, Roman coffee cream in goblet, strawberry shortcake,
banana kirsch sherbet and, in right foreground, eggs à *la neige*.

Low-calorie desserts, starting at back row left, are small fruits, zabaglione (90 calories a serving), strawberry whip (65 calories). On scale are zabaglione ingredients and at right is nine-calorie coffee jelly. On board

are fruits for tropical compote (57 calories); on gold-rimmed plate
is sherry jelly (79 calories); in center foreground, cherry crown (42 calories)
and at right, *petits fours* (54 calories) and chocolate roll (20 calories).

Surrounded by purple grapes, champagne is poured bubbling
into a crystal goblet half full of brandied fruit to make a cool and quick
summertime dessert. This tall *coupe de luxe* takes a cook only three minutes
to assemble from frozen strawberries, peaches and pineapple chunks.
It can be brandy-marinated and chilled in the refrigerator for an hour
or the whole day. Iced champagne is poured over it at the table.

# PARTY
# BRUNCHES

**O**NCE upon a time the big meal of the week was Sunday dinner,
usually a roast served with potatoes and vegetables and topped off
by a dessert such as apple pie. Most of the afternoon
was spent sleeping it off. Today in many families the big Sunday dinner
has given way to brunch, a leisurely late morning meal
that combines the best of both breakfast and lunch.

Weekday breakfasts are often eaten on the run, but many cooks
find that, on Sunday, brunch followed by a light supper is more convenient
than cooking three meals. It makes the afternoon much longer
and becomes a pleasant time for the family to get together.
Brunch parties are now an accepted way of entertaining.
The menu is usually simpler than for a luncheon or dinner,
and is easier on the hostess since most of the food can be cooked
on short order or prepared ahead of time.

Brunch is a flexible meal that adapts itself to almost
any household. It can be quite formal, a buffet or guests can sit
on cushions around the coffee table. It can be served indoors
or out, with or without alcoholic drinks.

Some brunches can be very spectacular. The Chinese-style party
shown on the next page includes 12 dishes, one of which
is a fabulous winter melon broth, a soup which calls for such delicacies
as squab, water chestnuts and abalone, and takes eight hours
to cook. This fancy meal was whipped up by a caterer,
but with the exception of the soup its dishes are quite easy to prepare.
Most of them could have been done in advance, and three or four of them
would easily be adequate for a less fancy party.

A fruit course usually starts off the brunch. This is followed
by a main course that is generally built around some such
traditional breakfast fare as sausages, pancakes or codfish balls.
But there are no serious rules for a brunch, and some people like to make it
more lunch than breakfast, with dishes like a chicken casserole,
veal or a fish in sauce. It may be accompanied by a simple or even
a fancy dessert, but this is optional; coffee is a must.

Outdoor Chinese brunch party is
given by Mr. and Mrs. James Ludwig
on a San Francisco terrace.
The authentic Cantonese menu has
12 dishes ranging from appetizers
to desserts. On buffet table
in front row, left to right,
are "maiden's prayer," a low-calorie
vegetable dish; winter melon
broth served in melon shell;
dim sum, a meat appetizer;
casserole of lobster Tientsin;
Szechuan noodles and sauce;
"Lamps of China delight," a chicken
and crab meat dish served
in a footed bowl. In back row,
from left, are "shrimp fantasy,"
a shrimp-filled pastry;
iced tangerines (partly hidden
by melon); jo chon bau,
buns stuffed with barbecued pork;
"bit of Formosa," a variety
of sweet and sour pork;
iced lichee fruit;
and "filet opalescence," beef
with noodles. Mrs. Ludwig serves
soup to Barnaby Conrad who passes
bowl to Mr. Ludwig. Next to him
is Elisabeth Vincent,
and at right are Wakefield Baker Jr.
and Mrs. Conrad.

New England brunch consists of traditional favorites from the area.
In silver dish are bite-sized codfish balls. Baked beans are in dish in center.
These are served with corn and brown breads, tomato juice and coffee.

Pennsylvania Dutch brunch is built around potato pancakes (*lower right*). They
are served with pork sausages and bacon, cinnamon bun, in plate at left.
In glass mug is apple cider. At top are applesauce, coffee, sausages, bacon, jams.

French-style brunch has as main dish chicken Bordeaux (*top left*), a casserole
of chicken breasts, grapes and wine. It is served over pancakes,
with extra sauce from casserole. In glass is orange juice with pineapple stick.

Eighteenth Century New Orleans was devoted to Creole brunches, which are being revived by Brennan's, a New Orleans restaurant. A typical menu, served with champagne, is shown above. Clockwise from bottom left are pompano in herb sauce, eggs and artichoke hearts in hollandaise, pineapple with fresh fruit, flamed brandy in an orange, sautéed bananas. In center is hominy with parsley.

Indoor brunch is served
around the coffee table
in TV Commentator Ben Grauer's
New York apartment. From left
are Moss Hart, Ben Grauer,
Kitty Carlisle (Mrs. Hart),
Madge Evans and her husband
Sidney Kingsley, Melanie Kahane
(Mrs. Grauer). The party was
informal but the menu,
shown below, quite elaborate.

The brunch shown above began
with orange slices and
shredded coconut in curaçao,
at lower left. This was followed
by quiche lorraine,
in scalloped serving dish, and,
on blue plate, veal chasseur
with brandied pear. Dessert was
crepes with orange maple
sauce (top, right). Wine, coffee
and brandy were served.

# WINE BUYING

**A**LL the talk and mystery and ritual that seems to go with wine
often intimidates people who would like to buy it. They feel insecure
when faced with vintage years and rules about proper serving,
they get the idea that any good wine must be frightfully expensive.
Then they sigh and have a highball. Actually
they need not worry. The best of the experts agree on one simple,
cardinal rule. If a wine tastes good, it is good.

To clear up some false impressions, LIFE turned to a jury
of six prominent wine experts and asked them to set up a practical guide
to wine buying—even for those on a limited budget. The jury consisted
of internationally known authorities on wine: importers, buyers,
vineyard owners and restaurateurs. They were Importer Alexis Lichine;
Maxwell Kriendler of New York's "21" club, now of "21" Brands, Inc.;
the late Charles Codman of Boston's S.S. Pierce; Frank Schoonmaker,
wine buyer and importer; Ella Brennan Martin of New Orleans' famous
Brennan's restaurant; and Sam Aaron of Sherry Wine & Spirits,
whose company's ideal cellar is shown on the next page.

The jury's advice to beginners is: try enough different wines
to know what you like best. Then stick with it. Color, aroma and taste
should be considered. Wine should be allowed to rest
for about a week after being brought from the store since it never
travels well. For this reason the panel suggests keeping
a cellar, or store of wines, on hand. The bottles should be kept
in a cool place, on their sides so the corks do not shrink and let in air.
After intensive tasting sessions, the experts came up with
a suggested $25 cellar which includes a wide sampling of good wines,
and a $100 cellar, which goes in for some more impressive ones.
The contents of these cellars are listed in detail on page 134.

The jury had some tips on serving wine but again agreed
that personal taste was the only important guide. In general
they suggest that white and *rosé* wines be chilled before serving
and that the better brands of red wine be served at room temperature.
But when inexpensive red wine is served, they suggest
that slight chilling will improve its flavor.

Ideal glassware, selected by wine jury is, on top shelf, sherry or port (*left*),
white wine; second shelf, Burgundy, Rhine wine, champagne; third row,
brandy snifters, red wine glasses. All-purpose wine glasses are behind decanter.

**Ideal wine cellars, recently discovered by Sherry Wine & Spirits beneath an old
New York warehouse, have constant year-round temperature of 55°,
perfect for maturing wine. Equal to the best in Europe, cellars date back to the Civil War.**

# CHEESE

CHEESE is the only food in the world that can turn up at any point during a meal—as an appetizer, on a soup, with a salad, in casseroles or sauces or as dessert. A meal without it, according to Brillat-Savarin, is like a beautiful woman with one eye missing.

Like its classic companions, bread and wine, cheese is made by the process of fermentation. which can turn one substance, just as it is about to spoil, into something better than it was in the first place. Legend has it that cheese was discovered by an Arab merchant who put milk into a pouch made of the stomach of a suckling calf. When he went to drink the milk he found curds of cheese. (The transformation had been accomplished by an enzyme called rennet in the calf's stomach.) As the easiest way of preserving milk, cheese was useful and soon became popular. Among the Vikings it had such status that sailors were sometimes paid off in cheese at the end of a voyage. There is even a tale which gives cheese a place in history: supposedly the Montevidean navy once defeated the Buenos Aires navy by using cheeses as cannon balls.

From its accidental beginnings, cheesemaking developed into a fine skill. Around 1000 A.D. monks near the town of Roquefort in southern France found that milk left in local caves—cool, humid limestone caverns—would in a matter of months turn into a delicious cheese veined with blue mold. Other monasteries began developing varieties of cheese as a source of income. Today there are over 500 kinds of cheese, most of them of European origin, although cream and cottage cheeses and Liederkranz are native to America.

Cheeses vary enormously in texture and taste. They can be soft and creamy like Brie, Bel Paese or Camembert, which are best when runny. They can be firm like Gouda or Cheddar, or as hard as Parmesan, which can hardly be cut with a knife and must be grated. They can be mild like Edam or Muenster, sharp like Cheddar, odorous like Liederkranz or Limburger, tangy like Roquefort or Gorgonzola. Almost all are at their best when served as a dessert with crusty French bread, fruit and wine. To bring out its full flavor, ripened cheese should be removed from the refrigerator and kept at room temperature for at least two hours before serving.

**Nine popular cheeses are shown here with fruit, red wine, crusty bread.
    Beneath the apple perched on top of the pile are, from top down,
Gouda, Provolone and Cheddar. The Cheddar rests on an almost hidden**
Muenster. On left side of plate a wedge of Port du Salut
sits on some Gorgonzola. On right, Liederkranz is resting on bar
of smoked cheese, which sits on wheel of Bel Paese.

Dishes from appetizers to desserts, all prepared with cheese, are shown here.
In left-hand side of picture, clockwise from bottom left, are: blintzes
and jelly, eggplant Parmesan, Roquefort mousse, Welsh rarebit with toast,
Swiss cheese toast with rum sauce, hot cheese dunk with shrimp,
and cheesecake. In center of this circle are cheese and wine casserole,
Camembert French bread. At top left in right-hand side of picture is onion

and cheese pie. In top right-hand corner are brandied cherries and cheese,
and at lower right are cheese tarts and Camembert balls and crackers.
Cheeses on board running through center of right-hand half of picture are used
in these dishes. They are, from the top down, Parmesan,
Swiss with mozzarella on top of it, Roquefort, Gruyère, Cheddar, which is
the most popular U.S. cheese, cottage, Camembert and cream cheese.

# DRINKS AND HORS D'OEUVRE

**T**HERE are lots of ways to drink. You can just plain drink, without any fuss. You can dress up your drinking with a bit of ceremony. Or you can go through the full ritual of crushed ice, chilled glasses, obscure ingredients and show off your deftness with the shaker before your expectant guests. Most drinks shown on the opposite page deserve this kind of fanfare. Some are old classics. Some, like the bright blue brand-new Mediterranée and the Green Dragon, are for special tastes. They range from drinks for lazy afternoons, like the Bull Shot, to drinks for after dinner, like the stinger, and they include that subject of so much purist controversy, the dry martini. Recipes for them (page 137) have been contributed by great bartenders who mix their wares judiciously. They scorn the home bar expert who pours freely from the bottle and hopes for the best, a method, they feel, which has ruined a lot of good liquor, not to mention innocent drinkers.

The pre-dinner drinks, whether the occasion is a cocktail party or a simple gathering of the grownups in a family, should always be accompanied by something to nibble on. This is not only pleasant for the drinkers but even fun for the cook. She or he can experiment freely, and a failure is no disaster.

Such hors d'oeuvre, seven hot and seven cold, are shown on these pages. The number is purposely large, to show variety. Actually at a small party no more than one hot and two cold snacks should be served. Even at a large party it is wiser to concentrate on producing an ample supply of a few varieties. One of the commonest faults of a cocktail party is that there is no food left for the hungry latecomers.

So many cocktail parties are less than festive that a few simple rules may be valuable. The room should not be crowded with too many guests. The host should have plenty of ice. He should not try to offer more than three kinds of drinks without a professional bartender. There should be plenty of food stashed away in case the guests turn out to be voracious. There should be spare glasses. And the host himself should be abstemious and not ply his guests beyond reason.

On the bottom shelf, from left, are a stinger, Irish coffee, Grasshopper, martini on the rocks and Scotch mist. Second shelf: a pink tequila, Mediterranée and Bull Shot. Third shelf: crème de cacao, apricot liqueur, white crème de menthe, cognac, green chartreuse, cherry liqueur, mint julep and rum swizzle. Top shelf: brandy float, green crème de menthe, gimlet, Green Dragon and Scotch sour on the rocks.

Hors d'oeuvre that look elegant
are easy and quick to make,
thanks to frozen, canned
and packaged foods. In top row,
from left, are crab meat
in canapé shells served in
a square skillet, avocado dunk
with corn chips, and
stuffed celery. In next row:
shrimp with remolade sauce,
hot fish bites with chili
dunking sauce, clam
and cream cheese dunk
with potato chips,
and broiled anchovy fillets
on toast. In foreground
are cucumber slices
with smoked salmon, cheesed
potato chips, steak Tartare
with pumpernickel bread,
curried meat balls,
garlic tomatoes,
wedges of melon wrapped
in prosciutto ham and broiled
deviled ham with chutney.

# RECIPES FOR ENTERTAINING

FLAMING FOOD

FULL-SUPPER SANDWICHES

GAME BIRDS

EGG DISHES

DESSERTS

PARTY BRUNCHES

WINE BUYING

CHEESE

DRINKS AND HORS D'OEUVRE

# FLAMING FOOD

## FLAMING BEEF COLLOPS

| | |
|---|---|
| 3 pounds beef, | Cayenne pepper |
| cut in 2-inch cubes | 6 small tomatoes |
| 1 cup dry red wine | Whole mushroom caps |
| 2 tablespoons vinegar | 2 green peppers, cut up |
| ½ cup oil | Lemon, cut in 6 sections |
| 2 onions, thinly sliced | Brandy |
| 1 garlic clove, crushed | 2 teaspoons salt |
| ¼ teaspoon marjoram | Freshly ground black pepper |
| ¼ teaspoon rosemary | |

Marinate beef at room temperature for at least 4 hours in wine, vinegar, oil, onions, garlic, marjoram, rosemary, a few grains of cayenne pepper, salt and black pepper. Drain beef and save marinade. Put a tomato on each of 6 skewers, add beef alternately with mushroom caps and green pepper. Put a section of lemon at the end of each skewer. Broil under moderate heat for 10 minutes, turning frequently and basting with marinade. To serve, put a piece of absorbent cotton moistened with brandy on the end of each skewer and light the cotton. Serves 6.

## FLAMING PEACHES

| | |
|---|---|
| 12 canned peach halves, | 1 cup brandy |
| drained | |

Preheat top pan of chafing dish. Arrange peach halves, cut side down, in the pan. Pour some brandy into a ladle and the rest over the peaches. Warm the brandy in the ladle over a match, light it, then flame the peaches with it. Serves 6.

## SUKIYAKI

| | |
|---|---|
| 2 pounds round steak, | 6 scallions, cut up |
| sliced thin | 2 cups canned bean sprouts, |
| 2 ounces beef suet, cut up | drained |
| 2 onions, sliced thin | ½ cup beef bouillon |
| 1 cup chopped celery | ¼ cup soy sauce |
| 2 cups canned | 1 teaspoon sugar |
| sliced mushrooms, drained | Freshly ground black pepper |
| 1 pound spinach, cut in | Boiled rice |
| 1-inch strips | |

Heat large iron skillet. Rub inside of skillet with suet, then fry suet for 5 minutes or until skillet is well greased. Remaining bits of suet may be removed and discarded. Sauté onions for 5 minutes. Add celery, mushrooms, spinach, scallions and bean sprouts and cook over high heat for 5 minutes, stirring frequently. Push vegetables to one side of pan, add beef and fry for 3 minutes. Stir beef and vegetables together. Add bouillon, soy sauce, sugar and pepper and cook for 5 minutes, stirring frequently. Serve with rice. Serves 6.

## CHICKEN WITH BROCCOLI

| | |
|---|---|
| 4 cups canned | ½ cup grated Swiss cheese |
| chicken fricassee | ½ cup light cream |
| 1 bunch broccoli, cooked | 1 teaspoon curry powder |

Combine chicken fricassee, cheese, cream and curry powder and cook in a chafing dish for 10 minutes, stirring frequently. Serve on hot platter, surrounded with broccoli. Serves 6.

## CREPES SUZETTE

| | |
|---|---|
| 2 eggs | ¼ cup Cointreau |
| 2 egg yolks | ½ cup orange juice |
| 6 tablespoons flour | 1 tablespoon |
| Sugar | grated lemon rind |
| 2 cups milk | ¼ cup brandy |
| ¾ cup butter | 1 teaspoon salt |

Beat eggs and egg yolks together lightly. Sift in flour, 2 teaspoons sugar and salt. Add milk and beat well. Strain through a fine sieve. For each crepe melt 1 teaspoon butter in a small skillet, add 2 tablespoons batter and cook over high heat for 2 minutes on each side. Makes 12. To serve, melt remaining ½ cup butter in chafing dish. Add Cointreau, orange juice and lemon rind and cook for 5 minutes or until mixture comes to a boil. Add a few crepes and cook them for 2 or 3 minutes, basting frequently with the Cointreau sauce. Fold each crepe in quarters and push to one side. Repeat until all crepes are used. Pour brandy into a ladle and warm it over a match. Light the brandy and pour it over the crepes to flame them. When the flame dies, serve the crepes with the sauce. Serves 6. Canned crepes and their sauce may be used if desired. Heat them in a chafing dish and flame them with ½ cup brandy.

## FLAMING FRUITCAKE

| | |
|---|---|
| 1 fruitcake ring | ½ cup brandy |

Fit a heatproof cup or bowl in center of cake and pour in warmed brandy. (Scoop out the cake if the cup is too large.) Light the brandy and ladle brandy over each piece of cake as it is cut and served. Serves 6.

## MEXICAN CORN CASSEROLE

### CORN MEAL STRIPS

| | |
|---|---|
| 1 cup yellow corn meal | Freshly ground black pepper |
| 1 teaspoon salt | |

Bring 2 cups of water to a boil in a saucepan. Mix corn meal, salt and pepper with 1 cup of cold water. Pour into boiling water, stirring constantly. Cook until thickened, stirring frequently. Pour into greased 10-inch-square baking pan. Chill overnight or for at least 4 hours. Cut into 1x2-inch strips.

### MEAT FILLING

| | |
|---|---|
| 2 pounds ground beef | 2½ cups canned |
| 1 can condensed | whole kernel corn |
| cream of chicken soup | ½ cup sliced stuffed olives |
| 1 cup finely chopped onion | 1 green pepper, sliced thin |
| 2 garlic cloves, minced | 1 teaspoon salt |
| 1 teaspoon chili powder | Freshly ground black pepper |

Combine beef, ½ cup of chicken soup, ½ cup onion, garlic, chili powder, salt, pepper and 2 cups of water in a saucepan. Bring to a boil, reduce heat and simmer for 15 minutes, stirring occasionally. Combine the canned corn, remaining chicken soup and remaining ½ cup onion in a bowl and mix well. Stir in ¼ cup olives. Line a large casserole with corn meal strips. Pour in the meat mixture. Top with the corn and olive mixture. Arrange green pepper slices and remaining ¼ cup olive slices on top. Cook in a hot oven (400°) for 30 minutes. Serves 6.

## SHRIMP NEWBURG

| | |
|---|---|
| 2 pounds shrimp, shelled | Freshly grated nutmeg |
| 6 tablespoons butter | Paprika |
| ½ cup sherry | Cayenne pepper |
| 3 egg yolks, beaten | Salt |
| ¾ cup heavy cream | Toast |

Sauté shrimp in butter in the top pan of a chafing dish for 5 minutes, stirring constantly. Stir in sherry. Remove from heat. Put the bottom pan of the chafing dish on the stand and fill it with boiling water. Set the top pan over the boiling water. Beat egg yolks with cream until thick and foamy. Stir the egg yolks and cream mixture into the shrimp mixture. Add a dash of nutmeg and paprika, a few grains of cayenne pepper and a little salt. Cook for 5 minutes or until the sauce thickens, stirring constantly. Serve on toast. Serves 6. Cooked scallops or oysters or cooked and cut up lobster, crab meat, sweetbreads or brains may be used instead of shrimp.

## MEAT BALLS ON FLAMING CABBAGE

| | |
|---|---|
| 1 large cabbage | 2 eggs, lightly beaten |
| 2 pounds round steak, ground | ½ cup butter |
| ½ cup dry red wine | 1 teaspoon salt |
| ½ cup chopped onion | Freshly ground black pepper |
| 2 garlic cloves, minced | Garlic tomato sauce |

First make the meat balls. Combine round steak, wine, onion, garlic, eggs, salt and pepper. Shape into bite-sized balls. Sauté in butter for 10 minutes or until golden brown. Keep meat balls hot. Then turn back the outer leaves of the cabbage. Out of its center scoop a hollow large enough to hold a container of canned heat. To serve, set the cabbage on a tray. Put the hot meat balls on toothpicks and stick the picks into the cabbage. Light the canned heat. Serve the meat balls with garlic tomato sauce. Serves 6.

## GARLIC TOMATO SAUCE

| | |
|---|---|
| 2 garlic cloves | 2 tablespoons minced onion |
| ½ cup tomato juice | ½ teaspoon cumin seed |
| ½ cup oil | ¼ teaspoon crushed |
| ½ cup red wine vinegar | chili peppers |
| ½ cup beef bouillon | Tabasco sauce |
| ¼ cup finely chopped | Cayenne pepper |
| green pepper | 1 teaspoon salt |

Crush garlic with salt and combine in saucepan with tomato juice, oil, vinegar, bouillon, green pepper, onion, cumin seed, chili peppers, a dash of Tabasco and a few grains of cayenne pepper. Bring to a boil, reduce heat and simmer for 15 minutes, stirring occasionally. Makes about 2 cups.

## SWISS FONDUE

| | |
|---|---|
| 2 pounds Swiss cheese, grated | 6 tablespoons brandy |
| | Ground nutmeg |
| 6 tablespoons flour | 1 teaspoon salt |
| 1 garlic clove, cut | Freshly ground black pepper |
| 4 cups dry white wine | French bread, cut in pieces |

Combine Swiss cheese and flour and mix until cheese is coated with flour. Rub inside of chafing dish pan with garlic. Pour in wine and cook over low heat until bubbles of wine rise to the surface. Stir in cheese, a few spoonfuls at a time, and continue stirring until the cheese is thoroughly melted and the mixture starts bubbling. Add brandy, a dash of nutmeg, salt and pepper. To serve, dip pieces of French bread into fondue. Serves 6.

## FLAMING KIPPERS

| | |
|---|---|
| 6 smoked kippers | Freshly ground black pepper |
| ¼ cup butter | ½ cup bourbon whisky |
| Lemon juice | |

Sauté kippers in butter in chafing dish for 5 minutes. Season with lemon juice and pepper. Pour some warmed bourbon into a ladle and the rest over the kippers. Warm the bourbon in the ladle over a match, light it and flame the kippers. Baste the kippers with burning bourbon. Serves 6.

## CHIPPED BEEF IN MUSHROOM SAUCE

| | |
|---|---|
| ¾ pound dried chipped beef | 1 teaspoon Worcestershire sauce |
| 2 cans condensed cream of mushroom soup | Freshly ground black pepper |
| ¼ cup butter | ½ cup toasted almonds |
| 2 cups milk | Toast |

Soak chipped beef in 2 cups of hot water for 10 minutes. Drain and discard water. Sauté beef in butter in chafing dish for 5 minutes, stirring constantly. Combine soup with milk and stir until smooth and thoroughly blended. Stir soup mixture and Worcestershire into beef. Season with pepper. Simmer for 10 minutes, stirring occasionally. Sprinkle with toasted almonds. Serve on toast. Serves 6.

## FLAMING DUCK

| | |
|---|---|
| 2 five-pound oven-ready ducks | 1 cup red currant jelly |
| 6 carrots, sliced | ¼ cup dry red wine |
| 4 large onions, sliced | 1 cup brandy |
| 6 tablespoons butter | 1 teaspoon salt |
| 2 oranges | Freshly ground black pepper |

Rub cavities of ducks with salt and pepper. Put ducks on a rack in a shallow baking pan. Roast in a slow oven (325°) for 2½ hours or until done. Meanwhile sauté carrots and onions in butter for 10 minutes or until onions are golden brown. Squeeze the oranges and save the juice. Scrape white pulp from orange rind and discard. Cut rind into thin strips. Simmer the rind in 2 cups of water for 15 minutes. Strain and reserve rind and water. When the ducks are done, remove them from the roasting pan and keep them hot. Drain fat from pan. Add the carrot and onion mixture, orange juice, orange rind water, jelly and wine to juices left in pan. Cook over low heat until the jelly melts, stirring constantly. Strain sauce and add orange rind. To serve, place ducks on a heated platter. Pour some of the brandy into a ladle and the rest over the ducks. Warm the brandy in the ladle over a match, light it and flame the ducks with it. Spoon the blazing brandy over the ducks so the flavor penetrates. Pour hot sauce into a sauceboat and serve with the ducks. Serves 6.

## FARMER'S PUNCH

| | |
|---|---|
| 1 fifth port | 1 tablespoon honey |
| 3 oranges | ½ cup brandy |
| Whole cloves | |

Stud 2 oranges with cloves and roast over a fire or in a moderate oven (350°) for 20 minutes or until the oranges are soft and begin to brown. Put one roasted orange in a pan. Add port and honey. Simmer over low heat for 15 minutes. Pour the port mixture into a warm punch bowl. Set the second orange in a large ladle. Pour warmed brandy over the orange and light it. Lower the blazing orange into the hot punch. Slice the third orange and garnish the punch with these slices. Serve the drink in warm mugs. Serves 6.

## FLAMING SUNDAES

Any ice cream sundae may be served flaming. Dip a lump of sugar into lemon extract and press it into a marshmallow. Put the marshmallow on the sundae and light the sugar lump. The flaming sugar will toast the marshmallow.

## CAFE DIABLE

| | |
|---|---|
| 3 cups hot black coffee | Thin outer peel 1 lemon |
| ½ cup brandy | 4 whole cloves |
| 7 lumps of sugar | Stick of cinnamon |
| Thin outer peel 1 orange | |

Heat brandy, 6 lumps of sugar, orange and lemon peel, cloves and cinnamon in chafing dish or café diable pan until the sugar is dissolved, stirring occasionally. Heat the bowl of a ladle over a match. Dip up a little of the mixture. Put 1 sugar lump in the ladle and light it. Lower the ladle into the chafing dish to light the brandy. While the brandy is flaming, pour the hot coffee into the chafing dish. When the flames die, ladle the coffee into demitasse cups. Serves 6.

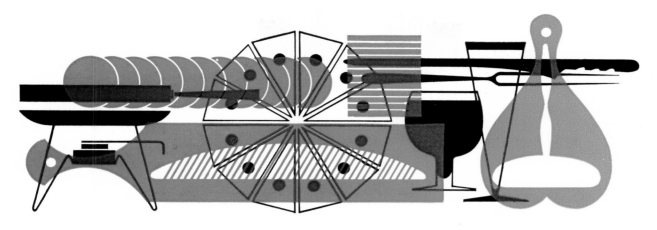

# FULL-SUPPER SANDWICHES

### ONION AND LIEDERKRANZ SANDWICH

| | |
|---|---|
| 6 red onions, sliced | 2 teaspoons salt |
| 6 four-ounce packages | Freshly ground black pepper |
| Liederkranz cheese | Rye, pumpernickel |
| 1 cup olive oil | or Kommissbrot bread |
| ¼ cup wine vinegar | |

Let cheese stand at room temperature for at least 2 hours or until soft. Marinate onions in oil, vinegar, salt and pepper at room temperature for at least 1 hour. To serve, slice bread, spread it with Liederkranz cheese and top it with drained onion slices. Serves 6.

### POOR BOY SANDWICH

| | |
|---|---|
| French or Italian bread | Sliced boiled ham |
| Butter | Dry mustard |
| Sliced salami | Dry wine |
| Sliced cheese | |

Cut bread in half lengthwise. Spread with butter. Put layers of salami, cheese and ham on bottom half of loaf. Cover with top half. Cut into serving pieces. Combine 3 parts of dry mustard with 1 part of dry wine and serve with sandwich. Serves 6.

### PIZZA SANDWICH

| | |
|---|---|
| Small loaves French bread | Sliced mozzarella cheese |
| Olive oil | Anchovy fillets |
| Canned Italian tomatoes, | Canned meat balls, drained |
| drained and cut up | Oregano |
| Grated Parmesan cheese | Thyme |

Cut loaves of bread in half lengthwise. Scoop out the soft centers, leaving shells about ½ inch thick. Brush inside of shells with olive oil. Spread shells with tomatoes and sprinkle with Parmesan cheese. Put mozzarella and anchovies on some shells, mozzarella and sliced meat balls on others. Sprinkle with oregano, thyme and oil. Bake in a hot oven (400°) for 15 minutes.

### FISH FRY SANDWICH

| | |
|---|---|
| 2 pounds flounder fillets | Oil or vegetable shortening |
| ½ cup flour | 1 teaspoon salt |
| 2 eggs, lightly beaten | Freshly ground black pepper |
| 1 cup cracker crumbs | 6 slices buttered white bread |

Cut flounder fillets into 6 pieces. Season with salt and pepper. Dip in flour, then in eggs, finally in cracker crumbs. Fry in 1 inch hot oil (375°) for 10 minutes. Drain and serve 1 piece of flounder on each slice of buttered bread. Serves 6.

### CHICKEN ROLL SANDWICH

| | |
|---|---|
| 2 cups diced cooked chicken | Lettuce or other salad greens |
| 2 cups diced celery | White grapes |
| 1 green pepper, chopped | 1 teaspoon salt |
| 1 cup mayonnaise | Freshly ground black pepper |
| 1 cup sour cream | Large hard rolls |
| 1 teaspoon curry powder | Pink pickled eggs |

Combine chicken, celery, green pepper, mayonnaise, sour cream, curry powder, salt and pepper. Line a salad bowl with lettuce leaves and put this chicken salad in the center. Arrange grapes around the chicken. Cut a ½-inch slice from the top of each roll and scoop out the soft center. To serve, fill the hollow rolls with chicken salad. Serve with grapes and pink pickled eggs. Serves 6.

### PINK PICKLED EGGS

| | |
|---|---|
| 6 eggs | ½ bay leaf |
| 1 cup canned beet juice | ¼ teaspoon ground allspice |
| 1 cup cider vinegar | 1 teaspoon salt |
| 1 garlic clove, crushed | Freshly ground black pepper |

Hard cook eggs, plunge into cold water and shell immediately. Put eggs in a quart jar. Combine remaining ingredients and pour over eggs. Cover, cool and refrigerate overnight or for at least 8 hours.

### RIVIERA SANDWICH

| | |
|---|---|
| Large round loaf | Chopped chives |
| of white bread | Sardines |
| Butter | Pitted ripe olives, halved |
| Thin tomato slices | Salt |
| Chopped parsley | Freshly ground black pepper |

Cut bread in half crosswise. Butter cut surface of each half and arrange tomato slices on the edge. Sprinkle the tomatoes with parsley, chives, salt and pepper. Drain sardines and save the oil. Arrange sardines like the spokes of a wheel in the center of each half loaf. Decorate with olives. Sprinkle sardine oil over each half. To serve, cut in pie-shaped wedges.

### CHEESE AND CHILI-BURGERS

| | |
|---|---|
| 3 pounds ground beef | Butter |
| ½ cup dry red wine | Onion rings |
| 1 teaspoon salt | Cheese sauce |
| Freshly ground black pepper | Chili sauce |
| 12 hamburger buns | |

Combine ground beef, wine, salt and pepper, mix well. Divide into 12 burgers and broil. Butter the hamburger buns. Serve the burgers on buns with onion rings and a choice of cheese sauce or chili sauce. Serves 6.

### CHEESE SAUCE

| | |
|---|---|
| ½ pound Cheddar cheese, | 1 teaspoon dry mustard |
| grated | ½ teaspoon basil |
| 1 cup milk or beer | |

Combine cheese, milk or beer, mustard and basil in the top of a double boiler and cook over boiling water for 15 minutes or until smooth, stirring frequently. Serve hot. Makes about 2 cups. If the sauce becomes too thick, add a few additional tablespoonfuls of milk or beer.

### CHILI SAUCE

| | |
|---|---|
| 2 cups canned | ¼ teaspoon chili powder |
| chili con carne | ½ teaspoon cumin seed |
| 1 tomato, peeled and chopped | |

Combine chili con carne, tomato, chili powder and cumin seed and simmer for 10 minutes, stirring frequently. Serve hot. Makes about 2 cups.

# GAME BIRDS

## ROAST PHEASANT WITH BRANDY AND CREAM

| | |
|---|---|
| 3 pheasants | 2 cups chicken bouillon |
| ½ cup brandy | 6 slices bacon |
| 2 cups heavy cream | ¼ cup horseradish |
| 8 shallots, thinly sliced | 1 teaspoon salt |
| ¼ cup butter | Freshly ground black pepper |

Sauté shallots in butter in a roasting pan for 5 minutes. Add pheasants and sauté over high heat for 15 minutes or until brown on all sides. Pour some brandy into a ladle and the rest over the pheasants. Warm the ladle over a match, light the brandy and flame the pheasants. When flames die, add bouillon, salt and pepper. Put bacon over pheasants' breasts and roast uncovered in a moderate oven (375°) for 45 minutes, basting frequently. Stir cream and horseradish into pan juices and continue roasting for 15 minutes, basting frequently. Serve pheasants and sauce with popped wild rice. Serves 6.

## POPPED WILD RICE

| | |
|---|---|
| 2 cups wild rice | Salt |
| Oil or vegetable shortening | |

Wash rice and dry thoroughly. Fry 1 tablespoonful at a time in 2 inches of hot oil (375°) for about 5 minutes or until rice pops. Drain on paper towels. Sprinkle with salt and serve hot. Serves 6.

## PHEASANT WITH MUSHROOMS

| | |
|---|---|
| 3 pheasants, split | 2 tablespoons lemon juice |
| 2 cups sliced mushrooms | ½ cup chopped scallions |
| ½ cup butter | 1 teaspoon salt |
| 1 cup dry white wine | Freshly ground black pepper |

Sauté pheasant in butter for 10 minutes. Remove pheasant and sauté mushrooms in butter remaining in skillet for 10 minutes or until golden brown. Return pheasant to skillet. Add wine, lemon juice, scallions, salt and pepper. Cover and simmer for 1 hour or until tender. Serves 6.

## PHEASANT POT PIE

| | |
|---|---|
| 2 pheasants, cut up | 12 small onions, parboiled |
| 2 onions, quartered | 2 carrots, sliced |
| 1 celery stalk, cut up | 1 cup peas |
| 1 bay leaf | 2 tablespoons pimento strips |
| 2 cloves | ½ recipe baking powder |
| 1 teaspoon thyme | biscuits |
| 2 tablespoons lemon juice | 1 teaspoon salt |
| 6 tablespoons flour | Freshly ground black pepper |

Combine pheasant, quartered onions, celery, bay leaf, cloves, thyme, salt and pepper in a large saucepan with 4 cups of water. Bring to a boil, reduce heat, cover and simmer for 45 minutes or until pheasant is tender. Remove pheasant and strain broth. Add lemon juice and stir well. Add flour and cook, stirring until broth thickens. Arrange pheasant, whole onions, carrot slices, peas and pimento in a casserole. Pour sauce over them. Roll biscuit dough ¼ inch thick and fit it over casserole. Cut slits in dough to let steam escape. Bake in a hot oven (425°) for 30 minutes. Serves 6.

## SALMIS OF PHEASANT

| | |
|---|---|
| 2 pheasants | 1 cup mushroom caps |
| 1½ cups beef bouillon | 2 tablespoons |
| 1 onion, quartered | chopped parsley |
| 1 carrot, cut up | 1 teaspoon salt |
| 1 cup chopped celery | Freshly ground black pepper |

Roast pheasants in a moderate oven (375°) for 1 hour or until done. Slice breasts, cover them and keep hot over boiling water. Remove legs. Combine legs and carcasses with bouillon, onion, carrot, celery, salt and pepper. Bring to a boil, reduce heat, cover and simmer for 15 minutes. Remove legs from stock, slice off meat and keep it hot with breast slices. Strain stock, add mushroom caps and parsley and simmer 15 minutes. Serve sliced pheasant meat with sauce. Serves 6.

## PAN FRIED PHEASANT WITH GRAVY

| | |
|---|---|
| 2 pheasants, cut up | 2 cups light cream |
| 12 slices bacon | 2 teaspoons salt |
| Flour | Freshly ground black pepper |
| 1 tablespoon cornstarch | |

Sauté bacon in large skillet until bacon is crisp. Remove bacon, drain and save it. Dust pheasant lightly with flour, season with salt and pepper. Fry pheasant in ½ cup bacon fat over high heat for 10 minutes, turning frequently. Reduce heat, cover pan and simmer for about 20 minutes, turning occasionally. Remove pheasant and keep hot. Add cornstarch dissolved in 2 tablespoons water to the pan juices and mix well. Add cream gradually and cook, stirring constantly, until gravy is thickened. Serve gravy and bacon slices with pheasant. Serves 6.

## ROAST WILD DUCK

| | |
|---|---|
| 3 wild ducks | 1 teaspoon salt |
| Celery leaves | Freshly ground black pepper |
| 1 cup butter, melted | Apricot sauce |
| ½ cup dry red wine | Baked hominy grits |

Rub cavities of ducks with salt and pepper. Fill the cavities with celery leaves. Brush skin with ½ cup butter. Roast ducks breast side up in a hot oven (450°) for 30 minutes, basting every 5 minutes with wine and remaining ½ cup butter. Carve ducks and keep them hot over boiling water. Save the juices to add to apricot sauce. Serve with apricot sauce and baked hominy grits. Serves 6.

## APRICOT SAUCE

| | |
|---|---|
| 2½ cups canned peeled | 6 tablespoons butter |
| apricots, drained | 3 duck livers, cut up |
| 1 teaspoon grated orange rind | Duck juices |
| 2 cups dry red wine | Freshly ground black pepper |

Press apricots through a coarse sieve. Combine apricots, orange rind, wine, butter and pepper in the top of a double boiler. Cook over direct heat for 5 minutes. Press duck livers through a coarse sieve and add to apricot mixture with duck juices. Place over hot water and simmer for 5 minutes, stirring constantly, until smooth and slightly thickened. Pour over duck, serve immediately. Makes about 5 cups.

## BAKED HOMINY GRITS

| | |
|---|---|
| 1 cup dried hominy grits | 1 teaspoon salt |
| 2 tablespoons butter | |

Stir hominy grits slowly into 4 cups boiling salted water and cook until thickened, stirring constantly. Pour into greased casserole, dot with butter and bake in a moderate oven (375°) for 45 minutes. Serves 6.

## BROILED WILD DUCK

| | |
|---|---|
| 3 wild ducks, split | 3 whole cloves |
| 1 cup dry white wine | ½ teaspoon thyme |
| 2 tablespoons | ¼ teaspoon ground mace |
| chopped parsley | 1 cup butter, melted |
| 2 tablespoons | Salt |
| chopped chives | Freshly ground black pepper |
| 2 bay leaves, crumbled | |

Marinate ducks in the refrigerator overnight or for at least 8 hours in mixture of wine, parsley, chives, bay leaves, cloves, thyme, mace, salt and pepper. Drain and dry the ducks. Dip in melted butter and broil under medium heat for 30 minutes or until done, turning once and basting with butter. Serves 6.

## OVEN BARBECUED DUCK

| | |
|---|---|
| 2 large wild ducks, | 1 garlic clove, crushed |
| quartered | 1 tablespoon paprika |
| ¼ cup lemon juice | 1 teaspoon Worcestershire |
| ¼ cup oil | sauce |
| 1 tablespoon grated onion | Freshly ground black pepper |

Arrange duck quarters on shallow baking pan. Combine remaining ingredients and brush mixture over ducks. Roast ducks in a moderate oven (350°) for 1 hour or until tender, basting frequently. Serves 6.

## SAUTEED QUAIL

| | |
|---|---|
| 6 quail, split | 1 teaspoon salt |
| 6 club rolls | Freshly ground black pepper |
| ¾ cup butter | Grape sauce |

Split rolls in half and hollow out centers. Toast in a low oven (325°) until brown. Melt ¼ cup butter and brush the rolls with the butter. Sauté the quail over high heat in the remaining ½ cup of butter for 10 minutes or until golden brown. Sprinkle them with salt and pepper. Arrange quail on rolls and serve with grape sauce. Serves 6.

## GRAPE SAUCE

| | |
|---|---|
| 1 cup seedless white grapes | 2 tablespoons finely |
| 4 tablespoons butter | chopped mushrooms |
| ½ cup port wine | ½ cup finely chopped |
| ⅛ teaspoon ground cloves | hazelnuts |

Bring grapes and 1 cup of water to a boil. Cover, reduce heat and simmer for 5 minutes. Drain off water. Add butter, wine and cloves. Cover and simmer for 5 minutes. Stir in mushrooms and simmer for 5 minutes. Add hazelnuts and serve immediately. Makes about 2½ cups.

## ROAST QUAIL

| | |
|---|---|
| 6 quail | ½ teaspoon thyme |
| 6 chicken livers | Salt |
| Butter | Freshly ground black pepper |

Sauté chicken livers in 2 tablespoons butter for 10 minutes or until golden brown. Remove from stove and stir in thyme, salt and pepper. Stuff each quail with 1 chicken liver and a teaspoon of the butter sauce. Tie legs close to body. Rub quail with butter and roast them in a very hot oven (450°) for 15 to 20 minutes or until done. Serves 6.

## SHERRIED QUAIL CASSEROLE

| | |
|---|---|
| 6 quail, quartered | 1 tablespoon cornstarch |
| 2 tablespoons dry sherry | 1 cup chicken bouillon |
| ¼ cup butter | 2 tablespoons |
| ½ cup chopped onion | chopped parsley |
| ½ cup chopped celery | |

Sauté quail in butter for 10 minutes. Remove quail and sauté onion and celery in butter remaining in skillet for 5 minutes. Add cornstarch dissolved in bouillon and cook, stirring constantly, until thickened. Stir in sherry and parsley. Arrange quail in shallow casserole and pour sauce over them. Bake in a moderate oven (350°) for 15 minutes. Serves 6.

## ROAST WILD TURKEY

| | |
|---|---|
| 1 wild turkey | Freshly ground black pepper |
| 1 cup butter, melted | Peanut or potato stuffing |
| 1 cup dry white wine | Mashed acorn squash |
| 1 teaspoon salt | |

Rub cavity of turkey with salt and pepper. Fill loosely with peanut or potato stuffing. Brush skin with ½ cup butter. Roast in a moderate oven (375°) for 2 hours or until done. Baste frequently with remaining ½ cup butter and wine. Serve with mashed acorn squash. Serves 6.

## PEANUT STUFFING

| | |
|---|---|
| 3 cups shelled | ½ cup dry white wine |
| roasted peanuts | ½ cup chicken bouillon |
| 4 cups dry bread crumbs | 1 egg, beaten |
| 1 medium onion, | 3 tablespoons butter, melted |
| finely chopped | Freshly ground black pepper |

Chop peanuts and brown them in a moderate oven (375°) for 15 minutes. Add remaining ingredients, toss lightly together. Makes about 8 cups.

## POTATO STUFFING

| | |
|---|---|
| 4 cups hot mashed potatoes | 1 tablespoon |
| 2 ounces salt pork, minced | poultry seasoning |
| 3 cups soft bread crumbs | 1 tablespoon salt |
| 1 cup chopped onion | |

Sauté salt pork for 5 minutes. Add bread crumbs and onion and sauté for 10 minutes, stirring constantly. Add to potatoes and mix lightly. Add poultry seasoning and salt. Makes about 8 cups.

## MASHED ACORN SQUASH

| | |
|---|---|
| 3 acorn squashes | 1 cup heavy cream |
| ¼ cup butter | Ground nutmeg |
| 1 tablespoon minced onion | Salt |

Cut squashes in half lengthwise and remove seeds and fibers. Put 1 teaspoon butter, ½ teaspoon minced onion and a dash of salt in each half. Cover and bake in a moderate oven (350°) for 30 minutes or until tender. Scoop cooked squash from shells and mash with cream and the remaining 2 tablespoons of butter. Sprinkle with nutmeg. Serves 6.

## SWEET AND SOUR TURKEY

| | |
|---|---|
| 1 wild turkey, cut up | 2 tablespoons cornstarch |
| 2 onions, cut up | ¼ cup sugar |
| 1 garlic clove | ½ cup vinegar |
| 1 bay leaf | 2 teaspoons salt |
| 2 whole cloves | 10 peppercorns |
| ½ teaspoon mustard seed | |

Place turkey in pot with 4 cups of water. Add onion, garlic, bay leaf, cloves, mustard, salt and peppercorns. Bring to a boil, reduce heat, cover and simmer for 2 hours. Remove turkey and strain broth. Return broth to pot, add cornstarch combined with sugar and vinegar. Cook, stirring constantly, until the sauce thickens. Add turkey and simmer for 15 minutes. Serves 6.

## ROAST WILD GOOSE

| | |
|---|---|
| 1 wild goose | Freshly ground black pepper |
| ½ cup butter, softened | Chestnut or apple |
| ½ cup gin | and sour cream stuffing |
| 3 juniper berries | Glazed apple slices |
| 1 teaspoon salt | Red cabbage |

Rub cavity of goose with salt and pepper. Fill loosely with chestnut or apple and sour cream stuffing. Rub skin with butter. Roast in a moderate oven (375°) for 3 hours or until done. Baste frequently with mixture of gin, juniper berries and ¼ cup of water. Serve with glazed apple slices and red cabbage. Serves 6.

## CHESTNUT STUFFING

| | |
|---|---|
| 4 pounds chestnuts | 1 cup heavy cream |
| ½ cup finely chopped celery | 2 teaspoons salt |
| ¼ cup butter, melted | Freshly ground black pepper |
| 1 cup soft bread crumbs | |

Cut slits in chestnut shells. Cover chestnuts with water, boil for 20 minutes, drain and peel off both shell and skin. Put the chestnuts through a food grinder using a coarse blade. Sauté celery in butter for 10 minutes. Add chestnuts and remaining ingredients and mix lightly. Makes about 8 cups.

## APPLE AND SOUR CREAM STUFFING

| | |
|---|---|
| 2 cups chopped apple | 1 tablespoon lemon juice |
| Sour cream | 1 teaspoon ground sage |
| ½ cup chopped onion | Cayenne pepper |
| ¼ cup butter | 2 teaspoons salt |
| 6 cups soft bread crumbs | |

Sauté apple and onion in butter for 5 minutes. Add to bread crumbs and mix lightly. Add lemon juice, sage, a dash of cayenne and salt. Moisten with sour cream. Makes about 8 cups.

## GLAZED APPLE SLICES

| | |
|---|---|
| 2 pounds cooking apples | ¼ teaspoon ground nutmeg |
| 1 lemon | ⅛ teaspoon ground cloves |
| 2 cups brown sugar | ½ teaspoon ground cinnamon |

Peel, core and slice apples. Grate the lemon peel and squeeze the lemon. Arrange apple slices in a shallow baking dish. Combine 1 cup sugar, lemon peel and juice and spices with 1½ cups of water. Pour over apples. Bake in a moderate oven (375°) for 25 minutes. Sprinkle with the remaining 1 cup sugar and broil under low heat for 5 minutes. Serve warm or chilled. Serves 6.

## RED CABBAGE

| | |
|---|---|
| 1 three-pound red cabbage | ¼ cup vinegar |
| 2 green apples, peeled | 2 tablespoons bacon fat |
| and chopped | 1 teaspoon salt |
| 1 onion, finely chopped | Freshly ground black pepper |
| ¼ cup sugar | |

Shred cabbage. Put in saucepan with apples, onion, sugar, vinegar, bacon fat, salt and pepper and ½ cup boiling water. Bring to a boil, reduce heat, cover and simmer for 1 hour, stirring occasionally. Serves 6.

## WILD GOOSE IN WINE

| | |
|---|---|
| 1 wild goose, cut up | 2 bay leaves, crumbled |
| 2 cups dry white wine | 2 slices bacon, minced |
| 2 onions, sliced | 1 garlic clove, crushed |
| 2 tablespoons | 2 cups chicken bouillon |
| chopped parsley | 1 teaspoon salt |
| 1 teaspoon thyme | 6 peppercorns |

Marinate goose in the refrigerator overnight or for at least 8 hours in mixture of wine, onions, parsley, thyme, bay leaves, salt and peppercorns. Dry goose and save the marinade. Put it in a casserole with the bacon and roast in a hot oven (425°) for 25 minutes or until brown, turning the goose frequently. Add the marinade, garlic and bouillon. Cover and bake in a moderate oven (325°) for 1 hour or until goose is tender. Serves 6.

## ROAST GROUSE WITH RED WINE SAUCE

| | |
|---|---|
| 6 grouse | 2 tablespoons minced onion |
| ¾ cup dry red wine | ¾ cup beef bouillon |
| Celery leaves | 1 teaspoon salt |
| 12 slices bacon | Freshly ground black pepper |
| 2 tablespoons butter | |

Rub cavities of grouse with salt and pepper. Stuff each grouse with celery leaves and 1 teaspoon butter. Cover breasts with bacon slices. Roast in a moderate oven (375°) for 15 minutes. Remove grouse and keep hot. Sauté onion in juices remaining in roasting pan over low heat for 5 minutes or until onions are golden brown. Add wine and bouillon. Bring to a boil and cook for 5 minutes, stirring and scraping the pan. Serve sauce with grouse. Serves 6.

## GROUSE CASSEROLE

| | |
|---|---|
| 6 grouse, split | 2 cans condensed |
| ¼ cup flour | cream of chicken soup |
| ½ cup butter | ¼ cup sherry |
| 1 cup chicken bouillon | Freshly ground black pepper |

Dust grouse with flour and sauté in butter for 10 minutes. Arrange grouse in casserole. Add bouillon to butter in skillet, stir well and pour over grouse. Cover casserole and bake in a slow oven (325°) for 30 minutes. Take casserole out of the oven and remove grouse. Stir chicken soup, sherry and pepper into sauce remaining in the casserole and blend well. Return grouse to sauce. Bake uncovered for 15 minutes. Serves 6.

## BROILED GROUSE

| | |
|---|---|
| 6 grouse | 2 tablespoons |
| ½ cup olive oil | chopped chives |
| ¼ cup lemon juice | 1 teaspoon salt |
| 2 tablespoons | Freshly ground black pepper |
| chopped parsley | Currant jelly |

Split grouse down the back without separating halves. Press the birds flat. Marinate in oil, lemon juice, herbs, salt and pepper at room temperature for 1 hour, turning frequently. Remove grouse from marinade and place skin side down on unheated broiler rack. Broil for 10 minutes, basting several times with marinade. Turn and broil skin side up for 10 to 15 minutes, basting frequently. Serve with currant jelly. Serves 6.

## MOURNING DOVE CASSEROLE

| | |
|---|---|
| 6 doves | 1 six-ounce can mushrooms |
| 6 small onions | 1 large onion, chopped |
| 6 tablespoons | ½ teaspoon thyme |
| chopped parsley | ¼ teaspoon dried basil |
| ½ cup butter | 1 teaspoon salt |
| 1 garlic clove, minced | Freshly ground black pepper |
| 2½ cups canned tomatoes | Polenta |

Stuff each dove with 1 onion, 1 tablespoon parsley and 1 teaspoon butter. Sauté garlic in remaining 6 tablespoons butter for 5 minutes. Add doves and sauté for 10 minutes or until brown on all sides. Put doves and garlic butter in a deep casserole and add the rest of the ingredients. Cover and bake in a moderate oven (375°) for 1 hour or until done. Serve on a platter with a border of polenta. Serves 6.

## POLENTA

| | |
|---|---|
| 1 cup yellow corn meal | 2 tablespoons butter |
| 4 tablespoons grated | 1 teaspoon salt |
| Parmesan cheese | Freshly ground black pepper |

Bring 4 cups salted water to a boil in the top part of a double boiler. Add corn meal slowly and cook until slightly thickened, stirring constantly. Place over boiling water and cook for 45 minutes. Add cheese, butter and black pepper. Cook for 5 minutes. Serves 6.

## SAUTEED DOVES

| | |
|---|---|
| 6 doves, split | 2 tablespoons |
| ½ cup butter | minced celery leaves |
| 1 cup dry white wine | ½ teaspoon tarragon |
| ¼ cup minced onion | Salt |

Sauté doves in butter for 5 minutes or until lightly browned. Add wine, onion, celery leaves and salt. Cover and simmer over low heat for 20 minutes. Add tarragon and simmer, uncovered, for 15 minutes. Serves 6.

## BROILED DOVES

| | |
|---|---|
| 6 doves | Freshly ground black pepper |
| Butter | Toast |
| 6 slices bacon | Chopped parsley |
| Salt | Lemon wedges |

Season doves inside and out with salt and pepper and rub skins with butter. Wrap each dove in a slice of bacon held in place with a toothpick. Broil under low heat for 20 minutes, turning frequently. Serve on toast with parsley and lemon. Serves 6.

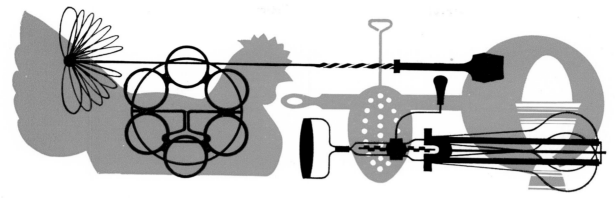

# EGG DISHES

## HUEVOS RANCHEROS

| | |
|---|---|
| 6 eggs | 4 tomatoes, peeled |
| 6 canned tortillas | and chopped |
| 1½ cups chopped onion | ¾ cup finely chopped |
| 1 garlic clove, minced | hot pepper |
| ½ cup bacon fat | ½ teaspoon salt |

Sauté onion and garlic in ¼ cup bacon fat for 5 minutes. Add tomatoes, hot pepper and salt. Cover and simmer for 10 minutes. Remove cover and simmer for 10 minutes. Meanwhile sauté tortillas in remaining ¼ cup bacon fat for 30 seconds on each side. Remove and keep hot. Fry eggs in fat remaining in skillet. Put 1 egg on each tortilla and spoon sauce over it. Serves 6.

## EGGS FLORENTINE

| | |
|---|---|
| 6 eggs, poached | Tabasco sauce |
| 2 packages chopped | 1 teaspoon salt |
| frozen spinach | Mornay sauce |
| ¾ cup heavy cream | Grated Parmesan cheese |

Cook spinach and drain. Combine spinach, cream, 2 drops of Tabasco and salt. Spoon spinach mixture into 6 buttered ramekins or individual ovenproof dishes. Put 1 egg in each ramekin and top with about ⅓ cup Mornay sauce. Sprinkle with Parmesan cheese. Broil under medium heat for 5 minutes or until brown.

## MORNAY SAUCE

| | |
|---|---|
| 2 tablespoons minced onion | 3 egg yolks, beaten |
| 6 tablespoons butter | 1 tablespoon heavy cream |
| 4 tablespoons flour | 2 tablespoons grated |
| 2 cups milk | Parmesan cheese |

Sauté onion in 4 tablespoons butter in top of double boiler for 5 minutes. Place over boiling water and stir in flour. Add milk and cook until sauce thickens, stirring constantly. Cook for 15 minutes, stirring frequently. Strain through a fine sieve and return to top of double boiler. Beat egg yolks and cream together and add to sauce. Cook over hot, not boiling, water for 10 minutes, stirring constantly. Stir in Parmesan cheese and the remaining 2 tablespoons butter. Makes about 2 cups.

## SAUSAGE AND EGG PIE

| | |
|---|---|
| 6 eggs | Cayenne pepper |
| 6 link sausages, cooked | ½ teaspoon dry mustard |
| 2 tablespoons butter | ½ cup cream sauce |
| 1 teaspoon anchovy paste | ½ recipe of pie crust |
| 1 cup canned sliced | 2 tablespoons heavy cream |
| mushrooms, drained | ¼ cup dry sherry |
| Ground cloves | 1 teaspoon salt |

Blend butter and anchovy paste together and spread mixture on the bottom of a 9-inch pie plate. Cover with mushroom slices. Arrange sausages spoke-fashion on the mushrooms and break an egg into each space between the sausages. Season with a dash of cloves, a few grains of cayenne pepper and salt. Add mustard to cream sauce and pour over the eggs. Roll the pie crust ⅛ inch thick and cover the pie with the crust. Make a hole the size of a dime in the center and prick crust with a fork to let steam escape. Brush the crust with cream. Bake in a moderate oven (350°) for 30 minutes or until the crust is lightly browned. Remove pie from oven. Pour sherry through the hole in the crust. Return pie to the oven and bake for 10 minutes. Serves 6. This recipe is based on one included in Louis P. de Gouy's *The Gold Cook Book*.

## CREAM SAUCE

| | |
|---|---|
| 1 cup heavy cream | Ground cloves |
| 1 tablespoon butter | ½ teaspoon salt |
| 1 tablespoon flour | Freshly ground black pepper |
| 1 bay leaf | |

Melt butter in the top of a double boiler, add the flour and stir until smooth. Put over hot water and stir in cream. Cook until thickened, stirring constantly. Add bay leaf, a pinch of cloves, salt and pepper. Cook for 5 minutes. Remove bay leaf. Makes about 1 cup.

## FLUFFY BAKED OMELET

| | |
|---|---|
| 6 eggs, separated | 2 tablespoons butter |
| 1 tablespoon flour | ½ teaspoon salt |
| 1 tablespoon cornstarch | Freshly ground black pepper |
| 1 cup milk | |

Beat egg yolks. Add flour, cornstarch, salt and pepper and beat until smooth. Add milk gradually, beating constantly. Beat egg whites until stiff but not dry, fold into egg yolk mixture. Melt butter in a heavy 9-inch skillet. Pour in egg mixture and bake in a moderate oven (350°) for 20 minutes. Fold onto hot platter. Serve immediately. Serves 6.

## LIFE's SPECIAL OMELET

| | |
|---|---|
| 6 eggs | 6 walnuts, chopped |
| 2 slices French bread | 1 teaspoon salt |
| 6 tablespoons butter | Freshly ground black pepper |
| ¼ cup red caviar | |

First, to make croutons, cut French bread into ½-inch pieces and sauté in 2 tablespoons butter until brown. Keep hot. Then beat eggs, salt, pepper and ¼ cup of water together with a whisk or fork until mixed but not foamy. Melt the remaining 4 tablespoons butter in a skillet. Add egg mixture and as eggs begin to set lift them gently with the flat of a fork or a spatula. Shake the skillet to keep the omelet from sticking to it. Cook until eggs are thoroughly set but slightly moist in the center. Put croutons, caviar and walnuts on the omelet. Fold one side of the omelet over the other and slide the folded omelet onto a hot platter. Serves 6. This recipe was especially devised for LIFE by Madame Romaine de Lyon whose New York restaurant features 320 other omelets.

## EGGS BENEDICT

| | |
|---|---|
| 6 eggs, poached | 6 slices toast or toasted |
| 6 thin slices boiled ham | English muffins |
| 2 tablespoons butter | Hollandaise sauce |

Sauté ham in butter for 5 minutes or until lightly browned. Place a slice of ham on each slice of toast, top with an egg and spoon hollandaise sauce over.

## HOLLANDAISE SAUCE

2 cups butter
6 egg yolks, lightly beaten
½ cup lemon juice

Cayenne pepper
1 teaspoon salt

Melt butter over hot (not boiling) water. Slowly beat in egg yolks, lemon juice, a few grains of cayenne pepper and salt. Continue beating until thickened. Makes about 3 cups.

## SHIRRED EGGS DUCHESSE

6 eggs
4 egg yolks
3 cups mashed potatoes
6 tablespoons grated
  Gruyère cheese

6 tablespoons melted butter
Salt
Freshly ground black pepper
Madeira sauce

Beat 3 egg yolks lightly. Beat in potatoes and blend thoroughly. Put potato mixture through a pastry bag with a rose tip to form borders around the edges of 6 shirred egg dishes. Put 1 table-spoon butter in the bottom of each dish and break 1 egg into each dish. Cook over low heat until eggs begin to set. Remove from heat and sprinkle each egg with 1 tablespoon grated cheese, salt and pepper. Beat the remaining egg yolk and brush the potato borders with it. Broil under moderate heat until potatoes are brown. Serve with hot Madeira sauce.

## MADEIRA SAUCE

⅓ cup Madeira wine
2 tablespoons butter
2 tablespoons flour

2 cups beef bouillon
Salt
Freshly ground black pepper

Melt butter over low heat. Add flour and stir until smooth. Add bouillon and cook until thickened, stirring constantly. Stir in Madeira, salt and pepper and simmer for 5 minutes. Makes about 2 cups.

## FRENCH FRIED DEVILED EGGS

12 eggs, hard cooked
1 egg, beaten
4 tablespoons
  crumbled bleu cheese
½ cup heavy cream
¼ cup minced celery
1 tablespoon minced parsley
1 teaspoon grated onion

1 tablespoon Worcestershire
  sauce
Cayenne pepper
1 cup dry bread crumbs
¼ cup dry white wine
Oil or vegetable shortening
½ teaspoon salt
Tomato celery sauce

Cut eggs in half lengthwise. Remove yolks and mash them. Add cheese, cream, celery, parsley, onion, Worcestershire, a few grains of cayenne pepper and salt. Stir until thoroughly mixed. Fill egg whites with yolk mixture and press halves together. Roll eggs in crumbs. Add wine to beaten egg and dip the eggs in it. Roll again in crumbs. Fry in 3 inches of hot oil (375°) for 5 minutes or until lightly browned. Serve immediately with tomato celery sauce. Serves 6.

## TOMATO CELERY SAUCE

2½ cups canned tomatoes
½ cup finely chopped
  celery leaves
¼ cup finely chopped onion
½ teaspoon sugar

Tabasco sauce
2 tablespoons cornstarch
1 teaspoon salt
Freshly ground black pepper

Combine tomatoes, celery leaves, onion, sugar, 4 drops of Tabasco, salt and pepper in a saucepan. Bring to a boil, reduce heat, cover and simmer for 10 minutes, stirring occasionally. Strain sauce through a sieve and return to saucepan. Dissolve cornstarch in ¼ cup of cold water and stir it into the sauce. Return to heat and cook until thickened, stirring constantly. Makes about 2 cups.

## EGGS IN ASPIC

6 eggs, poached
2 envelopes
  unflavored gelatine
2½ cups chicken bouillon
1 bay leaf
1 tablespoon lemon juice

1 stalk celery with leaves,
  cut up
3 ounces pâté
  de foie gras
Salt

Soften gelatine in 1 cup of cold water. Combine bouillon, bay leaf, lemon juice, celery and salt in saucepan. Bring to a boil, reduce heat and simmer for 10 minutes. Strain and add broth to softened gelatine. Stir until gelatine is dissolved. Cool mixture for 30 minutes or until syrupy. Pour about ½ inch of gelatine mixture into 6 individual custard cups. Chill for 30 minutes or until gelatine is set. Put 1 tablespoonful of pâté in each cup. Put a poached egg in each cup on top of the pâté and add the remaining gelatine. Chill for at least 3 hours. Unmold before serving.

## SCOTCH WOODCOCK

12 eggs, lightly beaten
2 tablespoons butter
⅓ cup dry sherry
Salt

Freshly ground black pepper
6 slices toast
Anchovy paste

Beat eggs with salt and pepper until foamy. Cook in butter over low heat until the eggs begin to set, stirring gently. Stir in sherry and continue cooking until eggs are done. Meanwhile spread toast with anchovy paste. Serve eggs on top of toast. Serves 6.

## EGGS CASTELLANE

6 eggs, hard cooked
2 tablespoons dry sherry
1 tablespoon finely
  chopped onion
1 bay leaf
6 peppercorns
2 tablespoons butter
1 tablespoon flour
1 cup beef bouillon

½ cup finely
  chopped mushrooms
1 teaspoon minced parsley
1 teaspoon lemon juice
¼ cup cream, whipped
Ground nutmeg
1 teaspoon salt
Freshly ground black pepper

Combine sherry, onion, bay leaf, peppercorns and 1 tablespoon butter in saucepan and simmer for 5 minutes. Stir in flour and mix thoroughly. Add bouillon and cook until thickened, stirring constantly. Strain and return to saucepan. Add mushrooms and simmer for 5 minutes. Add parsley and lemon juice. Meanwhile cut eggs in half lengthwise. Remove yolks and mash them. Add the remaining 1 tablespoon butter, whipped cream, a dash of nutmeg, the salt and freshly ground black pepper and blend thoroughly. Fill egg whites with yolk mixture and arrange them in a shallow baking dish. Pour the hot sherry sauce over the eggs. Bake in a hot oven (400°) for 15 minutes. Serves 6.

## BAKED EGGS

6 eggs
1 slice bacon
6 chicken livers
Butter
Cayenne pepper

Dry mustard
6 tablespoons heavy cream
Salt
Freshly ground black pepper

Cut bacon into 6 pieces and sauté until crisp. Drain and save bacon, discard fat. Sauté chicken livers in 2 tablespoons butter for 5 minutes or until lightly browned. Put 1 liver in each of 6 buttered individual baking dishes. Add a few grains of cayenne and pinch of mustard to cream and stir well. Put 1 tablespoon cream into each dish and break 1 egg in on top of the cream. Season with salt and pepper. Put a piece of bacon on top of each egg. Cover the baking dishes and bake eggs in a moderate oven (375°) for 10 minutes or until eggs are set. Custard cups covered with foil may be used instead of individual china baking dishes.

## EGGS IN SOUR CREAM

6 eggs
1½ cups sour cream
¼ cup melted butter
¾ cup chili sauce

Cayenne pepper
Seasoned salt
Freshly ground black pepper

Put 2 teaspoons melted butter in each of 6 *plats* (individual metal or earthenware baking dishes). Combine sour cream, chili sauce, a few grains of cayenne, the salt and black pepper. Spoon into *plats*. Break 1 egg into each *plat*. Bake in a hot oven (400°) for about 10 minutes or until eggs are done. Custard cups may be substituted for *plats*.

# DESSERTS

## COUPE DE LUXE

1 package frozen whole
strawberries, defrosted
1 package frozen sliced
peaches, defrosted
1 package frozen pineapple
chunks, defrosted
¼ cup brandy
1 fifth champagne, iced

Combine fruit and add brandy. Marinate in the refrigerator for at least 1 hour. To serve, fill large glasses or goblets half full of fruit and marinade. Pour champagne over the fruit at the table. Serves 6.

## PEPPERMINT CHOCOLATE ICE CREAM

1 package chocolate frozen
dessert mix
Light cream
2 ounces chocolate-coated
mint patties

Prepare frozen dessert mix as directed on the package, using cream instead of milk. Melt mint patties in 2 additional tablespoonfuls of cream. Add to mix. Pour into refrigerator tray and freeze until firm. Turn ice cream out into a chilled bowl and beat with rotary beater until smooth. Return to tray and freeze until firm enough to serve. Serves 6.

## CRANBERRY SHERBET

2 cups cranberry juice
1 envelope unflavored
gelatine
1 cup sugar
¼ cup lemon juice

Soften gelatine in ½ cup of cold water. Add ¾ cup of boiling water and stir until gelatine is dissolved. Dissolve sugar in cranberry and lemon juice and add to gelatine mixture. Pour into refrigerator tray and freeze until firm. Turn sherbet out into a chilled bowl and beat with rotary beater until smooth. Return to tray and freeze until firm enough to serve. Before serving, remove from refrigerator tray and beat again until creamy. Serves 6.

## RUM AND BUTTERSCOTCH PIE

1 tablespoon rum
1 package butterscotch
instant pudding
18 gingersnaps
2 tablespoons sugar
2 tablespoons melted butter
Light cream

Crush 12 gingersnaps and mix with sugar, butter and 1 tablespoon of water. Spread over bottom of 8-inch pie plate. Cut 6 gingersnaps in half, arrange around edge of pie plate. Prepare pudding according to package directions, using combined rum and cream instead of milk. Pour pudding into gingersnap shell. Chill for at least 2 hours. Serves 6.

## BAKED ALASKA

1 eight-inch cake layer
4 egg whites
½ cup sugar
1 quart firm ice cream

Beat egg whites until foamy, add sugar and beat until stiff but not dry. Place cake on heavy unfinished wooden tray or heat-proof platter. Spoon ice cream on the cake leaving a 1-inch border all around. Cover ice cream and cake completely with egg white meringue. Brown meringue lightly in a very hot oven (500°) for 2 minutes. Serve immediately. Serves 6.

## ICEBOX CAKE

2 eight-inch cake layers
2 cups heavy cream
½ cup instant cocoa mix
2 tablespoons crème de
cacao

Split cake layers in half crosswise. Beat cream until slightly thickened, add cocoa mix and beat until thick. Stir in crème de cacao. Spread mixture between layers and on top of cake. Chill for at least 1 hour. Serves 6.

## SOUR CREAM AND CHERRY JAM

1 pint sour cream
1 cup cherry jam

Stir cream and jam together and spoon mixture into refrigerator tray. Chill for 30 minutes. Do not freeze. Serves 6.

## COEUR A LA CREME

1 eight-ounce package
cream cheese
1 pound cottage cheese
1 cup heavy cream
1 quart fresh strawberries,
hulled
Confectioners' sugar

Let cream cheese stand at room temperature for at least 1 hour. Beat until smooth. Add cottage cheese and heavy cream slowly, beating constantly, until thoroughly blended. Spoon into 6 individual heart-shaped baskets lined with cheesecloth. Set on tray and chill overnight or for at least 8 hours. To serve, unmold coeurs and arrange fresh strawberries around them. Sprinkle berries with sugar if desired. Serves 6.

## ICE CREAM CUP

1 pint ice cream
6 ounces semisweet
chocolate bits
2 tablespoons butter
¼ cup crushed
peppermint candy

Melt chocolate and butter over hot water. Line 6 fluted paper baking cups with chocolate mixture. Set in muffin pan to keep shape. Chill for at least 1 hour. Peel away paper, leaving chocolate cups. Fill with ice cream and sprinkle with peppermint candy. Serves 6.

## ROMAN COFFEE CREAM

1 tablespoon instant coffee
4 tablespoons heavy cream
3 cups ricotta cheese
1 tablespoon brandy
4 tablespoons
confectioners' sugar

Combine ingredients and beat until smooth. Chill for at least 1 hour. Serves 6.

## FROSTY STRAWBERRY SHORTCAKE

1 pint strawberries, crushed
6 individual spongecake shells
1 package vanilla
frozen dessert mix
Light cream
2 tablespoons curaçao
Sugar

Prepare frozen dessert mix as directed on the package, using cream instead of milk. Beat in curaçao. Pour into refrigerator tray and freeze until firm. Turn ice cream out into a chilled bowl and beat with a rotary beater until smooth. Return to tray and freeze until firm enough to serve. Spoon into cake shells and top with sugared crushed strawberries. Serves 6.

## BANANA KIRSCH SHERBET

| | |
|---|---|
| 2 cups mashed banana | 2 cups milk |
| ½ cup kirsch | 2 egg whites |
| ¼ cup light corn syrup | ½ cup sugar |

Combine banana, kirsch, syrup and milk. Beat egg whites until foamy, add sugar and beat until stiff but not dry. Fold into banana mixture. Pour into refrigerator tray and freeze until firm. Turn out into a chilled bowl and beat until smooth. Return to tray and freeze until firm enough to serve. Serves 6.

## EGGS A LA NEIGE

| | |
|---|---|
| 3 egg whites | 3 cups milk |
| 2 tablespoons sugar | 1 package vanilla pudding mix |

Beat egg whites until foamy, add sugar and beat until stiff but not dry. Scald the milk. Drop egg white meringue by teaspoonfuls into the hot milk. Cover and let stand for 3 minutes. Remove meringues carefully and put them on a towel to drain and cool. Combine pudding mix and the milk in which the meringues were cooked and cook until mixture boils, stirring constantly. Remove from heat, cool for 10 minutes, stirring once. Pour the pudding into a shallow serving bowl. Top with meringues. Serve warm or chilled. Serves 6.

## ZABAGLIONE

| | |
|---|---|
| 6 eggs, separated | 6 noncaloric sweetener |
| 3 tablespoons sweet | tablets, crushed |
| Marsala wine | |

Beat egg yolks lightly with a rotary beater in top of double boiler. Beat in wine and sweetener tablets. Place over hot (not boiling) water and cook, beating constantly, until mixture is thick and light. Beat egg whites until stiff but not dry. Fold egg yolk and wine mixture slowly into the egg whites. Serve warm or chilled. Serves 6. Noncaloric sweetener liquid equivalent to 6 teaspoons of sugar may be used instead of crushed sweetener tablets.

## STRAWBERRY WHIP

| | |
|---|---|
| 1 cup strawberries, crushed | 12 noncaloric sweetener |
| 6 whole strawberries | tablets, crushed |
| 1½ envelopes | ¼ teaspoon grated lemon rind |
| unflavored gelatine | 2 teaspoons lemon juice |
| ¾ cup ginger ale | ½ cup nonfat dry milk powder |

Soften gelatine in ½ cup of cold water. Place over hot water and stir until gelatine dissolves. Combine crushed strawberries, ginger ale, sweetener tablets and lemon rind. Stir in gelatine. Chill for 30 minutes or until syrupy. Meanwhile combine lemon juice and ½ cup of ice water in a small bowl and sprinkle milk powder on top. Beat with a rotary beater until stiff. Fold beaten milk mixture into the chilled gelatine syrup. Chill for at least 1 hour. Serve topped with whole strawberries. Serves 6. Noncaloric sweetener liquid equivalent to 12 teaspoons of sugar may be used instead of sweetener tablets.

## COFFEE JELLY

| | |
|---|---|
| 3 tablespoons instant coffee | 1 teaspoon grated lemon rind |
| 2 envelopes unflavored gelatine | 1-inch stick cinnamon |
| ½ teaspoon grated | 12 noncaloric sweetener |
| orange rind | tablets, crushed |

Soften gelatine in ½ cup of cold water. Combine coffee, orange and lemon rind, cinnamon and sweetener tablets in 3 cups of boiling water. Simmer for 5 minutes. Add softened gelatine and stir until it is dissolved. Remove cinnamon stick. Chill jelly for 1 hour or until firm. Break up with fork before serving. Serves 6. Noncaloric sweetener liquid equivalent to 12 teaspoons of sugar may be used instead of crushed sweetener tablets.

## TROPICAL COMPOTE

| | |
|---|---|
| 1½ cups cubed fresh pineapple | 1 cup cubed papaya |
| ½ cup cubed cherimoya | or 1 cup sliced fresh peach |
| or 1 banana, sliced | ½ cup dry white wine |

Combine fruit with wine and marinate at room temperature for 1 hour. Chill for at least 1 hour. Serves 6.

## SHERRY JELLY

| | |
|---|---|
| 1 cup sweet sherry | 16 noncaloric sweetener |
| 2 envelopes | tablets |
| unflavored gelatine | ¼ cup lemon juice |
| 1½ cups orange juice | |

Soften gelatine in ½ cup of orange juice. Dissolve sweetener tablets in 1 cup of hot water, add to gelatine and stir until gelatine and tablets are dissolved. Add sherry, remaining 1 cup orange juice and the lemon juice. Pour into 6 individual molds. Chill for 1 hour or until firm. Noncaloric sweetener liquid equivalent to 16 teaspoons of sugar may be used instead of sweetener tablets.

## CHERRY CROWN

| | |
|---|---|
| 2 cups canned | 2 envelopes low-calorie |
| water pack cherries | lemon-flavored gelatin |

Drain cherries and measure juice. Add enough boiling water to make 2 cups of liquid. Add gelatin and stir until dissolved. Chill for about 30 minutes or until slightly thickened. Stir in cherries. Pour into 6 individual molds and chill for 1 hour or until firm.

## PETITS FOURS

| | |
|---|---|
| 7 eggs, separated | ¾ teaspoon cream of tartar |
| 2 tablespoons lemon juice | 1½ cups sifted cake flour |
| 3 tablespoons liquid Sucaryl | ¼ teaspoon salt |
| ½ teaspoon vanilla extract | Petits fours icing |
| ½ teaspoon almond extract | |

Beat egg yolks for about 5 minutes or until thick and lemon colored. Combine lemon juice, Sucaryl, vanilla extract, almond extract and ½ cup cold water. Add slowly to egg yolks, beating constantly until mixture is thick and fluffy. Beat egg whites until foamy, add cream of tartar and beat until stiff but not dry. Fold carefully into the egg yolk mixture. Combine sifted flour and salt. Sift flour a little at a time over egg mixture and fold it in gently. Pour batter into two ungreased 9-inch-square cake pans and bake in a moderate oven (350°) for 30 minutes or until cake springs back when touched lightly. Invert tins on cooling racks. When cakes are cold, remove them from the pans and cut each cake into 24 pieces. Frost with petits fours icing.

## PETITS FOURS ICING

| | |
|---|---|
| 1 egg white | Food colorings |
| 2 cups sifted | Flavoring extracts |
| confectioners' sugar | |

Stir egg white into sugar. Add about ½ cup water, a little at a time, stirring constantly until a thin frosting is formed. Divide frosting into several bowls and tint and flavor each with a few drops of different colorings and extracts. Arrange cake squares 1 inch apart on cooling racks set on waxed paper. Pour frosting over the cakes to coat tops and sides. Decorate with nuts, coconut or chocolate bits. Let the cakes stand at least 10 minutes before taking them off the racks. The frosting which collects on the waxed paper may be reused by heating it in a small bowl set over warm water for a few minutes, adding a drop or two of warm water if necessary to thin it.

## CHOCOLATE ROLLS

| | |
|---|---|
| 1 package low-calorie | 1 teaspoon |
| chocolate cake | unflavored gelatine |
| and frosting mix | |

Mix cake as directed on package. Pour into 2 heavily greased and floured 12x18-inch pans. Bake in a hot oven (400°) for 8 minutes. Turn out onto lightly floured towels; cover cakes with pans until cool. Cut each cake in half to make 4 strips about 5x16 inches. Trim off crisp edges. Roll cakes with towels into 16-inch-long rolls. When cakes are cool, soften gelatine in ¾ cup water and bring to boil, stirring constantly. Add frosting mix. Beat in warm bowl until fluffy. Unroll cakes and spread with frosting. Let set for 20 minutes. Reroll cakes, wrap loosely in towels and chill for at least 2 hours. Cut rolls into ¾-inch slices with a sharp, wet knife. Makes about 88 slices.

# PARTY BRUNCHES

## MAIDEN'S PRAYER

| | |
|---|---|
| ½ pound chicken breasts, boned and diced | ½ cup thickly sliced canned bamboo shoots |
| ⅛ teaspoon ground ginger | ½ cup thinly sliced scallions |
| 2 tablespoons dry sherry | ½ cup canned button mushrooms, drained |
| 1 teaspoon soy sauce | |
| ¼ cup peanut oil | 1 cup chicken bouillon |
| 3 cups snow peas | ½ teaspoon salt |
| ½ cup thinly sliced celery | Freshly ground black pepper |

Season chicken with ginger, sherry, soy sauce, salt and pepper. Cook in 2 tablespoons oil in large skillet over high heat for 5 minutes, stirring constantly. Remove chicken mixture and keep hot. Put 2 tablespoons oil in skillet and add remaining ingredients. Cook over high heat for 5 minutes, stirring constantly. Remove from heat. Put chicken on top of vegetables and allow juices from chicken to soak into vegetables for 5 minutes. Return skillet to high heat and cook for 5 minutes, stirring constantly. Serves 6.

## WINTER MELON BROTH

| | |
|---|---|
| 1 ten-pound winter melon | 2 tablespoons dry sherry |
| 1 squab | 1 teaspoon soy sauce |
| ¼ pound canned abalone, diced | Chicken bouillon |
| ½ cup chopped mushrooms | 1 teaspoon salt |
| ½ cup chopped canned water chestnuts | Freshly ground black pepper |
| | 1 cup cooked peas |
| ½ cup chopped canned bamboo shoots | 2 tablespoons finely chopped lean Smithfield ham |

Wash melon and cut off the top, using a zig-zag pattern. Remove melon seeds. Put whole squab, abalone, mushrooms, chestnuts, bamboo shoots, sherry, soy sauce, salt and pepper in melon. Add bouillon until it comes to within ½ inch of top of melon. Set melon on a rack in a deep kettle over 1 inch of boiling water. Cover and steam over medium heat for 8 hours, adding more water when necessary to keep it at the 1-inch level. Remove melon. Skim fat from soup. Before serving, sprinkle soup with peas and ham. Serves 6.

## DIM SUM

| | |
|---|---|
| 1 cup rice flour | 1 tablespoon cornstarch |
| ½ cup chopped cooked pork | 2 hard-cooked egg yolks, sieved |
| ¼ cup chopped boiled ham | |
| ¼ cup finely chopped canned bamboo shoots | 2 tablespoons minced Smithfield ham |

Combine rice flour and 1¼ cups of boiling water. Cool slightly and place on board heavily sprinkled with rice flour. Knead for 2 or 3 minutes. Roll out pastry ⅛ inch thick. Cut into 2-inch squares. Makes about 24. Mix all the other ingredients, except Smithfield ham, and form into small balls. Wrap the pastry squares around the balls, leaving the tops open. Sprinkle the tops with Smithfield ham. Put on rack over 1 inch of boiling water, cover pan and steam over high heat for 10 minutes. Dim sum may be prepared and steamed a day ahead of time, stored covered in the refrigerator, and resteamed before serving.

## LOBSTER TIENTSIN

| | |
|---|---|
| 1 three-pound lobster | ¼ cup chicken bouillon |
| 4 cups finely chopped Chinese cabbage | 2 tablespoons dry sherry |
| | 1 teaspoon soy sauce |
| Peanut oil | ¼ teaspoon ground ginger |
| 2 egg whites | Freshly ground black pepper |
| 2 tablespoons cornstarch | |

Blanch cabbage in hot oil. Rinse with cold water and drain. Remove meat from raw lobster and cut it into ½-inch pieces. Combine egg whites and cornstarch and marinate lobster in this mixture for 30 minutes. Stir in 2 tablespoons bouillon, sherry, soy sauce, ginger and pepper. Cook in 2 tablespoons oil in a large skillet over high heat for 5 minutes, stirring constantly. Remove lobster mixture and keep hot. Cook cabbage, remaining 6 tablespoons chicken bouillon and 2 tablespoons oil in the skillet over high heat for 5 minutes, stirring constantly. Add lobster mixture and cook for 5 minutes, stirring constantly. Serves 6.

## SZECHUAN NOODLES

| | |
|---|---|
| 1 pound narrow egg noodles, boiled and drained | 1 tablespoon finely chopped green pepper |
| ¼ pound cooked shrimp, cut up | 2 tablespoons finely chopped parsley |
| 2 tablespoons finely chopped cooked ham | 2 teaspoons ground ginger |
| 2 tablespoons finely chopped cooked pork | ½ teaspoon Tabasco sauce |
| | 1 tablespoon soy sauce |
| 2 tablespoons finely chopped cooked chicken | 2 tablespoons cornstarch |
| | ¼ cup chicken bouillon |
| 2 tablespoons dry sherry | 2 tablespoons peanut oil |

Combine shrimp, ham, pork, chicken, sherry, vegetables and seasonings. Mix cornstarch and bouillon together. Add to shrimp and meat mixture. Cook in oil in a large skillet over high heat for 5 minutes, stirring constantly. Serve with noodles. Serves 6.

## LAMPS OF CHINA DELIGHT

| | |
|---|---|
| ½ cup finely chopped cooked chicken | ¼ cup finely chopped scallions |
| ½ cup cooked crab meat | 6 eggs, lightly beaten |
| ¼ cup finely chopped canned bamboo shoots | 4 tablespoons cornstarch |
| | Peanut oil |
| ¼ cup chopped mushrooms | 1 teaspoon salt |
| 1 tablespoon chopped parsley | Freshly ground black pepper |

Combine chicken, crab meat, vegetables, eggs, salt and pepper. Spoon into 18 buttered Chinese porcelain spoons or heat-proof custard cups. Steam on rack in covered pan over 1 inch boiling water for 10 minutes. Cool. Remove cakes from spoons and roll in cornstarch. Fry in 1-inch hot oil (375°) for 5 minutes or until brown. Serve with Lamps of China sauce. Serves 6.

## LAMPS OF CHINA SAUCE

| | |
|---|---|
| ¾ cup liquid strained from canned, cream-style corn | 2 teaspoons cornstarch |
| | ½ teaspoon salt |
| ¾ cup heavy cream | Freshly ground black pepper |

Combine all ingredients and cook over low heat for 5 minutes or until thickened, stirring constantly. Makes about 2 cups.

## SHRIMP FANTASY

| | |
|---|---|
| 1 cup chopped cooked shrimp | 1 teaspoon soy sauce |
| 1 cup rice flour | 1 tablespoon dry sherry |
| ¼ cup chopped scallions | Freshly ground black pepper |
| ¼ cup chopped mushrooms | |

Combine rice flour and 1¼ cups of boiling water. Cool slightly and place on board heavily sprinkled with rice flour. Knead for 2 or 3 minutes. Roll out pastry ⅛ inch thick. Cut into 2-inch squares. Combine shrimp with the rest of the ingredients. Put a teaspoonful on each pastry square and fold the pastry around it. Put on rack over 1 inch of boiling water. Cover pan and steam over high heat for 10 minutes. Makes about 24. Shrimp fantasy may be prepared and steamed a day ahead of time, stored tightly covered in the refrigerator and resteamed for 10 to 15 minutes before serving.

## JO CHON BAU

| | |
|---|---|
| 3 loin pork chops, cut 1 inch thick | ¼ teaspoon ground ginger |
| ¼ cup barbecue sauce | ¼ cup finely chopped scallions |
| ½ cup canned oyster sauce | 2 tablespoons peanut oil |
| 1 tablespoon honey | 2 tablespoons butter, melted |
| 1 tablespoon sherry | 1 package yeast roll mix |

Prepare roll mix according to package directions. Meanwhile brush chops with barbecue sauce. Put them on a wire rack over a pan containing 1 inch of water. Bake in hot oven (400°) for 30 minutes, turning once. Cool. Bone chops and cut meat into bite-size pieces. Marinate for 1 hour in mixture of oyster sauce, honey, sherry and ginger. Add scallions and cook in oil in large skillet over high heat for 3 minutes, stirring briskly. Divide roll-mix dough into 6 pieces. Flatten each piece and brush with butter. Top with pork mixture. Fold dough over pork and twist top to seal. Let buns rise in a warm place for 30 minutes. Put a square of foil on the bottom of each bun. Place buns on rack over 1 inch of boiling water. Cover pan and steam over high heat for 15 minutes. Jo chon bau may be prepared and steamed a day ahead of time, stored tightly covered in the refrigerator and resteamed for 10 to 15 minutes before serving.

## BIT OF FORMOSA

| | |
|---|---|
| 1 pound pork tenderloin, cooked | 1 tablespoon catsup |
| 3 eggs, beaten | 4 slices canned pineapple, cut in wedges |
| 4 tablespoons cornstarch | 1 large green pepper, cut in squares |
| Peanut oil | |
| 2 tablespoons wine vinegar | ½ cup thinly sliced carrot |
| 2 tablespoons sugar | 1 teaspoon salt |
| 1 cup chicken bouillon | Freshly ground black pepper |

Cut pork into ½-inch cubes. Dip into eggs, then roll in 2 table-spoons cornstarch. Fry in 1 inch of hot oil (375°) for 10 minutes. Drain. Add pork to remaining ingredients and cook in 2 tablespoons oil in large skillet over high heat for 5 minutes, stirring constantly. Serves 6.

## FILET OPALESCENCE

| | |
|---|---|
| 1 pound top sirloin of beef, sliced 1 inch thick | ½ cup snow peas, cut in ½-inch pieces |
| ¼ cup dry sherry | ½ cup thinly sliced mushrooms |
| 1 teaspoon soy sauce | |
| 2 tablespoons cornstarch | ½ cup finely chopped chives |
| ⅛ teaspoon ground ginger | 1 cup chicken bouillon |
| 2 tablespoons peanut oil | Chow mein noodles |
| ½ cup thinly sliced asparagus | |

Cut beef into 2-inch strips and slice strips across grain about ⅛ inch thick. Combine sherry, soy sauce, cornstarch and ginger. Marinate beef in this mixture for 1 hour. Fry in oil in large skillet over high heat for 5 minutes, stirring constantly. Remove beef and keep hot. Add vegetables and bouillon to liquid remaining in skillet and cook over high heat for 5 minutes, stirring constantly. Add beef to vegetable mixture and cook for 5 minutes, stirring constantly. Serve the filet opalescence with chow mein noodles. Serves 6.

## GLOUCESTER CODFISH BALLS

| | |
|---|---|
| 1½ cups fibered salt codfish | 2 eggs, well beaten |
| 3 cups diced potatoes | Freshly ground black pepper |
| ⅓ cup milk | Oil or vegetable shortening |

Soak codfish in cold water for 10 minutes. Drain. Repeat twice. Add cod to potatoes with 1 cup of water. Boil for 15 minutes or until potatoes are soft. Drain and mash. Add milk, eggs and pepper. Drop mixture by teaspoonfuls into 1 inch of hot oil (375°). Fry for 5 to 8 minutes or until golden brown. Drain. Serve hot. Serves 6.

## PENNSYLVANIA DUTCH POTATO PANCAKES

| | |
|---|---|
| 4 pounds potatoes, peeled | 1 teaspoon lemon juice |
| 2 large onions | Ground nutmeg |
| 1 egg | Oil or vegetable shortening |
| 1½ cups flour | 1 tablespoon salt |
| 2 teaspoons baking powder | |

Put raw potatoes and onions through food grinder, using fine blade. Drain thoroughly. Mix egg, flour, baking powder, lemon juice, a pinch of nutmeg and salt. Drop mixture by tablespoon-fuls into 2 inches of hot oil (375°). Fry for about 10 minutes or until golden brown. Drain. Serves 6.

## CINNAMON BUNS

| | |
|---|---|
| 2 envelopes granular yeast | 4 to 4½ cups sifted flour |
| 1 cup milk | 2 teaspoons ground cinnamon |
| 6 tablespoons sugar | ½ cup raisins |
| 2 eggs | 2 teaspoons salt |
| 6 tablespoons butter | |

Soften yeast in ½ cup lukewarm water. Scald milk. Add 2 table-spoons sugar and the salt. Cool to lukewarm and add yeast. Stir well. Beat in eggs and 4 tablespoons butter. Add flour, stirring until a moderately firm dough is formed. Turn dough out on a lightly floured board and knead until the dough is smooth and not sticky. Roll the dough out into an oblong about ¼ inch thick. Spread with the remaining 2 tablespoons butter and sprinkle with the 4 tablespoons sugar combined with cinnamon. Sprinkle with raisins. Roll up and cut into slices. Put the buns on a buttered baking sheet, cover and let rise for about 30 minutes or until double in bulk. Bake in a hot oven (400°) for 20 minutes or until brown. Makes about 24.

## CHICKEN CASSEROLE BORDEAUX

| | |
|---|---|
| 3 pounds chicken breasts | 2 cups gooseberry jam |
| 1 pound white seedless grapes | 1 tablespoon horseradish |
| 2 cups dry white wine | 1 teaspoon salt |
| 1 cup red currant jelly | Freshly ground black pepper |
| | Lemon pancakes |

Crush grapes in a deep saucepan. Arrange chicken breasts on crushed grapes and pour wine over them. Add salt and pepper. Bring to a boil, reduce heat, cover and simmer for 1 hour. Remove breasts and cut meat from bones. Cut into pieces and keep hot. Strain broth from grapes, keep grapes hot. Add jelly, jam and horseradish to broth. Boil for 15 minutes. Arrange chicken in casserole surrounded with grapes. Pour sauce over. Serve with lemon pancakes. Serves 6.

## LEMON PANCAKES

| | |
|---|---|
| 1 teaspoon grated lemon rind | 2 eggs, beaten |
| 2½ cups sifted flour | 2 cups milk |
| 4½ teaspoons double-acting baking powder | ¼ cup melted shortening |
| 1 teaspoon sugar | 1 teaspoon salt |

Sift flour, baking powder, sugar and salt into a bowl. Combine eggs, milk, shortening. Stir in lemon rind. Add to dry ingredients. Beat only until flour is dampened (batter will be lumpy). Fry pancakes on an ungreased griddle. To fry each pancake, pour about ¼ cup of batter on hot griddle. When the edges become dry and some of the bubbles break, turn the pancake and cook until brown on the other side. The pancake batter may be prepared in advance and kept overnight, tightly covered, in the refrigerator. Makes about 12 four-inch pancakes.

## POMPANO CLAUDET

| | |
|---|---|
| 3 two-pound pompanos | ¼ cup butter |
| 1 lemon slice | ¼ cup chopped chives |
| 1 bay leaf | 2 tablespoons chopped parsley |
| ½ pound mushrooms, chopped | 1 tablespoon Worcestershire sauce |
| ¼ cup chopped onion | 2 tablespoons lemon juice |
| 3 canned pimento, chopped | 1 teaspoon salt |
| 2 green peppers, chopped | 6 peppercorns |
| 2 tablespoons capers | Freshly ground black pepper |

Wash fish and cut off heads and tails. Split fish and set aside. Put fish heads and tails, lemon slice, bay leaf and peppercorns in a saucepan with 2 cups of water. Bring to a boil, reduce heat, cover and simmer for 20 minutes. Strain. Season the fish with salt and freshly ground black pepper. Broil under medium heat for 10 minutes, turning once. Meanwhile sauté chopped vegetables and capers in butter for 5 minutes. Add chives, parsley, Worcestershire, lemon juice and fish stock. Cover and simmer for 5 minutes. Serve sauce over fish. Serves 6.

## EGGS WITH ARTICHOKE HEARTS

| | |
|---|---|
| 6 eggs, poached | 6 artichoke hearts, cooked |
| 1 pound spinach, cooked and chopped | ¼ cup heavy cream |
| | 3 cups hollandaise sauce |

Combine spinach with cream. Spoon over hot artichoke hearts. Top with eggs and pour hot hollandaise sauce over. Serves 6.

## PINEAPPLE CUP

| | |
|---|---|
| 1 large pineapple | 1 cup cantaloupe balls |
| 1 cup whole strawberries | 1 cup cherry liqueur |
| 1 cup honeydew balls | |

Cut the pineapple in half lengthwise. Scoop out center, leaving a 1-inch shell, remove core and cut the rest in cubes. Chill the pineapple shells. Combine pineapple cubes with strawberries, melon balls and liqueur and let stand at room temperature for 1 hour. Then chill for at least 4 hours. To serve, spoon fruit and marinade into the pineapple shells. Serves 6.

## FLAMING BRANDY IN ORANGE CUPS

| | |
|---|---|
| Cognac | 6 sugar cubes |
| 6 oranges | 6 whole cloves |

Cut through rind around middle of oranges. Plunge oranges into boiling water and let stand for 5 minutes. Remove oranges and cool slightly. Discard water. Carefully pull half of the rind up to form a cup on the top of each orange, pull the other half down to form a base. Put a sugar cube and clove in each orange cup. Warm brandy, pour into orange cups and light. Serve flaming. Serves 6.

## SAUTEED BANANAS

| | |
|---|---|
| 6 bananas | ½ cup sugar |
| 2 tablespoons lemon juice | ¼ cup butter |

Select bananas which are all yellow or slightly green tipped. Peel bananas and brush with lemon juice then roll bananas in sugar. Sauté in butter over low heat for 5 minutes or until golden brown. Serves 6.

## ORANGE SLICES IN CURACAO

| | |
|---|---|
| 6 oranges | ½ cup fresh grated coconut |
| ¼ cup Curaçao | |

Peel, slice and seed oranges. Marinate in Curaçao for at least 12 hours. Arrange orange slices in serving dishes, pour marinade over them and sprinkle with coconut. Serves 6.

## QUICHE LORRAINE

| | |
|---|---|
| 6 thick slices bacon | Ground nutmeg |
| 12 thin slices Swiss cheese | Ground cayenne pepper |
| 4 eggs, lightly beaten | Freshly ground black pepper |
| 2 cups light cream | 1 unbaked 9-inch pie shell |
| 1 tablespoon flour | |

Cut bacon slices in half. Cut Swiss cheese into pieces same size as bacon. Fry bacon until crisp, drain. Line 9-inch pie plate with unbaked pie shell. Overlap bacon and cheese slices to cover bottom of crust. Combine the eggs, cream, flour, a pinch of nutmeg, a few grains of cayenne pepper and black pepper. Beat well. Strain and pour over bacon and cheese slices. Bake in a hot oven (400°) for 15 minutes. Reduce heat to 325° and bake for 30 minutes. Serves 6. To prepare quiche lorraine in advance, line pastry shell with bacon and cheese and mix the rest of the ingredients together for the custard. Refrigerate separately. Let pie shell and custard mixture stand at room temperature for about 30 minutes before combining and baking.

## PIE CRUST PASTRY

| | |
|---|---|
| 1½ cups sifted flour | ½ teaspoon salt |
| ½ cup shortening | |

Sift flour with salt. Cut the shortening in with pastry blender or two knives until mixture resembles coarse meal. Sprinkle 4 tablespoons ice water, one tablespoonful at a time, over the flour mixture and blend it in with a fork. Wrap the dough in waxed paper and chill it for at least 15 minutes. Makes enough pastry for 2-crust pie or 2 eight-inch or nine-inch pie shells. When wrapped or placed in a covered container, chilled dough will keep in the refrigerator for 2 days.

## VEAL CHASSEUR

| | |
|---|---|
| 2 pounds veal cutlet, sliced ¼ inch thick | 1 pound mushrooms, sliced |
| ¼ cup butter | ½ cup dry white wine |
| 2 shallots, minced or 2 tablespoons minced onion and 1 small garlic clove, minced | 2 tablespoons chopped parsley |
| | 1 teaspoon salt |
| | Freshly ground black pepper |
| | Brown sauce |

Trim fat from veal and cut the meat into 1-inch pieces. Sauté veal in butter for 10 minutes or until golden brown. Remove from skillet and keep hot. Sauté shallots and mushrooms in butter remaining in skillet for 5 minutes. Add wine and simmer for 15 minutes or until the liquid is reduced one half. Stir in brown sauce, parsley, salt and pepper. Add meat and simmer for 5 minutes. Serves 6.

## BROWN SAUCE

| | |
|---|---|
| 1 onion, chopped | 2 tablespoons dry Madeira wine |
| ¼ cup diced celery | ½ teaspoon ground thyme |
| 1 large carrot, chopped | 1 large bay leaf |
| 1 garlic clove, chopped | ½ teaspoon salt |
| ½ cup butter | 6 peppercorns |
| 3 tablespoons cornstarch | |
| 3 cups beef bouillon | |

Sauté onion, celery, carrot and garlic in butter for 10 minutes or until onion is golden brown. Add cornstarch to ½ cup cold bouillon and stir into onion mixture. Add remaining 2½ cups of bouillon, wine, thyme, bay leaf, salt and pepper. Bring to a boil, reduce heat, cover and simmer for 30 minutes, stirring occasionally. Strain. Makes about 2 cups.

## CREPES

| | |
|---|---|
| 4 eggs | 4 cups milk |
| 4 egg yolks | ½ cup butter |
| ¾ cup flour | 2 teaspoons salt |
| 1 tablespoon sugar | Orange maple sauce |

Beat eggs and egg yolks together lightly. Sift in flour, sugar and salt. Add milk and beat well. Strain through a fine sieve. To cook each crepe melt 1 teaspoon butter in small skillet, add 2 tablespoons batter and cook over high heat for 2 minutes on each side. Makes 24. Serve with orange maple sauce.

## ORANGE MAPLE SAUCE

| | |
|---|---|
| 1 cup orange juice | 1 cup maple syrup |
| 2 tablespoons grated orange rind | ⅓ cup Curaçao |

Combine ingredients and let stand at room temperature for 1 hour. Heat in chafing dish. Dip crepes in hot sauce, fold first in half then in quarters and simmer in sauce for 5 minutes. Serves 6.

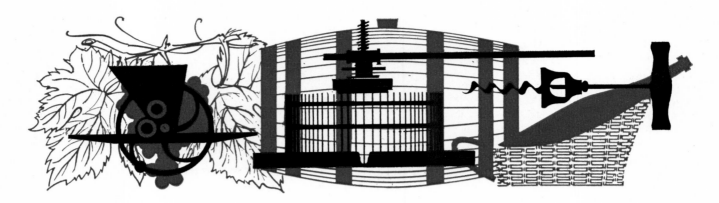

# WINE BUYING

## A $25 WINE CELLAR

**DRY SHERRY**, one bottle. This is served before dinner like a cocktail, chilled if preferred. Choose a good American brand such as Almadén, Beaulieu, L. M. Martini, Widmer's or a modestly priced dry sherry from a reputable Spanish firm such as Bobadilla, Domecq, Duff Gordon, Garvey, Gonzalez Byass, Harvey's, Sandeman, Williams & Humbert.

**CALIFORNIA RED WINE**, one gallon. Buying by the gallon means lower cost per bottle. To prevent spoiling, decant into five bottles or 10 half bottles, corking tightly. California's best red wines come from the north coast counties, Napa, Sonoma, Santa Clara, Mendocino, Alameda, and are bottled at the winery. California claret and Burgundy are often almost identical, but Burgundy usually has more body.

**CALIFORNIA WHITE WINE**, one gallon. Decant as above. Good white wine in gallon size is more difficult to find than red. Look for a wine bottled and shipped by a north coast county winery. Almadén, L. M. Martini and Charles Krug are among those nationally distributed. American Chablis and American sauterne, unlike French Chablis and sauternes, are sometimes impossible to tell apart.

**CHILEAN RIESLING**, one bottle, a low-cost dry white wine.

**VIN ROSE**, two bottles. This all-purpose pink wine goes with almost any food. Serve chilled. The pink wines of California are excellent, particularly those of Almadén, Beaulieu, Krug and Martini; or get a French *rosé*, from Alsace, Anjou, Côtes du Rhône (the best is Tavel) or Provence, of recent year such as 1957.

**CHIANTI**, one bottle. An economical all-purpose Italian red wine. Choose among such reliable shippers as Antinori, Bertolli, Brolio, Martini & Rossi, Ruffino and Serristori. Very cheap Chianti is not recommended since it is generally not as good as ordinary red wine from California.

**CALIFORNIA CABERNET OR PINOT NOIR RED WINE**, one bottle. Most of the good red Bordeaux is made from the Cabernet grape, just as the finer red Burgundy is produced from the Pinot Noir grape. These flourish best in northern California at the vineyards of Almadén, Beaulieu, Hallcrest, Inglenook, Krug, Martini, Paul Masson and M. Ray.

**AMERICAN DRY WHITE WINE**, one bottle. America's best dry white wines generally bear the name of the grape variety such as Delaware, Pinot Blanc, Pinot Chardonnay, Riesling, Sauvignon Blanc, Semillon, Traminer. Among the better growers of these wines are Almadén, Beaulieu, Buena Vista, Inglenook, Krug, Martini, Wente and, in New York State, Widmer's.

**RED BORDEAUX (FRENCH) OF 1952, '53, '55 VINTAGE**, one bottle. When buying this wine, first look for one that has *Mis en bouteilles au Château* on the label. This means it was bottled by the owner of the château. Dependable châteaux include Beychevelle, Calon-Ségur, Gruaud-Larose, Lascombes, Léoville-Las-Cases, Palmer, Pichon Longueville. If you cannot find one so labeled or if this turns out to be too expensive, then look for one named after a specific town such as Margaux, St. Julien or St. Estèphe. Failing this, settle for a wine simply named after a district, such as Médoc or St. Emilion.

**RED BURGUNDY (FRENCH), 1952, '53, '55**, one bottle. Wines from many of the less famous vineyards of Burgundy are good and not too expensive. District names include Beaujolais, Côte de Beaune, Mâconnais. For best wines look for an "estate bottling" with a phrase such as *Mis du Domaine* or *Propriétaire* next to the producer's name on the label.

**RHINE WINE (GERMAN), 1953, '55, '57**, one bottle. Liebfraumilch is what the average American usually asks for when buying a German wine. The word connotes very little, except that the wine comes from a part of the Rhine area. So ask for wines that carry the name of a specific town and a specific vineyard such as Hochheimer (for name of town), Daubhaus (for name of vineyard) or Eltviller Sonnenberg, Niersteiner Rehbach, Johannisberger Klaus or Rüdesheimer Schlossberg.

## A $100 WINE CELLAR

**DRY AMONTILLADO SHERRY**, one bottle. Choose from among the Spanish shippers listed under $25 cellar.

**TAWNY PORT**, one bottle. An excellent wine for after dinner. Choose from among such Portuguese shippers as Cockburn, Harvey's, Robertson, Sandeman, Fonseca and Delaforce.

**CALIFORNIA RED WINE**, two gallons. See $25 cellar.

**CALIFORNIA WHITE WINE**, two gallons. See $25 cellar.

**BETTER CALIFORNIA RED WINES**, four bottles. Choose Cabernet or Pinot Noir from better vineyards listed under $25 cellar.

**BETTER AMERICAN WHITE WINES**, four bottles. See $25 cellar.

**IMPORTED CHIANTI**, two bottles. See $25 cellar.

**WHITE BORDEAUX OF 1952, '53, '55 VINTAGE**, three bottles. Pick Graves for moderately dry, Barsac for semisweet and sauternes for sweet. For better wines select a château bottling such as Carbonnieux (Graves), Coutet (Barsac), and Filhot, La Tour Blanche and d'Yquem among the sauternes.

**RED BORDEAUX, 1949, '52, '53**, four bottles. Two bottles of a good château (see $25 cellar). Two bottles from one of the top vineyards—Château Lafite-Rothschild, Latour, Margaux, Haut Brion, Mouton-Rothschild, Cheval Blanc—for special occasions.

**VIN ROSE**, four bottles. See $25 cellar.

**WHITE BURGUNDIES, 1952, '53, '55,** three bottles. All white Burgundies are dry. Choose among Chablis (the driest), Pouilly-Fuissé, Meursault, Corton Charlemagne, Puligny- or Chassagne-Montrachet. To obtain the best, look for an estate bottling.

**ALSATIAN WINES, 1955, '57,** two bottles. These are dry white wines bearing the name of the grape, rather than the district, on the label. Choose Traminer or Gewurztraminer for full flavor, fruitiness and aroma; Riesling for dryness, and Sylvaner for lightness and lower cost.

**RHONE VALLEY RED WINES,** two bottles. Pick Châteauneuf-du-Pape, Côte-Rôtie, Hermitage of 1950, '52, '55 vintage, estate bottled.

**ESTATE-BOTTLED RED BURGUNDIES, 1952, '53, '55,** two bottles. These superb wines are produced by great vineyards in small quantity. Look for estate bottling. Among the greatest vineyards are Chambertin, Clos Vougeot, Corton, Musigny, Grands Echézeaux, La Tâche, Richebourg and Romanée-St.-Vivant. Red Burgundies mature relatively fast; 1955s are ready to drink now.

**RHINE OR MOSELLES, 1953, '55, '57,** two bottles. Give preference to wines bearing the name of a vineyard as well as a town (see $25 cellar). Also look for the words *Original Abfüllung*, which mean "bottled by the vineyard owner." In addition, look for *Spätlese*, which means the grapes have matured on the vine, and *Auslese*, which means they have also been picked with extra care.

**CHAMPAGNES,** two bottles. One good American champagne such as Almadén, Fournier, Gold Seal, Great Western, Korbel or Masson, and one imported, vintage or nonvintage, such as Bollinger, Clicquot, Charles Heidsieck, Heidsieck Dry Monopole, Irroy, Krug, Lanson, Moët & Chandon, Mumm's, Perrier Jouet, Piper Heidsieck, Pol Roger, Pommery & Greno, Louis Roederer and Taittinger. Strangely, a champagne that is labeled extra dry is actually less dry than one labeled *brut*.

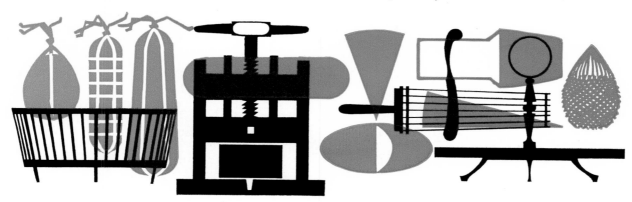

# CHEESE

## CHEESE BLINTZES

| | |
|---|---|
| 1 pound cottage cheese | 1 teaspoon vanilla extract |
| 2 eggs | 1 teaspoon ground cinnamon |
| 1 cup milk | ½ teaspoon salt |
| Butter | Sour cream |
| 1 cup sifted flour | Jam |
| ½ cup sugar | |

To make the blintzes, beat the eggs until foamy. Add milk and 2 tablespoons melted butter. Add flour and salt and beat with a rotary beater until smooth. Fry the blintzes one at a time in a hot lightly buttered 8-inch skillet. For each blintz pour 3 tablespoons batter into skillet, tipping to spread batter thinly. Fry over high heat for 2 minutes or until lightly browned on one side. Remove from pan. Lay blintzes on towels to cool. To make the filling, stir cottage cheese, sugar, vanilla and cinnamon together until well blended. Put 2 tablespoons of the filling on the browned side of each blintz and fold the sides over to completely cover the filling. Sauté blintzes in butter over medium heat for 5 minutes or until golden brown. Serve with sour cream and jam. Makes 12.

## EGGPLANT PARMESAN

| | |
|---|---|
| 1 large eggplant | ¼ cup olive oil |
| ¼ cup grated Parmesan cheese | 2 cups canned tomato sauce |
| ¼ pound mozzarella cheese, sliced | 2 tablespoons minced parsley |
| 1 egg, lightly beaten | ¼ teaspoon basil |
| ¼ cup dry white wine | ¼ teaspoon oregano |
| 1 cup cracker crumbs | 1 bay leaf, crumbled |
| 1 garlic clove, minced | 1 teaspoon salt |

Pare eggplant and cut it crosswise into ¼-inch slices. Beat egg with wine. Dip eggplant slices in egg and wine, then dip them in cracker crumbs. Sauté garlic in oil for 5 minutes. Add eggplant and sauté for 10 minutes or until golden brown. Remove eggplant and keep hot. Add tomato sauce, parsley, basil, oregano, bay leaf and salt to oil remaining in skillet and simmer for 15 minutes, stirring frequently. Arrange alternate layers of eggplant, Parmesan and mozzarella cheese, and sauce in a casserole. Top with mozzarella. Bake in a moderate oven (350°) for 30 minutes. Serves 6.

## ROQUEFORT MOUSSE

| | |
|---|---|
| ¼ pound Roquefort cheese | 2 tablespoons minced pimento |
| 1 envelope unflavored gelatine | 1 tablespoon minced capers |
| ¼ cup lemon juice | 1 teaspoon grated onion |
| 1 cup grated cucumber, drained | 1 cup heavy cream, whipped |
| 4 tablespoons minced parsley | 1 teaspoon salt |
| | Freshly ground black pepper |

Soften gelatine in lemon juice. Add 1 cup of boiling water and stir until gelatine is dissolved. Mash cheese. Add cucumber, parsley, pimento, capers, onion, salt and pepper and mix well. Combine with gelatine mixture. Chill for 20 minutes or until mixture is slightly thickened. Fold in whipped cream. Pour into mold and chill for at least 4 hours or until firm. Serves 6.

## WELSH RAREBIT

| | |
|---|---|
| 1 pound Cheddar cheese, grated | 2 teaspoons Worcestershire sauce |
| 1 cup beer | Cayenne pepper |
| 2 tablespoons butter | Toast |
| ½ teaspoon dry mustard | |

Combine beer, butter, mustard, Worcestershire sauce and a few grains of cayenne pepper in the top of a double boiler. Cook over hot, not boiling, water for 5 minutes or until butter melts, stirring constantly. Add grated cheese and cook for 10 minutes or until cheese melts and mixture is thoroughly blended, stirring frequently. Serve over toast. Serves 6.

## SWISS TOAST

| | |
|---|---|
| 6 slices Swiss cheese | 1 cup milk |
| 12 slices white bread | 1 teaspoon salt |
| ¾ cup butter | Rum sauce |
| 2 eggs | |

Spread the bread with ¼ cup softened butter and make 6 Swiss cheese sandwiches. Beat eggs until foamy and beat in milk and salt. Dip sandwiches in egg mixture to coat them thoroughly. Sauté in the remaining ½ cup butter for 10 minutes or until golden brown on both sides. Serve immediately with hot rum sauce. Serves 6.

## RUM SAUCE

| | |
|---|---|
| ¼ cup dark rum | 1 cup sugar |
| 2 tablespoons butter | |

Combine rum, butter and sugar with ⅓ cup of water and cook over low heat, stirring constantly, until sugar is dissolved and sauce is hot. Makes about 1½ cups.

## HOT CHEESE DUNK

| | |
|---|---|
| ½ pound Swiss cheese, grated | ¼ cup butter |
| ¼ pound Parmesan cheese, grated | 6 tablespoons flour |
| | 1 teaspoon A-1 sauce |
| 2 chicken bouillon cubes | Cooked shrimp |
| 2 cups heavy cream | or bite-sized pieces |
| 2 tablespoons grated onion | of French bread |

Scald cream, add bouillon cubes and stir until cubes are dissolved. Sauté onion in butter for 5 minutes or until soft. Add flour and mix well. Add cream mixture to onion mixture and cook for 5 minutes or until thickened, stirring constantly. Stir in cheese and A-1 sauce and simmer over low heat for 10 minutes or until cheese melts, stirring constantly. Serve hot with shrimp or bite-sized pieces of French bread. Makes about 3 cups.

## CHEESE CAKE

| | |
|---|---|
| 3 cups cottage cheese | 4 tablespoons lemon juice |
| 3 eggs | 1 teaspoon almond extract |
| ½ cup milk | 1 cup heavy cream |
| 1 cup sugar | 2 cups graham cracker |
| 2 envelopes | crumbs |
| unflavored gelatine | ½ cup light brown sugar |
| 1 tablespoon grated | ½ cup butter, melted |
| lemon rind | ½ teaspoon salt |

Separate eggs and set whites aside. Beat egg yolks in top of a double boiler until thick and lemon colored. Stir in milk and ½ cup sugar. Place over hot water and cook for 10 minutes or until thickened, stirring constantly. Soften gelatine in ½ cup cold water. Add to egg yolk custard and stir until gelatine is dissolved. Cool. Press cheese through coarse strainer or food mill and stir lemon rind, lemon juice and almond extract into it. Stir cheese mixture into custard. Beat cream with salt until stiff. Fold into cheese custard. Beat egg whites until foamy, add the remaining ½ cup sugar and beat until stiff but not dry. Fold egg white mixture into cheese custard. Combine cracker crumbs, brown sugar and melted butter. Spread crumb mixture over bottom and sides of an 8-inch spring-form pan. Pour in cheese custard. Chill for at least 4 hours. Serves 6.

## CHEESE AND WHITE WINE CASSEROLE

| | |
|---|---|
| ½ pound Gruyère cheese, grated | 6 eggs |
| | ½ cup heavy cream |
| 1½ cups dry white wine | ½ cup chicken bouillon |
| 6 slices bread | ¼ teaspoon dry mustard |
| 6 tablespoons butter | 1 teaspoon paprika |
| 1 garlic clove, crushed | |

Trim crusts from bread. Cream butter and garlic together and spread on bread. Arrange bread in casserole buttered side down. Beat eggs until foamy, beat in cream. Add cheese, wine, bouillon, mustard and paprika, stirring only enough to mix. Pour over bread. Bake in a moderate oven (350°) for 30 minutes or until puffed and brown. Serve immediately. Serves 6.

## CAMEMBERT FRENCH BREAD

| | |
|---|---|
| 4 ounces Camembert cheese | ¼ teaspoon basil |
| 1 large loaf French bread | ½ teaspoon onion salt |
| ½ cup butter | |

Combine cheese, butter, basil and onion salt in a saucepan and simmer over low heat for 5 minutes or until thoroughly blended, stirring constantly. Remove from heat and cool for 10 minutes or until mixture starts to thicken, stirring occasionally. Slice bread in half lengthwise. Spread some cheese mixture on cut surfaces of bread, put loaf together and spread remaining cheese mixture on top and sides of the loaf. Wrap bread in foil and bake in a moderate oven (325°) for 20 minutes. Turn back foil to expose crust and bake for 5 minutes. Serve hot. Serves 6.

## ONION AND CHEESE PIE

| | |
|---|---|
| ½ pound Swiss cheese, grated | 1 cup milk |
| | ½ teaspoon curry powder |
| 1 large onion, sliced | ¼ teaspoon ground nutmeg |
| ½ recipe of pie crust | Tabasco sauce |
| 2 tablespoons flour | 1 teaspoon salt |
| 4 eggs, lightly beaten | Freshly ground black pepper |
| 1 cup heavy cream | |

Roll pie crust ⅛ inch thick and line 10-inch pie plate with it. Flute edges of crust. Mix cheese thoroughly with flour and spread in bottom of pie shell. Separate onion slices into rings and arrange rings on cheese mixture. Beat eggs lightly. Beat in cream, milk, curry powder, nutmeg, 2 drops of Tabasco, salt and pepper. Pour egg mixture over cheese and onion rings. Bake in a moderate oven (350°) for 45 minutes. Serves 6.

## BRANDIED CHERRIES AND CHEESE

| | |
|---|---|
| 1 pound cottage cheese | 1 cup heavy cream |
| 2½ cups canned Bing cherries | 1 teaspoon salt |
| ½ cup brandy | |

Press cottage cheese through a coarse sieve to break up curds. Line colander or strainer with cheesecloth. Put cheese in colander, set on a plate and refrigerate overnight or for at least 8 hours to drain off whey. Combine brandy with cherries and cherry juice and cook over high heat, stirring occasionally, until mixture comes to a boil. Remove from heat, cover and cool for 30 minutes. Chill for at least 1 hour. Whip cream with salt until stiff. Break up drained cottage cheese with a fork and add whipped cream. Stir lightly until mixed. Serve cheese and cream mixture on a platter and arrange the chilled brandied cherries around it. Serves 6.

## SWISS CHEESE TARTS

| | |
|---|---|
| ½ pound Swiss cheese, grated | ⅛ teaspoon dry mustard |
| | Cayenne pepper |
| ¼ cup grated onion | 1 teaspoon salt |
| 2 tablespoons butter | Freshly ground black pepper |
| 3 eggs | 1 recipe of pie crust |
| 1½ cups light cream | |

Roll pie crust ⅛ inch thick. Fit pie crust into 24 two-inch tart pans. Sauté onion in butter for 5 minutes or until soft. Add to cheese and toss to mix well. Beat eggs until foamy. Beat in cream, mustard, a few grains of cayenne pepper, the salt and black pepper. Stir egg mixture into cheese mixture and pour into tart shells. Bake in a hot oven (400°) for 20 minutes or until golden brown. Serve hot or cold.

## CAMEMBERT ALMOND BALLS

| | |
|---|---|
| 8 ounces Camembert cheese | ½ cup sweet butter, softened |
| 1 cup salted almonds, ground | Toasted crackers |
| 1 cup dry white wine | |

Place whole cheese in bowl, pour wine over it and let stand at room temperature overnight or for at least 8 hours, turning cheese once or twice. Drain and discard liquid. Press cheese through a coarse sieve or food mill and blend in softened butter. Chill for at least 3 hours. Shape the cheese into about 24 small balls. Roll the balls in ground almonds, and serve them at once with toasted crackers.

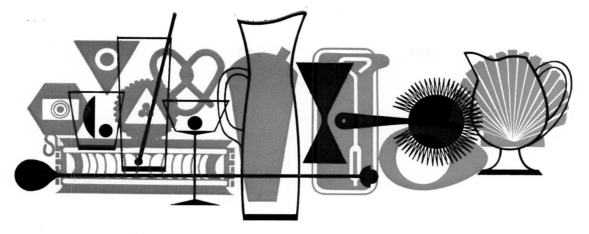

# DRINKS AND HORS D'OEUVRE

### STINGER

5 parts brandy      1 part white crème de menthe

Shake vigorously with ice cubes. Strain into chilled glass.

### IRISH COFFEE

Irish whisky      Sugar

Hot strong black coffee      Whipped cream

Put sugar lump or 1 teaspoon sugar in glass. Add 1 jigger whisky. Add coffee to within 1 inch of top. Stir. Float cream on top.

### GRASSHOPPER

1 part green crème de menthe      1 part heavy cream

1 part white crème de cacao

Shake or whirl in blender with ice. Strain into chilled glass.

### MARTINI ON THE ROCKS

5 parts gin      1 part dry vermouth

Stir well with ice cubes. Strain into old-fashioned glass filled with ice cubes. Add a twist of lemon peel, a pickled onion or a pitted olive if desired. Vodka or tequila may be substituted for gin, dry sherry may be substituted for vermouth. For a drier dry martini, some bartenders use 6 or more parts of gin to 1 part of vermouth.

### SCOTCH MIST

Scotch whisky

Fill glass with crushed ice and pour Scotch whisky over it. Bourbon, rye, brandy or vodka also may be served as mist drinks.

### PINK TEQUILA

2 parts tequila      Grenadine to taste

1 part fresh lime juice

Shake or whirl in blender with ice cubes. Strain into glass filled with ice cubes.

### MEDITERRANEE

2 parts gin      Blue Curaçao to taste

1 part lemon juice

Shake gin, lemon juice and Curaçao with ice cubes until frothy. Pour into chilled glass over ice cubes.

### BULL SHOT

2 parts vodka      Dash of Worcestershire

3 parts beef bouillon      sauce

Dash of lemon juice      Pinch of salt and pepper

Dash of Tabasco sauce

Stir ingredients with a spoon and pour into glass filled with ice cubes.

### MINT JULEP

Bourbon or rye whisky      Mint leaves

Sugar

Chill glasses thoroughly in the refrigerator. For 6 drinks make a syrup of 3 ounces of bourbon or rye, 3 ounces of water, 2 teaspoons sugar and mint leaves. Muddle syrup thoroughly. Pack chilled glasses with crushed ice and pour 2 tablespoons of strained syrup into each glass. Fill the glasses with bourbon or rye. Work a long-handled spoon up and down in the glasses until they begin to frost. Add more crushed ice and stick a sprig of mint in the top. If desired, dip the mint sprigs in water, coat them with sugar and chill until frosty.

### RUM SWIZZLE

3 parts light rum      Dash Angostura bitters

1 part fresh lime juice      Sugar to taste

Pour into glass and stir with a swizzle stick until foamy. Add ice cubes.

### BRANDY FLOAT

Brandy      White crème de menthe

Pour about ¾ of a glass of crème de menthe. Add a little brandy, which will float on top.

### GIMLET

3 parts gin      Sugar to taste

1 part lime juice

Stir ingredients with a spoon. Pour over ice cubes in chilled glass.

### GREEN DRAGON

1 part green chartreuse      1 part cognac

Mix the ingredients and pour over crushed ice.

### SCOTCH SOUR ON THE ROCKS

4 parts Scotch whisky      Sugar to taste

1 part lemon juice

Shake thoroughly and strain into old-fashioned glass filled with ice cubes.

### CRAB MEAT IN CANAPE SHELLS

½ cup cooked crab meat      ¾ cup light cream

48 packaged canapé shells      1 egg yolk

1 tablespoon butter      2 tablespoons dry sherry

2 tablespoons flour      ½ teaspoon salt

2 tablespoons grated      Freshly ground black pepper

    Parmesan cheese

Melt butter over low heat. Add flour and stir until smooth. Add cheese and cream and cook until thickened, stirring constantly. Remove from heat. Stir in crab meat, salt and pepper. Beat egg yolk with sherry and add to crab meat mixture. Spoon into canapé shells and broil under medium heat for 3 minutes or until brown on top.

### AVOCADO DUNK

2 avocados      1 garlic clove, mashed

¼ cup mayonnaise      Freshly ground black pepper

2 tablespoons lemon juice      Corn chips

1 teaspoon chili powder

Peel avocados and mash the pulp. Add other ingredients and mix well. Cover and let stand for at least 1 hour. Serve with corn chips. Makes about 2 cups.

## STUFFED CELERY

| | |
|---|---|
| Celery stalks | 2 tablespoons minced capers |
| 2 eight-ounce packages | 1 teaspoon anchovy paste |
| cream cheese | 1 teaspoon minced onion |
| ½ cup sour cream | 1 teaspoon dry mustard |
| ½ cup butter, softened | 1 teaspoon paprika |

Combine cream cheese, sour cream and butter and stir until smooth. Add capers, anchovy paste, onion, mustard, paprika. Fill celery stalks with cheese mixture. This cheese mixture can be kept in a covered container in the refrigerator for at least 1 week. Makes about 3 cups.

## SHRIMP WITH REMOLADE SAUCE

| | |
|---|---|
| 3 pounds cooked shrimp | 1 garlic clove, minced |
| 1 cup mayonnaise | 1 tablespoon anchovy paste |
| 2 hard-cooked eggs, | 1 teaspoon Worcestershire |
| finely chopped | sauce |
| 6 stuffed olives, chopped | 1 teaspoon dry mustard |
| 1 tablespoon chopped | Salt |
| green pepper | Freshly ground black pepper |

Shell shrimp and chill for at least 1 hour. Combine the rest of the ingredients to make the sauce and mix thoroughly. Chill for at least 1 hour. Serve sauce with shrimp.

## FISH BITES WITH CHILI DUNK

| | |
|---|---|
| 2 eight-ounce packages | 1 teaspoon chili powder |
| frozen fish bites | 1 cup mayonnaise |
| 1 tablespoon chili sauce | 1 garlic clove, crushed |

Mix chili sauce, chili powder, mayonnaise and garlic and let stand for at least 1 hour. Spread fish bites on baking sheet and heat in a hot oven (425°) for 10 minutes. Serve hot fish bites with chili dunking sauce.

## CLAM CHEESE DUNK

| | |
|---|---|
| 1 ten-ounce can | 1 garlic clove, minced |
| chopped clams | 1 tablespoon lemon juice |
| 3 eight-ounce packages | Potato chips |
| cream cheese | |

Mash cheese. Drain clams and save juice. Add the clams, garlic and lemon juice to the cheese and mix in enough clam juice to make the mixture the right consistency for dunking. Serve with potato chips.

## BROILED ANCHOVIES

| | |
|---|---|
| 2 two-ounce cans | Minced parsley |
| flat anchovy fillets | Lemon wedges |
| 3 slices white bread | |

Trim crusts from bread. Toast bread on one side only in a broiler under low heat. Cut each slice into 6 strips. Put one anchovy fillet on the untoasted side of each strip. Broil under moderate heat for 3 minutes or until hot. Sprinkle with minced parsley and serve with lemon wedges.

## CUCUMBER AND SALMON

| | |
|---|---|
| 2 medium cucumbers | Freshly ground black pepper |
| ¼ pound smoked salmon, | Lemon wedges |
| sliced | |

Score cucumber skin with a fork. Cut cucumbers into ¼-inch slices. Put a piece of sliced salmon on each cucumber. Serve with pepper and lemon wedges.

## CHEESED POTATO CHIPS

| | |
|---|---|
| Potato chips | Grated Parmesan cheese |

Spread potato chips on a baking sheet and sprinkle with Parmesan cheese. Bake in a hot oven (400°) for 5 minutes or until piping hot.

## STEAK TARTARE

| | |
|---|---|
| 2 pounds ground beef | 2 teaspoons salt |
| 2 eggs | Freshly ground black pepper |
| ½ cup capers | Pumpernickel bread |
| ½ cup minced onion | |

Mix ingredients together. Garnish with additional capers and serve raw with thinly sliced pumpernickel.

## CURRIED MEAT BALLS

| | |
|---|---|
| 1 pound ground beef | ½ cup butter |
| 2 teaspoons curry powder | ½ teaspoon salt |
| 1 cup stuffing mix | Freshly ground black pepper |

Mix beef, curry powder, stuffing mix, salt and pepper together. Shape into 32 small balls and sauté in butter over high heat for 5 minutes or until brown. Drain.

## GARLIC TOMATO

| | |
|---|---|
| 3 small tomatoes | Toast |
| 1 garlic clove, mashed | ¾ cup mayonnaise |

Peel and slice tomatoes. Cut toast into rounds to fit tomato slices. Put a slice of tomato on each toast round. Mix mayonnaise with garlic and spread on tomatoes. Broil under moderate heat for 3 minutes or until brown and bubbling.

## PROSCIUTTO AND MELON

| | |
|---|---|
| ½ pound prosciutto, | 1 honeydew melon |
| thinly sliced | Freshly ground black pepper |

Cut melon into wedges or small pieces. Wrap each wedge in prosciutto. Serve with pepper. Crenshaw, cantaloupe, Persian or honeyball melons may be substituted for honeydew.

## BROILED HAM AND CHUTNEY

| | |
|---|---|
| 4 ounces canned deviled ham | ¼ cup mayonnaise |
| ⅓ cup chutney | 24 round crackers |

Drain chutney and save juice. Mince chutney and combine with ham and mayonnaise and chutney juice. Spread on crackers and broil under moderate heat for 5 minutes or until lightly browned and bubbling.

# SUMMER COOKING

THE RECIPES FOR ALL DISHES SHOWN
IN THIS SECTION ARE ON PAGES 159-164.

# COOKING ON ICE

**W**HEN hot weather comes and appetites slacken, consumption
of soft drinks and ice cream goes up while proteins and vitamins
are likely to be neglected. This is unfortunate because almost everybody
leads an active outdoor life during the summer and it is then
that the need for a proper diet is greater than ever.
Yet there is a simple way to correct this deficiency. The housewife
can prepare well-balanced meals for most of the week on one cool morning
and store them in the refrigerator to finish "cooking" there.

The most important thing about cooking on ice is careful,
thoughtful planning. The refrigerator should be kept defrosted so that
it operates at peak efficiency. Its contents should be kept
well organized so the dishes will all fit in. The housewife should have
a collection of attractive bowls and icebox containers.
And she should go in heavily for frozen, canned and packaged foods
and easy mixes. This will keep the cook cool and out of the kitchen,
and the house cool by avoiding much use of the stove.

There is nothing new about cold cooking. The Romans chilled their drinks
and made a kind of sherbet with snow from the mountains.
For centuries good cooks and chefs have been using gelatine molds
to turn out summer dishes. But it is only in recent years,
as big refrigerators with roomy freezing compartments have moved
into the average home, that regular summer cooking on ice has become
really feasible. Now almost anyone can undertake the fancier dishes
shown on the following pages, from duck in aspic to apple mint mousse.

A good cook always tries to make food look as attractive as possible.
In the cold of winter she tempts the eye with heat and makes a pretty sight
of a steaming roast and brown potatoes. But in summer she has
a lot more leeway. Then fresh fruits and vegetables are easily available.
She can cut them into decorative shapes and use bright radishes,
sliced eggs and strawberries to decorate the food. Cooking on ice,
she can give meat and fowl main dishes an icy look by coating them
with aspic. She can deck dishes with flowers as well as fruits
and, with ice and imagination, can easily and inexpensively come up with
as pretty a showpiece as the watermelon on the opposite page.

Party watermelon was chilled thoroughly, cut in half lengthwise.
The four scooped-out circles hold roses, sweet sliced
strawberries, honeydew melon balls and orange sherbet.

Cold summer dishes, starting in the bottom row at left, are:
roast duck in aspic in front of champagne, herbed green salad,
chicken soup Senegalese, cold ham with brandied peaches, tongue and olives
in wine aspic. The circular pudding is a lemon Bavarian mold;
to the right are sliced beef *en gelée*; raw vegetables with herbed eggs;
poached salmon with mayonnaise *verte* and a glass of white wine

and seltzer. In right foreground is a brandied pâté in a casserole
with a rabbit-head top. Left to right, on the cakes of ice, are
apple mint mousse in an individual glass and a red bowl, a basket of cherries,
fresh fruit salad. On the center block are five summer drinks:
iced coffee with rum, spiced iced tea, tea punch, lemonade and grape juice.
In the basket above them is chervil bread; and at right, four parfaits.

# SALADS

A FAMOUS old saying has it that it takes four people to make a salad.
You need a spendthrift for the oil, a miser for the vinegar,
a counselor for the salt and a madman to mix it all up.
The salad-conscious sage who first made this observation
should perhaps have added a botanist to the group. Twenty-nine of
the different kinds of leaves which can go into a green salad are shown
on these pages. Their proper blending is just as important as the dressing.

To the purist, of course, the word salad has only one meaning.
It stands for green lettuce leaves with olive oil and vinegar
served in a wooden bowl that is rinsed, not soaped, after using.
The best basic leaves for this are the head lettuces,
tender Boston lettuce and the crisper iceberg. The taste
of this green salad is then varied by mixing these leaves with some
of the others—Bibb, romaine, raab, endive, chicory, celery cabbage,
dandelion and many more. While the head lettuces are bland, some greens,
like water cress, are sweet. Collards are cabbagy, escarole is sharp
and mustard greens are bitter. A careful blend of leaves
will yield a tempting bowl like that shown on the opposite page.

To salad lovers of the less-than-purist school,
the word has a lot more meanings. To them a salad can be made
of almost anything from potatoes, with no greens at all,
to greens with mixtures of meat, eggs, vegetables, fruit or fish.
Such salads can make tempting side dishes or fine main courses
for a meal. In them the dressing is not limited: it can be French,
Russian, Thousand Island, sour cream, mayonnaise or anything you like.

For both kinds of salads there are only a few rules to follow.
The greens should be meticulously washed of grit and sand and tossed
gently in a French salad basket or swung gently in a towel until dry.
Then they may be crisped in the refrigerator. As for the dressing,
if French is used, the oil should be put in first
and the salad tossed until its leaves are covered. Then add
a little vinegar and some salt and pepper. If bottled
or premade dressing is used, it should be added a little at a time.
And a green salad should be tossed lightly at the table, just before serving.

This mixed greens salad uses (*left, from top down*) mustard greens, Swiss chard,
collards and (*right*) chicory and dandelion greens. Cruets hold
pure olive oil and pure wine vinegar. A little garlic may be rubbed on bowl.

## BOUILLABAISSE SALAD

This sea food and fish salad with mixed greens is
substantial enough for a full meal, especially good in summer.
It uses five greens. Mounted on colored sticks, they are, from left,
scallion tops, water cress, celery tops, celery cabbage
and iceberg lettuce which is too often served alone in salad
after salad. The lobster, shrimp, crab meat and whitefish
are broken into bite-sized pieces, garnished with ripe olives,
tomatoes. Serve with French or hot spice dressing.

## AVOCADO FRUIT SALAD

Melon balls and various fruits in season fill avocado cups
and are arranged in salad bowl on top of the greens. The four greens
shown with them are, behind the bowl, from left, Belgian endive,
land cress, field salad and escarole. In some U.S. towns
these greens may be easiest to find in Italian markets.
This fruit salad goes well with low-calorie, hot spice
or sour cream dressing. The avocado cups are actually already sliced
so they will separate into thin pieces when the salad is tossed.

146

## VEAL AND CHICKEN SALAD

A tasty summer supper is made of greens with strips of cold veal and chicken. Greens used in this salad are, from left, behind bowl, Bibb lettuce, raab (*broccoli di rape*), romaine lettuce and sorrel (sour grass). This salad also contains cut-up apples and celery, a pistachio nut garnish. Almost any other cooked or canned meats can be substituted for the cold veal and chicken and filled out with cheese strips or chunks. Meats can be marinated overnight in French or sweet-and-sour dressing.

## VEGETABLE SALAD BOWL

A good nonfattening but satisfying dish, this salad has only 65 calories per serving, not counting the dressing. The five greens used in it, on sticks behind it, are parsley, turnip tops, Boston lettuce, beet tops and spinach. This salad uses a wide variety of vegetables—tomatoes, cucumber, mushrooms, broccoli, carrots, radishes and onions—raw and cooked. Serve with a classic French dressing, or sweet-and-sour or low-calorie dressing in which vegetables have been marinated overnight.

## FIVE GREAT SALAD DRESSINGS

On the five shelves above are ranged ingredients for salad dressings to suit almost every salad—with a pint of the finished product at the right. On top shelf are the makings for classic French dressing: oil, vinegar, garlic (optional), salt and pepper. This dressing is usually made with the salad but can be prepared in advance. Next shelf is low-calorie dressing, with oil, vinegar, lemon, pepper, parsley, herbs and spices. On third shelf is sour cream dressing, made with sour cream, vinegar, oil, spices, horseradish, pepper, salt, onion capers. On fourth shelf is hot spice dressing: tarragon vinegar, oil, chili powder, onion, bay leaves, cayenne. On bottom shelf is sweet-and-sour dressing, which includes sugar, chives, celery, green pepper, mustard, Worcestershire sauce.

# ELEGANT PICNICS

**T**HERE is a moment at most picnics when a man finds himself perched
on a pointed stone with a top-heavy plate on his knees.
He gamely makes a stab at the food with his plastic knife—only to feel
the plate tilt and the warm juices run freely over his pants leg.
This is a needless sacrifice to the false but prevalent idea
that because a picnic is informal it must also be uncomfortable.
A picnic can be an occasion of ease and grace.

In older days picnics could be very elegant indeed, and the romance
that still goes with dining out of doors inspired great artists like Manet
and Watteau. Their picnics went in heavily for leafy bowers
and sylvan glades and men with lutes. Once in a while they put in
an undraped nymph and, as such artists will, they underemphasized the food.
They left that up to painters like Bruegel; his idea of an elegant picnic
was a groaning board and hungry guests by the hundreds.

The elegant picnic that is back in style in the U.S. today is something
of a cross between the two conceptions. There are a number
of guests, there is plenty of food and it is well in evidence. The setting
is chosen with an eye to beauty and romance. The elegant picnic
bears no resemblance to the workaday kind, where the emphasis is
maximum efficiency and nourishment and a minimum of load—perhaps
only a sandwich stuffed in a pocket to take the edge off a hiker's hunger.
Nor is it the kind served on the tail gate of a station wagon
at a horse show or a football game. Instead it is set up in a cool,
attractive place. There is a natural table or a place for a portable one.
Since there is a good deal of hauling to do, it is not
too far from a parking place. Once set up it will range, like the picnic
on page 152, from icy cocktails to cold squab.

All the new coolers, camp stoves, plastic plates and forks make
this kind of picnic a lot less trouble than it was in Manet's day. The menu
should be as carefully planned as for a fancy dinner. The food should
be packed so that the dishes needed first will be on top, leaving
the others to stay fresh in their containers. And, as a final trick
of strategy, bring some hot dogs if there are children around. Then the
children can be sent off to cook them as inelegantly as they like.

An elegant picnic is set
on a stone table in a park picnic
ground. The meal is to begin
with chilled chicken avocado soup,
which is served in thick
restaurant mugs. The main dish
is ham, baked in a crust
that keeps juices and flavor in.
Casserole keeping hot by fireplace
in background holds lentils,
cooked with salami, scallions
and parsley. The salad is romaine,
doused with mustard and
mayonnaise, to be served with
thin sandwiches of Bermuda onion
brushed with mayonnaise.
There is pink lemonade for children,
who are cooking their own
hot dogs, and wine for the adults.
Dessert melons for children are
flavored with lime juice,
for adults are touched with wine.

An adult beach picnic is set on folding tables. Rattan back rests permit guests to eat in normal posture. The main course is cold squab with red pepper strips, but the meal starts with cocktails, carried in vacuum jug and served in mugs at right. Liver pâté, in crock behind squab, is served with several breads—Russian pumpernickel (big loaf), Kommissbrot, crispbread, crackers, salty rye. There are scallions and little unpeeled tomatoes. Butters in crocks at right are flavored with parsley, tomato. Dessert is Canadian Cheddar cheese, Swiss Emmentaler (*left*), pears and apples (*right*).

# OUTDOOR
# COOKING

**T**HE barbecue and the ballot were once almost synonymous in the U.S. Every candidate for office was feted with an outdoor meal and it was considered the citizen's duty "to holler right, vote straight, and eat as much barbecue as any man in the country." Now this democratic institution has moved from the public square to the patio or the plain backyard. During the past 10 years increasing numbers of housewives have discovered that it is more fun to hang over an outdoor grill with a husband than over an indoor stove alone. Today, wherever the weather is fine, the barbecue boom is smoking up all outdoors.

As barbecue equipment has become better designed, lighter and less expensive, millions of families all over the country have acquired grills costing anywhere from $2 to $200 and have laid in supplies of charcoal. Almost any sort of meat or fish can be grilled out of doors. In general, both meat and fish cooked this way need to be basted frequently or they will dry out. The classic basting mixtures are hot barbecue, tomato-wine and chili sauces. Steak sauce is good not only for basting but may also be served hot with steak, lamb and hamburgers. Sauces may be made up in large quantities and kept in the refrigerator for future use. The most convenient way to baste is with a paintbrush which slathers a lot of sauce on the food.

Barbecue experts say that in teaching the barbecue cook how to handle his coals there is no substitute for experience. But a few rules will help novices and maybe even some old hands. Never grill over an open flame. Instead, wait until the fuel has burned down to form a red-hot bed of embers. A bulb syringe filled with water should be kept handy to tamp flames when they arise from drippings. Charcoal or hardwoods such as oak, hickory or maple are best for barbecuing because they burn slowly and make a lasting bed of coals.

Outdoor barbecuing does not really require special skillets, ladles, forks and other paraphernalia, but a lot of *aficionados* like to perform the cooking ceremony in full regalia. Elaborate barbecue equipment is part of the fun. Barbecue menus, however, are better kept on the simple side. Here and on the following pages are 15 dishes and four basic barbecue sauces to give outdoor meals variety and flavor.

# WELL-BASTED LAMB THE EASY WAY

The scene above is a guest's-eye view of a simple yet attractive outdoor meal in the course of cooking. The host is carefully spreading basting sauce on a leg of lamb. The hostess is contemplating a spurt of flame that the sauce has caused to leap from the embers. Wine is chilling in a cooler under the table. It is a cool day, so the grill is in the sun. But it is the kind that can be moved, still cooking, into the shade or even into a covered patio. On it, some corn in husk has been turned with its brown side up, some await turning, and the meal is nearly done. The six-pound lamb has been cooking for about two hours, the corn for a matter of minutes. This lamb has been marinated in oil and wine vinegar. The host is basting it with hot barbecue sauce, but he could just as well have chosen any of the basic sauces whose ingredients are shown on the opposite page.

**HOT BARBECUE SAUCE**

**STEAK SAUCE**

**CHILI SAUCE**

**TOMATO WINE SAUCE**

Assembled on weathered planks are some barbecue standbys. At lower left
are ham steaks with a sherry marinade. Above them, to right, are
chili pork chops with soy sauce and garlic marinade and basting sauce
in jar. At upper left basket holds spareribs with a pineapple marinade
and basting sauce. Stuck in the cork disk are five different skewer meals—kebabs—
and one skewer dessert. Their sauces are in cups around them. From left:
kidney and liver kebab (with no sauce); shrimp and bacon kebab
(served with soy marinade); eggplant lamb kebab (with tomato wine sauce);

dessert fruit kebab (with Cointreau honey marinade); lamb and pineapple *teriyaki*
(sweet-and-sour marinade); fish kebab (tart marinade). To right
of kebabs is duck on a spit with orange sauce in a white beaker. On platter
at upper right are a rib roast cut into 1½-inch steaks and
a thick sirloin steak. Garlic and salt are in wooden bowl, olive oil
for steaks in yellow one. In center are garlic hot dogs. Chicken
with white wine and herb marinade is in right foreground
and in center foreground are Tabasco hamburgers with hot barbecue sauce.

# RECIPES FOR
## SUMMER COOKING

COOKING ON ICE

SALADS

ELEGANT PICNICS

OUTDOOR COOKING

# COOKING ON ICE

## BRANDIED PATE

1 cup canned liver pâté
¼ cup brandy
1 cup finely chopped mushrooms
½ cup butter
2 tablespoons chopped parsley
Salt
Freshly ground black pepper
Chopped chives

Sauté mushrooms in butter over low heat for 5 minutes or until lightly browned. Add mushrooms and butter to pâté and mix well. Stir in brandy, parsley, salt and pepper and blend thoroughly. Let stand at room temperature for at least 1 hour. Chill in the refrigerator overnight or for at least 4 hours. Serve sprinkled with chopped chives. Serves 6.

## CHICKEN SOUP SENEGALESE

2 cans condensed cream of chicken soup
2 cups light cream
1 tablespoon curry powder
¼ cup lemon juice
1 teaspoon salt
Freshly ground black pepper
Chopped chives or parsley

Combine chicken soup and cream in a saucepan and stir until smooth and well blended. Mix curry powder with ¼ cup of water and add to soup mixture. Simmer over low heat for 10 minutes, stirring frequently. Remove from heat and stir in lemon juice, salt and pepper. Cool for 30 minutes. Chill in the refrigerator for at least 1 hour. Serve the soup garnished with chopped chives or parsley. Serves 6.

## ROAST DUCK IN ASPIC

2 five-pound oven-ready ducks
2 oranges, quartered
2 onions, quartered
8 whole cloves
2 envelopes unflavored gelatine
½ cup Cointreau
3 cans condensed consommé
1 teaspoon salt
Freshly ground black pepper
Water cress
Orange slices

Stuff ducks with orange quarters and onions studded with cloves. Place ducks on a rack in a shallow baking pan and roast in a slow oven (325°) for 2½ hours or until done. Cool ducks and discard stuffing. Cut ducks into serving pieces with poultry shears and arrange pieces in a shallow dish. Soften gelatine in Cointreau. Bring 1 can of consommé to a boil, pour into gelatine and Cointreau mixture and stir until gelatine is dissolved. Stir in the remaining 2 cans of cold consommé, salt and pepper and pour this mixture over duck. Chill in the refrigerator for at least 2 hours or until the aspic has set. Serve garnished with water cress and orange slices. Serves 6.

## HAM WITH BRANDIED PEACHES

1 eight-pound precooked boned ham
6 canned brandied peaches
Whole cloves
1 cup honey
1 teaspoon dry mustard
Cayenne pepper

Score ham and stud with cloves. Combine ¼ cup of the brandied peach juice, honey, mustard and a few grains of cayenne pepper. Spread mixture over top and sides of ham. Bake in a hot oven (425°) for 15 minutes or until well glazed, basting once or twice with pan juices. Cool. Chill in the refrigerator for at least 1 hour. Serve the ham with chilled brandied peaches. Serves 6.

## TONGUE IN WHITE WINE ASPIC

1½ pounds sliced cooked tongue
1 cup dry white wine
2 cans condensed consommé
2 envelopes unflavored gelatine
Stuffed olives

Arrange overlapping slices of tongue in two rows along either side of a shallow serving dish. Arrange a row of stuffed olives in the center. Soften gelatine in ½ cup of cold water. Bring 1 can of consommé to a boil and add it to the gelatine, stirring until the gelatine is dissolved. Stir in the wine and remaining 1 can of cold consommé. Cool for 30 minutes until the wine and gelatine mixture is slightly syrupy. Pour over the tongue and chill in the refrigerator for at least 2 hours or until the wine aspic has set. Serves 6.

## SLICED BEEF EN GELEE

6 slices cold roast beef or pot roast
½ teaspoon thyme
½ teaspoon basil
Carrot slices
Green pepper strips
2 cans condensed consommé
2 envelopes unflavored gelatine
1 teaspoon Worcestershire sauce
Cayenne pepper
½ teaspoon salt
Freshly ground black pepper

Arrange overlapping slices of beef in a shallow serving dish. Sprinkle with thyme, basil, salt and black pepper. Garnish with carrot slices and green pepper strips. Soften gelatine in ½ cup of cold water. Bring 1 can consommé to a boil and add it to the gelatine, stirring until the gelatine is dissolved. Add the remaining 1 can of cold consommé, 1 cup of cold water, Worcestershire sauce and a few grains of cayenne pepper. Cool for 30 minutes or until the gelatine mixture is syrupy. Pour the mixture over the beef slices and chill in the refrigerator for at least 2 hours or until the gelatine is set. Serves 6.

## COLD POACHED SALMON

6 salmon steaks
2 onions, chopped
2 carrots, chopped
2 stalks celery with leaves, cut up
¼ cup butter
¼ cup vinegar
2 tablespoons chopped parsley
2 cloves
½ bay leaf, crumbled
1 tablespoon salt
10 peppercorns
Water cress
Lemon or lime wedges
Cucumber slices
Mayonnaise verte

Sauté onions, carrots and celery in butter in a large skillet for 5 minutes or until onion is soft. Add vinegar, parsley, cloves, bay leaf, salt and peppercorns, and 2 quarts of water. Bring to a boil and cook for 10 minutes, stirring occasionally. Reduce heat and add salmon steaks. Cover skillet and simmer for 10 minutes. Cool salmon in the stock. Remove salmon and discard stock. Chill salmon in the refrigerator for at least 1 hour. Serve with mayonnaise verte. Garnish with water cress, lemon or lime wedges and cucumber slices. Serves 6.

## HERBED EGGS

| | |
|---|---|
| 12 eggs | Cayenne pepper |
| 2 tablespoons minced chives | Celery curls |
| 2 tablespoons minced parsley | Carrot sticks |
| ¼ cup sour cream | Cucumber sticks |
| 1 tablespoon lemon juice | Cauliflowerets |
| ½ teaspoon curry powder | Radishes |
| Salt | Scallions |
| Freshly ground black pepper | |

Hard cook eggs, plunge into cold water and shell immediately. Cut eggs in half lengthwise. Remove and mash yolks. Add chives, parsley, sour cream, lemon juice, curry powder, salt, pepper and a few grains of cayenne pepper to the yolks and mix well. Spoon yolk mixture into egg whites. Chill at least 1 hour. Serve with raw celery curls, carrot and cucumber sticks, cauliflowerets, radishes and scallions. Serves 6.

## FRESH FRUIT SALAD

| | |
|---|---|
| 1 cup sliced strawberries | 2 pears, cubed |
| 1 pineapple, cubed | 2 peaches, sliced |
| 2 oranges, sliced | Mixed greens |
| 12 plums, halved | Mayonnaise |

Arrange fruit and greens in a salad bowl. To serve, add mayonnaise and toss well. Serves 6.

## HERBED GREEN SALAD

| | |
|---|---|
| Romaine | Freshly chopped tarragon |
| Chicory | Freshly chopped chervil |
| Belgian endive | Freshly chopped dill |
| Freshly chopped parsley | Champagne dressing |

Arrange romaine, chicory and endive in a salad bowl and sprinkle generously with freshly chopped herbs. To serve, toss well with champagne or classic French dressing. Fresh basil, water cress, chives or rosemary may be added to the salad or substituted for the other herbs.

## CHAMPAGNE DRESSING

| | |
|---|---|
| ½ cup iced champagne | Salt |
| ½ cup olive oil | Freshly ground black pepper |
| 1 tablespoon lemon juice | |

Make this dressing at the table when serving champagne. Combine oil, lemon juice, salt and pepper in a small bowl and blend them together well with a fork. Pour in champagne and stir briskly, just enough to mix the champagne with the other ingredients. Serve immediately.

## MAYONNAISE

| | |
|---|---|
| 2 egg yolks | 1 teaspoon lemon juice |
| 1 cup olive oil | Salt |
| ¼ teaspoon dry mustard | Freshly ground black pepper |
| Cayenne pepper | |

Beat egg yolks with a rotary beater or whisk until frothy. Beat in mustard, a few grains of cayenne pepper, salt and black pepper. Add lemon juice and beat until egg yolk mixture is thick and lemon colored. Add olive oil, 1 teaspoon at a time, beating constantly. Makes about 2 cups.

## MAYONNAISE VERTE

| | |
|---|---|
| 2 cups mayonnaise | 1 tablespoon freshly |
| 2 tablespoons dry white wine | chopped dill |
| 2 tablespoons freshly | 1 tablespoon freshly |
| chopped parsley | chopped chives |

Combine ingredients and mix well. Chill for at least 30 minutes. Makes about 2½ cups.

## CHERVIL BREAD

| | |
|---|---|
| 3 small loaves brown-and- | 3 tablespoons |
| serve French bread | chopped chervil |
| ½ cup butter, softened | |

Combine chervil and butter and spread on top and sides of bread. Wrap loaves in foil and bake in a hot oven (425°) for 15 minutes or until well browned. Serves 6.

## LEMON BAVARIAN

| | |
|---|---|
| 2 packages lemon pie filling | Whole strawberries |
| 1 cup heavy cream, whipped | Powdered sugar |
| Sliced strawberries | |

Prepare lemon pie filling according to package directions for lemon pudding. Cool for 10 minutes. Fold in whipped cream and pour into a ring mold. Chill overnight or for at least 6 hours. To serve, unmold and fill center with sliced strawberries. Arrange whole strawberries around the ring and dust them with powdered sugar. Serves 6.

## APPLE MINT MOUSSE

| | |
|---|---|
| 2 cups applesauce | ⅛ teaspoon ground mace |
| ½ teaspoon | 1 tablespoon lemon juice |
| peppermint extract | Green food coloring |
| ½ cup sugar | 1 cup heavy cream, whipped |
| 1 teaspoon ground cinnamon | |

Combine sugar, cinnamon and mace. Add to applesauce and stir until sugar is dissolved. Add lemon juice, peppermint extract and enough food coloring to tint the mixture green. Fold in whipped cream. Spoon into an ice tray and freeze for 2 hours or until firm enough to serve. Serves 6.

## PINK ALMOND PARFAIT

To make each parfait, put alternate spoonfuls of several flavors of ice cream in parfait glasses. Top with sweetened whipped cream, flavored with almond extract and tinted with a few drops of red food coloring.

## ICED COFFEE WITH RUM

| | |
|---|---|
| 4 tablespoons instant coffee | Sweetened whipped cream |
| 4 tablespoons rum | Ground nutmeg |
| 1 tablespoon sugar | |

Pour 4 cups of boiling water over the coffee. Stir in rum and sugar. Pour into glasses filled with ice. Top with whipped cream and sprinkle with nutmeg. Make ice cubes by freezing coffee in trays to make a stronger drink. Serves 6.

## SPICED ICED TEA

| | |
|---|---|
| 2 tablespoons tea leaves | 1 tablespoon sugar |
| 1 teaspoon ground cinnamon | Lemon wedges |
| ¼ teaspoon ground ginger | |

Pour 4 cups of rapidly boiling water over the tea leaves, cinnamon, ginger and sugar. Let stand for 5 minutes. Strain into pitcher. Pour into glasses filled with ice. Serve the tea with lemon wedges. Serves 6.

## TEA PUNCH

| | |
|---|---|
| 3 tablespoons tea leaves | Orange slices |
| 4 cups sweet white wine | Lemon slices |
| ½ cup lemon juice | Whole strawberries |
| Pineapple sticks | |

Pour 1 quart of briskly boiling water over tea leaves. Let stand for 5 minutes. Strain. Add wine and lemon juice and pour over ice. Garnish with fruit. Makes about 2 quarts.

## MINTED LEMONADE

| | |
|---|---|
| 1 can unsweetened | 1 cup sugar |
| frozen lemon juice | Mint leaves |

Combine sugar with ½ cup of water, bring to a boil, reduce heat and cook until sugar is dissolved, stirring constantly. Pour it over 1 tablespoon chopped mint leaves and let stand for 5 minutes. Strain into a pitcher. Defrost lemon juice and add it to the mint syrup. Add 3½ cups of water and mix well. Pour into glasses filled with ice cubes and garnish with mint leaves. Serves 6.

## LIMED GRAPE JUICE

| | |
|---|---|
| 4 cups grape juice | 2 tablespoons lemon juice |
| 1 tablespoon lime juice | Soda water or ginger ale |

Combine grape juice with lemon and lime juice. Pour into glasses filled with ice until the glasses are about two thirds full. Add soda water or ginger ale. Serves 6.

# SALADS

## CLASSIC FRENCH DRESSING

| | |
|---|---|
| 3 parts olive oil | Salt |
| 1 part wine vinegar | Freshly ground black pepper |

When making the dressing at the dinner table: Pour olive oil over greens and toss until greens are coated. Add vinegar, salt and pepper and toss well. When making the dressing in advance, simply combine all the ingredients in a jar or cruet. Cover. Shake well before using.

## VARIATIONS ON FRENCH DRESSING

**CAPER:** Add chopped capers, crushed garlic or garlic salt, and a few drops of Tabasco sauce.
**CHILI:** Add chili sauce and a dash of paprika.
**CHUTNEY:** Add finely chopped chutney.
**CURRY AND ONION:** Add curry powder and finely minced or grated onion.
**EGG AND OLIVE:** Add chopped or sieved hard-cooked egg and minced ripe olives.
**GARLIC:** Sprinkle salt in salad bowl and rub salt around bowl with a cut garlic clove until the clove is crushed.
**HERB:** Add some dried herbs or finely chopped fresh herbs. Try dill, basil, chervil, marjoram, parsley, oregano, tarragon or water cress separately or in combination.
**HORSERADISH:** Add prepared horseradish and a few drops of Tabasco sauce.
**LEMON:** Substitute lemon juice for the vinegar or use half lemon juice and half vinegar and add grated lemon rind.
**MUSTARD:** Add a pinch of dry mustard and a few grains of cayenne pepper.
**ONION:** Add onion juice and a few drops of Tabasco sauce or substitute onion salt for plain salt.
**ROQUEFORT OR BLEU CHEESE:** Add softened, crumbled Roquefort or bleu cheese.
**TARRAGON:** Use tarragon vinegar and add some finely chopped fresh tarragon.
**WINE:** Substitute dry white or red wine for the vinegar.

## LOW CALORIE DRESSING

| | |
|---|---|
| 1 cup salad oil | 1 tablespoon minced fennel |
| 1½ cups garlic vinegar | 1 tablespoon celery salt |
| 3 tablespoons grated lemon rind | 1 teaspoon oregano |
| 3 tablespoons chopped parsley | 1 teaspoon ground chervil |
| | 1 teaspoon dry mustard |
| | Freshly ground black pepper |

Combine all ingredients in a jar or cruet. Cover. Shake well before using. Makes about 3 cups.

## SOUR CREAM DRESSING

| | |
|---|---|
| 1½ cups sour cream | 2 tablespoons capers |
| ½ cup cider vinegar | 1 teaspoon dill seeds |
| ¾ cup oil | 1 teaspoon paprika |
| 2 tablespoons grated onion | 1 teaspoon salt |
| 2 tablespoons horseradish | Freshly ground black pepper |

Combine all ingredients in a jar. Cover. Shake well before using. Makes about 3 cups.

## HOT SPICE DRESSING

| | |
|---|---|
| ¾ cup tarragon vinegar | 1 teaspoon chili powder |
| 1¾ cups oil | ½ teaspoon cayenne pepper |
| ¼ cup grated onion | 1 teaspoon salt |
| 3 bay leaves, crumbled | Freshly ground black pepper |

Combine all ingredients in a jar or cruet. Cover. Shake well before using. Makes about 3 cups.

## SWEET AND SOUR DRESSING

| | |
|---|---|
| 1 cup oil | 2 tablespoons minced water cress |
| 1 cup red wine vinegar | 2 teaspoons dry mustard |
| ½ cup sugar | 1 tablespoon Worcestershire sauce |
| ¼ cup minced chives | |
| ¼ cup minced celery | 2 teaspoons salt |
| 2 tablespoons minced green pepper | Freshly ground black pepper |

Combine all ingredients in a jar or cruet. Cover. Shake well before using. Makes about 3 cups.

## TOSSED GREEN SALAD

| | |
|---|---|
| Mustard greens | Dandelion greens |
| Swiss chard | Chopped chives |
| Collards | Chopped dill |
| Chicory | Classic French dressing |

Wash greens well. Dry in a lettuce basket or in a towel. Arrange in a salad bowl. Sprinkle with chives and dill. Add French dressing and toss until leaves are well coated. Head lettuce, water cress, spinach, parsley, beet tops, celery tops, Belgian endive, escarole, sorrel or romaine may also be used. Add tomato wedges if desired.

## BOUILLABAISSE SALAD

| | |
|---|---|
| 1 cup cooked crab meat | 2 tomatoes, sliced |
| 1 cup cooked lobster meat | 6 ripe olives, halved |
| ½ pound cooked shrimp | Mixed greens |
| 1 cup cooked whitefish | Salad dressing |

Arrange crab, lobster, shrimp, whitefish and tomatoes on a bed of mixed greens. Garnish with olives. To serve, toss with classic French or hot spice dressing. Serves 6.

## AVOCADO FRUIT SALAD

| | |
|---|---|
| 3 avocados | 1 grapefruit, sectioned |
| 1 cup watermelon balls | 1 cup fresh pineapple cubes |
| 1 cup honeydew melon balls | Mixed greens |
| 3 bananas, scored and sliced | Cherries |
| 1 mango, cubed | Salad dressing |

Peel the avocados and cut them in half lengthwise. Slice the halves lengthwise into narrow wedges. Then put the wedges back together to form avocado cups. Fill a salad bowl with mixed greens and arrange the avocado cups in a ring around the edge of the bowl. Fill each cup with one kind of cut fruit and arrange the remaining cut fruit in the center of the bowl. Garnish the salad with whole cherries. When the salad is tossed, the avocado cups will fall apart. Serve with hot spice, classic French, or sour cream dressing. Serves 6.

## VEAL AND CHICKEN SALAD

| | |
|---|---|
| 1 cup cooked veal strips | 1 tablespoon minced chives |
| 1 cup cooked chicken strips | Pistachio nuts |
| ½ cup sliced celery | Mixed greens |
| 2 medium apples, cubed | Salad dressing |
| 6 stuffed olives, sliced | |

Arrange veal, chicken, celery, apples and olives on a bed of mixed greens. Garnish with chives and a few pistachio nuts. To serve, toss with classic French or sweet and sour dressing. Serves 6. Any leftover meat or fowl may be substituted for veal and chicken.

## VEGETABLE SALAD BOWL

| | |
|---|---|
| 2 tomatoes, sliced | Broccoli flowerets |
| ½ cup cooked snap beans | 2 carrots, cut in thin strips |
| ½ cup cooked lima beans | 1 cup radish slices |
| ½ cucumber, sliced | 1 onion, sliced |
| 1 zucchini squash, sliced | Mixed greens |
| ¼ cup sliced raw mushrooms | Salad dressing |

Marinate tomatoes and cooked vegetables in the refrigerator for at least 4 hours in classic French or low-calorie dressing. Drain and save marinade. Arrange marinated and raw vegetables on greens. To serve, use the marinade as dressing. Serves 6.

# ELEGANT PICNICS

## CHICKEN AVOCADO SOUP

| | |
|---|---|
| 4 cups cold chicken bouillon | 1 teaspoon salt |
| 2 cups diced avocado | Freshly ground black pepper |
| ¼ cup lime juice | |

Combine ingredients. Blend in an electric blender or with a rotary beater until smooth. Chill for at least 1 hour. Serves 6.

## JAMBON EN CROUTE

| | |
|---|---|
| 1 ten-pound precooked ham | 1 egg, beaten |
| 1 package pastry mix | 2 tablespoons heavy cream |

Trim fat from ham. Prepare pastry dough according to directions on the package. Roll about three quarters of the dough into an oval shape ⅛ inch thick. Put the ham on the dough and fold dough up around the lower two thirds of the ham. Roll remaining dough into a small oval to cover top of ham and overlap the other dough by about 1 inch. Press edges of dough together and flute. Brush dough with combined egg and cream. Cut flowers and leaves from dough scraps and decorate ham with them. Brush with egg mixture, bake in a hot oven (450°) for 30 minutes.

## LENTIL CASSEROLE

| | |
|---|---|
| 1 pound dried lentils | ½ cup chopped parsley |
| 1 large onion | ½ pound salami, |
| 4 cloves | cut in julienne strips |
| 1 bay leaf | 3 bacon slices, halved |
| 1 cup chopped scallions | 1 teaspoon salt |

Put lentils in saucepan with onion studded with cloves, bay leaf and salt. Cover with water. Bring to a boil, reduce heat and simmer for 30 minutes. Strain lentils and keep the liquid. Discard onion and bay leaf. Combine lentils, scallions and parsley. Put about ⅓ of the lentil mixture in a casserole, top with half of the salami, add another third of lentil mixture, top with the remaining salami and cover with remaining lentil mixture. Add lentil liquid with enough water to make 2 cups. Arrange bacon on top. Bake in a moderate oven (350°) for 30 minutes. Serves 6.

## STUFFED HONEYDEW MELONS

| | |
|---|---|
| 3 honeydew melons | 1 cup honeydew balls |
| 1 cup watermelon balls | 1 cup port wine or lime juice |
| 1 cup cantaloupe balls | |

Cut 1 inch off top of each honeydew. Scoop out seeds and fill with mixed melon balls. Pour ⅓ cup wine or lime juice in each melon. Replace tops. Chill at least 2 hours. To serve, cut each melon in half and serve with melon balls and marinade.

## CAMP COFFEE

| | |
|---|---|
| ¾ cup regular grind coffee | 1 egg |

Crush the egg—shell and all—into ground coffee in old-fashioned coffee pot. Add 5½ cups of cold water. Bring to a boil; then set back of grill to simmer for 10 minutes. Add ½ cup cold water to settle the coffee grounds. Serves 6.

## ROAST SQUAB

| | |
|---|---|
| 12 squabs | Paprika |
| 12 slices bacon, halved | Salt |
| ½ cup dry white wine | Freshly ground black pepper |
| 1 onion, sliced | Sweet red pepper strips |

Place squabs in roasting pan. Sprinkle with paprika, salt and pepper. Cover each squab with 2 half-slices of bacon. Pour wine and ½ cup water into pan. Add onion. Roast in a moderate oven (350°) for 45 minutes, basting every 15 minutes with pan juices. Remove the bacon after 30 minutes. Serve cold with red pepper strips. Allow 2 squabs per person.

## MOCK LIVER PATE

| | |
|---|---|
| 1 pound liverwurst | ¼ cup grated onion |
| ¼ cup brandy | 1 teaspoon prepared mustard |
| ½ cup sour cream | |

Mash the liverwurst. Add the rest of the ingredients and mix until smooth and well blended. Chill for at least 2 hours.

## PARSLEY BUTTER

| | |
|---|---|
| 1 pound soft butter | 2 teaspoons lemon juice |
| 1 cup chopped parsley | ¼ teaspoon garlic powder |
| ¼ cup chopped chives | |

Combine ingredients. Chill for 1 hour. Makes about 3 cups.

## TOMATO BUTTER

| | |
|---|---|
| 1 pound soft butter | ¼ teaspoon basil |
| 4 tomatoes, | Freshly ground black pepper |
| peeled and chopped | |

Combine ingredients. Chill for 1 hour. Makes about 3 cups.

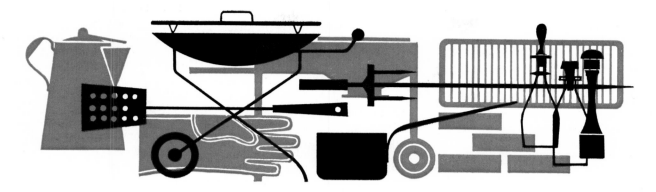

# OUTDOOR COOKING

## HOT BARBECUE SAUCE

| | |
|---|---|
| 2 teaspoons Tabasco sauce | 2 cups chopped onion |
| 2½ cups bottled chili sauce | 2 garlic cloves, minced |
| 1 teaspoon chili peppers, minced | 1 tablespoon brown sugar |
| ¾ cup oil | 1 bay leaf, crumbled |
| ½ cup lemon juice | 1 teaspoon dry mustard |
| 2 tablespoons tarragon vinegar | 1 teaspoon salt |

Combine ingredients with ½ cup water. Bring to a boil, reduce heat and simmer for 15 minutes. Serve with hamburgers, spareribs, lamb or chicken. Makes about 6 cups. Sauce may be kept covered in a refrigerator for at least 1 week.

## STEAK SAUCE

| | |
|---|---|
| 1 cup chopped mushrooms | ½ cup brandy |
| 12 anchovy fillets | ¾ cup tomato paste |
| 3 garlic cloves, minced | ½ cup finely chopped parsley |
| 1 cup olive oil | Freshly ground black pepper |
| 3 cups dry red wine | |

Sauté mushrooms, anchovy fillets and garlic in olive oil for 5 minutes. Add remaining ingredients. Bring to a boil, reduce heat and simmer for 15 minutes, stirring frequently. Serve with steak or hamburgers. Makes about 6 cups. Sauce may be kept covered in a refrigerator for at least 1 week.

## CHILI BARBECUE SAUCE

| | |
|---|---|
| 1½ tablespoons chili powder | 4 cups canned tomatoes |
| ¾ cup finely chopped onion | ¾ cup red wine |
| 2 garlic cloves, finely chopped | 2 tablespoons cornstarch |
| ¾ cup finely chopped green pepper | ¾ cup bouillon |
| | 1 teaspoon sugar |
| 6 tablespoons butter | 1 tablespoon salt |
| | Freshly ground black pepper |

Sauté onion, garlic and green pepper in butter for 5 minutes. Add chili powder, tomatoes, wine, salt and pepper. Combine cornstarch, cold bouillon and sugar and stir into chili mixture. Bring to a boil, reduce heat and cook until thickened, stirring constantly. Cover and simmer for 10 minutes. Serve with hot dogs, ham, pork or spareribs. Makes about 6 cups. Sauce may be kept covered in a refrigerator for at least 1 week.

## TOMATO-WINE SAUCE

| | |
|---|---|
| 1 cup canned tomatoes | 1 tablespoon sugar |
| 1 cup dry white wine | 1 bay leaf, crumbled |
| 1 cup thinly sliced okra | ½ teaspoon oregano |
| 1½ cups beef bouillon | ¼ teaspoon Tabasco sauce |
| ½ cup finely chopped celery | ½ teaspoon basil |
| 1 tablespoon lemon juice | ½ cup finely chopped onion |
| 1 teaspoon chili powder | 2 garlic cloves, minced |
| ¼ cup Worcestershire sauce | 1 teaspoon salt |
| ½ cup oil | Freshly ground black pepper |

Combine all ingredients and bring to a boil. Reduce heat and simmer for 45 minutes. Strain. Serve with chicken, ham, pork, hot dogs or lamb. Makes about 6 cups. Sauce may be kept covered in a refrigerator for at least 1 week.

## BARBECUED LEG OF LAMB

| | |
|---|---|
| 1 six-pound leg of lamb, boned and flattened | 2 garlic cloves, crushed |
| | 1 tablespoon salt |
| 1 cup oil | Freshly ground black pepper |
| ¼ cup wine vinegar | Hot barbecue sauce |

Marinate lamb at room temperature for 2 hours in combined oil, vinegar, garlic, salt and pepper. Turn the lamb once or twice and baste occasionally with the marinade. Remove from marinade and broil for 2 hours or until done, turning frequently and basting with hot barbecue sauce. Serves 6.

## BARBECUED HAM STEAKS

| | |
|---|---|
| 6 one-inch ham steaks | ½ cup brown sugar |
| 4 cups sherry | 2 garlic cloves, minced |
| ½ cup butter, melted | 1 tablespoon paprika |
| ½ cup dry mustard | |

Marinate ham steaks at room temperature for 2 hours in combined sherry, butter, mustard, brown sugar, garlic and paprika. Turn steaks once or twice and baste with the marinade. Broil for 10 minutes on each side, basting frequently with the marinade. Serves 6.

## BARBECUED PORK CHOPS

| | |
|---|---|
| 6 one-inch pork chops | Freshly ground black pepper |
| 1 cup soy sauce | 1 cup chili barbecue sauce |
| 1 garlic clove, crushed | |

Marinate pork chops at room temperature for 1 hour in combined soy sauce, garlic and pepper. Turn chops once or twice and baste with the marinade. Broil for 30 minutes on each side, basting frequently with chili barbecue sauce. Serves 6.

## BARBECUED SPARERIBS

| | |
|---|---|
| 5 pounds spareribs | ½ cup wine vinegar |
| ½ cup Cointreau | 1 lemon, sliced |
| ½ cup soy sauce | 2 teaspoons ground ginger |
| ½ cup honey | 2 garlic cloves, minced |
| 1 cup canned crushed pineapple | Freshly ground black pepper |

Marinate spareribs at room temperature for 1 hour in combined Cointreau, soy sauce, honey, pineapple, vinegar, lemon slices, ginger, garlic and pepper. Remove lemon from marinade. Broil spareribs for 20 minutes on each side, basting frequently with the marinade. Serves 6.

## KIDNEY-LIVER KEBAB

| | |
|---|---|
| 1 pound lamb kidney, cut in 1-inch cubes | 6 tomatoes, cut in wedges |
| | 12 mushroom caps |
| 1 pound liver, cut in 1-inch cubes | 3 onions, sliced |
| | 1 cup butter, melted |
| 1 pound lamb, cut in 1-inch cubes | 2 garlic cloves, minced |

Thread kidney, liver and lamb cubes on skewers alternating with tomato wedges, mushroom caps and onion slices. Broil for 15 minutes, turning frequently and basting with combined butter and garlic. Serves 6.

## SHRIMP AND BACON KEBAB

3 pounds shrimp, shelled
1 pound sliced bacon
1 cup soy sauce
½ cup lemon juice
2 cups canned
   pineapple chunks, drained

Marinate shrimp at room temperature for 30 minutes in soy sauce and lemon juice. Cut bacon slices in half. Thread shrimp on skewers, alternating with pineapple chunks and folded bacon slices. Broil until bacon is crisp. Serves 6.

## EGGPLANT LAMB KEBAB

2 pounds lamb, cut
   in 2-inch cubes
1 eggplant, cut
   in 2-inch cubes
12 small boiled potatoes
3 green peppers, each cut
   in 6 sections
12 small whole onions
12 mushroom caps
2 cups tomato-wine sauce

Marinate lamb overnight in tomato-wine sauce. Thread on skewers, alternating lamb with vegetables. Broil for 20 minutes, basting frequently with the marinade. Serves 6.

## FRUIT KEBAB

6 canned peach halves,
   drained and cut in half
3 bananas, sliced thick
2 apples, cut in wedges
1 fresh pineapple, cubed
3 grapefruits, sectioned
1 cup grapefruit juice
½ cup honey
2 tablespoons Cointreau
1 teaspoon chopped mint

Marinate fruit in grapefruit juice, honey, Cointreau and mint at room temperature for 30 minutes. Thread on skewers, alternating fruits. Broil for about 5 minutes, basting frequently with the marinade. Serves 6.

## TERIYAKI KEBAB

3 pounds lamb, cut
   in 2-inch cubes
¾ cup canned pineapple juice
2 tablespoons soy sauce
2 tablespoons lemon juice
1 garlic clove, minced
2 cups canned
   pineapple chunks, drained
Stuffed olives

Marinate lamb at room temperature for 2 hours in pineapple juice, soy sauce, lemon juice and garlic. Thread lamb on skewers alternating it with pineapple chunks and olives. Broil for 10 minutes, basting frequently with the marinade. Serves 6. Top sirloin may be used instead of lamb.

## FISH KEBAB

2 pounds swordfish, cut
   in 1-inch cubes
¾ cup oil
½ cup lemon juice
1 bay leaf, crumbled
Tabasco sauce
2 cucumbers, cut
   in 1-inch slices
Stuffed olives

Marinate fish at room temperature for 30 minutes in combined oil, lemon juice, bay leaf and 4 drops of Tabasco sauce. Stir once or twice to coat fish thoroughly with marinade. Thread on skewers, alternating fish with cucumbers and olives. Broil for 10 minutes, turning frequently and basting with marinade. Serves 6.

## DUCK ON A SPIT

2 five-pound ducks
4 oranges, quartered
½ cup oil
1 cup butter
1 cup orange juice
2 tablespoons grated
   orange rind
2 tablespoons chopped
   water cress

Stuff ducks with quartered oranges. Brush with oil and broil for 1½ hours or until done, turning spit frequently. Meanwhile combine butter, orange juice, orange rind and water cress and simmer for 15 minutes, stirring occasionally. Serve ducks with hot orange-butter sauce. Serves 6.

## RIB ROAST OR STEAK

3-rib roast separated into
   steaks or 1 four-pound steak
½ cup olive oil
2 garlic cloves, crushed
2 teaspoons salt
Steak sauce

Combine oil with garlic and salt and spread on meat. Broil. Serve with steak sauce. Serves 6.

## HOT DOGS

12 kosher-style garlic
   hot dogs
Chili barbecue sauce

Broil for 10 minutes, turning frequently. Serve with sauce.

## BARBECUED CHICKEN

3 two-pound chickens, cut up
½ cup dry white wine
½ cup oil
1 teaspoon chopped chives
2 tablespoons
   chopped parsley
Tomato-wine sauce

Marinate chicken at room temperature for 1 hour in combined wine, oil, chives and parsley. Turn chicken once or twice and baste with the marinade. Broil for 30 minutes or until done, turning frequently and basting with tomato-wine sauce. Serves 6.

## TABASCO HAMBURGERS

3 pounds round steak,
   ground
1 cup chopped onion
¾ cup chopped green pepper
2 cups hot barbecue sauce

Combine round steak, onion and green pepper with ½ cup hot barbecue sauce. Shape into 12 hamburgers. Broil, turning once and basting frequently with hot barbecue sauce. Serve with remaining barbecue sauce.

# SEASONING

THE RECIPES FOR ALL DISHES SHOWN
IN THIS SECTION ARE ON PAGES 181-184

# SPICES

FIFTY years ago it would have been hard to find a half dozen different
spices in a grocery store. By then they were not
in much demand because the basic need for them had gone. In older days,
in fact throughout all history, spices were prized beyond belief.
They even gave the grocer his name—he was a man who bought spices
by the gross. They were prized for their preservative powers
and for the pleasant flavor they could add to salted or aging meat.
But by the turn of the century new methods of preserving
and canning food had changed them from a necessity to a luxury.

Now spices are back again in force. Today some supermarkets carry
as many as 70 different varieties, and since the 1930s the per capita use
of spices in the U.S. has increased by more than 35%. This growth
owes much to the tourists who come back from their travels
with exotic recipes. It owes even more to the present-day housewife
who is growing more daring in cooking as she tries to vary
familiar dishes—especially leftovers.

In its pure sense, the word "spice" refers only to parts of aromatic plants
grown in the tropics—"true" spices like ginger, pepper, turmeric,
cinnamon and mace. But nowadays, for the purpose of buying
and cooking, the word has come to include aromatic seeds
like anise, fennel and coriander and even the whole family of herbs,
discussed on pages 170-173. Such an assortment of spices
is shown on the opposite page, arranged as they might have appeared
in a fragrant old spice store generations ago.

Many popular spices are blends, such as the pickling spice, which is
used for pickles and relishes. It also serves to add flavor to meat
and vegetables when placed in a cheesecloth bag and put
in the cooking pot. Spices should be bought in small amounts
because they start losing flavor in three to six months, depending
on their container. Long exposure to heat, moisture or air
should be avoided. In cooking, spices need careful measuring so that
they will improve the flavor of the food rather than smother it. With foods
that require long cooking, spices are generally added near the end.
With uncooked foods they are added well in advance of serving.

Traditional oak bins and bags hold spices that are widely available in the U.S. today—from hot chili powder and mild fennel to sweet anise seed. On top of bin are implements for grinding, weighing, measuring and storing them, and in the center, beside a decorative jar of bay leaves, are sticks of cinnamon bark, which add delicious flavor to hot drinks like spiced wine.

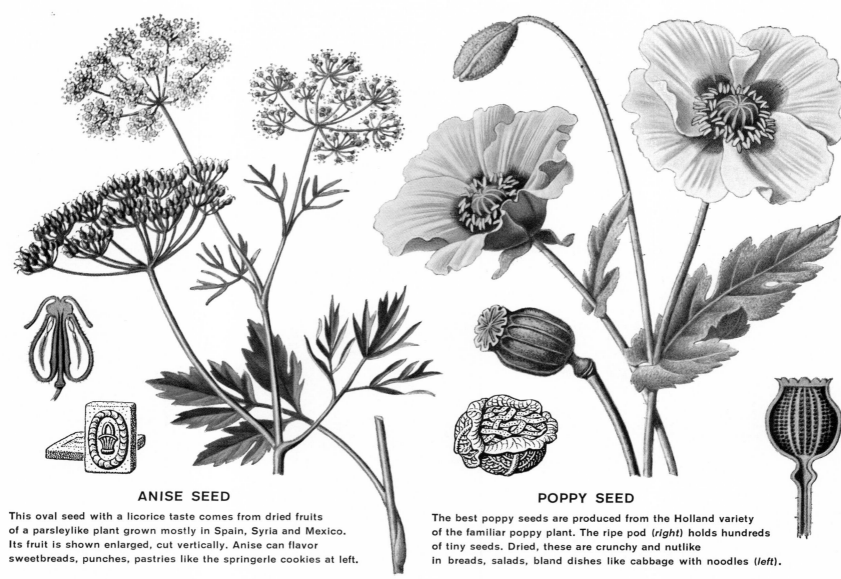

## ANISE SEED

This oval seed with a licorice taste comes from dried fruits
of a parsleylike plant grown mostly in Spain, Syria and Mexico.
Its fruit is shown enlarged, cut vertically. Anise can flavor
sweetbreads, punches, pastries like the springerle cookies at left.

## POPPY SEED

The best poppy seeds are produced from the Holland variety
of the familiar poppy plant. The ripe pod (*right*) holds hundreds
of tiny seeds. Dried, these are crunchy and nutlike
in breads, salads, bland dishes like cabbage with noodles (*left*).

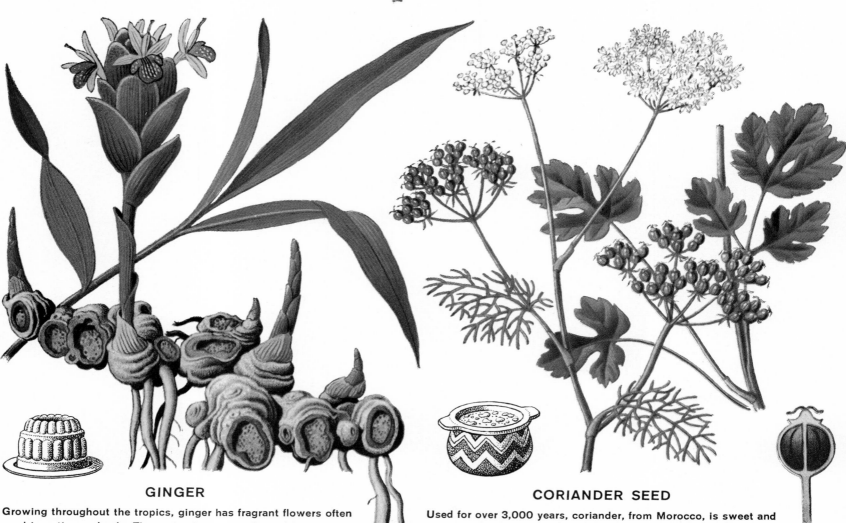

## GINGER

Growing throughout the tropics, ginger has fragrant flowers often
used in native garlands. The seasoning comes from the roots
called "hands" which are sun-bleached, then shipped whole, broken
or ground. It is excellent in roasts, biscuits, puddings.

## CORIANDER SEED

Used for over 3,000 years, coriander, from Morocco, is sweet and
tart. The dried seeds are fruit segments shown as clusters
on the plant and enlarged (*lower right*). They help flavor salads,
pickles, pastry, soups like Mexican Menudo soup shown here.

## MARJORAM

The most versatile of herbs, marjoram, a member of the mint family, is aromatic and a bit bitter. It is excellent on lamb, with cheese dishes, in poultry stuffings, soups and vegetables. Mushroom casserole at lower left is seasoned with marjoram, salt, chives.

## THYME

The finest herb for fish and shellfish soups like clam chowder and oyster stew (*left*), thyme may be sprinkled in the cooking water of a lobster or added to a poultry dressing. Thyme is aromatic and pungent, goes well with tomatoes, fricasees, chipped beef.

## ROSEMARY

Primarily a meat herb, as used on the roast of beef at lower left, rosemary is the leaf of an evergreen shrub and shaped like a curved pine needle. It has a fresh, sweet flavor, is better fresh from the garden than when dried. It is excellent with lamb, fish and poultry.

## OREGANO

Closely related to marjoram, oregano has a similar flavor—strong, aromatic, pleasantly bitter. It is an important ingredient in Italian dishes like pizza, veal scallopini, and pasta sauces and is fine in omelets. Some gourmets use it for pork, chicken Mexican.

## TARRAGON

Best known as a flavoring for vinegar, tarragon is good in sea food, such as lobster Figaro at lower left. Sprinkle also over broiled chicken before removing from stove. Both the dried leaves and the flowering tops may be used for their faintly aniselike flavor.

## MINT

A staple in lamb sauce and mint jelly, this strong, sweet tangy and cool-tasting herb has unusual use as flavor for ice cream with crème de menthe (*lower left*). Mint came originally from Europe and Asia, achieved fame in the U.S. in the South's mint julep.

# COOKING
# WITH WINE

THERE is always something impressive about cooking with wine, and many people feel that it is an art best left to master chefs. Actually it often means no more than just adding wine to whatever is cooking in the pot. The simple addition of wine can change the taste of a familiar favorite and can lend an air of distinction to an otherwise straightforward dish. There are many recipes in this book that call for cooking with wine and all of these dishes, from game birds to vegetables as well as the ones on the following pages, are prepared in one of two quite different basic methods.

The first, and most common, is to cook the food with wine or in a wine sauce. This adds the wine's own flavor while the wine, like salt, brings out the flavor of the food itself. The alcohol evaporates when the wine is cooked. No matter how much wine is used in a dish, the effect is never heady. But most of the taste of the wine remains even after hours of cooking so it is usually wise to add the wine early and let its flavor blend into the dish. Some uncooked dishes, like the sherry soufflé shown on the opposite page, use wine as their principal flavoring.

The second method is to flavor the food with wine before cooking. This began as a way to pickle and preserve food and is still a tasty means of tenderizing it. It is generally done with a marinade, or sauce, in which the food is soaked and which may be used for basting. The process can make inexpensive cuts like the barbecued lamb shanks on page 178 as tender and delicious as meats that cost far more.

Full-bodied Burgundies and clarets are usually used in sturdy dishes like beef stew, kidney pie. Lighter white wines, such as a dry Bordeaux, are excellent with fowl or fish. Marinated fruits, one of the most popular wine-food dishes, are usually soaked in a light wine like *rosé* or a fortified wine like port or sherry. The wine served with the meal should be of the same type as that used in cooking the food. Even the connoisseurs admit that it is not necessary to use choice vintages for cooking. But at the same time there is no such thing as a cooking wine. Wine that is not good enough to drink is not good enough to eat.

Sherry soufflé, a chilled dessert with whipped cream and lady fingers, is shown in the wine-tasting room of the Inglenook vineyard in California's Napa Valley. The antique chairs and table and the stained-glass window were brought from wine-growing regions of Europe. The wine basket and glass hold an Inglenook sherry made from the Palomino grapes (p. 178) that decorate the table.

# WINE GRAPES

**GAMAY**

The Gamay thrives only in cool,
hilly, upland country and it yields
a smooth, red Burgundy-type wine.

**PINOT BLANC**

This grape, used in making some
of the finest California champagnes,
also makes a light, white wine.

# TABLE GRAPES

**FLAME TOKAY**

Sweet in taste, rich in color, it is
a familiar fixture in fruit salad.
Because of its thick skin it is easy to ship.

**THOMPSON SEEDLESS**

A table favorite, it outsells
all the others, makes most of world's
raisins and goes into neutral white wines.

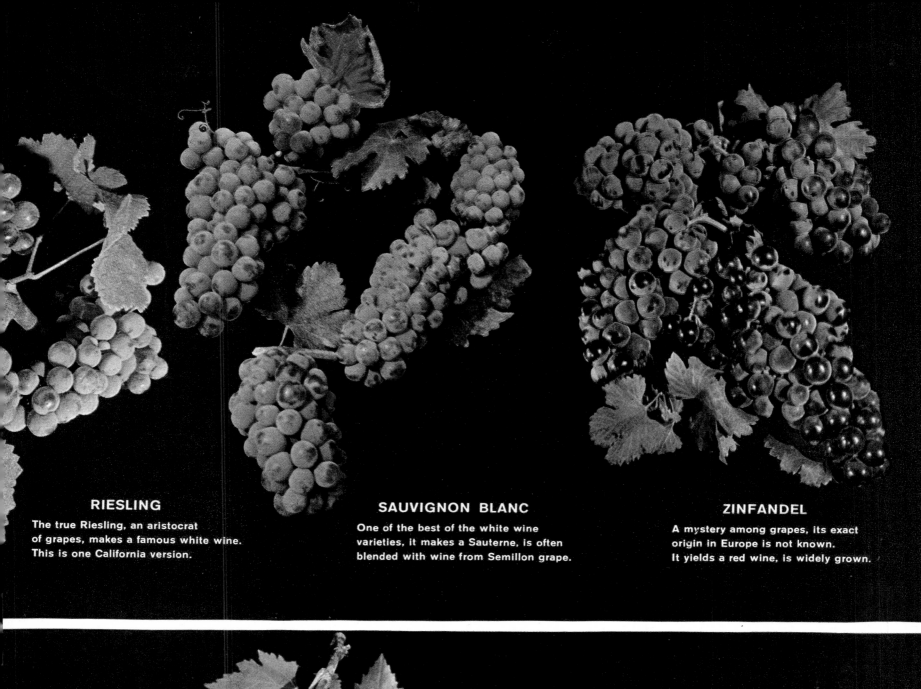

**RIESLING**
The true Riesling, an aristocrat of grapes, makes a famous white wine. This is one California version.

**SAUVIGNON BLANC**
One of the best of the white wine varieties, it makes a Sauterne, is often blended with wine from Semillon grape.

**ZINFANDEL**
A mystery among grapes, its exact origin in Europe is not known. It yields a red wine, is widely grown.

**RIBIER**
It was rare commercially in U. S. 25 years ago, grows more popular yearly, now ranks fourth in acreage.

**OLIVETTE BLANCHE**
Known as "ladyfingers," these graceful grapes are thin-skinned and hard to ship but are sweet to taste.

**RED MALAGA**
Since it ripens earlier than most red grapes, it beats Tokays to market, enjoys an early-season demand.

Lamb shanks are barbecued outdoors in a vineyard and basted with a vermouth sauce in which they have been marinated overnight. Sauce also contains garlic, shallots and is seasoned with herbs. In the background are trellises of Palomino grapes.

Wine and cheese are an unbeatable combination, and almost any wine is suitable company for almost any cheese. Here on a lug, or crate for shipping grapes, grouped around a wedge of Port du Salut, are (*left to right*) glasses of sherry, *rosé*, Burgundy, Pinot Blanc, Rhine wine.

Fruits for marinating in wine are shown in the vineyards of Mr. and Mrs. Jerome Draper of St. Helena, Calif. The flavor of almost any fruit is heightened by wine. Shown here (*left to right*) are cantaloupe, pineapple, honeydew melon filled with grapes, grapefruit and oranges, and behind them watermelon. Small glass holds *rosé* wine and large one holds marinade of *rosé*.

# RECIPES FOR
## SEASONING

**SPICES**

**HERBS**

**COOKING WITH WINE**

# SPICES

## SPRINGERLE COOKIES

2 teaspoons ground anise  
2 teaspoons anise seed  
2 eggs  
1 cup sugar  
2 cups sifted flour  

Beat eggs until thick and lemon colored. Add sugar gradually, beating constantly, until mixture is thoroughly blended. Combine flour and ground anise and stir into egg mixture. Knead on lightly floured board until it forms a stiff dough, adding a little more flour if necessary. Roll dough ⅛ inch thick and cut into about 24 squares. Place squares on a greased baking sheet which has been sprinkled with anise seed. Let them stand at room temperature for 8 hours to dry. Bake in a slow oven (325°) for 10 minutes.

## CABBAGE AND NOODLES WITH POPPY SEED

¼ cup poppy seed  
1 large cabbage  
8 ounces broad noodles, boiled and drained  
¾ cup butter  
1 teaspoon salt  
Freshly ground black pepper  

Scoop out center of cabbage, leaving shell about 1 inch thick, and chop center coarsely. Cover chopped cabbage with boiling water and cook over high heat for 5 minutes. Drain. Sauté chopped cabbage in ½ cup butter over low heat for 15 minutes, stirring frequently. Season with salt and freshly ground black pepper. Combine hot noodles with poppy seed and remaining ¼ cup of butter. Serve cooked cabbage in raw cabbage shell and top with noodles. Serves 6.

## GINGER PUDDING

2 teaspoons ground ginger  
¼ cup butter  
½ cup brown sugar  
2 eggs, beaten  
3½ cups sifted flour  
3½ teaspoons double-acting baking powder  
1 cup milk  
¼ teaspoon salt  

Cream butter with brown sugar until light and fluffy. Add eggs and mix well. Sift flour with ginger, baking powder and salt. Add flour and milk alternately to butter mixture, mixing well after each addition. Pour into greased 2-quart mold, cover mold and place it on a rack in a large pot over 1 inch of hot water. Cover pot and steam for 2 hours adding more water if necessary. Serves 6.

## MEXICAN MENUDO SOUP

1 teaspoon coriander seed  
3 pounds tripe  
1 pound veal, cubed  
3 large onions, chopped  
3 garlic cloves, minced  
1 teaspoon chili powder  
1 teaspoon oregano  
2 cups canned whole hominy  
¼ cup chopped parsley  
1 tablespoon salt  
Freshly ground black pepper  

Cut tripe into thin strips. Combine with veal cubes, onions, garlic, chili powder, coriander, oregano, salt and pepper and 4 quarts of water in large saucepan. Bring to a boil and continue boiling for 5 minutes. Skim. Reduce heat, cover and simmer for 5 hours. Add hominy. Simmer for 30 minutes. Sprinkle with parsley. Serves 12.

## SAFFRON BUNS

Whole saffron  
1 cup milk  
Butter  
2 tablespoons sugar  
1 envelope granular yeast  
4 cups sifted flour  
2 eggs, beaten  
½ cup raisins  
½ cup chopped citron  
½ teaspoon grated lemon rind  
1 egg white  
½ teaspoon salt  

Scald milk. Add ½ cup butter, sugar and salt and stir until sugar is dissolved. Cool to lukewarm. Dissolve yeast in ¼ cup lukewarm water and add to milk mixture. Stir in flour. Add eggs, raisins, citron, lemon rind and a pinch of saffron. Turn out on a lightly floured board. Knead for 5 minutes. Place in a greased bowl. Melt 1 tablespoon butter, brush dough with butter and cover bowl with towel. Let dough rise in a warm place until double in bulk. Punch dough down. Shape it into 24 round buns and top each bun with a small ball of dough about the size of a marble. Arrange buns 2 inches apart on a greased baking sheet and let them rise, uncovered, until double in bulk. Brush buns with slightly beaten egg white. Bake in a moderate oven (350°) for 20 minutes.

## FISH FLAMBE WITH FENNEL

1 teaspoon fennel seed  
1 three-pound bluefish  
1 teaspoon dried thyme  
1 tablespoon dried parsley  
¼ cup brandy  

Broil fish under medium heat on a foil-lined broiler rack for 30 minutes, turning once. Serve on hot platter and sprinkle with herbs. Pour some of the brandy into a ladle and the rest over the fish. Warm the brandy in the ladle over a match, light it, then flame the fish with it. Serves 6.

## SESAME BREAD

2 tablespoons sesame seed  
1 large loaf French bread  
¼ cup butter  
¼ cup finely chopped parsley  
¼ cup finely chopped chives  

Slice bread lengthwise. Combine butter, parsley and chives and spread on cut surfaces of bread. Sprinkle with sesame seed and bake in a moderate oven (350°) for 20 minutes or until loaf is crisp. Serves 6.

## SLICED CUCUMBER PICKLES

1½ teaspoons ground turmeric  
20 medium cucumbers, sliced  
12 onions, sliced  
5 cups cider vinegar  
4 cups sugar  
1 teaspoon celery seed  
4 one-inch pieces stick cinnamon  
1 tablespoon mustard seed  
6 cloves  
4 tablespoons salt  
1 teaspoon peppercorns  

Sprinkle sliced cucumbers and onions with salt and let stand at room temperature 1½ hours. Drain well. Combine remaining ingredients in a large saucepan and bring to a boil. Add cucumbers and onions, reduce heat and simmer 10 minutes. Remove cinnamon sticks. Ladle into hot sterilized jars and seal immediately. Makes about 8 pints.

# HERBS

### SAVORY WITH STRING BEANS

| | |
|---|---|
| 1 teaspoon minced savory | 1 tablespoon minced celery |
| 1 onion, chopped | 1 tablespoon chopped parsley |
| 1 garlic clove, minced | 1 tablespoon dry white wine |
| 2 tablespoons oil | Salt |
| 1 tomato, peeled and diced | Freshly ground black pepper |
| 1 tablespoon minced green pepper | 1 pound string beans, cooked |

Sauté onion and garlic in oil for 5 minutes or until lightly browned. Add savory, tomato, green pepper, celery, parsley, white wine, salt and black pepper. Mix well. Simmer for 10 minutes, stirring occasionally. Pour sauce over hot string beans and mix well. Serves 6.

### BASIL AND TOMATO SALAD

| | |
|---|---|
| 2 tablespoons chopped basil | 1 teaspoon salt |
| 6 tomatoes, quartered | Freshly ground black pepper |
| ½ cup olive oil | Mixed greens |
| 2 tablespoons wine vinegar | |

Marinate tomatoes in mixture of 1 tablespoon basil, the oil, vinegar, salt and pepper for 4 hours. Stir tomatoes once or twice and baste with the marinade. Combine greens with remaining 1 tablespoon basil and arrange in salad bowl. Arrange tomato quarters on greens and pour marinade over them. Before serving, toss well. Serves 6.

### SAGE STUFFING FOR DUCK

| | |
|---|---|
| 2 teaspoons chopped sage | 6 cups coarse bread crumbs |
| 2 five-pound oven-ready ducks | ½ cup sour cream |
| ½ cup butter | Salt |
| 8 apples, chopped | Freshly ground black pepper |
| 6 onions, chopped | |

Chop duck livers, hearts and gizzards. Sauté in butter for 10 minutes or until tender. Remove and set aside. Sauté the apples and onions in butter remaining in skillet for 10 minutes or until onions are lightly browned. Add apples, onions and liquid from skillet to bread crumbs. Stir in the livers, hearts and gizzards, sage, sour cream, salt and pepper. Mix lightly. Stuff ducks with this mixture and set them on a rack in a shallow baking pan. Roast in a slow oven (325°) for 2½ hours or until done. Serves 6.

### DILL SAUCE FOR FISH

| | |
|---|---|
| 2 tablespoons chopped dill | ½ cup, butter, melted |
| 1 teaspoon dill seed | 1 teaspoon salt |
| 2 tablespoons chopped parsley | Freshly ground black pepper |
| 2 tablespoons lemon juice | 1 three-pound halibut, mackerel or salmon |
| 1 teaspoon paprika | |

Make dill sauce by combining chopped dill, dill seed, parsley, lemon juice, paprika, salt and pepper with melted butter. Spread half the sauce on one side of the fish and broil on a foil-lined rack under medium heat for 15 minutes. Then turn the fish, spread the other side with the remaining sauce and broil 15 minutes or until done. Serves 6.

### CHERVIL WITH FRIED EGGS

| | |
|---|---|
| 1 tablespoon finely chopped chervil | ½ cup melted butter |
| | Fried eggs |

Mix chervil with melted butter and spoon over eggs.

### HERBED COTTAGE CHEESE SALAD

| | |
|---|---|
| 1 tablespoon minced chives | 1 green pepper, diced |
| 1 tablespoon minced dill | 1 tablespoon minced onion |
| 1 tablespoon minced basil | 1 teaspoon salt |
| 1 tablespoon minced tarragon | Freshly ground black pepper |
| 1 pound cottage cheese | Mixed greens |
| 1 cup sour cream | Salad dressing |
| 1 cucumber, diced | |

Combine cottage cheese with sour cream, herbs, cucumber, green pepper, onion, salt and black pepper. Arrange greens on plate and spoon the herbed cottage cheese mixture on top. Serve with any desired salad dressing. Serves 6.

### MUSHROOM CASSEROLE WITH MARJORAM

| | |
|---|---|
| 1 tablespoon chopped marjoram | ½ cup chicken bouillon |
| 1 teaspoon minced chives | ¼ cup dry white wine |
| 1 pound mushrooms | 1 teaspoon salt |
| ½ cup butter, melted | Freshly ground black pepper |

Put mushrooms in casserole. Combine butter with marjoram, chives, salt and pepper. Add chicken bouillon and wine. Stir well and pour over mushrooms. Cover and bake in a moderate oven (350°) for 20 minutes. Serves 6.

### OYSTER STEW WITH THYME

| | |
|---|---|
| ½ teaspoon thyme | 2 cups cream |
| 1 quart oysters | 2 teaspoons salt |
| ½ cup butter | Freshly ground black pepper |
| 4 cups milk | |

Simmer oysters and their liquor with butter until oysters begin to curl around the edges. Combine and scald milk and cream. Add thyme, salt and pepper. Add to the oysters and simmer for 10 minutes. Do not allow stew to boil. Serves 6.

### ROSEMARY WITH MEAT

Sprinkle roasts of beef, lamb, pork or veal lightly with freshly chopped or dried rosemary before cooking them. Or sprinkle the cut surfaces of beef steaks before broiling them. Be careful not to overseason; too much rosemary can make food taste bitter. Rosemary can also be used to season meat or poultry stuffing or sauces for beef or lamb.

### MARINARA SAUCE

| | |
|---|---|
| 1 teaspoon oregano | 1 garlic clove, minced |
| 3 cups canned Italian tomatoes, drained | ¼ cup olive oil |
| ½ cup chopped onion | 1 teaspoon salt |
| | Freshly ground black pepper |

Sauté onion and garlic in olive oil for 5 minutes. Add tomatoes, oregano, salt and pepper. Bring to a boil, reduce heat and simmer for 30 minutes, stirring occasionally. Makes about 3 cups.

## LOBSTER FIGARO

1 tablespoon
chopped tarragon
3 two-pound lobsters, boiled
and split

2 cups cooked crab meat
1 cup mayonnaise
1 tablespoon tomato paste
1 tablespoon lemon juice

Remove lobster meat and chop. Save shells. Combine lobster and crab meat. Mix mayonnaise, tarragon, tomato paste and lemon juice. Add to sea food and fill shells with this mixture. Serves 6.

## MINT ICE CREAM

1 cup chopped mint leaves
1 tablespoon
crème de menthe
2 cups milk

8 egg yolks, beaten
1 cup sugar
2 cups cream, whipped
Green food coloring

Scald milk. Remove from heat, add mint leaves and let stand for 20 minutes. Strain. Beat egg yolks until slightly thickened. Add sugar gradually, beating until thick and lemon colored. Add scalded milk gradually. Cook over very low heat for 10 minutes, stirring constantly. Cool and stir in a few drops of green coloring. Fold mixture into whipped cream. Pour into freezing trays and freeze until mushy. Turn out into chilled bowl, add crème de menthe and mix well. Return to trays and freeze until firm. Makes about 2 quarts.

## OMELET AUX FINES HERBES

½ teaspoon minced chives
½ teaspoon minced basil
½ teaspoon minced oregano
6 eggs

½ cup milk
3 tablespoons butter
1 teaspoon salt
Freshly ground black pepper

Beat eggs thoroughly. Stir in milk, salt and pepper. Melt butter in skillet, add egg mixture, and cook over low heat. As eggs begin to set, lift them gently from the sides to let the uncooked portion flow underneath. Cook until eggs are thoroughly set but slightly moist in the center. Sprinkle omelet with chives, basil and oregano. Fold the omelet in half and slide it onto a hot platter. Serves 6.

## CHIVE AND CHERVIL DUMPLINGS

2 tablespoons chopped chives
2 tablespoons chopped chervil
1½ cups sifted flour
2 teaspoons double-acting
baking powder

¾ cup milk
3 teaspoons shortening
1 teaspoon salt
Freshly ground black pepper
Chicken or beef stew

Sift flour, baking powder, salt and pepper together. Cut in shortening with a pastry blender or two knives until the dough resembles coarse meal. Stir in chives and chervil. Add the milk, stirring only enough to blend. Drop by the tablespoonfuls into boiling stew. Cover and cook for 15 minutes. Serves 6.

## HERBED ROAST LEG OF LAMB

1 teaspoon minced marjoram
1 teaspoon minced thyme
1 teaspoon minced rosemary
1 garlic clove, crushed
1 six-pound leg of lamb

2 tablespoons olive oil
2 tablespoons flour
1 cup dry white wine
1 teaspoon salt
Freshly ground black pepper

Crush garlic with salt and pepper. Mix with olive oil. Spread on lamb. Sprinkle lamb with marjoram, thyme, rosemary and flour. Pour wine and 1 cup of water in roasting pan with lamb. Roast in a slow oven (325°) for 2½ hours, basting frequently. Serves 6.

# COOKING WITH WINE

## COLD SHERRY SOUFFLE

1½ cups sweet sherry
6 eggs, separated
¾ cup sugar
1 tablespoon lemon juice

2 envelopes
unflavored gelatine
1 cup heavy cream
Lady fingers

Soften gelatine in ½ cup cold water for 5 minutes. Place over boiling water and stir until dissolved. Remove from heat and add sherry. Cool. Chill for 30 minutes or until mixture begins to thicken. Meanwhile beat egg whites until foamy. Add ½ cup sugar gradually, beating constantly. Add lemon juice and beat until mixture is stiff but not dry. Beat egg yolks until frothy, add ¼ cup sugar gradually and beat until yolks are thick and lemon colored. Add slightly thickened wine gelatine slowly to egg yolks and continue beating until thick and light. Fold beaten egg whites into gelatine mixture. Whip cream and fold in. Pour into a collared 7-inch soufflé dish lined with lady fingers. Chill for 3 hours or until firm. Remove paper collar before serving. Serve with additional whipped cream if desired. Serves 12.

To make a collar for the soufflé dish, cut a strip of waxed paper 6 inches wide and long enough to fit around the top of the dish. Fold over to make a double strip 3 inches wide. Butter one side and tie the strip around the dish, buttered side in, so that it stands like a collar above the edge.

## BARBECUED LAMB SHANKS WITH VERMOUTH

1 cup dry vermouth
6 lamb shanks
1 cup oil
1 tablespoon lemon juice
3 shallots or 1 medium onion,
chopped

2 garlic cloves, minced
1 teaspoon chopped tarragon
1 teaspoon chopped basil
1 teaspoon salt
10 peppercorns, crushed

Marinate lamb shanks in vermouth, oil, lemon juice, shallots, garlic, herbs, salt and pepper. Let stand at room temperature for at least 4 hours. Turn lamb shanks once or twice and spoon marinade over. Broil lamb for about 30 minutes, turning frequently and basting with the marinade. This marinade may also be used for chicken, turkey, pork or other cuts of lamb.

## ROSE SAUCE

1 cup rosé wine
1 cup honey
Ground cardamom

2 tablespoons lemon juice
12 mint leaves, chopped
1 teaspoon salt

Combine honey with a pinch of cardamom and ½ cup of water. Simmer for 5 minutes. Add mint and salt. Cool, strain. Add *rosé* and lemon juice, stir well. Makes about 2 cups. Pour sauce over pineapple, grapefruit, oranges or melons. Let fruit stand at room temperature for at least 2 hours. Chill before serving.

# A GUIDE TO COOKING WITH WINE

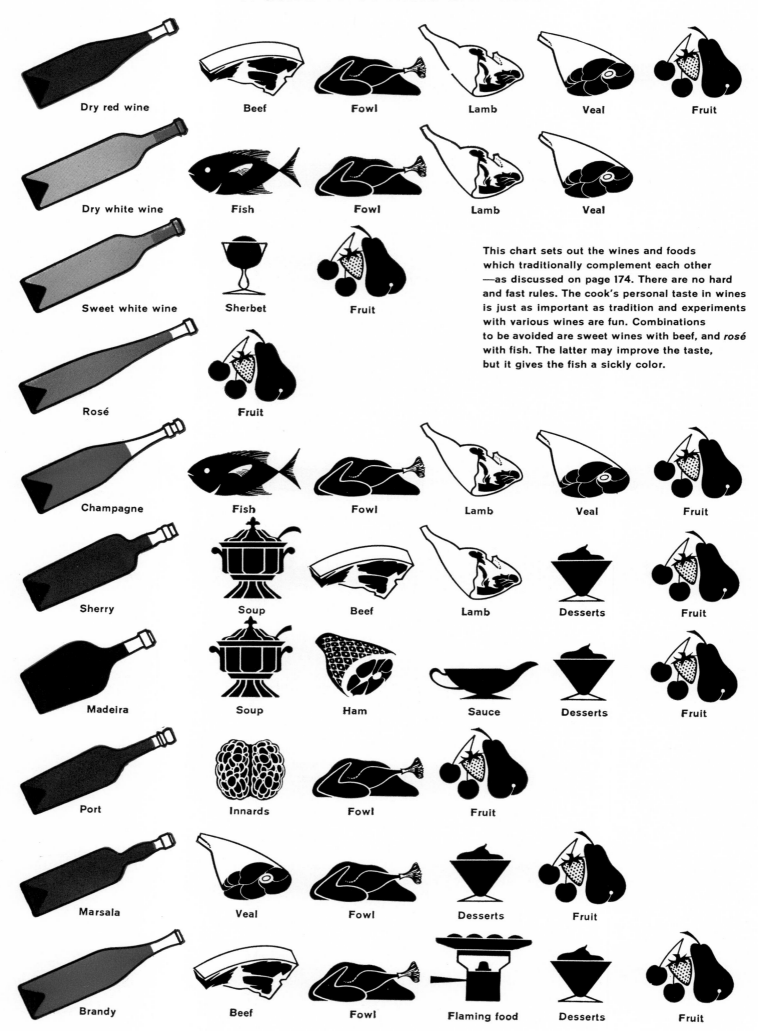

| | | | | | |
|---|---|---|---|---|---|
| Dry red wine | Beef | Fowl | Lamb | Veal | Fruit |
| Dry white wine | Fish | Fowl | Lamb | Veal | |
| Sweet white wine | Sherbet | Fruit | | | |
| Rosé | Fruit | | | | |
| Champagne | Fish | Fowl | Lamb | Veal | Fruit |
| Sherry | Soup | Beef | Lamb | Desserts | Fruit |
| Madeira | Soup | Ham | Sauce | Desserts | Fruit |
| Port | Innards | Fowl | Fruit | | |
| Marsala | Veal | Fowl | Desserts | Fruit | |
| Brandy | Beef | Fowl | Flaming food | Desserts | Fruit |

This chart sets out the wines and foods which traditionally complement each other —as discussed on page 174. There are no hard and fast rules. The cook's personal taste in wines is just as important as tradition and experiments with various wines are fun. Combinations to be avoided are sweet wines with beef, and *rosé* with fish. The latter may improve the taste, but it gives the fish a sickly color.

# CHILDREN'S FOOD

THE RECIPES FOR ALL DISHES SHOWN
IN THIS SECTION ARE ON PAGES 197-200

# CHILDREN'S DESSERTS

THE simple satisfaction of mud-pie-making gives way at an early age to a desire to turn out something with a more edible end product, and by the age of 4 most children want to "help" in the kitchen. Soon licking the frosting off the pan is not creative enough for them and they want to stir the batter, wield the eggbeater and in general become a nuisance to mothers who are trying to get something on the table in time for dinner.

The best way to cope with their culinary cravings, and one that is entirely feasible from the age of 7 on, is to devote an occasional afternoon to letting the children cook. Quite naturally, the things that children enjoy making most are desserts. Happily, these are often easy to make and are a good place for neophyte chefs to begin. But when starting the children off, it is best not to try to cut corners. Instead, use recipes that, no matter how simple, will teach children some of the basic methods and theories of cooking.

All the desserts shown on the opposite page are made from "real" recipes—they are products made from scratch without benefit of mixes—and the results ought to be tasty enough to be served to the whole family. In fact the cookies, cupcakes, mousse and ice cream are often made by adults for dessert. When teaching children to cook this way with the basic raw materials, mothers must be willing to help separate eggs or cream butter. They must also be patient when it comes to cleaning up the kitchen.

All of these desserts can be made in less than an hour, which is about the limit of a child's ability to concentrate on a single project. Some need extra time for chilling. With some, especially the gingerbread men and the cupcakes, the best fun of all comes in the decorating process, so it is a good idea to have an assortment of nuts, candy sprinkles and raisins on hand. Children are apt to have their own strong, and often unorthodox, ideas of decoration, but as long as the results are edible there is no reason to stick to any rules. The more encouragement children get to experiment, the better cooks they will eventually turn out to be.

Two small cooks are shown with a group of easy-to-make desserts. Clockwise from the lower left are cupcakes, some trimmed with nutmeats and some in the process of being decorated with sprinkles; peach ice cream in bowl and freezer tray; gingerbread men; raisin-stuffed baked apples; brownies; chocolate-cooky roll with whipped cream; strawberry mousse and chocolate-chip cookies.

# SCHOOL LUNCHES, BREAKFASTS

OPENING his lunch box can be a daily treat for a child at school, or it can be such a depressing moment that he will somehow ditch the box's contents and spend his carfare on popcorn. Almost half the mothers in America with children of school age are faced with the task of putting up lunches for their youngsters. Planning one that is packable, nutritious and has some variety—which many children inherently resist—can be as taxing as ordering a seven-course dinner.

More often than not the lunch box staple is a sandwich. The daily chore of making this can be lightened by an occasional sandwich production line. Sandwiches that are made in advance and frozen taste just as fresh by lunchtime as those that have been made and packed the same day. Almost any sandwich can be frozen except those with lettuce, tomatoes, hard-cooked eggs or mayonnaise, but these extras can be packed in a separate container in the lunch box. One way to provide variety and still not make anything too exotic for a child's taste is to vary the bread. Wheat germ, dark brown or protein bread have a delicious flavor and are highly nutritious. Most children consider a sandwich on a roll a treat.

On cold days it is a good idea to have the lunch box contain something hot. This is a good thing to keep in mind when making such dinners as casseroles or beef stew. Make an extra portion, freeze it and use it in the lunch box a day or two later. Extra servings of salad, particularly chicken or vegetable which are popular with youngsters, can also be made in advance.

Any child who does not eat his main meal in the middle of the day should have a hearty breakfast. Some suggestions for breakfasts that will appeal to children are shown on pages 192, 193. Most children will happily eat a dried cereal for breakfast— which one depends on which box top they are collecting at the moment. But if he is going to eat a lunch-box lunch, the child should also get an egg, perhaps with sausages, bacon or corned beef hash.

Lunch box sandwiches are, from top in left row, liverwurst on protein bread, cream cheese on date nut, cucumber and radish on wheat germ, carrot and celery on white. In center row are bacon on cheese bread, deviled ham and egg on Italian, salmon salad on roll. At right are banana and cottage cheese, corned beef on a roll, tongue on whole wheat, baked beans on brown bread, Gouda cheese on rye. At bottom are mustard, marmalade, catsup and mayonnaise.

Farm-style beef stew, to be packed in wide mouth vacuum bottle, is main dish of this lunch which includes bread and butter sandwich, banana, package of cookies. Coated paper plate makes stew easy to manage.

Two sandwiches, meat loaf on rye, and pimento cheese spread with olives, are eaten with carrot sticks and celery. Grapes and chocolate milk, to which an egg may be added, are dessert and beverage.

Chicken and vegetable salad from vacuum bottle is eaten with lettuce wrapped separately in plastic bag. Since milk is often available at school, a jam sandwich and an apple complete the lunch menu.

Hot bouillon starts off a box lunch that includes an American cheese and bologna sandwich on French bread, a tomato and applesauce. Tomato may be eaten whole or sliced and put in sandwich.

Breakfasts that children enjoy
helping to make and
like to eat are shown at right.
In background girl looks on
as boy stirs a pan of hot cereal.
On table, clockwise from lower left,
are helpings of baked fish and
cream, made from leftover fish;
fig French toast served
with bacon and a dollop of jam;
two pitchers of fruit juice;
waffles and maple syrup; a pitcher
of milk; a frying pan filled
with corned beef hash; eggs fried
in the center of pieces of bread,
called "toad in the hole."
Children's breakfasts should include
fruit, either juice or whole.
Though a glass of milk is standard,
hot cocoa with a marshmallow
or a cup of hot bouillon is a good
substitute on very cold days.

# CANDY FOR CHILDREN

EVEN though candymaking is an enormous business in the U.S. today, children still get a special enjoyment from homemade sweets. Homemade candies were giving American youngsters sticky fingers and spoons to lick and tempting them with the smell of vanilla and maple sugar long before candy bars had been heard of.

New Englanders were pulling taffy almost as soon as the first molasses came in from the West Indies. And New Orleans, which already knew the Marshal du Plessis-Praslin's recipe for almond pralines, tried making pralines with southern pecans and created a national delight. America's favorite candy was invented, it is said, by a legendary Pennsylvania cook who stirred a batch of caramels too long, tasted the result and uttered a disgusted "Fudge!"— and the expletive stuck to the mixture as a name.

Cooking candy is mainly a matter of heat; if the temperature isn't exactly right, neither is the candy. Even cooks who only intend to make candy on occasion are well advised to invest in a good inexpensive candy thermometer. The thermometer should be put in the pan before the candy starts to cook. Candy recipes (page 199) call for the same ingredients used in everyday cooking and young confectioners will achieve surprisingly professional results if recipes are followed exactly. The most common ingredients—they should always be of the best quality—are sugar, butter, cream, nuts, flavoring extracts, food colors, fruit juices and rinds and dried fruits. In ancient times, before sugar was known, honey was used to make sweet candy treats.

Candy cooking with children is mostly a matter of common sense. Because candymaking involves cooking at high heat, the children should be old enough to understand and follow instructions, and they need adult supervision. Feed everybody beforehand to discourage overzealous tasting. See that all children have on washable clothes. Set out a minimum number of pots and all ingredients that will be needed. And lay in a supply of patience. With it, making candy with kids can be a delightful way to spend an afternoon. The sweet results, which can keep for long periods, are fun to serve and make excellent and inexpensive gifts.

On the plates above are 11 of America's favorite homemade candies.
Plates in top row hold, left to right, caramels, apricot coconut balls, pralines
(behind jar) and truffles. In second row are butter crunch, fudge
and peanut brittle. Behind girl's head is a bowl of taffy. On the table
are a few candy spirals and lollipops and, at right, caramel apples.
Girl in foreground is engaged in one of the nicest candymaking jobs—pulling taffy.

# RECIPES FOR CHILDREN'S FOOD

**CHILDREN'S DESSERTS**

**SCHOOL LUNCHES, BREAKFASTS**

**CANDY FOR CHILDREN**

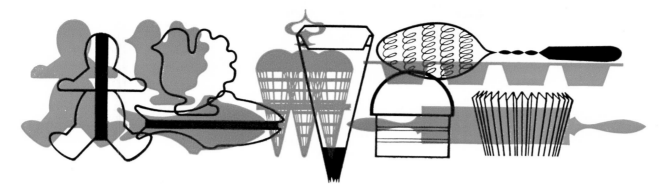

# CHILDREN'S DESSERTS

## CUPCAKES

| | |
|---|---|
| 2 cups sifted cake flour | ⅔ cup milk |
| 2 teaspoons double-acting baking powder | 1 teaspoon vanilla extract |
| ⅓ cup shortening | ½ teaspoon salt |
| 1 cup sugar | Confectioners' sugar icing |
| 1 egg | Candy sprinkles |
| | Nuts |

Add baking powder and salt to the sifted flour and sift again. Cream the shortening until it is soft, add the sugar gradually and cream until light and fluffy. Add the egg and beat well. Add the flour alternately with the milk, a little at a time, beating after each addition until the batter is smooth. Stir in the vanilla. Set fluted paper baking cups in a cupcake pan and fill them about two thirds full. Bake the cupcakes in a moderate oven (375°) for 20 minutes. Remove the cupcakes from the pans and cool them on cake racks. Makes 18 to 24. When cold, frost the cupcakes with confectioners' sugar icing and decorate them with candy sprinkles and nuts.

## CONFECTIONERS' SUGAR ICING

| | |
|---|---|
| 2 cups confectioners' sugar | 1 teaspoon vanilla extract |
| Heavy cream | Food colorings |

Sift the sugar into a large bowl. Add about ⅓ cup of cream, a few spoonfuls at a time, stirring constantly until the icing is thick enough to spread. Stir in the vanilla. Put the icing in several small bowls and stir a few drops of different colorings into each bowl of icing.

## PEACH ICE CREAM

| | |
|---|---|
| 1 package frozen peaches | 1 cup heavy cream |
| 1 cup milk | 1 teaspoon vanilla extract |
| ½ cup sugar | Salt |
| 2 egg yolks, beaten | |

Defrost and drain the peaches. Put the milk in the top part of a double boiler and cook over very low heat until a light film forms on top of the milk. Add the sugar and salt to the milk and stir until the sugar dissolves. Remove from heat and beat slowly into the egg yolks. Set over hot water and cook, stirring constantly, for 5 minutes or until the mixture coats the spoon. Remove from heat and cool the custard. Then chill it for 30 minutes. Whip the cream until thick, add the peaches, vanilla and chilled custard. Pour into an ice tray and freeze for 1 hour. Turn the ice cream out into a chilled bowl and stir well. Return it to the ice tray and freeze until it is firm enough to serve. Makes about 1 quart.

## GINGERBREAD MEN

| | |
|---|---|
| 2 cups sifted flour | ½ cup shortening |
| 1 teaspoon baking powder | ½ cup sugar |
| ½ teaspoon soda | ½ cup molasses |
| 1 teaspoon ground ginger | 1 egg yolk |
| 1 teaspoon ground cloves | ½ teaspoon salt |
| 1½ teaspoons ground cinnamon | Currants |
| ½ teaspoon ground nutmeg | Ornamental frosting |
| | Cinnamon drops |

Sift the flour, baking powder, soda, spices and salt together. Cream the shortening until it is soft. Stir in the sugar and molasses. Add the egg yolk and mix well. Stir in the flour mixture. Roll the dough about ¼ inch thick on a lightly floured board or pastry cloth. Cut it with a gingerbread-man cooky cutter. Arrange the cookies on ungreased cooky sheets and put currants in for eyes. Bake in a moderate oven (350°) for 10 minutes. Cool. Decorate the gingerbread men with ornamental frosting and cinnamon drops.

## ORNAMENTAL FROSTING

| | |
|---|---|
| 1 cup confectioners' sugar | 1 egg white |
| ⅛ teaspoon cream of tartar | ¼ teaspoon vanilla extract |

Sift the sugar and cream of tartar into a bowl. Add the egg white and vanilla. Beat with a rotary or electric beater until thickened. Cover the bowl with a damp cloth until ready to use.

## RAISIN-STUFFED BAKED APPLES

| | |
|---|---|
| 4 baking apples | ¼ teaspoon ground cinnamon |
| ½ cup seedless raisins | ¼ teaspoon ground nutmeg |
| ¼ cup honey | Red food coloring |
| 2 teaspoons melted butter | |

Core each apple and peel the top half. Arrange the apples in a baking pan. Combine the raisins, honey, butter, cinnamon and nutmeg and fill the apples with this raisin mixture. Pour 2 cups of hot water into the pan around the apples. Add a few drops of red food coloring to the water. Bake in a moderate oven (375°) for about 45 minutes or until the apples are tender, basting them frequently with the colored water. Serve hot or cold.

## CHOCOLATE-COOKY ROLL

| | |
|---|---|
| 12 thin chocolate cookies | ½ teaspoon vanilla extract |
| 1 cup heavy cream | 1 teaspoon sugar |

Whip the cream until frothy. Add the vanilla and sugar and beat until thick. Spread one side of each cooky with cream and arrange the cookies on edge on a serving platter to make a long roll. Frost the cooky roll with the rest of the cream. Put the roll in the refrigerator and chill it for 4 hours. To serve, slice the roll at an angle so that the pieces have stripes of cream and chocolate cooky.

## STRAWBERRY MOUSSE

| | |
|---|---|
| 1 package frozen sliced strawberries | 1 cup heavy cream |
| 1 envelope unflavored gelatine | ½ cup sugar |
| | 1 teaspoon vanilla extract |

Defrost and drain the strawberries. Put the juice in a measuring cup and add enough cold water to make 1 cup of liquid. Soften the gelatine in this liquid for 5 minutes, then add 1 cup of boiling water and stir until the gelatine is dissolved. Add the strawberries. Cool the mixture for 30 minutes or until it is slightly thickened. Meanwhile whip the cream until slightly thickened. Add the sugar gradually, beating constantly, until the cream is thick. Add the vanilla. Fold the whipped cream into the strawberry and gelatine mixture. Pour into a fancy mold. Chill in the refrigerator for 2 hours or until firm. Serves 6.

## BROWNIES

| | |
|---|---|
| **2 squares** | **½ teaspoon vanilla extract** |
| **unsweetened chocolate** | **⅔ cup flour** |
| **¼ cup butter** | **1 cup chopped nuts** |
| **1 cup sugar** | **Salt** |
| **2 eggs** | |

Melt the chocolate in a mixing bowl over hot water. Remove from heat. Add the butter and stir until melted. Cool for 5 minutes. Add the sugar, eggs and vanilla and beat thoroughly. Mix in the flour and a pinch of salt. Stir in the nut meats. Put into a greased 8-inch-square pan and bake in a slow oven (300°) for 40 minutes. Cut into squares.

## CHOCOLATE-CHIP COOKIES

| | |
|---|---|
| **1 cup chocolate chips** | **1 cup sifted flour** |
| **½ cup butter** | **½ teaspoon soda** |
| **¼ cup sugar** | **½ cup chopped nuts** |
| **½ cup brown sugar** | **½ teaspoon vanilla extract** |
| **1 egg** | **½ teaspoon salt** |

Cream butter until soft. Add both sugars gradually and cream until light and fluffy. Stir in egg. Sift flour with soda and salt and add it. Stir in chocolate chips, nuts and vanilla. Mix thoroughly. Drop teaspoonfuls of batter onto greased cooky sheet about 2 inches apart. Bake in a moderate oven (375°) for 10 minutes or until lightly browned. Makes about 4 dozen.

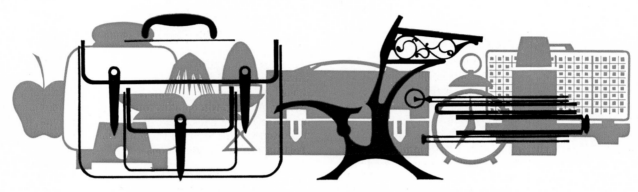

# SCHOOL LUNCHES, BREAKFASTS

## LUNCH BOX SANDWICHES

**LIVERWURST SPREAD:** Mash liverwurst. Add minced onion and sandwich spread. Spread on protein bread.

**CREAM CHEESE:** Mix cream cheese with a little orange juice. Spread on date nut bread. Add marmalade if desired.

**CUCUMBER AND RADISH:** Spread wheat germ bread with butter or mayonnaise. Arrange thin slices of cucumber and radish on bread and sprinkle them with lemon juice and salt.

**CARROT AND CELERY:** Combine chopped carrot and chopped celery with mayonnaise and a little apple juice. Spread on white bread.

**BACON AND LETTUCE:** Spread cheese bread with butter or mayonnaise. Arrange cooked bacon slices and lettuce on bread.

**DEVILED HAM AND EGG:** Slice small loaf of Italian bread lengthwise. Combine deviled ham with chopped hard-cooked egg and mayonnaise. Season with lemon juice. Spread on bread.

**SALMON SALAD:** Slice soft finger roll lengthwise. Mash salmon and add chopped green pepper, chopped celery, mayonnaise and a little lemon juice. Spread on roll.

**BANANA AND COTTAGE CHEESE:** Slice small loaf of Italian bread lengthwise. Mash banana with lemon juice. Mix cottage cheese with chopped stuffed olives and a little mayonnaise. Spread the banana mixture on one end of the sandwich and the cheese mixture on the other.

**CORNED BEEF:** Slice graham roll lengthwise and spread with mustard or mayonnaise. Arrange sliced corned beef and pickle relish on roll.

**TONGUE:** Spread whole wheat bread with mayonnaise or butter. Arrange sliced tongue and water cress on bread.

**BAKED BEANS:** Mash baked beans with chili sauce. Spread on brown bread.

**GOUDA CHEESE:** Spread rye bread with mustard or butter. Arrange sliced Gouda cheese on bread.

**PIMENTO CHEESE AND OLIVE:** Spread pimento cheese spread on white bread. Arrange sliced stuffed olives on top.

**MEAT LOAF:** Spread rye bread with butter or mustard. Arrange sliced meat loaf on bread.

**CHEESE AND BOLOGNA:** Slice small loaf of Italian or French bread lengthwise. Spread with butter or mayonnaise. Arrange sliced cheese and bologna on bread. Add mustard if desired.

## BAKED FISH AND CREAM

| | |
|---|---|
| **½ cup flaked cooked fish** | **Salt** |
| **¼ cup light cream** | **Freshly ground black pepper** |
| **Butter** | |

Place fish and cream in shallow individual baking dish. Dot with butter. Sprinkle with salt and pepper. Bake in a hot oven (400°) for 10 minutes. Serves 1.

## FIG FRENCH TOAST

| | |
|---|---|
| **½ cup bottled fig juice** | **2 slices bread** |
| **1 egg** | **Butter** |

Beat fig juice and egg together. Soak the bread in this mixture for 5 minutes. Sauté bread in butter over low heat for 10 minutes or until golden brown. Serves 1.

## BUTTERMILK WAFFLES

| | |
|---|---|
| **1½ cups buttermilk** | **1 teaspoon soda** |
| **3 eggs** | **1 tablespoon grated** |
| **1¾ cups sifted flour** | **orange rind** |
| **2 teaspoons double-acting** | **½ cup oil** |
| **baking powder** | **1 teaspoon salt** |

Beat eggs thoroughly. Add buttermilk and remaining ingredients. Mix only until batter is smooth. Bake in preheated waffle iron until steaming stops and waffle is golden brown. Serves 4.

## CORNED BEEF HASH

| | |
|---|---|
| **½ cup canned** | **½ teaspoon dried onion flakes** |
| **corned beef hash** | **2 tablespoons bacon fat** |
| **1 tablespoon catsup** | |

Combine hash, catsup and dried onion flakes thoroughly. Sauté in bacon fat in covered skillet over low heat for 10 minutes. Serves 1.

## TOAD IN THE HOLE

| | |
|---|---|
| **1 egg** | **3 tablespoons butter** |
| **1 slice bread** | |

Cut a circle out of the center of the bread. Fry bread in butter until brown and crisp on one side. Turn it over and break an egg into the circle. Fry over low heat about 5 minutes or until the egg is cooked. Serves 1.

# HOME HELPS

THE RECIPES FOR ALL DISHES SHOWN
IN THIS SECTION ARE ON PAGES 229-232

# WORKMANLIKE KITCHENS

**A**S cooks go," a British wit once wrote of a cherished servant,
"she went." And that about sums up the situation in the U.S. today.
Now the disappearance of domestic help has sent most householders
into their own kitchens—and some have been surprised at what they found.
In the 19th Century, when cooks were plentiful, the American kitchen
was a remote, inefficient enclosure, totally lacking in charm.
When the housewife went to work in it, she found herself in the position
of a hostess who tries her own guest room and finds that the bed
sags badly. So by the millions housewives set out to make some changes.

At first the whole emphasis was on efficiency. This led
to a burst of aseptic white kitchens that had the look of laboratories.
Then, as it dawned on the housewives that this was the place
where they would spend a lot of their lives, the kitchen began to take on
new glamor. Finally it emerged as a central part of the house,
an easy place to work, a pleasant place to entertain and really a place
to live. Most modern kitchens today are part of the living area.
Trick lighting shoots from walls and ceilings. And
the furniture is as comfortable as the engineering is exact.

Old-fashioned kitchens had to be enormous. The cook needed
lots of room to chop, peel, mash, soak, trim and clean the food.
Some of the new ones are enormous, too, but they are mostly living space.
They cash in on all the modern studies of efficiency. They are planned
for all the new laborsaving devices and premixed and frozen foods.
They unify work areas for different tasks and eliminate unnecessary motions,
such as walking or bending. They provide plenty of storage space
for the housewife to arrange dishes and cans efficiently.
A well-planned kitchen can become a servant in itself.

But almost as important as their efficiency is their decorative effect
in the house. The modern kitchen makes a virtue of shiny pots
and pans. It exploits rather than hides the simmering dishes, supplies them
with a background of rich brick, fine paneling, glistening copper
or stainless steel. As in Colonial days the kitchen,
like those on the following pages, has once again become the busiest,
most charming and often the prettiest room in the house.

In a handsome kitchen-dining room, two little girls stir onion soup in chafing dish while the hostess lights the candles. This 20-minute party meal is example of modern kitchen efficiency. The soup was bought dehydrated, the trout and potato puffs on the table frozen and the bread semibaked. The same meal, started from scratch, would have taken the three eight hours to prepare.

# RUSTIC CHARM FROM PINE AND PEWTER

This cheerful kitchen in a 200-year-old remodeled farmhouse has nothing of the laboratory look. It has a flexible lighting arrangement, and at night it can be converted from kitchen to dining room and back with the flick of a switch. Pinhole lights in the ceiling on the dining-fireplace side direct light downward, leaving the rest of the area dark, and on the opposite side of the room concealed fluorescent fixtures similarly concentrate light for cooking. The owner's eye for antiques produced a collection of pewter and most of this handsome old furniture at less than present-day prices. Though no attempt was made to hide modern appliances, the room was paneled with wide pine boards from a century-old barn. This kitchen was planned by C. C. Philippe, a vice president of New York's Waldorf-Astoria hotel, for his country home in Peekskill, N.Y.

Copper hood over range conceals light fixtures. Wood cornice extends around three sides of room to hide continuous run of fluorescent lighting. Ceiling color comes from pigment added to plaster.

Antique furnishings for kitchen include English pewter dinner plates on mantel, long-handled omelet pan from Brittany (*left*) and early American harvest table (*right*) once red, now natural pine.

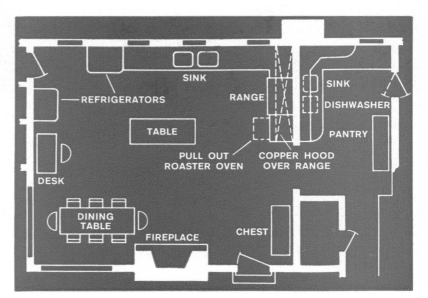

Rectangular room is divided into working and dining sections. When guests assemble for dinner or cocktails around fireplace, servant can work in pantry (*top right*). There are two refrigerators.

Skylighted kitchen is spacious and functional, with appliances and working space in the foreground area and a fully equipped bar in the rear. Dining area is behind brick partition at left.

All of the cabinets are made of rift-oak, but the 3-foot chopping counter is of more durable maple. The open spice shelves within easy reach of the stove add a practical note of color.

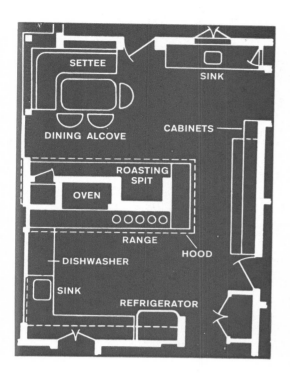

Over-all kitchen plan shows how central island divides the kitchen with a passage between cook's domain and dining area (*at top*).

Stainless range has five electric burners in a row. A large warming oven for dishes and two roasting ovens at waist height eliminate stooping. Floor is tile brick in a herringbone pattern.

# PRACTICAL LUXURY IN A 'GALLEY'

A kitchen right out of a high-budget movie was designed for the $80,000 home of Novelist Robert Buckner on California's Monterey peninsula. Functional as a ship's galley, it is a handsome blend of brick, oak, mahogany and metal.

Details like rift-oak cabinets with metal-lined drawers, painted refrigerator and custom-made hardware ran kitchen's cost up to $20,000, but its compact design could be copied for far less. Except for skylights, all lighting is indirect, with fixtures put under cabinets and directed down to eliminate glare.

A partial brick wall and copper hood divide the space for cooking and for dining (*see plan*), allowing the family to enjoy leisurely Sunday breakfasts or to entertain informally at the indoor barbecue (*right*) while remaining completely apart from the kitchen's work area. The owners of this kitchen find guests usually have to be pried away from the kitchen and into other parts of the house.

Brick partition giving privacy to both cooking and dining areas contains stainless steel range (*above*) and, on this side, an indoor roasting spit which is the owner's favorite single feature.

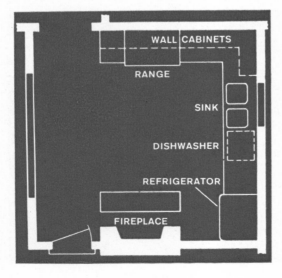

Compact kitchen in a rambling country house makes it easy for cook to feed a large family. Cabinets are natural birch; bench is pine rubbed with beeswax and shellacked. Note passthrough in rear.

WALL CABINETS

RANGE

SINK

DISHWASHER

REFRIGERATOR

FIREPLACE

Plan for kitchen above shows how the fireplace with pine bench dominates wall opposite the range.

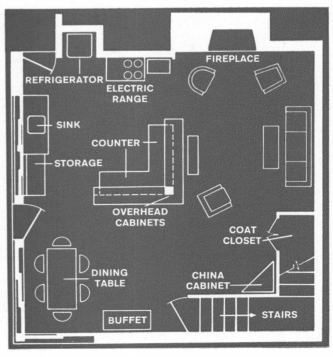

REFRIGERATOR

ELECTRIC RANGE

FIREPLACE

SINK

COUNTER

STORAGE

OVERHEAD CABINETS

COAT CLOSET

DINING TABLE

CHINA CABINET

BUFFET

STAIRS

Plan for the kitchen on opposite page shows how central counter divides the interior into separate living areas.

In a reconstructed barn an L-shaped bar of weathered pine provides semiseparation of the modern kitchen (*in background*) from the dining and living areas and allows the hostess to stay with her guests while she is cooking. Kitchen area floor is covered with easy-to-clean linoleum. The beamlike structure above the counter conceals cabinets which are used for storage.

Almost all U.S. kitchens are designed by men. That housewives are not
entirely happy with man's conception of woman's domain was made clear
at a U.S. housing administration forum at which women explained
what they think ails modern houses. Having considered their complaints,
one of the country's few successful women architects, Margaret King Hunter
of Hanover, N.H., planned an interior to suit her own needs. Her design

so impressed General Electric Company executives that they built it.
Mrs. Hunter's kitchen does away with walls and is stationed in the middle
of the living space. Motor-driven shades lower to enclose kitchen
or screen any side. A ventilating fan is in plastic skylight over kitchen.
Here Mrs. Hunter stands in the hub of her house while son Christopher
and friends have supper. Dining area is in foreground, living room at right.

# LUXURY WITH LEFTOVERS

**M**ANY of the world's most delicious dishes have been developed by cooks who went to the cupboard and found it not bare but full of leftovers. Inventively scrambling and combining the odds and ends, they came up with new culinary triumphs. Today most busy cooks make a stab at camouflaging last night's meal for tonight's serving, but their second-go dishes are rarely distinguished. Too many serve leftovers in unadorned cold slices or slap them together in a "stew" concocted of chunks of meat and a can of peas. As a result most families accept leftover dishes only as a necessary economy.

Of course the leftover dish is a real economy. Meat is cheaper when bought in large roasts. But there is no reason why the second crack at a roast should inevitably produce a second rate dish. Leftovers are things to strive for, not to avoid. They should be planned in advance as part of the week's menu. They will make meals that actually have more excitement and savor than the original dish. Some fine dishes, like shepherd's pie and deviled beef bones, can only be made from leftovers.

Such time-honored dishes have another great advantage. They are quick and easy to prepare, since the meat does not need much more cooking. Confronted with the remains of a roast, the cook has an opportunity to try recipes that seem too time-consuming when started with raw meat. As a matter of fact, one of the tricks of leftover cooking is not to recook the meat too long.

An important thing to consider is that the leftover does not necessarily have to be consumed the very next day, nor, if there is a lot of it, does the cook have to strain her wits to disguise it three days in a row. Once cooked a roast can be stored at least five days in the fresh food section of the refrigerator. Smoked leftovers, like ham, can easily be stretched from one week to the next. Households that have freezers are perfectly equipped to handle leftovers. They can resurrect a leftover a month after the family has forgotten the original dish. On these pages are 12 dishes made from roasts of beef, ham, veal and lamb. In themselves they prove that some of the world's greatest dishes are encores.

Baked ham on board at upper left keeps in the refrigerator
for two weeks after cooking. Three hot dishes made from its leftovers
include at lower left, a ham casserole with sherry, ground ham,
green pepper, rice; a ham and cheese soufflé in oval dish in center,
good for a quick supper or Sunday brunch; and
a Creole jambalaya at lower right, with diced ham, rice, tomatoes, wine.

Two roasts—a 10-pound veal shoulder at upper left and a 7½-pound leg of lamb
at upper right—are shown with six fine meals made from their leftovers.
At right of the veal roast is an Italian dish, a platter of veal
and mozzarella cheese sandwiches to serve with tomato wedges;
In oval casserole at lower left is Hungarian veal goulash with white wine
and thin onion slices; to its right are veal-stuffed peppers

with buckwheat groats, canned tomatoes, onion. Below the leg of lamb
at right is shepherd's pie, a luxury claimed by Scotland
and England, made of cubed lamb and leftover mashed potatoes
which form a "pie shell." To its left is a rich Scotch broth
which uses bones, diced lamb and leeks and makes a full meal soup.
Above the broth is a delicious dish, French lamb cassoulet.

Rib roast in the oval platter at top right produces leftovers even from its bones. To left of the roast are beef bones *diable* —saved up in the freezer from several roasts. Below these is a casserole of baked beef hash, made according to a special Austrian recipe. At lower right, for Sunday supper or lunch, is beef vinaigrette topped with onion rings, as served in France.

# THE NATION'S BOUNTY

IN this rich land there are some foods which, just because they are
so very plentiful, are often unappreciated. All year round
they are on hand in every store and almost every larder. Yet no matter
how many times they are brought to the table they turn up as the same drab,
familiar dishes. They are the Cinderellas of the food world.

Among the leading ones are pork, potatoes, rice, tomatoes and apples.
All of these tumble into the nation's food basket at a fantastic
annual rate. Tomatoes alone are measured in billions of pounds a year.
Pork comes in tens of billions of pounds, apples and potatoes
in millions of bushels. Even rice, which is normally considered to be
a product of Asia, runs into the millions of tons. And each
of these foods, with a little knowledge and imagination, can be transformed,
like Cinderella, into the highlight of an evening.

The pictures on the following pages show these foods with their
Cinderella look. Pork is no longer a plain chop or roast. Instead
it emerges served with apricots, cooked in beer or doused with wine.
Potatoes are not just mashed. They turn up as hot breads,
pancakes, curried casseroles. Rice is served with almonds, cheese and clams.
Apples are stuffed and candied and tomatoes broiled and sautéed.

With the exception of tomatoes and pork, all these potential delicacies
are remarkably easy to store. Rice can be kept for months
on the shelf. Apples and potatoes are so tough that in years gone by
farmers just stuck them away for the winter packed in some sand
in a barrel. New dwarf apple trees which yield fine fruit can be
grown in a small backyard. And tomatoes can be grown anywhere
in the U.S., in the smallest garden or even in a window box.

Apples are one of the most familiar American foods. There are
almost endless varieties of them, 7,000 of which have been named.
Tomatoes, oddly enough, are a relative novelty
in the world of food. They were grown for years by the Indians,
but it took a long time to make the white man realize that they were
something more than a garden ornament. A little more than 100 years ago
in this country they were almost unknown as a vegetable.

Pork in 11 dishes is shown above. Starting at left from top to bottom are: roast fresh shoulder of pork stuffed and garnished with apricots; creamed pork with mushrooms in corn bread ring; Bohemian beer casserole with cubed pork, onions, celery; pork chops chatelaine with a dry white wine sauce, garnished with chestnuts and small onions. Next right row, starting at top: roast fresh ham; Creole pork skillet with chili powder, onions, celery, green peppers; pork steak with garlic sauce; classic roast suckling pig with special stuffing made with cider. In right row: pork birds (pork shoulder sliced thin and wrapped around pieces of pineapple); a pork crown roast with cranberry stuffing; Javanese pork *sates* on skewers with kumquats.

Potatoes and rice are shown above in 12 versions. In the center are potato pancakes with lingonberries. Casserole at top left holds sweet potatoes baked with dry sherry and brown sugar. At lower left is Swedish rice pudding with raisins and slivered almonds. Circling clockwise from it are: a curried potato casserole; Italian potatoes with tomatoes; rice amandine with chicken; hot potato salad with diced bacon; rice flamingo with mushrooms and Parmesan cheese; risotto with pork and dry white wine; potato rolls; paella with clams, chicken and shrimp; and an emerald rice ring.

Tomatoes and apples are most often eaten raw but can be served as any of the dishes shown here. In top row from left are fresh tomato relish; broiled tomatoes with onion and curry powder; and sautéed tomato slices with sour cream. In center row from left is a crock of *gazpacho*, a Spanish soup made with raw vegetables; apple and raisin conserve; and a deep dish apple pie with brown sugar and spices. In front row at left are candied baked apples stuffed with figs and dates and topped with a nut and caramel sauce. At right is baked applesauce amandine with almonds and macaroons and whipped cream.

# HOW TO BUY MEAT

THE price of meat has gone up a lot since World War II and nowadays, to get the most out of the meat money, the American housewife has to know her business. The average family insists on meat as a staple of its diet. The average housewife spends about a quarter of her food money on it. If she learns to select her cuts of meat knowingly she will feed her family interestingly and well—and stretch her money doing it.

Currently about 80% of all meat sold is government inspected. Most kinds of meat are also stamped with Department of Agriculture grade marks. If these stamps are not visible on retail cuts it is possible to tell quality by the appearance of the meat—as is explained on the following pages. Although the top grades are the tenderest meat, less expensive grades are just as nutritious. The less expensive cuts, however, require different treatment. Tender cuts like rib roast and porterhouse are good for roasting or broiling—dry heat cooking. But less tender ones like short ribs, chuck and brisket are better cooked with moist heat—braised or stewed. Most of the cheaper cuts and grades improve in flavor when they have been marinated before cooking in a cup of olive or peanut oil, a cup of wine or a third of a cup of vinegar, a crushed clove of garlic, some pepper and salt.

Any cut of meat can be cooked so that it is attractive in appearance and tender and tasty to eat. Because coarser cuts usually take longer to cook, the housewife when selecting her meat should consider not only its quality but the length of time she is able to give it. If she has plenty of time she can make fine dishes out of economical cuts like lamb neck, beef plate, pork hock and oxtail. Butchers sometimes do not display these and have to be asked for them.

Meat to be stored at home should be loosely wrapped and kept in the coldest part of the refrigerator. A standing rib roast thus stored will safely last up to five days. Things like liver and ground beef should be cooked within 48 hours. Partially cooked smoked meats like ham and sausage last the longest and may be kept about a week. No one should try to age meat at home; unless humidity and temperature are scientifically controlled, it will spoil.

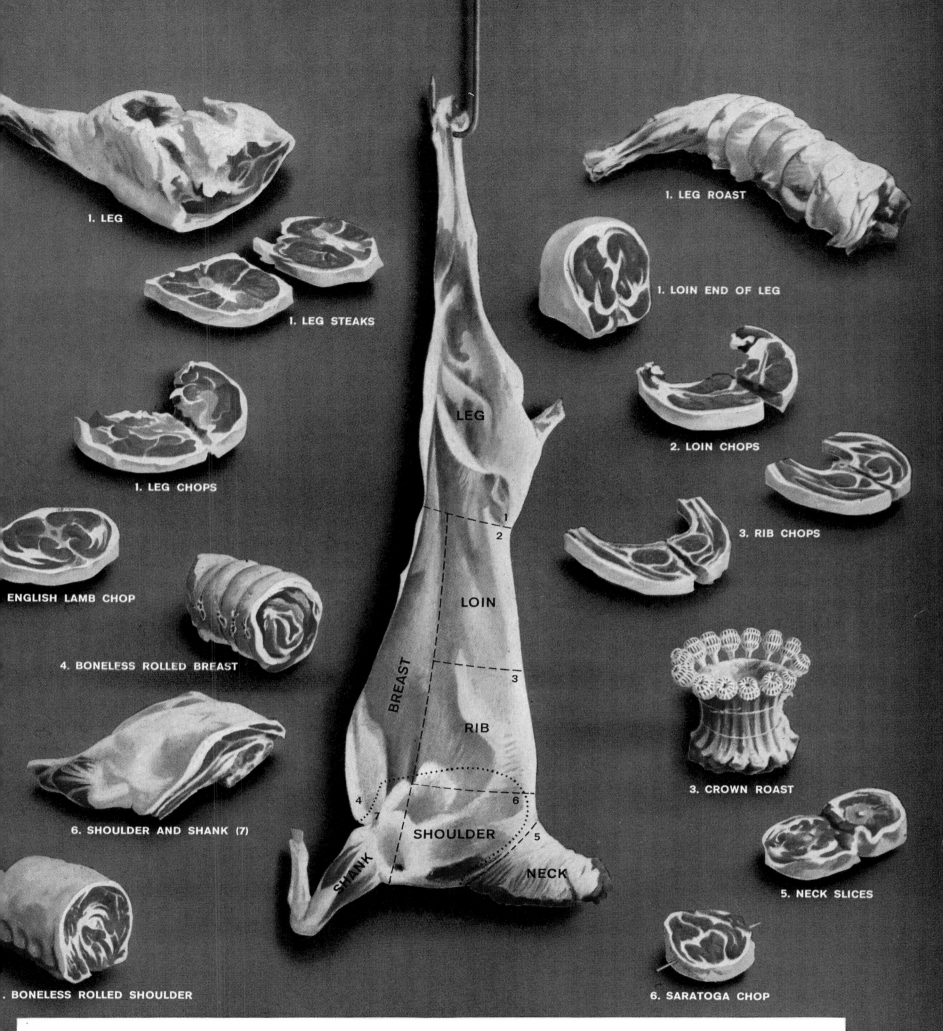

1. LEG

1. LEG STEAKS

1. LEG CHOPS

ENGLISH LAMB CHOP

4. BONELESS ROLLED BREAST

6. SHOULDER AND SHANK (7)

. BONELESS ROLLED SHOULDER

LEG

LOIN

BREAST

RIB

SHANK

SHOULDER

NECK

1. LEG ROAST

1. LOIN END OF LEG

2. LOIN CHOPS

3. RIB CHOPS

3. CROWN ROAST

5. NECK SLICES

6. SARATOGA CHOP

## HOW TO IDENTIFY CUTS OF LAMB

Popular in the northeast and on the western seaboard, lamb is not properly appreciated in the Midwest. On a national average Americans eat only about 4½ pounds of it a year. Cuts of lamb are shown above, keyed to the part of the carcass from which they come. The most expensive are leg, rib and loin chops, English lamb chops, leg and crown roasts, leg steaks and loin end of leg. Medium-priced cuts are neck slices, boneless rolled breast and the shoulder and shank. U.S. Prime is the top grade. U.S. Choice has less fat and generally costs as much. U.S. Good has little fat, is less juicy and less expensive. Utility meat, the cheapest grade, is lean and needs longer cooking, may be braised or stewed. Top quality lamb is pinkish red and fine textured. The fat is clear, crisp looking and creamy white in color. Spring lamb is less than six months old and some markets have it all year. Mutton, which comes from older animals, can be recognized by its dark red meat and hard, white fat.

# BEEF HAS BECOME THE NATION'S FAVORITE

Most popular meat in the country (Americans eat about 85 pounds a year apiece), beef is generally the most expensive. But prices vary according to quality and cuts and beef has more cuts than any other meat. Below are the most familiar cuts, with numbers keying them to the carcass. The most expensive are rib roast, tip roast, tenderloin, eye round and all the steaks except top and bottom round, blade and arm, which are medium priced. Other medium-priced cuts are boneless and standing rump, blade roast, heel of round, arm roast, boneless stew, boneless chuck, brisket. The rest are low-cost cuts. Top quality beef is graded as U.S. Prime. U.S. Choice, the grade of beef most in demand, is almost as juicy as Prime but has less fat. U.S. Good usually has little fat, is less succulent. U.S. Commercial and Utility come from older animals, require long, slow cooking. Beef of good quality is distinguishable by its bright red, firm, fine-grained meat and is liberally marbled with fat which is white rather than yellow.

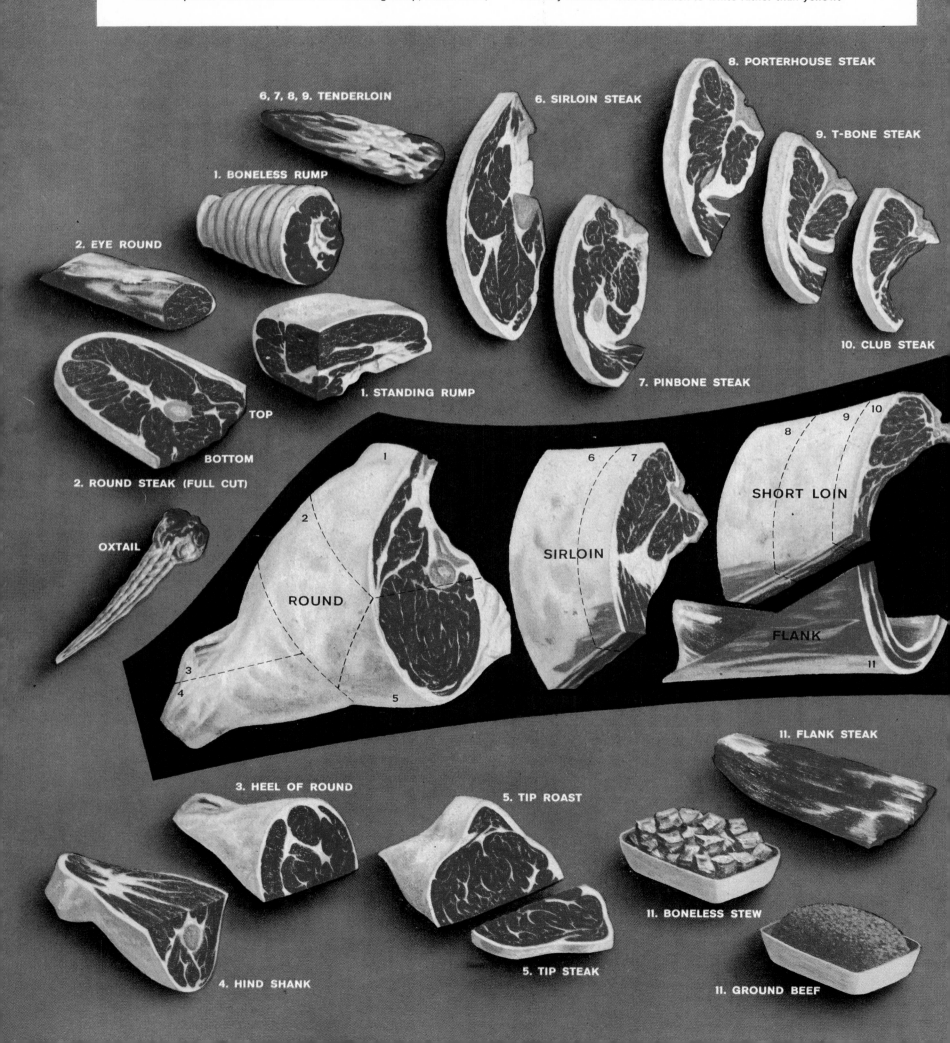

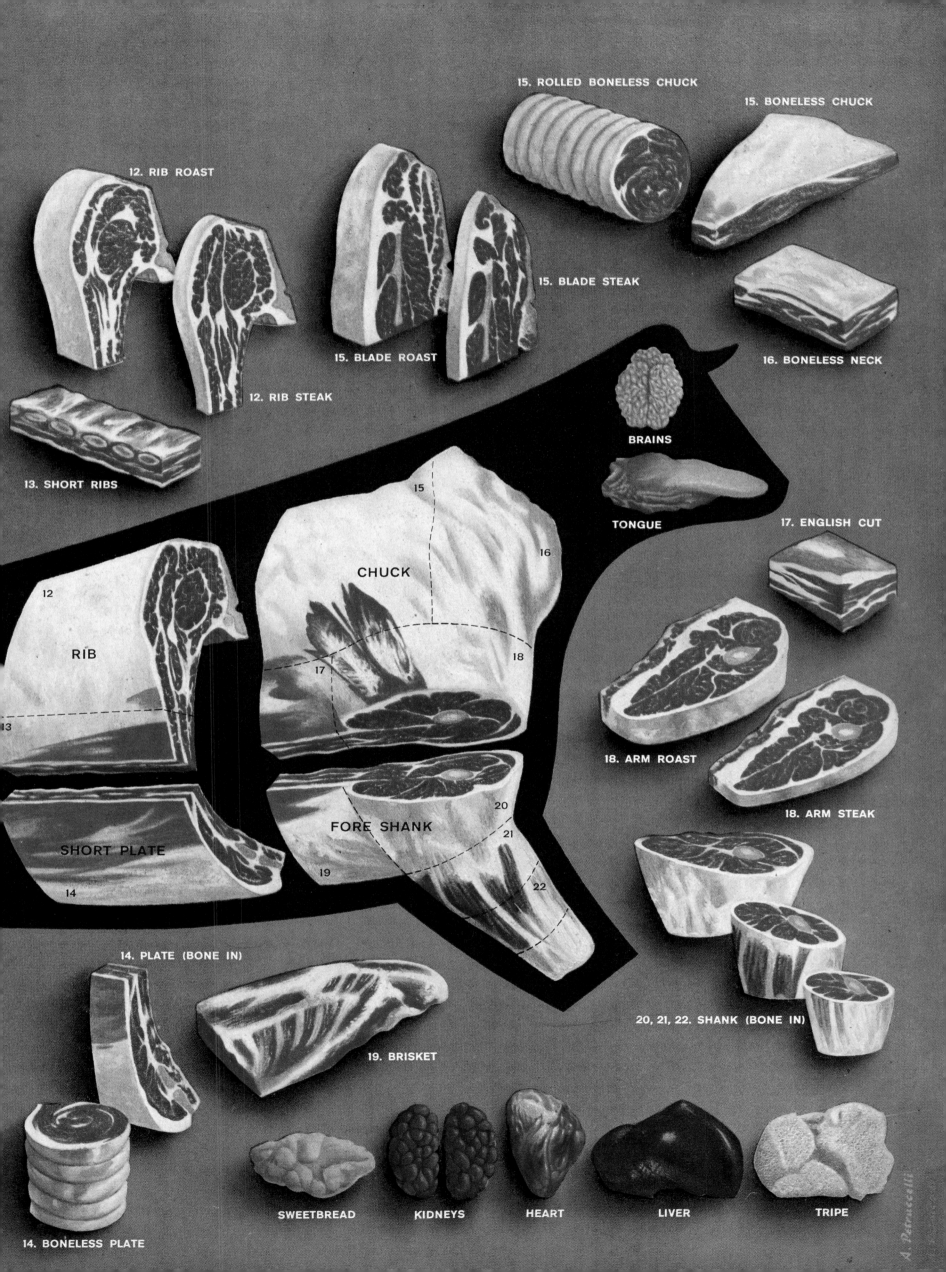

12. RIB ROAST

15. ROLLED BONELESS CHUCK

15. BONELESS CHUCK

15. BLADE STEAK

12. RIB STEAK

15. BLADE ROAST

16. BONELESS NECK

13. SHORT RIBS

BRAINS

TONGUE

17. ENGLISH CUT

15

CHUCK

16

12

RIB

17

18

13

18. ARM ROAST

SHORT PLATE

FORE SHANK

20

21

18. ARM STEAK

14

19

22

14. PLATE (BONE IN)

20, 21, 22. SHANK (BONE IN)

19. BRISKET

SWEETBREAD

KIDNEYS

HEART

LIVER

TRIPE

14. BONELESS PLATE

3. PORK TENDERLOIN

1. BONELESS HAM ROAST

1. BAKING HAM

3. PORK CHOPS

1. HAM SLICE

HAM

1. HAM BUTT (DOUBLE SLICES)

3. LOIN ROAST

BACON

FAT BACK

PORK LOINS

4. BACON

5. SPARERIBS

SPARE RIBS

6. SHOULDER BUTT

9. JOWL BUTT

SHOULDER BUTT

PICNIC SHOULDER

7. PICNIC SHOULDER

HOCK

6. SHOULDER SLICE

FORE FOOT

JOWL BUTT

8. PORK HOCK

6. BONELESS SHOULDER BUTT

# PORK IS PLENTIFUL AND POPULAR

Pork is the second most popular meat in the country and in many cases the least expensive. It is available all year round but most plentiful in late fall and winter when fresh pork is often a housewife's best buy. The average American eats about 65 pounds of pork a year. The most expensive cuts are loin roast, tenderloin, chops, boneless ham roast, baking ham, ham slice, ham butt double slices. Medium-cost cuts are spareribs, shoulder butt, picnic shoulder, shoulder slice and bacon. Popular cheap cuts are

jowl butt and pork hock. Most hogs are less than a year old when slaughtered so pork is fairly uniform in tenderness. A good guide to quality smoked pork is the packer's brand name. One of the best buys is a smoked ham, which keeps well and has little waste since even the bone can be used for soup. For a small family smoked shoulder butt, which has no bone, is a good investment. In buying fresh pork look for flesh that is grayish pink, firm and fine grained. Fresh pork should always be served well done.

# HOW
# TO CARVE

AN expert carver at work is a pleasant sight to see. His fork
seeks out the perfect place to grab the roast or bird and hold it
steady. His knife glides through the meat and around the bones,
and thin, precise slices pile up on the platter. For the moment
he is the envy of the other men at the table. But his deft motions
are not a show-off's tricks. A well-carved roast is much more appetizing
to look at than one that has been hacked up; it serves more people,
retains its juices and actually tastes better.

The thought of carving in public before guests alarms some men
but there is no real reason why carving should be hard. All that is needed
is practice and the proper materials. Successful carving
depends partly on the cook. An overdone or underdone roast cannot
be carved tidily. Neither can a turkey or a pig if the skin
has become dry and hard. And the carver needs the proper tools,
a very sharp carving knife or a slicer, depending on the roast,
a carving fork with long tines, and a steel to keep the knife's edge true.

Thus armed, he should proceed to make things as easy for himself
as possible. After the roast is done, the meat will be firmer
and easier to carve if it is allowed to sit in the kitchen for 15 minutes
before it is brought to the table. The serving platter
should be flat and large enough to hold the meat with some space
left over. Garnishes ought to be put on a separate plate,
where they will be out of the carver's way. Then the meat should
be dissected, not haphazardly but according to a well thought out plan
like the ones on the following pages.

The average carver functions best standing up, although a man
with confidence in his ability sits down when carving. If there is
too little elbow room at the table he should work
at a side table. It is best not to try to serve each slice as it is cut
when many guests are present, but to carve enough for all, stacking
the slices on a warm side dish where they will retain their heat.
This avoids that annoying moment when the first guest comes up
for seconds just as the last is served. It also resolves
the carver's age-old problem and gives him a chance to eat a bite himself.

## VEAL SHOULDER IS TIPPED FOR CARVING

The butcher has cracked the ribs and removed the blade bone.
The pocket has been stuffed. To carve, tip the shoulder on its side and
steady it with a fork. Slice from the rib end until the big bone
(*at right*) is reached. Release slices by drawing knife along dotted line.

## HAM SLICES START WITH SMALL WEDGE

Ham is placed on platter with shank bone at the carver's left.
Slices begin with small wedge followed by even, thin slices until aitchbone
is reached. Then thin slices are taken off the butt end,
after which ham may be turned over and carved from the other side.

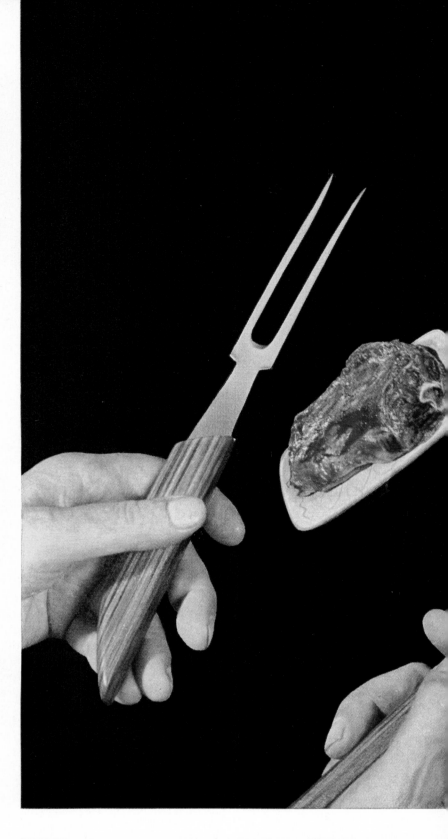

## ROAST BEEF IS SLICED THICK OR THIN

Arrange rib roast of beef so the rib bones are at left. Take
a firm grip on fork and stick it securely between two ribs. Start slicing
at right edge, moving against grain horizontally toward ribs.
Draw knife point along ribs. To save juices do not change fork position.

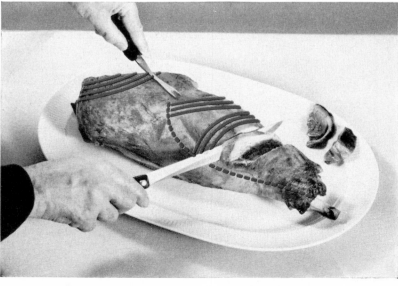

## LEG OF LAMB IS SLICED CROSS GRAIN

Leg of lamb should be placed on platter thick side up with leg bone
at carver's right. Cut a slice off bottom if necessary to hold leg steady.
Then start at shank end and slice until aitchbone is reached.
Run knife along bone to release the slices, and finally slice butt end.

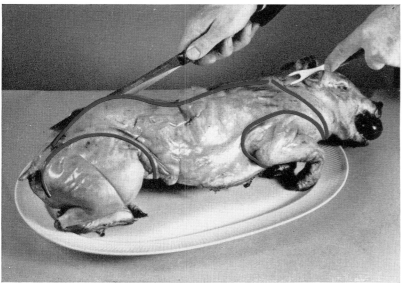

## SUCKLING PIG IS CARVED WHOLE

First cut suckling pig along spine, cracking the tender backbone. Next, cut off the legs as indicated above. Then cut ribs, two for each diner. Some skin and meat are cut from ham and shoulder for each serving. Meat on head is considered a great delicacy—some like ears, some jowls.

## TURKEY IS CARVED ON FAR SIDE FIRST

Turkey is placed on platter with legs toward the carver's right. First remove the far leg and thigh, cutting to joint along lines indicated above. Then cut off the far wing. Next, cut long, thin slices along the breast on the far side. Repeat on other side of bird.

# HOME HELPS: RECIPES

**LUXURY WITH LEFTOVERS**

**THE NATION'S BOUNTY**

# LUXURY WITH LEFTOVERS

## HAM CASSEROLE WITH SHERRY

| | |
|---|---|
| 4 cups ground leftover ham | 1 tablespoon grated onion |
| ½ cup sherry | 1 teaspoon prepared mustard |
| 2 eggs, well beaten | 1 teaspoon Worcestershire |
| 2 cups cooked rice | sauce |
| 2 tomatoes, chopped | 1 cup soft bread crumbs |
| ¼ cup diced green pepper | ¼ cup butter, melted |
| ½ cup heavy cream | Paprika |

Combine all ingredients except bread crumbs, butter and paprika and mix well. Put the mixture in a casserole. Toss crumbs with butter. Sprinkle top of casserole with buttered crumbs and paprika. Bake in a moderate oven (350°) for 45 minutes.

## HAM AND CHEESE SOUFFLE

| | |
|---|---|
| 1 cup chopped leftover ham | ½ cup butter |
| 2 cups grated | 6 eggs, separated |
| Parmesan cheese | 2 tablespoons chopped chives |

Cream the butter and add the egg yolks one at a time, beating well until the mixture is light and fluffy. Stir in ham, cheese and chives and mix well. Beat egg whites until stiff but not dry. Fold into ham and cheese mixture. Pour into a well-greased baking dish. Bake in a moderate oven (350°) for 30 minutes. Serves 6.

## JAMBALAYA

| | |
|---|---|
| 2 cups diced leftover ham | 3½ cups canned tomatoes |
| 3 onions, sliced | ½ teaspoon thyme |
| 1 green pepper, diced | ¼ teaspoon basil |
| 1 garlic clove, minced | ¼ teaspoon paprika |
| ¼ cup butter | ¼ teaspoon Tabasco sauce |
| ½ cup dry white wine | 1 cup rice |

Sauté onions, green pepper and garlic in butter for 10 minutes. Add ham, wine, tomatoes and seasonings and mix well. Bring to a boil and add rice gradually, stirring constantly. Reduce the heat, cover and simmer for 25 minutes. Serves 6.

## VEAL AND MOZZARELLA SANDWICHES

| | |
|---|---|
| 12 thin slices leftover veal | ½ cup butter |
| 12 thin slices | 1 teaspoon anchovy paste |
| mozzarella cheese | 1 teaspoon dry mustard |
| 12 slices white bread, toasted | 1 teaspoon oregano |

Cream butter with anchovy paste, mustard and oregano. Spread on toast. Top with veal and cheese. Broil under low heat until cheese melts. Serves 6.

## VEAL GOULASH

| | |
|---|---|
| 4 cups diced leftover veal | 1 teaspoon Kitchen Bouquet |
| 2 cups thinly sliced onion | 2 cups beef bouillon |
| ¼ cup butter | ½ cup dry white wine |
| 1 tablespoon paprika | 3 tablespoons flour |
| ½ teaspoon thyme | Hot buttered noodles |

Sauté onion in butter for 5 minutes. Add veal, paprika, thyme and Kitchen Bouquet. Cook for 10 minutes, stirring frequently. Mix bouillon and wine with flour and add slowly to veal mixture. Cook, stirring constantly, until thickened. Serve over noodles. Serves 6.

## VEAL STUFFED PEPPERS

| | |
|---|---|
| 2 cups diced leftover veal | 2 teaspoons chili powder |
| 6 green peppers | 2 teaspoons Worcestershire |
| 2 cups cooked | sauce |
| buckwheat groats | ½ teaspoon basil |
| ¼ cup chopped parsley | ½ teaspoon thyme |
| 2 tablespoons grated onion | Parmesan cheese |
| 3½ cups canned tomatoes | Paprika |

Cut off top of peppers. Remove seeds. Parboil peppers for 10 minutes. Drain. Combine veal, groats, parsley, onion, 1 cup tomatoes and seasonings. Stuff peppers with mixture, sprinkle with Parmesan and paprika. Set in baking dish with remaining tomatoes. Bake in moderate oven (350°) for 30 minutes. Serves 6.

## SHEPHERD'S PIE

| | |
|---|---|
| 3 cups cubed leftover lamb | 2 tablespoons butter |
| 3 cups leftover gravy | ½ cup chopped parsley |
| 2 tablespoons minced onion | 3 egg yolks, beaten |
| ¾ cup thinly sliced celery | 3 cups mashed potatoes |
| 1 garlic clove, minced | Freshly ground black pepper |

Sauté onion, celery and garlic in butter for 10 minutes. Stir in lamb, gravy, parsley and pepper. Add egg yolks to potatoes and mix well. Line sides of a casserole with potato. Pour in lamb mixture. Spoon remaining potatoes around the top. Bake in a moderate oven (350°) for 30 minutes. Serves 6.

## SCOTCH BROTH

| | |
|---|---|
| 2 cups diced leftover lamb | ½ cup pearl barley |
| Bone from lamb roast | 1 cup diced carrots |
| 3 leeks, thinly sliced | 1 cup chopped celery |
| ¼ cup butter | ½ cup chopped parsley |
| 4 chicken bouillon cubes | Freshly ground black pepper |

Crack bone. Sauté lamb, leeks and bone in butter for 10 minutes, stirring frequently. Add 3 quarts of water, bouillon cubes and pepper. Bring to a boil, reduce heat, cover and simmer for 1 hour. Add barley and simmer for 1 hour. Add carrots, celery and parsley and simmer uncovered for 30 minutes. Serves 6.

## LAMB CASSOULET

| | |
|---|---|
| 2 cups cubed leftover lamb | 1½ cups dried lentils |
| 2 ounces salt pork, diced | 3 cups chicken bouillon |
| ¼ cup finely chopped onion | 3 cups canned tomatoes |
| 1 garlic clove, minced | 1 tablespoon chopped parsley |

Sauté pork, onion and garlic until pork is crisp. Add all remaining ingredients except lamb. Bring to a boil, reduce heat, cover and simmer for 2 hours. Add lamb and pour into casserole. Bake in moderate oven (350°) for 20 minutes. Serves 6.

## BEEF BONES DIABLE

| | |
|---|---|
| 12 leftover rib roast bones | 2 tablespoons vinegar |
| ½ cup prepared mustard | ½ cup Worcestershire sauce |
| 2 teaspoons dry mustard | 1 teaspoon Tabasco sauce |
| 3 tablespoons molasses | 1 teaspoon salt |

Mix ingredients and brush on bones. Roast in a hot oven (400°) for 20 minutes. Serve hot or cold. Serves 6.

## BAKED BEEF HASH

| | |
|---|---|
| 4 cups diced leftover roast beef | 2 tablespoons soy sauce |
| ¼ cup finely chopped onion | 2 tablespoons chopped parsley |
| ¼ cup butter | ¼ teaspoon ground marjoram |
| ½ cup dry red wine | ¼ teaspoon ground thyme |
| 6 large boiled potatoes, diced | ¼ teaspoon ground savory |
| ½ cup heavy cream | Paprika |

Sauté onion in butter for 10 minutes or until tender. Add diced beef and all of the rest of the ingredients except paprika. Mix well. Turn into a casserole. Sprinkle generously with paprika and bake in a moderate oven (350°) for 30 minutes. Serves 6.

## BEEF VINAIGRETTE

| | |
|---|---|
| 2 cups julienne strips of leftover roast beef | 2 teaspoons chopped tarragon |
| 2 onions, sliced | 2 teaspoons chopped chervil |
| ¼ cup wine vinegar | 2 teaspoons chopped chives |
| ½ cup olive oil | ¼ teaspoon dry mustard |
| 4 tablespoons capers | Tabasco sauce |
| 2 tablespoons chopped parsley | Freshly ground black pepper |

Separate onion slices into rings. Combine with beef, vinegar, oil, capers, herbs, mustard, a few drops of Tabasco, and pepper. Let stand at room temperature for at least 3 hours, stirring occasionally. Chill thoroughly. Serves 6.

# THE NATION'S BOUNTY

## ROAST FRESH PORK WITH APRICOTS

| | |
|---|---|
| 1 four-pound pork shoulder | 2 tablespoons butter |
| 6 canned apricots | 2 cups toasted bread cubes |
| 2 tablespoons chopped onion | Ground nutmeg |
| 2 tablespoons chopped celery | ½ teaspoon salt |

Have butcher bone and cut pocket in pork shoulder. Sauté onion and celery in butter for 5 minutes. Add ¼ cup canned apricot juice, bread cubes, salt and a pinch of nutmeg. Stuff pork shoulder with this mixture. Roast in slow oven (325°) for 3 hours. Add apricots and cook for 15 minutes. Serves 6.

## PORK AND CORN BREAD RING

| | |
|---|---|
| 3 cups diced cooked pork | 4 tablespoons flour |
| 1 package corn muffin mix | 2 cups milk |
| 1 cup sliced mushrooms | 2 egg yolks, well beaten |
| 2 tablespoons minced onion | ½ teaspoon salt |
| 4 tablespoons butter | |

Prepare mix as directed on the package. Bake in a ring mold in a hot oven (400°) for 30 minutes. Meanwhile, sauté mushrooms and onion in butter for 5 minutes. Add flour, stir until smooth. Add milk and cook, stirring, until thickened. Stir some of this sauce into egg yolks. Stir egg yolk mixture into sauce. Add pork and salt and cook over hot (not boiling) water for 20 minutes, stirring occasionally. Serve in hot corn bread ring. Serves 6.

## BOHEMIAN BEER CASSEROLE

| | |
|---|---|
| 3 cups cubed cooked pork | 1½ cups pumpernickel bread crumbs |
| 12 ounces flat beer | ¼ teaspoon sugar |
| ¼ cup chopped onion | 1 teaspoon salt |
| ¼ cup chopped celery | Freshly ground black pepper |
| 2 tablespoons butter | |

Sauté onion and celery in butter for 5 minutes. Add cubed pork, beer and remaining ingredients. Place in casserole. Cover and bake in a moderate oven (375°) for 40 minutes. Serves 6.

## PORK CHOPS CHATELAINE

| | |
|---|---|
| 6 pork chops | 12 chestnuts, boiled and peeled |
| 2 tablespoons butter | White wine sauce |
| 6 small white onions, boiled | |

Sauté chops in butter for 40 minutes. Remove and keep warm. Add onions, chestnuts and white wine sauce to drippings in pan. Heat thoroughly. Serve with chops. Serves 6.

## WHITE WINE SAUCE

| | |
|---|---|
| ½ cup dry white wine | ¼ cup flour |
| 1 onion, chopped | 1¼ cups beef bouillon |
| 1 small carrot, chopped | 2 tablespoons chopped parsley |
| ¼ cup chopped celery | |
| 1 garlic clove, minced | 1 bay leaf, crumbled |
| 2 tablespoons butter | 6 peppercorns |

Sauté onion, carrot, celery and garlic in butter for 10 minutes. Add flour and cook, stirring constantly, until brown. Add bouillon and stir until thickened. Add wine and remaining ingredients, cover and simmer for 1 hour. Strain. Makes about 2 cups.

## ROAST FRESH HAM

| | |
|---|---|
| 1 twelve-pound fresh ham, skinned and scored | 3 cloves |
| 2 large onions, sliced | 2 cups dry white wine |
| 1 stalk celery, cut up | ¼ cup flour |
| 2 garlic cloves, sliced | 3 cups chicken bouillon |
| | Orange sections |

Roast ham with onions, celery, garlic, cloves and wine in a slow oven (325°) for 5 hours or until meat thermometer registers 185°. Baste frequently. Remove ham from pan and pour off all but 2 tablespoons fat. Add flour and stir until smooth. Add bouillon and cook, stirring constantly, until thickened. Serve sauce with ham. Garnish ham with orange sections. Serves 12.

## CREOLE PORK SKILLET

| | |
|---|---|
| 4 cups diced cooked pork | ¼ cup oil |
| 3 cups canned tomatoes | 1 teaspoon chili powder |
| 2 large onions, sliced | 1 teaspoon sugar |
| ½ cup chopped green pepper | 2 tablespoons flour |
| ½ cup chopped celery | 1½ teaspoons salt |

Sauté onions, green pepper and celery in oil for 10 minutes. Add pork, tomatoes, chili powder, sugar and salt. Bring to a boil, reduce heat, cover and simmer for 45 minutes. Combine flour and ¼ cup water and stir into mixture. Cook, stirring, until slightly thickened. Serves 6.

## PORK STEAK WITH GARLIC SAUCE

| | |
|---|---|
| 2 pork steaks | ¾ cup beef bouillon |
| 3 garlic cloves, minced | ¼ cup chopped celery leaves |
| 1 onion, chopped | ¼ cup chopped parsley |
| 2 tablespoons butter | 1 small bay leaf, crumbled |
| 2 tablespoons flour | ¼ teaspoon thyme |
| 1 cup canned tomatoes | Freshly ground black pepper |

Sauté garlic and onion in butter for 10 minutes. Add flour and stir until smooth. Add remaining ingredients. Cover and simmer for 1 hour. Fry steaks for 40 minutes. Serve with sauce. Serves 6.

## ROAST SUCKLING PIG

| | |
|---|---|
| 1 ten-pound suckling pig | 3 cups soft bread crumbs |
| ½ cup chopped celery | ¼ teaspoon thyme |
| ¼ cup chopped onion | Apple juice |
| 1 garlic clove, cut | ½ teaspoon salt |
| 3 tablespoons butter | Apple |

Sauté celery, onion and garlic in butter for 5 minutes. Combine with bread crumbs, thyme and salt and enough apple juice to moisten. Stuff pig and close cavity. Place piece of wood in pig's mouth. Cover ears and tail with foil to prevent burning. Roast in a moderate oven (325°) for 4 hours, basting frequently. To serve, remove piece of wood and insert apple. Serves 6.

## PORK BIRDS

| | |
|---|---|
| 12 slices lean pork shoulder | ½ cup chopped parsley |
| ½ teaspoon oregano | ¼ cup chopped celery leaves |
| ½ teaspoon thyme | 2 tablespoons grated onion |
| 6 slices canned pineapple, cut in half | 1 bay leaf, crumbled |
| ½ cup dry white wine | 1 tablespoon cornstarch |
| 2 tablespoons bacon fat | 1 teaspoon salt |
| | Freshly ground black pepper |

Sprinkle pork slices with oregano, thyme, salt and pepper. Place a piece of pineapple on each pork slice, roll and fasten with a toothpick. Brown in fat. Arrange in roasting pan. Combine 1 cup canned pineapple juice, wine, parsley, celery leaves, onion and bay leaf. Pour over meat. Cover and bake in a moderate oven (350°) for 1 hour. Remove pork and put on a platter. Strain sauce. Add cornstarch mixed with ¼ cup water. Cook, stirring, until thickened. Serve with pork. Serves 6.

## PORK CROWN ROAST WITH CRANBERRIES

| | |
|---|---|
| 7-pound pork crown roast | ½ cup dry white wine |
| 1½ cups raw cranberries | ¼ cup sugar |
| 4 cups bread cubes | ½ teaspoon marjoram |
| 2 tablespoons grated onion | ¼ teaspoon thyme |
| 1 garlic clove, minced | 1 teaspoon salt |
| ½ cup butter | Freshly ground black pepper |

Chop cranberries. Sauté bread cubes, onion and garlic in butter for 10 minutes. Add cranberries and remaining ingredients. Fill center of roast with this mixture. Roast in slow oven (325°) for 3½ hours or until meat thermometer registers 185°. Serves 6.

## PORK SATES

| | |
|---|---|
| 2 pounds lean pork, cubed | 2 tablespoons ground coriander |
| 6 Brazil nuts, grated | |
| 1 cup minced onion | ¼ teaspoon crushed red pepper |
| 2 garlic cloves, minced | |
| ¼ cup lemon juice | ¼ cup olive oil |
| ¼ cup soy sauce | Kumquats |
| 2 tablespoons brown sugar | |

Marinate pork cubes in combined nuts, onion, garlic, lemon juice, soy sauce, sugar and seasonings for 10 minutes. Put pork on skewers. Bake in a very hot oven (450°) for 20 minutes, basting frequently with oil. Garnish with kumquats. Serves 6.

## POTATO PANCAKES

| | |
|---|---|
| 1½ cups grated potatoes | ½ cup flour |
| 2 eggs | 1 teaspoon salt |
| 2 cups milk | Canned lingonberries |

Beat eggs with ¼ cup milk. Blend in flour. Add remaining milk and salt. Beat until smooth. Squeeze potatoes dry and add to batter. Bake on lightly greased griddle using ¼ cup batter for each pancake. Fold cooked pancakes in quarters. Serve with lingonberries. Serves 6.

## SHERRIED SWEET POTATOES

| | |
|---|---|
| 6 sweet potatoes | Butter |
| ¾ cup light-brown sugar | 1½ cups dry sherry |

Parboil sweet potatoes. Peel and slice. Arrange potatoes in a greased casserole, topping each layer with brown sugar and butter. Pour sherry over potatoes. Bake in a hot oven (400°) for 45 minutes. Serves 6.

## CURRIED POTATO CASSEROLE

| | |
|---|---|
| 5 cups diced boiled potatoes | 5 tablespoons flour |
| 2 teaspoons curry powder | 2 tablespoons tomato paste |
| ½ cup chopped onion | 2½ cups chicken bouillon |
| ¼ cup butter | Freshly ground black pepper |

Sauté onion in butter for 5 minutes. Add curry, flour, tomato paste and pepper. Mix well. Add bouillon gradually and cook until thickened, stirring constantly. Add potatoes and pour into casserole. Bake in moderate oven (375°) for 30 minutes.

## ITALIAN POTATOES

| | |
|---|---|
| 6 potatoes, peeled | 1 teaspoon oregano |
| 2 tomatoes, peeled and cut up | 1½ teaspoons salt |
| 6 tablespoons olive oil | Freshly ground black pepper |
| 1 garlic clove, crushed | |

Boil potatoes in salted water for 30 minutes or until tender. Mash. Beat in remaining ingredients. Serve hot or cold. Serves 6.

## HOT POTATO SALAD

| | |
|---|---|
| 6 hot boiled potatoes | ½ cup cider vinegar |
| 6 strips bacon, diced | 2 tablespoons sugar |
| ¼ cup finely chopped onion | 1 teaspoon salt |

Fry bacon until crisp. Slice potatoes and add onion and salt. Add vinegar and sugar to bacon and fat in skillet and bring to a boil. Pour over potatoes and mix. Serve at once. Serves 6.

## POTATO ROLLS

| | |
|---|---|
| 2 large potatoes, boiled and mashed (1 cup) | ½ cup sugar |
| | 5½ cups sifted flour |
| 2 envelopes granular yeast | 2 eggs, beaten |
| 1 cup milk | 1½ teaspoons salt |
| ⅔ cup butter | |

Dissolve yeast in ½ cup lukewarm water. Scald milk and add butter, sugar and salt. Stir until sugar is dissolved. Add mashed potatoes and mix well. Cool to lukewarm. Add the yeast and half of the flour. Mix well. Beat in eggs. Add remaining flour and mix thoroughly. Knead dough on lightly floured board for 10 minutes or until smooth and elastic. Place in greased bowl turning once to bring greased side up. Cover with damp cloth. Let rise in warm place (80–85°) for 1 hour or until dough is doubled in bulk. Punch dough down. Form into 36 rolls. Place in greased muffin pans and let rise in warm place for 30 minutes. Brush rolls with melted butter. Bake in a moderate oven (375°) for 20 minutes.

## PAELLA

| | |
|---|---|
| 2 cups rice | 2 garlic cloves, crushed |
| 1 three-pound chicken, cut up | ¼ cup oil |
| 1 pound raw shrimp, shelled | 1 cup peas |
| 12 clams or mussels | ¼ cup diced pimento |
| 2 onions, quartered | ½ teaspoon oregano |
| 1 celery stalk with leaves, cut up | Whole saffron |
| | 2 teaspoons salt |
| 2 carrots, cut up | Freshly ground black pepper |

Combine chicken, onions, celery, carrots, salt and pepper in 6 cups of water. Bring to a boil, reduce heat, cover and simmer for 1 hour. Strain and save 4 cups of stock. Bone chicken and cut up meat. Fry rice and garlic in oil over medium heat, stirring constantly, until rice is lightly browned. Add chicken, chicken stock, peas, pimento, oregano and a pinch of saffron. Cover and cook over low heat for 15 minutes. Add shrimp and clams in the shells. Cover and cook for 10 minutes. Serves 6.

## SWEDISH RICE PUDDING

| | |
|---|---|
| 1 cup rice | 2 tablespoons butter |
| 5 cups milk | ⅓ cup slivered |
| 2 eggs, beaten | blanched almonds |
| ½ cup sugar | ⅓ cup raisins |
| ½ teaspoon ground cinnamon | 1 teaspoon salt |

Combine rice and 1 cup boiling water in a deep saucepan. Bring to a boil, reduce heat and simmer for 15 minutes. Add milk and simmer for 45 minutes. Add to eggs. Stir in remaining ingredients. Pour into casserole. Set in pan of hot water and bake in hot oven (400°) for 45 minutes. Serves 6.

## RICE AND CHICKEN AMANDINE

| | |
|---|---|
| 3 cups cooked rice | 6 tablespoons flour |
| 2½ cups diced cooked chicken | 2 cups chicken bouillon |
| ½ cup slivered | 1 cup heavy cream |
| blanched almonds | 2 tablespoons diced pimento |
| 1 tablespoon minced onion | 1 tablespoon minced parsley |
| ¼ cup butter or chicken fat | 1 teaspoon salt |

Sauté almonds and onion in butter for 10 minutes. Stir in flour. Add bouillon and cream. Cook, stirring until thickened. Add chicken and remaining ingredients. Pour into casserole. Bake in moderate oven (375°) for 30 minutes. Serves 6.

## RICE FLAMINGO

| | |
|---|---|
| 1½ cups rice | 6 tablespoons oil |
| 1 pound mushrooms, sliced | ½ cup tomato paste |
| ½ cup finely chopped onion | ½ cup grated Parmesan cheese |
| ½ cup finely chopped celery | 2 teaspoons salt |
| ½ cup grated carrots | Freshly ground black pepper |

Sauté mushrooms, onion, celery and carrots in 4 tablespoons of oil for 10 minutes. Add tomato paste, pepper and ⅓ cup water. Cover and simmer for 20 minutes. Sauté rice in remaining 2 tablespoons oil until lightly browned. Add salt, 3 cups of hot water. Cover and simmer for 15 minutes. Add vegetables and simmer for 10 minutes. Add cheese. Serves 6.

## RISOTTO WITH PORK

| | |
|---|---|
| 1½ cups rice | 2 tablespoons oil |
| 2 cups julienne strips | 3 cups beef bouillon |
| of cooked pork | 1 cup dry white wine |
| 1 garlic clove, minced | ¾ cup thinly sliced scallions |

Sauté rice and garlic in oil until rice is lightly browned. Add bouillon, pork, wine and scallions. Cover and simmer for 30 minutes. Serves 6.

## EMERALD RICE

| | |
|---|---|
| 4 cups cooked rice | ⅓ cup grated Parmesan cheese |
| 4 eggs, separated | 1 teaspoon paprika |
| 1 cup minced raw spinach | 1 teaspoon salt |
| ½ cup minced green pepper | 1 cup sour cream |
| ¼ cup minced onion | 3 tablespoons minced chives |
| 1 cup heavy cream, whipped | |

Beat egg yolks. Add rice, spinach, green pepper, onion, cream, cheese, paprika and salt. Fold in stiffly beaten egg whites. Pour into ring mold, set in pan of water and bake in moderate oven (350°) for 45 minutes. Serve with sour cream and chives. Serves 6.

## FRESH TOMATO RELISH

| | |
|---|---|
| 3 cups diced tomatoes | 3 tablespoons vinegar |
| ½ cup chopped onion | 1 teaspoon sugar |
| ½ cup chopped green pepper | Salt |
| 3 tablespoons olive oil | Freshly ground black pepper |

Combine ingredients and let stand at room temperature for 1 hour. Chill for at least 3 hours. Makes 4 cups.

## BROILED TOMATOES

| | |
|---|---|
| 6 tomatoes, cut in half | ¼ cup butter |
| ¾ cup minced onion | 2 tablespoons |
| ¼ teaspoon curry powder | chopped parsley |
| ¼ teaspoon sugar | ½ teaspoon salt |

Combine onion, curry powder, sugar and salt. Top each tomato half with 1 tablespoon of this onion mixture and 1 teaspoon butter. Broil under medium heat for 8 to 10 minutes. Sprinkle with chopped parsley before serving. Serves 6.

## SAUTEED TOMATOES WITH CREAM

| | |
|---|---|
| 12 tomato slices, 1 inch thick | 1 tablespoon grated onion |
| 1½ cups cream | ½ teaspoon salt |
| Flour | Freshly ground black pepper |
| ¼ cup bacon fat | |

Dip tomato slices in flour. Sauté in butter for 5 minutes. Remove from skillet. Sauté onion for 1 minute. Add cream, salt and pepper and simmer for 5 minutes, stirring constantly. Serve over tomatoes. Serves 6.

## GAZPACHO

| | |
|---|---|
| 4 cups diced tomato | ½ cup lemon juice |
| 1½ cups chopped | ¼ cup olive oil |
| green pepper | 1 tablespoon paprika |
| ¾ cup chopped onion | ½ cup sliced cucumber |
| 1 garlic clove, minced | 1 tablespoon salt |
| 2 cups beef bouillon | Freshly ground black pepper |

Combine all ingredients except cucumber. Let stand at room temperature for 1 hour, stirring frequently. Chill for at least 2 hours. Add cucumber just before serving. Serves 6.

## APPLE CONSERVE

| | |
|---|---|
| 1½ pounds apples, peeled | ½ teaspoon ground cinnamon |
| and sliced | ¼ teaspoon ground nutmeg |
| 1 cup raisins | Ground cloves |
| ½ lemon, sliced | 1 cup chopped nuts |
| 1 cup sugar | ½ teaspoon salt |

Combine apples, raisins, lemon, sugar, cinnamon, nutmeg, salt, a pinch of cloves and 1 cup water in large saucepan. Bring to a boil, reduce heat and simmer for 2 hours, stirring occasionally. Remove from heat and stir in nuts. Serve warm or cold. Makes about 3 cups.

## DEEP DISH APPLE PIE

| | |
|---|---|
| 6 cups peeled apple slices | 2 tablespoons butter |
| ½ cup brown sugar | ½ recipe pie crust |
| ½ teaspoon ground cinnamon | 2 tablespoons heavy cream |
| ¼ teaspoon ground nutmeg | |

Combine apples, sugar, cinnamon and nutmeg in deep baking dish. Dot with butter. Top with pie crust rolled ⅛ inch thick. Brush crust with cream and bake in a hot oven (425°) for 40 minutes. Serves 6.

## CANDIED BAKED APPLES

| | |
|---|---|
| 6 baking apples | ¾ cup granulated sugar |
| 3 figs, chopped | ¼ cup butter |
| 3 dates, chopped | ½ cup brown sugar |
| 2 tablespoons chopped | ¼ cup chopped pecans |
| candied ginger | |

Core apples and peel the top half. Combine figs, dates and ginger and stuff apples. Combine sugar with 1 cup of water and boil for 5 minutes. Place apples in shallow baking pan and pour sugar syrup over them. Bake for 45 minutes, basting frequently with syrup. Combine butter and brown sugar and cook over low heat for 5 minutes, stirring constantly. Stir in nuts. Top apples with mixture and broil under low heat for 5 minutes. Serves 6.

## BAKED APPLESAUCE AMANDINE

| | |
|---|---|
| 2 pounds apples, quartered, | ½ cup brown sugar |
| peeled and cored | ¼ teaspoon almond extract |
| 1 cup chopped | 1 cup macaroon crumbs |
| toasted almonds | 1 cup cream, whipped |

Simmer apples with 1 cup water for 20 minutes. Put through coarse sieve or food mill. Stir in sugar and extract. Put applesauce in shallow baking dish, sprinkle with macaroon crumbs and top with almonds. Bake in a moderate oven (350°) for 15 minutes. Serve with whipped cream. Serves 6.

# DINING OUT

THE RECIPES FOR ALL DISHES SHOWN
IN THIS SECTION ARE ON PAGES 273-283

# EUROPE'S RESTAURANTS

**T**HE greatest restaurants of Europe have no equals anywhere
in the world. Their chefs are dedicated to what they consider one
of man's noblest callings and their names reflect their fabled eminence—
like that of the Tower of Silver shown on the opposite page.

Thirteen of the Continent's finest eating places appear on these pages
with their specialties. These are not the out-of-the-way
little places that secretive gourmets cherish. They are the biggest
of the bigtime, standing full in the limelight, serving
fabulous food and charging plenty for it. Just to eat at any one of them
can be the high spot of a European trip and travelers often plan
their tours with these restaurants in mind.

In these restaurants the surroundings themselves add drama or delight
with spectacular vistas or warm charm. The waiters lift lids
with a flourish so that as the food is displayed the air
fills with the aroma of sauces and spices and herbs. The wine stewards
present the bottles as if they were handling crown jewels. The chefs
are autocrats. They have served long apprenticeships to culinary masters
and now they add their own touches to the secrets they have learned.
They will work magic for the guest who really appreciates food. They
have small respect for the guest who orders badly. Sometimes,
if a guest is late for a prearranged meal, they refuse to serve him.
Some have been known to eject customers caught smoking between courses.

The recipes for their greatest dishes have evolved
throughout the ages and many of them are guarded with great care.
Some of them, released especially for this article, may be found
on pages 273-276. By following their instructions carefully
and displaying the resulting dishes as the pictures show, the home cook
can practice the highest form of Europe's *haute cuisine*.

## TOUR D'ARGENT

### PARIS

One of the oldest eating places in this city famous for gastronomy is
the Tour d'Argent. Its dining rooms give a superb view of Notre Dame and
its kitchens dispense food worthy of the setting. Pressed duck—in the background—
is the specialty. Since 1890 every duck has been numbered, and more than
a quarter million ducks have been served. Tour d'Argent is as expensive as
any restaurant in Europe. A meal with duck specialty and wines costs about $16.

# BAUMANIERE

## LES BAUX

In southern France on a patio beneath craggy hills and 300-year-old ruins of Les Baux near Arles, the Baumanière serves classic French food with a country flavor. Some of the dishes reflect the spicy local Provencal cooking. A favorite, *gigot d'agneau* (leg of lamb), in foreground, is boned, stuffed with kidneys, mushrooms, truffles, *foie gras*, flavored with armagnac and cooked in a layer of puff pastry. Other specialties are chicken in bouillon (*left*), galantine of duck, which has been soaked in port, and Chantilly cream cake topped with grilled hazelnuts.

# PYRAMIDE

## VIENNE

Under its late owner, Fernand Point, the Pyramide earned the title "loftiest tabernacle of gastronomy in France." Set in an old Roman town 17 miles south of Lyon, the restaurant turns a gloomy facade to the street, serves its patrons in an elegant inside dining room or garden. Its menu is a roster of the classical dishes of France's great cuisine. Among its specialties are chicken *en gelée*, in foreground, and, clockwise from left, pâté of duck, *langouste* (crayfish), eggs *en gelée*. The guest is given no choice of main dishes, eats what is on the day's menu.

# PASSETTO
**ROME**

A few steps from the ancient Piazza Navona
with its great Bernini fountain is Passetto,
the most elegant restaurant in a city
which prizes elegance. Its specialties are Italian
and its most colorful feature is
this tremendous buffet. At front are three

antipasto trays, one at left, one to the right
behind it, another in the right foreground.
In center are chicken breasts in gelatine. At left
are wild raspberries with a cream puff dessert
behind them. In the center is a pyramid
of fresh figs and beside them stands a mousse

# PAPPAGALLO
## BOLOGNA

Pappagallo started out in Bologna as a market-street restaurant serving plain food to working people. It is now lodged in the handsome carriage house of a 14th Century palazzo and entertains world celebrities. Its cooking is in the honest Bolognese tradition with no hint of French cuisine. Among its dishes are veal cutlet *alla Bolognese*, in center of silver tray, flanked on left by supreme of chicken soufflé and, on right, by filet of turkey. In white bowl at right is baked green lasagne. Walls are covered with photographs of eminent guests who have eaten there. One noted doctor even recommended the restaurant to a declining patient as a cure better than any medicine he knew.

of *pâté de foie gras*. At right are three salads. In background are vegetables and fruits used in Passetto's kitchen, with a leg of calf in the middle. In the picture at right are fish from Italian waters that Passetto serves—fresh mullet, carp, grayling and sole.

# ROYAL DANIELI

**VENICE**

For drama at dinner no place can surpass Danieli's, set above the wide San Marco Canal in Venice. Its balustraded dining terrace and sumptuous dining rooms give a high clear view of the slim-spired island church of San Giorgio Maggiore.

## SCENE-STEALER SALAD

Set the stage for a star performance when you serve **Caesar Salad.** Here's where the man in the family will want to get into the act to show off his culinary skills at the table. You can help him by having all the ingredients ready—wine vinegar, and garlic olive oil (prepared a day ahead) in cruets, a lemon cut in half, 1 or 2 coddled eggs, and a cup of Caesar croutons that you've made beforehand. Fill the wooden salad bowl with drained, torn romaine, and let the show begin.

### CAESAR SALAD

3 medium heads romaine, chilled
2 to 3 tablespoons wine vinegar
1 lemon, halved
1 or 2 1-minute coddled eggs
6 tablespoons grated parmesan cheese

Break romaine leaves in 2- or 3-inch pieces into chilled salad bowl. Drizzle with ⅓ cup *Garlic Olive Oil,* then vinegar. Squeeze lemon over greens; break in eggs. Season with salt, freshly ground pepper and a dash of worcestershire sauce. Sprinkle with parmesan. Toss till well combined. Add 1 cup *Caesar Croutons;* toss lightly. Garnish with anchovies, if desired. Makes 6 main dish servings. For **Garlic Olive Oil:** Prepare a day ahead. Slice 6 cloves of garlic lengthwise into quarters; let stand in 1 cup olive oil. For **Caesar Croutons:** Cut each slice of bread in 5 strips one way, then across 5 times to make squares. Spread out on baking sheet; sprinkle with a little *Garlic Olive Oil.* Heat in extremely slow oven (225°) for 2 hours. Sprinkle with grated parmesan. Cool. Store, covered, in jar in refrigerator.

# DESSERT SHOWMANSHIP

When it comes to entertaining, there's no better combination than elegance, ease, and a little showmanship. This gourmet recipe—**Cherries Jubilee**—has all three ingredients, and it's delicious. Dramatic, too—you flame this chafing dish dessert with brandy right at the table as your guests watch. Cook-at-the-table elegance is a snap with today's great selection of cookware, designer styled and decorated, to go along with your best contemporary or traditional silver and china. *Continued on next page*

Photographs: de Gennaro

## CHERRIES JUBILEE

1 1-pound can (2 cups) pitted dark
    sweet cherries
¼ cup sugar
2 tablespoons cornstarch
. . .
¼ cup brandy, kirsch, or cherry brandy
. . .
Vanilla ice cream

Drain cherries, reserving syrup. In saucepan, blend sugar and cornstarch; gradually stir in reserved cherry syrup, mixing well. Cook and stir over medium heat till mixture thickens and bubbles. Remove from heat; stir in cherries. Turn into heatproof bowl or top pan of chafing dish. (Be sure bottom pan of chafing dish is filled with hot water; keep hot over flame.) Heat brandy or kirsch in small metal pan with long handle. (If desired, pour heated brandy into large ladle.) Carefully ignite heated brandy and pour over cherry mixture. Stir to blend brandy into sauce and serve immediately over ice cream. Makes 2 cups sauce. (For a most dramatic effect, dim the lights just before lighting brandy.)

Soft Italian dinner music plays, pungent aromas arise
from silver tureens and chafing dishes. The food
tends to be elaborate, like the *zuppa di pesce*
(fish soup), in front of the lamp, which contains squid,
prawns and lobster; or like *granseola* at lower right,
a native Venetian shellfish something like
an Alaska crab. The other dishes, from left, are polenta,
liver *alla Veneziana*, fried mixed fish and scampi
grilled over charcoal. In back in a crystal bowl
is the famous Danieli spun sugar dessert.

# RULE'S
## LONDON

As British as the bowlers that hang from the ancient hatracks, Rule's serves
substantial cooking in comfortable, cheery rooms cluttered with etchings
(above, London before the great 1666 fire) and cartoons.
Its nooks, named for past patrons, include a King Edward VII corner
and a Dickens corner. Rule's has changed neither address, decor nor menu
since it was founded on Maiden Lane in 1798. The steak and kidney pie
in foreground is a staple. At the left are parsley potatoes.
Behind are strawberry-topped trifle, English ale and Stilton cheese.

# STALLMASTAREGARDEN
## STOCKHOLM

Stallmästaregården, which means stablemaster's lodge (the house
once belonged to a stablemaster), is the oldest (1754) restaurant
in Stockholm. It has gained its reputation by serving superb smorgasbord
and other elaborately prepared Swedish dishes. Specialties on the table
are, in foreground from left, *gravad lax* (fresh salmon with dill),
*Västkustsallad* (lobster-shrimp-mushroom salad), smoked eel, chicken.
In background are roast beef, mustard sauce for *gravad lax*, shrimp,
*köttbullar* (meat balls), sour cream, Iceland herring on ice, Swedish bread.

# SPATENHAUS

## MUNICH

In the old Max-Joseph Square across from the National Theater, Spatenhaus serves hearty Bavarian meals rich in eggs, cream and sauces. The cooks do well with game and with the old German standby, sauerbraten (*right foreground*). As prepared by Spatenhaus, the beef is soaked in vinegar for several days, then stewed with carrots, parsnips and onions. Sauerkraut in right background and the white and red radishes at left are served with it. On the antlers hang homemade sausages. Spatenhaus serves only beer brewed by its owners, and many beerbibbers think it the best in Germany.

# KAHLENBERG
## VIENNA

High in the woods on the Kahlenberg hill, diners feast
their eyes on distant Vienna and the Danube,
their palates on specialties of one of Austria's most
spectacular restaurants. For the most part Kahlenberg
serves Viennese food. On table are Austrian specialties,
from left, *leberknödel suppe* (liver ball soup),
Viennese beef goulash spiced with caraway seed, marjoram,
garlic, and Salzburger *nockerl*, a fluffy rich dessert.

# KRONE
## ASSMANNSHAUSEN-RHINE

Krone, on the Rhine near Wiesbaden, serves some
of Europe's great fish dishes and the Rhine's best wines.
On the antique wine-testing table—the numbers
help tasters keep track of the wine—is a salmon ready
to be cooked and served with salad with mustard dressing.
Glass and bottle at left contain Steinberger 1949;
red wine at back is Assmannshausen 1952; white wine
is fabulous Berncasteler Doctor Spätlese 1953.

## WALTERSPIEL

### MUNICH

Walterspiel has such a variety of dishes that it puts out a completely new menu every day. Here, beaming over some of his specialties, is Herr Alfred Walterspiel, a top chef for 50 years. Framing him is a Nymphenburg tile door. On table, from left, are crepes Barbara with ice cream, melted chocolate, cream and nuts; boiled ham with sauce, spinach, potato soup and in right foreground, toast Walterspiel.

## HOTEL DE LA COTE-D'OR

### SAULIEU

In this ancient town 150 miles southeast of Paris, Alexandre Dumaine, the best-known chef in France, operates a small restaurant where all the flourish is saved for the food. M. Dumaine does all the cooking while Madame sees to the guests. If notified 24 hours in advance M. Dumaine can prepare anything from the entire French *haute cuisine*. Here he shows one creation—lobster thermidor with Parmesan cheese.

## BEAUMONT INN

### HARRODSBURG, KENTUCKY

The Beaumont Inn, in the heart of Kentucky's Bluegrass section, was built in 1845 as a private school for polite young ladies. For many years, after it became a restaurant in 1919, it traditionally served all its first-time guests "The Beaumont Dinner"— a meal of Southern fried chicken, Kentucky ham, corn pudding, Sally Lunn muffins and chess pie. The Beaumont dinner is still on the menu but nowadays first-timers can choose their own meals. The inn is famous for steaks and chops as well as for desserts like chocolate sherry cake and lemon orange cake. A popular breakfast is country sausage with fried apples.

## NEWFANE INN
### NEWFANE, VERMONT

Built in 1787, the inn has little changed since the days
when it was the only public building in town.
The manager and chef, René Chardain, serves
international food like vichyssoise, clams casino,
scampi, rum cake, but also has a New England repertoire
of dishes like clam chowder, Indian pudding.

## STAGE COACH INN
### SALADO, TEXAS

This inn (*below*) was built in the 1840s
along the Chisholm Trail to take care of stagecoach
travelers. Among the early patrons were
Jesse James, Sam Houston and General Custer.
The fare is strictly Texan: sirloin steaks, meat pies,
hush puppies, banana fritters, barbecued chicken.

# BONANZA INN

## GENOA, NEVADA

Founded in 1867 by a man named Walley, and called
Walley Hot Springs, this inn began as a spa
for wealthy people from the West Coast
and Virginia City, Nev. They went there for its
mineral waters. Now the inn caters
to many tastes with halibut brandade, sweetbreads,
water cress soup or, for people who like
variety in a single meal, a huge smorgasbord.

# THE
# BIRD & BOTTLE

## GARRISON, NEW YORK

Built in 1761 as Warren's Tavern, this inn,
55 miles up the Hudson from New York City,
preserves the original flooring, beams, paneling
and fireplaces. In fine weather its guests
may dine outdoors. It offers two types of fare—
Creole dishes like New Orleans deviled crab and
oyster-stuffed chicken and native dishes like
black bean soup and glazed ham with grape sauce.

# THE MILK PAIL

**DUNDEE, ILLINOIS**

Located in a private game preserve, the Milk Pail has a forest-to-table operation that provides patrons in the proper season with pheasant, mallard duck, trout. Two special game dishes are pheasant and egg drop soup and venison ragout with wine and sour cream.

The Milk Pail also goes in for steaks and chops and has become famous for its pancakes and waffles, which it serves three times a day, year round. It is in an area where big farm-style Sunday brunches are popular and the inn is locally celebrated for such meals.

# THE MILTON INN

## COCKEYSVILLE, MARYLAND

Built of native fieldstone and covered with English ivy, the Milton Inn
was once a manor house and later a boys' school. It has wide
fireplaces, 2-foot-thick walls, pine flooring and schoolboys' initials
carved in its old beams. The inn specializes in French
and Italian food. Two of its best-known dishes are beef Bourguignon
and striped bass Livornese, made with fish from Maryland waters.

# LA CREMAILLERE

## BANKSVILLE, NEW YORK

In a 130-year-old farmhouse 35 miles outside New York City, owner and
master chef Antoine Gilly runs La Crémaillère-à-la-Campagne. Here
he stands with his specialties. Clockwise from bottom center they are
lobster Armoricaine, golden terrine of pheasant, roast duck
with orange, *petits fours*, Charlotte Russe, ham and melon chilled
on a carved ice swan, roast filet of beef with truffles, and chicken in aspic.

# BIG CITY RESTAURANTS

**A** TRADITION of elegant dining out is, like opera going, one of the marks of the civilized nation. In America the mark is present. Scarcely a city exists without at least one restaurant aspiring to the *grande cuisine*. And in the centers of New York, Chicago, Los Angeles, San Francisco and New Orleans, there is a wealth of opulent public dining rooms, fine and subtle foods to match the decor and an educated clientele to savor it and select the proper wines.

It is a miracle this is so, for American eating habits have been subjected to many deleterious influences over the years. There was, first of all, the meat and potatoes levelism that swamped American kitchens in the Jacksonian era of democracy gone mad. The Delmonicos, opening their restaurant in New York in the 1820s, struck a blow against that. Then came the overexuberant period of the new rich when dinner at Sherry's for 30 men and 30 horses was considered fun. This was the time of the trencherman when glittering Diamond Jim Brady would singlehandedly toss off some melon, a whole sea bass and a duck, with soup, vegetables and three desserts. Then came Prohibition to kill fine restaurant cooking stone dead, or nearly so.

But *gourmandise* does not die easily. After the Noble Experiment was done some of the famous old restaurants reopened. A few of the better speakeasies came into the open to flourish and grow great. The New York World's Fair left behind another set of fine restaurants, sprung from those established by foreign governments to display national cookery and later triumphantly going it on their own.

A fair sampling of the culinary wealth thus accruing to America is set out on the pages that follow. The restaurants shown are located in the cities where dining out has been most developed. They are among the famous places where famous and knowledgeable people go to dine.

## SCANDIA

### HOLLYWOOD

The 11-year-old Scandia is a solid place in black walnut that serves he-man food—and rich desserts. It is so famous for Scandinavian food that Danish restaurant families have sent their sons there to learn their trade in its kitchens. Here a waiter ladles a cherry Heering and dark rum sauce for thin Norwegian pancakes with vanilla ice cream and strawberries, topped with meringue.

## PERINO'S

### LOS ANGELES

In the city's most elegant restaurant, Alex Perino proudly displays products of his kitchen. Dishes, clockwise from bottom, are veal cutlet Cordon Bleu (ham and cheese between veal slices), chicken Jeanette *en gelée*, salmon in aspic with shrimp salad in clamshells, fruit salad, *pâté en gelée*.

## CHASEN'S

### LOS ANGELES

One of the best-known actors' gathering places, Chasen's (*left*) selects its specialties from many cuisines. Here Dave Chasen serves beef Belmont, his Tuesday night special. This is a boiled beef dish. The broth is served first in soup bowls, then the meat. In background is Caesar salad.

## LA RUE

### HOLLYWOOD

Excelling in both French and Italian cuisines, La Rue has a separate menu for each. Here Bruno Petoletti and Orlando Figini, proprietors, display tournedos served with a Madeira and brandy sauce. In the background are pheasant, caviar, endive, and a dessert of fruit, kirsch, Cointreau, orange blossoms, candied violets.

# TRADER VIC'S

## SAN FRANCISCO

In the wild clutter of oriental and South Sea images and mementos at left, Trader Vic's specializes in Polynesian food and drink. Favorite drinks, starting with the glass in foreground and reading clockwise, are the Tahitian Pearl, coffee grog, Samoan Fog Cutter, Scorpion for four (with straws), Kamaaina (in coconut) and Mai Tai. All are made with rum.

# ERNIE'S

## SAN FRANCISCO

Adorned by a walnut sideboard that was brought around the Horn in a sailing ship, Ernie's second-floor Ambrosia Room is decorated in rich red Gay Nineties style. Ready for the diners, these dishes include cracked crab at right rear, salmon with black caviar at left rear, and in the foreground bay shrimp with avocado in a cognac sauce surrounded by its ingredients.

# AMELIO'S

## SAN FRANCISCO

In one of the rooms where Amelio's has held forth for 30 years Chef Ermete Lavino and Maître d'Hôtel Adolph Dianda inspect dishes. On the table are asparagus *della casa*, veal *al prosciutto* and zucchini Fiorentina beside *rosé* wine and fruit. The asparagus, especially grown for Amelio's, and veal, cooked in a wine sauce, are specialties of the house.

# PALACE HOTEL

### SAN FRANCISCO

The skylighted Garden Court in San Francisco's historic Sheraton-Palace Hotel is one of the nation's most gracious dining rooms. The elegance of the crystal chandeliers and carefully nurtured greenery matches the restaurant's cuisine which specializes in chicken, shrimp and crab salads but especially in such desserts as chocolate cream cakes, French pastries, beehive honey cakes, strawberry shortcakes, napoleons and light cakes called St. Honorés.

# PUMP ROOM

## CHICAGO

Famed for flaming swords that carry speared sustenance ranging from shashlik
to Alaska crab, the Pump Room in the Ambassador East Hotel
is one of America's most spectacular dining rooms. Bright-coated waiters
march back and forth bearing the sizzling swords to the tables
while (at night, not at lunch) the lights grow dim. In this picture
the array of hot swords from left carry shashlik, deep sea scallops,
broiled lamb chops, whole chicken livers, milk-fed chickens, crab meat
rolled in bacon, and filet mignon. Presiding is the coffee boy.

## IMPERIAL HOUSE
### CHICAGO

In his Garden Room at right owner Max Guggiari, experienced in restaurants from Shanghai to Rome, has here displayed his specialties. In foreground is chicken Kiev with asparagus, tomatoes topped by slices of hard-cooked egg and truffles, and peas in a pastry cup. In background is a tempting arrangement of fruits and vegetables.

## JACQUES
### CHICAGO

In a town that specializes in steak palaces, Jacques (*left*) goes in for Continental charm and sophisticated dishes. Here are frogs' legs Provençale with the sauce for them. Behind them is a duckling with orange slices and, in the rear, roast beef. The fine wines include 1918 Château Lafite Rothschild and a 1952 Richebourg at left, and a 1953 Meursault.

## CLUB BOYAR
### CHICAGO

By invitation only business executives dine here to music by Pianist Clarence Pirez (*right*). Club Boyar was organized 11 years ago by Paul Pfohl, himself a businessman, for his friends. On piano strings are some of its specialties: pepper steak, clams casino baked with bacon and Spanish pimientos, baked potatoes with sour cream, and cauliflower Polonaise.

## BRENNAN'S

### NEW ORLEANS

With dining rooms facing a beautiful patio, Brennan's is a famous city
show place. In the foreground is its baked redfish court bouillon
served with rice, garnished with lemon slices topped with olives
and pimiento. At left is crawfish bisque with whole boiled crawfish
on the platter, stuffed crawfish sunk in the pot and an unstuffed crawfish
floating on top. At rear are bananas Foster flamed in rum, café brûlot.

## ANTOINE'S

### NEW ORLEANS

Operated by the Alciatore family for 118 years, site of one of the most
distinguished wine cellars in the South, Antoine's is the historic kitchen
where oysters Rockefeller and pompano *en papillote* were invented.
In foreground are oysters Rockefeller on rock salt. At right is
*pigeonneaux sauce paradis*—in a sauce including Madeira, truffles, seedless
white grapes and currant jelly. At left is pompano *en papillote*.

# ARNAUD'S

## NEW ORLEANS

Arnaud's restaurant, a wonderful warren
of 15 dining rooms and 1,500 seats, helps give
New Orleans its special culinary reputation.
Its best dish in local opinion
is this one—shrimp Arnaud, a boiled shrimp
with a fiery remolade sauce
that contains shallots, celery, olive oil,
red pepper, parsley, mustard and vinegar.

# VOISIN

## NEW YORK

Quiet and elegant, Voisin has for 45 years
been famed for its desserts. Below
is an assortment: a chocolate soufflé (top)
served with vanilla sauce (in sauceboat),
a gâteau St. Honoré (at left), two chocolate boxes
of spongecake and chocolate butter cream
flanking a strawberry strip, eclairs,
strawberry tarts and a vanilla pot de crème.

# THE FORUM

## NEW YORK

A restaurant with an off-beat touch is
The Forum of the Twelve Caesars. In foreground
is alpine snow hare stewed in wine
and served with maize and lingonberries. At left
is an appetizer of clams, oysters, crab meat,
lobster, shrimp. Ramekin holds pike mousse. Menu
goes in for Latin (eggs Benedictus) and
flaming foods—"fiddler crab lump a la Nero."

## BRUSSELS

### NEW YORK

Born of the 1939-40 New York World's Fair where its managers operated the Belgian Pavilion restaurant, the Brussels has become one of the city's finest restaurants. Here Maître d'Hôtel Leon Lievens lifts a chateaubriand *en papillote* from the paper in which it was cooked. On side table are the asparagus with sauce mousseline of hollandaise and whipped cream, and *pommes soufflées* to go with it.

## LE PAVILLON

### NEW YORK

Owned by Henri Soulé, a great restaurateur, Le Pavillon rates as the finest French restaurant in America. In the copper dish are *quenelles de brochet Pavillon*, egg-shaped mousses of sieved pike poached and served with lobster sauce. On the serving platter at right is *mousse de sole Pavillon* which is served, as in foreground, half covered with lobster sauce and half covered with champagne sauce.

# DINING OUT: RECIPES

**EUROPE'S RESTAURANTS**

**AMERICA'S INNS**

**BIG CITY RESTAURANTS**

# EUROPE'S RESTAURANTS

The recipes below were supplied by the chefs of the great restaurants shown on pages 234-247. Some of them appear here in both their European and American versions. Some appear only in their American form, adapted to serve any competent U.S. cook. In all cases an American version was necessary because, for example, European weights and measures are different; some European ingredients are not readily available in the U.S.; and because all the recipes were originally designed for a restaurant, rather than a home kitchen and were often intended to serve a vast number of people. Where they are called for as ingredients, this book has added its own recipes for pastries, creams and sauces. But the basic recipes have not been altered.

## PRESSED DUCK: TOUR D'ARGENT

| | |
|---|---|
| 3 four-pound oven-ready ducks | Juice of 3 lemons |
| 1½ cups duck consommé | Salt |
| 1½ cups port wine | Freshly ground black pepper |
| 1½ cups cognac | |

First prepare a consommé from the duck wings, necks, gizzards and hearts. Put them in a saucepan with 2 cups of water, 1 onion, 1 tablespoon chopped parsley and 1 teaspoon salt. Bring to a boil, reduce the heat and simmer for 20 to 30 minutes. Strain and save the stock. Roast the ducks in a hot oven (425°) for 30 minutes. Crush the duck livers and put them in a chafing dish with port and cognac. Cut the duck breasts into thin slices and put them in the chafing dish. Cut off the legs and set them aside. Crush the carcasses in a duck press to extract the juices. Pour duck consommé through the press. Pour the juices and consommé over the duck slices, livers and the wine and cognac. Add the lemon juice. Cook in the chafing dish over a high flame for 20 to 25 minutes, stirring briskly until the sauce becomes thick and chocolate colored. Salt and pepper pressed duck to taste. Serve hot. Broil the legs under medium heat for 10 minutes. Serve them separately as a second course. Serves 6.

### IN THE WORDS OF THE CHEF

For this recipe, it is necessary to have a very young duck, 6 to 8 weeks old, fattened particularly for the last 15 days. The duck must be killed by suffocation so that it will keep its blood. A carefully seasoned consommé is prepared in advance with the carcass of another duck. The chef first roasts the duck for about 20 minutes. When this first operation is finished, the duck is handed by the chef to the waiter who carries it into the restaurant and presents it to the client. One places the chopped liver in a plate and adds to it a glass of port and a glass of cognac. The duck's legs are detached and grilled during the rest of the preparation. The duck is cut into slices. These slices are put into the sauce which has been prepared with the liver. The carcass is then put into a special press in order to extract the blood to which is added a glass of consommé. This juice coming from the press will be poured over the slices, the crushed liver, the mixture of port and cognac and the juice of a lemon. All this culinary "sacrifice" takes place on a silver platter which is heated by two alcohol lamps, until the sauce, beaten without interruption for 20 to 25 minutes, thickens and begins to look like melted chocolate. The filets are arranged on a hot platter,

covered with the sauce and served, very hot, with souffléed potatoes. The grilled legs are served with tender lettuce. This dish is accompanied with one of our good Burgundy wines.

## GIGOT D'AGNEAU EN CROUTE: BAUMANIERE

| | |
|---|---|
| 1 leg of lamb, boned; 3 pounds after boning | 1 tablespoon chopped truffles |
| 2 lamb kidneys, cubed | 2 tablespoons armagnac |
| ¼ cup chopped mushrooms | 1 teaspoon salt |
| 2 ounces pâté de foie gras, chopped | Freshly ground black pepper |
| | Unbaked puff paste |
| | Gratin dauphinois à la crème |

Combine kidneys, mushrooms, foie gras, truffles, armagnac, salt and pepper. Stuff lamb with this mixture and close opening. Roast in a slow oven (325°) for 1 hour. Remove and let stand for 15 minutes. Roll puff paste dough ¼ inch thick. Wrap lamb in dough. Bake in a hot oven (425°) for 15 minutes. Serve with gratin dauphinois à la crème. Serves 6.

### IN THE WORDS OF THE CHEF

Take a leg of lamb weighing not more than 1 kilo. It is useful to debone it, leaving only the knuckle bone. This is easy to do with a very sharp knife. Cut away the meat from the bone up to the joint, which should be cut off. Pack into this cavity a stuffing composed of a cubed lamb kidney, mushrooms, truffles and a little foie gras. Naturally this stuffing should be salted, peppered and lightly flavored with armagnac. Sew up leg of lamb with a very big larding needle. The lamb thus prepared is put into the oven to brown and "sweat." For it is indispensable that the leg of lamb shed all its "water" before being wrapped in a thin layer of puff paste dough. The leg is cooked first of all 10 to 15 minutes and then again for the same length of time. The second operation is to finish cooking the leg of lamb and the pastry shell. I advise serving a gratin dauphinois à la crème with the leg of lamb.

## PUFF PASTE

| | |
|---|---|
| 1 cup butter | ¼ teaspoon salt |
| 2 cups sifted flour | |

Work the butter with the hands under a stream of cold water until it is creamy and waxy. Put ¼ cup of the butter in a cold bowl and shape the rest of it into a square ½ inch thick. Put the butter square in the refrigerator to chill. Add flour and salt to the butter in the bowl. Work mixture with a pastry blender or 2 knives until butter is the size of small peas. Stir in about 6 tablespoons of ice water, a little at a time, until a dough is formed. Turn the dough out on a lightly floured board and knead it for 5 minutes or until it is smooth and elastic. Roll it out into an oblong ⅛ inch thick. Place the chilled butter square in the center. Fold the 2 longest sides of the dough over, one at a time, each time completely covering the butter square. Then fold one third of this strip over the top and the other one third under. Wrap in waxed paper and chill for 30 minutes. Roll out again to form oblong and fold ends over to make 3 layers of dough. Wrap in waxed paper and chill again for 30 minutes. Repeat until dough has been rolled and chilled 4 times. Roll out ¼ inch thick and cut into desired shapes. Chill again. Use as indicated in any recipe requiring puff paste.

## GRATIN DAUPHINOIS A LA CREME

| | |
|---|---|
| 4 large potatoes, peeled | ¼ cup grated |
| and sliced thin | Parmesan cheese |
| 2 cups milk | 1 teaspoon salt |
| ½ cup heavy cream | Freshly ground black pepper |

Cook potatoes, salt and pepper in milk in top of double boiler over boiling water for 30 minutes. Put in baking dish, pour cream over potatoes, top with Parmesan cheese. Bake in a moderate oven (350°) for 20 minutes. Serves 6.

## PATE OF DUCK: PYRAMIDE

| | |
|---|---|
| ¼ pound pâté de foie gras, | 2 cups dry white wine |
| chopped fine | ¼ cup cognac |
| 2 three-pound ducks, boned | 1 cup lard |
| 1 pound veal | 1 cup butter |
| 1 pound pork | 4 cups sifted flour |
| 2 onions, chopped | 2 envelopes |
| 2 carrots, sliced | unflavored gelatine |
| ½ cup chopped parsley | 1 teaspoon salt |
| 1 teaspoon thyme | |

Cube the ducks, ½ pound of veal and ½ pound of pork. Combine cubed meat, onion, carrots, parsley, thyme, wine and cognac and marinate in a cool place for 2 days. Drain. Save 4 cups of the marinade. Chop remaining ½ pound of veal and ½ pound of pork. Mix drained meat with chopped meat and foie gras. Meanwhile cut lard and butter into flour and salt until it resembles coarse meal. Add 6 tablespoons of water and mix lightly. Turn out on a floured board and roll thin. Line inside of a casserole with dough. Fill with meat mixture and cover with dough. Cut 2 dime-size holes in top. Bake in moderate oven (375°) for 1 hour. Cool. Soften gelatine in 1 cup of the marinade. Bring remaining 3 cups of marinade to a boil and pour over gelatine, stirring until gelatine is dissolved. Cool. Chill for 20 minutes. Pour through holes into pâté. Chill for 2 hours. Serves 12.

## CHICKEN BREASTS IN GELATINE: PASSETTO

| | |
|---|---|
| 2 three-pound chickens | 3 envelopes |
| 1 stalk celery with leaves | unflavored gelatine |
| 1 bay leaf, crumbled | 1 tablespoon salt |
| 1 garlic clove | 6 peppercorns |
| 2 onions, cut up | |

Place chickens in a saucepan and add water to cover. Add celery, bay leaf, garlic, onions, salt and peppercorns. Bring to a boil, reduce heat, cover and simmer for 1 hour. Remove the chickens from broth. Drain and cool. Cut the chickens in quarters. Chill the chicken for at least 1 hour. Strain the broth and set aside 1 quart. Soften the gelatine in 1 cup of cold water. Add this to the hot, strained broth and stir until the gelatine is dissolved. Cool. Chill for ½ hour or until slightly thickened. Spoon very carefully over the chilled chicken to coat it completely. Return to refrigerator and chill for 1 hour. When chicken is glazed, garnish it with anything from artichokes to mushrooms. Serves 6.

## VEAL CUTLETS ALLA BOLOGNESE: PAPPAGALLO

| | |
|---|---|
| 6 veal cutlets | 6 slices boiled ham |
| 1 egg, beaten | 1 cup milk |
| 1 cup bread crumbs | 1 cup canned tomato sauce |
| ½ cup grated Parmesan | ½ teaspoon salt |
| cheese | Freshly ground black pepper |
| ½ cup lard | |

Beat egg with 2 tablespoons of water. Dip cutlets into the egg mixture and then into bread crumbs which have been combined with 2 tablespoons cheese, salt and pepper. Sauté in boiling hot lard for 10 minutes. Top cutlets with ham and sprinkle with remaining cheese. Combine milk and tomato sauce and add to cutlets in skillet. Cover and simmer for 25 minutes. Serves 6.

## SUPREME OF CHICKEN SOUFFLE: PAPPAGALLO

| | |
|---|---|
| 6 small chicken breasts | ¼ cup grated |
| ½ cup butter | Parmesan cheese |
| 6 eggs, separated | Salt |
| White truffles, sliced | |

Bone chicken breasts and flatten them with a cleaver. Season lightly with salt. Sauté in butter for 10 minutes. Meanwhile beat egg yolks until thick and lemon colored. Beat egg whites until stiff but not dry. Add cheese to egg yolks and fold in egg whites. Place sautéed chicken breasts in 6 individual baking dishes. Cover them with sliced truffles and pour egg mixture over them. Bake in a very hot oven (450°) for about 10 minutes or until puffed and brown. Serves 6.

## TURKEY FILETS: PAPPAGALLO

| | |
|---|---|
| 6 filets of turkey breast | 6 thin slices |
| Unbaked puff paste | Emmentaler cheese |
| ½ cup butter | Salt |
| White truffles, sliced | |

Roll puff paste ⅛ inch thick. Cut 12 pieces large enough for turkey filets. Chill 30 minutes. Place on baking sheet lined with 2 layers of brown paper. Bake 10 minutes at 500°. Cover pastry with waxed paper. Bake 10 minutes. Salt filets, flatten with cleaver. Sauté in butter over low heat 10 minutes. Set each filet on a piece of baked puff paste, top with truffles, cheese. Cover with another piece of puff paste. Arrange on baking sheets. Bake 10 minutes at 375°. Serves 6.

### IN THE WORDS OF THE CHEF

Cook in a saucepan 1 filet of tom turkey, well flattened, with a small lump of butter and salt, being careful that the filet always remains white. Cover it with white truffles cut into slices and with Emmentaler cheese. Put it between two layers of cooked puff paste, not sweetened, and put it into the oven for about 10 minutes. Serve it with vegetables, dressed with butter and cheese.

## BAKED GREEN LASAGNE: PAPPAGALLO

| | |
|---|---|
| 8½ cups flour | ½ pound pork loin, diced |
| 1½ cups cooked spinach, | ¼ cup dry white wine |
| drained and chopped | 3 tablespoons tomato sauce |
| 4 eggs | Butter |
| 1 onion, finely chopped | 1 quart milk |
| ¼ cup finely chopped celery | Grated Parmesan cheese |
| 1 small carrot, chopped | Salt |
| ½ pound lean beef, diced | Freshly ground black pepper |

First make the lasagne. Mix 8 cups of flour with the spinach and eggs. Knead on a lightly floured board until a firm dough is formed. Roll out thin and cut into 4-inch squares. Cook squares in salted boiling water. Remove, dip into cold water, drain and dry. While the lasagne is drying, make a meat sauce (ragout) and a béchamel sauce. For the meat sauce, sauté onion, celery, carrot, salt and pepper in 2 tablespoons butter for 10 minutes or until the onion is lightly browned. Add beef, pork, wine and tomato sauce and simmer for 10 minutes. For the béchamel, melt ½ cup butter in a saucepan. Add ½ cup of flour and a pinch of salt and stir until smooth. Add milk gradually, stirring constantly, and cook, stirring, until thick and smooth. To make baked green lasagne, put alternate layers of lasagne, meat sauce, béchamel sauce and Parmesan cheese in a baking dish. Bake in a moderate oven (350°) for 15 minutes. Serves 6.

### IN THE WORDS OF THE CHEF

To make the dough, take 1 kilo of flour, 300 grams of boiled spinach, well pressed and minced, and 4 eggs. Knead the dough well, spread it on a board with a rolling pin and cut it in 10-centimeter squares. Boil them for 2 or 3 minutes, dip them into cold water and let them dry. Put the lasagne in layers in a buttered pan, cover them with ragout, béchamel and grated Parmesan cheese. Add layers of lasagne and the sauce until whole thing is 5 centimeters high. Then put the pan into the oven, under slow fire, and let the contents stand for about 15 minutes. To prepare the ragout, fry until slightly brown a finely cut onion, celery, a small carrot, salt and pepper. Add 200 grams of lean beef and 200 grams of pork loin cut in small cubes. Cook it on slow fire adding ½ glass of white wine and 2 or 3 spoonfuls of tomato sauce. To prepare béchamel, melt 200 grams of butter in a pan, add slowly 100 grams of flour, a pinch of salt and a liter of milk. Stir continuously so sauce does not change color. Let reach boiling point and remove sauce from fire.

## ZUPPA DI PESCE: ROYAL DANIELI

| | |
|---|---|
| 3 pounds of mixed haddock, trout, cod, salmon, red snapper, cut up | ½ teaspoon thyme |
| | 1 teaspoon basil |
| 1 one-pound lobster, cut up | 2 tablespoons minced parsley |
| ½ pound prawns or shrimp | ½ cup dry white wine |
| ½ pound squid, cut up | 1½ cups chopped peeled tomatoes |
| 1 onion, cut up | Whole saffron |
| 1 stalk celery with leaves | 1 tablespoon salt |
| 2 tablespoons vinegar | Freshly ground black pepper |
| ½ cup olive oil | 6 slices bread |
| 2 garlic cloves, minced | |
| 1 bay leaf, crumbled | |

Boil lobster and prawns for 5 minutes in 1 quart of water with onion, celery, vinegar and 2 teaspoons salt. Remove and shell lobster and prawns. Return shells to the broth with heads and tails of fish and simmer for 20 minutes. Strain and put broth aside. Meanwhile cut the fish, squid and lobster meat into bite-sized chunks. Sauté with prawns in ¼ cup oil with garlic, bay leaf, thyme, basil and parsley for 5 minutes, stirring constantly. Add fish broth, wine, tomatoes, a pinch of saffron, the remaining 1 teaspoon of salt and the pepper. Bring to a boil, reduce heat, cover and simmer for 10 minutes, stirring occasionally. Serve with slices of bread fried in the remaining ¼ cup olive oil. Serves 6.

## LIVER ALLA VENEZIANA: ROYAL DANIELI

| | |
|---|---|
| 1¾ pounds calf liver, thinly sliced | Flour |
| 3 cups thinly sliced onion | 1 tablespoon minced parsley |
| 1¾ cups butter | 1 tablespoon beef bouillon |
| ¼ cup olive oil | Salt |
| Sage | Freshly ground black pepper |

Sauté onion in combined butter and olive oil with a pinch of sage for 5 minutes or until onion is lightly browned. Sprinkle liver with flour, season with salt and pepper. Add liver slices to onion and cook over high heat for 5 minutes. Add parsley and bouillon. Serve immediately. Serves 6.

## CRYSTAL BOWL DANIELI: ROYAL DANIELI

| | |
|---|---|
| 1½ cups diced fresh fruit | Cream Chantilly |
| Kirsch or maraschino liqueur | Melba sauce |
| Ice cream | Sugar yarn |
| Sweetened whipped cream | Candied cherries |

Put fruit in 6 individual crystal bowls. Pour in some kirsch or maraschino. Add a ball of ice cream and top it with whipped cream. Garnish with cream Chantilly in the shape of a little horn. Put a teaspoonful of melba sauce in the horn. Cover everything with a skein of sugar yarn shaped like a dome and sprinkle with tiny pieces of candied cherry. Serves 6. Cream Chantilly is made by whipping ice cold heavy cream until it becomes very stiff—much stiffer than regular whipped cream.

## SUGAR YARN

| | |
|---|---|
| 2 cups sugar | ¼ teaspoon cream of tartar |
| 1 teaspoon white corn syrup | |

Combine sugar, cream of tartar, and corn syrup with ⅔ cup of water in saucepan. Cover and bring to a quick boil over high heat. Remove cover. Warm a candy thermometer in hot water and lower it carefully into the boiling syrup. Continue boiling until thermometer registers 312°. Remove immediately from heat and set pan into cold water for 2 or 3 minutes to stop the cooking. Remove from cold water and set the pan in a bowl of hot water. Butter the handles of 2 long wooden spoons (or use 2 clean thin sticks). Place spoons on table about 24 inches apart and let the handles extend 10 inches out from the table. Place weights on the bowls of the spoons so that the spoons will not fall. Cover the table and floor under the spoons with paper. Dip a wire whisk or rotary beater into the syrup and quickly move it back and forth so that syrup threads are spun over and between the handles. Remove the spun sugar yarn from the handles, trim the ends and form into any desired shape.

## STEAK AND KIDNEY PIE: RULE'S

| | |
|---|---|
| 1½ pounds stewing beef, diced | ½ bay leaf, crumbled |
| 6 ounces kidney, sliced | 1 cup butter |
| ½ pound mushrooms, sliced | 3 cups sifted self-rising flour |
| 1 cup chopped onion | 1 cup milk |
| ¼ cup parsley | 1 teaspoon salt |

Put beef, kidneys, mushrooms, onion, parsley, bay leaf and salt in baking dish with 2 cups of water. Cut butter into flour until it resembles coarse meal. Add milk and mix lightly to form soft dough. Turn out on floured board and roll ⅛ inch thick. Place on top of baking dish. Cut slits in dough to let steam escape. Bake in a slow oven (325°) for 1 hour and 45 minutes. Serves 6.

## STRAWBERRY TRIFLE: RULE'S

| | |
|---|---|
| 8 ounces spongecake | 2 cups boiled custard |
| ½ cup strawberry jam | 1 cup fresh strawberries |
| 2 cups whipped cream | ¼ cup candied cherries |
| ¼ cup sweet sherry | 2 ounces angelica, cut up |

Cut spongecake in pieces and make a layer of sponge in the bottom of a serving dish. Top with jam and half of the whipped cream. Pour sherry over it. Add a second layer of cake. Pour boiled custard over all. Cool. Top with remaining cream and garnish with strawberries, cherries and angelica. Serves 6.

## BOILED CUSTARD

| | |
|---|---|
| 3 eggs | ½ teaspoon vanilla extract |
| ¼ cup sugar | Salt |
| 2 cups milk, scalded | |

In the top part of a double boiler beat eggs until frothy. Stir in sugar and a pinch of salt. Add milk gradually, stirring constantly. Cook over hot (not boiling) water until mixture is smooth and coats the spoon. Stir in vanilla. Makes about 2 cups.

## GRAVAD LAX: STALLMASTAREGARDEN

| | |
|---|---|
| 5 pounds salmon | ¼ cup salt |
| ¾ cup sugar | Ground white pepper |
| Chopped fresh dill | |

Skin and bone salmon. Keep skin. Into salmon knead sugar, salt, pepper and a generous quantity of dill. Chill for at least 8 hours. To serve, cut into pieces or in slices. Broil the skin and serve it with salmon. Serve as appetizer with mustard sauce.

## MUSTARD SAUCE

| | |
|---|---|
| 1 tablespoon French mustard | Vinegar |
| 1 teaspoon sugar | Finely chopped dill |
| 6 tablespoons olive oil | Ground white pepper |

Mix mustard, sugar and oil together. Thin from time to time with a few drops of vinegar. Season with dill and pepper.

## VASTKUSTSALLAD: STALLMASTAREGARDEN

| | |
|---|---|
| 1 two-pound lobster, boiled | 6 tomatoes, sliced |
| 1½ cups cooked shelled shrimp | ½ cup cooked small green peas |
| 24 mussels, steamed | French salad dressing |
| ¾ cup chopped mushrooms | Shredded lettuce |

Remove meat from lobster and cut it in pieces. Chill lobster, shrimp and mussels. To serve, combine sea food, mushrooms, tomatoes, peas, dressing. Toss well. Serve on lettuce. Serves 6.

## KOTTBULLAR: STALLMASTAREGARDEN

| | |
|---|---|
| 1 pound ground lean beef | 4 egg yolks |
| ½ pound ground lean pork | 2 eggs |
| ¼ pound ground veal | ¼ cup butter |
| 2 slices white bread | Cayenne pepper |
| ½ cup heavy cream | 1 teaspoon salt |
| ½ cup slightly browned chopped onion | Freshly ground black pepper |

Remove crust from bread and crumble bread into cream. Soak for 10 minutes. Put beef, pork, veal and onion through a food grinder. Add soaked bread, eggs, egg yolks, a few grains of cayenne pepper, salt and black pepper and mix well. Shape into balls and sauté in butter. Serves 6.

## SAUERBRATEN: SPATENHAUS

| | |
|---|---|
| 3 pounds top round of beef | ½ cup flour |
| 1 cup vinegar | 2 tablespoons shortening |
| ½ cup chopped onion | ¼ cup sliced roasted carrot |
| 2 bay leaves | ¼ cup chopped parsnip |
| 1 tablespoon paprika | ¼ cup chopped celery |
| 2 cloves | ¼ cup dry red wine |
| ½ teaspoon thyme | 2 teaspoons salt |

Combine vinegar, 1 cup of water, ¼ cup onion, bay leaves, paprika, cloves and thyme. Heat but do not boil. Pour over meat. Cover and store in a cool place for several days, turning meat once each day. Remove meat, drain. Strain and save marinade. Coat the meat with ¼ cup of flour and sear in shortening. Add carrot, parsnip, celery and remaining ¼ cup of onion and cook for 5 minutes, stirring constantly. Pour marinade over meat. Cover and simmer for 3 hours. Remove meat and keep hot. Mix remaining ¼ cup of flour and the salt with ½ cup of water. Stir into sauce and cook until thickened. Strain gravy, add wine and serve over meat. Serves 6.

## VIENNESE BEEF GOULASH: KAHLENBERG

| | |
|---|---|
| 3 pounds stewing beef, cubed | 2 tablespoons paprika |
| 2 cups chopped onion | ¼ cup catsup |
| ½ cup lard | 1 teaspoon salt |
| 1½ teaspoons caraway seed | 6 hot boiled potatoes |
| ½ teaspoon marjoram | 3 hard-cooked eggs, sliced |
| 2 garlic cloves, minced | |

Sauté onion in fat for 5 minutes. Add beef, caraway, marjoram, garlic, salt and 2 cups of water. Bring to a boil, reduce heat, cover and simmer for 1 hour. Combine the paprika, catsup and 2 tablespoons of water. Add this mixture to the stew and simmer for 10 minutes. Serve with potatoes and egg slices. Serves 6.

## SALZBURGER NOCKERL: KAHLENBERG

| | |
|---|---|
| 6 egg whites, beaten | ⅓ cup flour |
| Powdered sugar | 1 teaspoon vanilla sugar |
| 4 egg yolks | ½ cup lard |

To ½ cup powdered sugar add beaten egg whites, beat until stiff but not dry. Add egg yolks, flour and vanilla sugar and mix gently. Shape dough into 4 large balls (nockerl). Fry in hot lard, turning frequently, until golden brown. Sprinkle with powdered sugar. Serves 4. To make vanilla sugar, split piece of vanilla bean, remove seeds, crush them into 1 teaspoon powdered sugar.

## SALMON: KRONE

| | |
|---|---|
| 6 salmon steaks | 1 teaspoon salt |
| 1 tablespoon vinegar | ¾ cup butter, melted |

Combine vinegar, salt and 2 quarts water in a skillet. Bring to a boil. Add salmon, reduce the heat and simmer for 12 minutes. Drain salmon and serve with melted butter. Serves 6.

## BOILED HAM: WALTERSPIEL

| | |
|---|---|
| 1 ten-pound smoked ham | 1 teaspoon sugar |
| 1 bottle dry Rhine wine | 1 cup demi-glace |
| 2 tablespoons bread crumbs | 3 tomatoes, peeled, chopped |

Soak ham overnight in water to cover. Drain. Cover ham with warm water, bring to a boil, reduce heat and simmer for about 2½ hours. Drain ham and remove skin leaving a pointed "crown" on the shank end. Trim off surplus fat. Put the ham in a roasting pan and pour in wine. Cover and bake in a moderate oven (375°) for 1 hour. Sprinkle ham with crumbs mixed with sugar. Bake uncovered until the crumbs are golden brown. Remove ham and keep hot. Skim fat from broth in pan. Add demi-glace and tomatoes to broth. Cook, stirring constantly, until sauce is hot. Serve with ham. Serves 15.

## DEMI-GLACE

| | |
|---|---|
| ½ pound chopped veal | 2 tablespoons |
| 1 onion, chopped | chopped parsley |
| 1 carrot, sliced | 1 bay leaf |
| 2 tablespoons flour | Salt |
| 2 cups beef bouillon | Freshly ground black pepper |

Sauté veal, onion and carrot in a covered pan over low heat for 15 minutes or until rich brown. Add flour, stirring constantly, and cook for 5 minutes. Add bouillon, parsley, bay leaf, salt and pepper, simmer for 2 hours. Strain. Makes about 1 cup.

### IN THE WORDS OF THE CHEF

Among boiled hams I prefer those that weigh between 10 to 12 pounds in raw state. The smoked ham is put into cold water overnight and the hip bone removed. I then put it to boil not in cold but in warm water, of about 40 degrees Centigrade, let it boil up just once and then put it aside to draw. Generally one allows 20 minutes per pound, but this is not always right. The experienced cook has another sign. He knows that if the small bone located above the main leg bone can be easily removed, so that no meat is on it, the ham is ready. There are various ways to prepare the warm ham. One hour before the ham is done, the skin is removed so that the hind part forms an indented, rather crownlike end. The surplus fat is removed, thereby giving the ham shape, and then the ham is baked in the oven with a bottle of dry Rhine wine, covered well with parchment paper. After 1 hour it is sprinkled with 2 spoonfuls of fresh *mie de pain* (fresh, sifted white bread crumbs) that have been mixed with a teaspoonful of sugar, and is left uncovered to get a beautiful brown frosting. From the broth I make a delicious sauce by adding a very good demi-glace that is prepared in every very good kitchen, and many fresh tomatoes. I serve this separately.

## POTATO SOUP: WALTERSPIEL

| | |
|---|---|
| 3 large potatoes, sliced thin | 2 egg yolks, beaten |
| 4 slices lean bacon, diced | 1 cup sour cream |
| 6 leeks, sliced thin | 1 tablespoon minced parsley |
| ¼ cup chopped onion | 1 tablespoon minced chervil |
| 2 tablespoons flour | Butter |
| 4 cups bouillon | Thinly sliced rolls |

Sauté bacon in a deep saucepan for 5 minutes. Add leeks and onion and sauté for 5 minutes. Stir in flour. Add bouillon slowly, stirring constantly. Add potatoes and simmer for 1 hour. Combine egg yolks and sour cream and stir into soup. Simmer for 10 minutes, stirring constantly. Add parsley and chervil. Melt butter and cook slowly until it is rich brown. Sauté slices of roll in butter until brown and hot. Serve with soup. Serves 6.

### IN THE WORDS OF THE CHEF

For this I cut the white parts of a large quantity of leeks, a little onion and several slices of lean bacon into small slices, start sautéing everything very slowly without letting it take on color, add a little white flour, continue sautéing a little and fill up the pan with hot meat broth. I cut potatoes into very thin slices, wash them very carefully and add them to the broth. I let everything boil approximately 1 hour, then thicken the soup with much fresh sour cream and several egg yolks and finally add minced parsley and chervil. I serve with this soup thin slices of small rolls that I don't simply put into the stove dry, as is frequently done, but that I carefully sauté in butter on the stove, for it is the noisette butter that gives the rolls their taste.

## LOBSTER THERMIDOR: COTE D'OR

| | |
|---|---|
| 3 two-pound lobsters | 1 cup milk |
| ¼ cup olive oil | ½ cup grated |
| ¾ cup butter | Parmesan cheese |
| ¼ cup prepared mustard | Salt |
| 2 cups heavy cream | Freshly ground black pepper |
| 3 tablespoons flour | |

Split the lobsters. Brush with oil and sprinkle with salt and pepper. Broil under medium heat for 5 minutes. Remove from broiler and dot with 6 tablespoons of butter. Bake in a hot oven (400°) for 10 minutes. Remove lobster meat from shells and slice it. Save coral. Brush inside of each shell lightly with mustard. Meanwhile simmer cream over low heat for 30 minutes, stirring occasionally. Melt 4 tablespoons of butter, stir in flour and ½ teaspoon salt. Add milk slowly. Cook until sauce thickens, stirring constantly. Mix in cream and lobster coral. Return lobster meat to shells and cover with sauce. Sprinkle with Parmesan cheese and dot with remaining 2 tablespoons of butter. Bake in hot oven (400°) for 10 minutes. Serves 6.

# AMERICA'S INNS

## SALLY LUNN MUFFINS: BEAUMONT INN

⅓ cup soft butter
⅓ cup sugar
1 egg
1½ cups sifted flour

1 tablespoon double-acting
 baking powder
⅔ cup milk

Combine butter, sugar and egg and beat until light and fluffy. Combine flour and baking powder and sift together. Add to butter mixture alternately with milk. Fill 12 greased muffin pans ⅔ full of batter. Bake in a hot oven (400°) for 20 minutes.

## CHESS PIE: BEAUMONT INN

½ recipe pie crust
1 cup sugar
1 egg
2 egg yolks
½ cup butter, melted

4 teaspoons vinegar
1 tablespoon flour
¼ teaspoon salt
Meringue

Roll pie crust dough ⅛ inch thick, fit into 8-inch pie plate, trim and flute edges. Prick dough well with fork. Bake in a hot oven (425°) for 8 minutes. Meanwhile combine sugar, egg and egg yolks, butter, vinegar, flour and salt and beat with rotary beater until smooth. Pour into baked pie shell. Increase oven heat to 550° and bake for 15 minutes. Reduce oven heat to 250° and bake for 15 minutes. Remove from oven, top with meringue. Bake in a hot oven (425°) for 3 minutes. Serves 6.

## MERINGUE

3 egg whites
½ cup sugar

Salt

Beat egg whites with a pinch of salt until foamy. Add sugar slowly, beating constantly, until thick and glossy.

## VICHYSSOISE: NEWFANE INN

4 leeks, thinly sliced
½ cup butter
2 pounds potatoes, peeled
 and thinly sliced
1 cup light cream

1 cup milk
1 tablespoon chopped chives
1 teaspoon salt
Freshly ground black pepper

Sauté leeks in butter for 5 minutes in deep saucepan. Add potatoes, salt and water to barely cover. Bring to a boil, reduce heat, cover and simmer for 45 minutes. Press through coarse sieve or food mill. Cool. Chill in refrigerator for at least 1 hour. Before serving, stir in chilled cream and milk. Sprinkle with chives and black pepper. Serves 6.

## RUM CAKE: NEWFANE INN

4 eggs
½ cup sugar
½ teaspoon vanilla extract
1 cup minus 2 tablespoons
 sifted cake flour

7 tablespoons butter,
 melted and cooled
Rum custard cream
2 tablespoons dark rum
Semisweet chocolate frosting

Combine eggs, sugar and vanilla in deep bowl. Beat with electric or rotary beater until thoroughly mixed. Set in another bowl containing very hot (not boiling) water and beat about 15 minutes or until mixture is high, light and fluffy. Remove from hot water and continue beating until mixture is cool. Sprinkle ⅓ of the flour over egg mixture and fold in gently with slotted spoon. Repeat until all flour is used. Fold in butter. Pour into buttered and floured 9-inch spring-form pan (or in 2 deep 9-inch layer pans) and bake in a moderate oven (350°) for 35 minutes. Turn out onto cake-cooling rack. When cold, cut into 2 layers. Put layers together with rum custard cream. Sprinkle top of cake with dark rum and then spread top with semisweet chocolate frosting.

## RUM CUSTARD CREAM

2 tablespoons dark rum
½ cup sugar
2 tablespoons flour

1 egg, beaten
⅔ cup light cream
1 cup heavy cream, whipped

In top part of double boiler combine sugar, flour, egg and light cream. Cook over boiling water, stirring constantly, for 5 minutes. Add rum and cook for 5 minutes. Remove from heat and cool. Chill for 1 hour. Fold in whipped cream.

## SEMISWEET FROSTING

½ cup semisweet
 chocolate bits
2 tablespoons soft butter

½ cup sifted
 confectioners' sugar
2 tablespoons dark rum

Melt chocolate over hot (not boiling) water. Add butter, sugar and rum and stir until smooth. Cool. Spread on cake.

## MEAT PIE: STAGE COACH INN

3 pounds beef tenderloin
½ cup flour
½ cup oil
1½ cups sliced onion
1 garlic clove, minced
2 cans condensed consommé
1 bay leaf, crumbled
1 tablespoon dry mustard
1 teaspoon Kitchen Bouquet

2 teaspoons soy sauce
2 teaspoons Worcestershire
 sauce
1½ cups peas
½ recipe pie crust
1 teaspoon Ac'cent
1 teaspoon salt
Freshly ground black pepper

Cut beef in cubes. Combine flour, Ac'cent, salt and pepper in a paper bag. Put beef cubes in bag with flour mixture and shake well to coat meat thoroughly. Brown meat in oil in large saucepan. Remove meat, add onion and garlic to oil remaining in pan and fry for 10 minutes, stirring constantly. Add meat, consommé, 1 can water and seasonings. Bring to a boil, reduce heat, cover and simmer for 1½ hours. Add peas and pour into casserole or individual baking dishes. Top with pie crust, rolled ⅛ inch thick, and bake in a hot oven (425°) for 30 minutes or until crust is brown. Serves 6.

## HUSH PUPPIES: STAGE COACH INN

2 cups waterground
 white corn meal
1 teaspoon double-acting
 baking powder

3 tablespoons sugar
¼ cup butter
1 tablespoon salt

Combine corn meal, baking powder, sugar and salt. Add slowly to 3½ cups boiling water, stirring briskly. As soon as mixture is smooth, remove from heat. Stir in butter. Cool. Form into finger-shaped rolls and fry in 2 inches hot fat (375°) until golden brown. Makes about 3 dozen.

## OYSTER-STUFFED CHICKEN: BIRD & BOTTLE

| | |
|---|---|
| 3 broiler chickens, split in half | 2 tablespoons chopped onion |
| 1 pint oysters | 1 garlic clove, crushed |
| 3 tablespoons chopped green pepper | Butter |
| | Bread crumbs |
| 2 tablespoons chopped celery | ¼ teaspoon cayenne pepper |
| | 1 teaspoon salt |
| 3 tablespoons chopped parsley | Freshly ground black pepper |
| | Cranberry or lingonberry preserve |

Drain and chop oysters and save their liquor. Sauté oysters and vegetables with seasonings in 4 tablespoons butter for 10 minutes. Add 1 cup bread crumbs and ½ cup oyster liquor. Meanwhile place chickens in shallow baking pan skin side up and dot with butter. Add ½ cup of water to pan. Bake in a moderate oven (375°) for 30 minutes or until brown. Remove chicken from oven. Turn chicken skin side down and fill each cavity with oyster stuffing. Sprinkle stuffing with bread crumbs and melted butter. Bake 20 minutes or until crumbs are golden brown. Serve with cranberry or lingonberry preserve. Serves 6.

## DEVILED CRAB: BIRD & BOTTLE

| | |
|---|---|
| 1 pound lump crab meat | 2 eggs, beaten |
| ½ cup minced onion | 1 hard-cooked egg, chopped |
| ¼ cup minced celery | 1 tablespoon white wine vinegar |
| ¼ cup minced green pepper | |
| 1 garlic clove, minced | 1 teaspoon Worcestershire sauce |
| 1 tablespoon chopped parsley | |
| ½ cup butter | ¼ teaspoon thyme |
| 2 cups soft bread crumbs | Tabasco sauce |
| ½ cup heavy cream | 1 teaspoon salt |

Sauté onion, celery, green pepper, garlic and parsley in 6 tablespoons of butter for 10 minutes. Cool. Combine 1 cup bread crumbs, cream, raw and cooked eggs, vinegar, Worcestershire, thyme, a few drops of Tabasco and salt with sautéed vegetables. Add crab meat and toss lightly to mix. Spoon into 12 scallop shells or individual baking dishes. Melt remaining 2 tablespoons butter and toss with remaining 1 cup bread crumbs. Top crab mixture with buttered crumbs. Place shells in shallow baking pan. Put ¼ inch water in bottom of pan. Bake in a hot oven (450°) for 10 minutes or until browned and hot. Serves 6.

## HALIBUT BRANDADE: BONANZA INN

| | |
|---|---|
| 6 cups finely flaked cooked halibut | 3 cups mashed potatoes |
| | 2 tablespoons butter |
| 1½ cups mayonnaise | Cayenne pepper |
| ¾ cup oil | 1½ teaspoons salt |
| 3 garlic cloves, minced | |

Combine halibut, mayonnaise, oil, garlic, salt and a few grains of cayenne. Mix thoroughly. Place mixture in shallow casserole and top with mashed potatoes. Dot potatoes with butter. Bake in a moderate oven (375°) for 30 minutes or until potatoes are browned. Serve at once. Serves 6.

## WATER CRESS SOUP: BONANZA INN

| | |
|---|---|
| 2 bunches water cress | 1 tablespoon sugar |
| 2 thick slices onion | 3 cups chicken bouillon |
| 1 three-inch piece of celery, cut up | 1 large can evaporated milk |
| | 2 tablespoons butter |
| 1 tablespoon cornstarch | 1 teaspoon salt |

Remove leaves from stems of cress. Place leaves, onion, celery, cornstarch, sugar, salt and 2 cups of bouillon in blender and blend until smooth. Place in saucepan, add remaining 1 cup of bouillon. Bring mixture to a boil, reduce heat and cook, for 10 minutes, stirring constantly. Add evaporated milk and butter and simmer for 5 minutes. Serves 6.

## PHEASANT BROTH: THE MILK PAIL

| | |
|---|---|
| 2 hen pheasants | Ac'cent |
| 1 large onion | Freshly ground black pepper |
| ½ stalk celery | Egg drops |
| 2 medium carrots | |

Cover pheasants with water. Add onion, celery, carrots, Ac'cent and pepper. Bring to a boil, reduce heat, cover and simmer for 45 minutes. Remove pheasants, cut off breasts and save breasts for another meal. Return pheasants to stock and simmer for 45 minutes or until meat falls from the bones. Remove pheasants and strain stock. Cut meat into small pieces and return to stock. Add egg drops before serving. Serves 12.

## EGG DROPS

| | |
|---|---|
| 3 eggs | Yellow food coloring |
| ¾ cup flour | 1 teaspoon salt |

Beat eggs lightly. Add flour, salt and 3 drops of food coloring and beat until smooth. Press through colander into boiling water and cook for 3 minutes or until egg drops are set. Skim out of water and add to pheasant broth or other soup.

## VENISON RAGOUT: THE MILK PAIL

| | |
|---|---|
| 3 pounds boned venison | ¼ cup melted butter |
| 1 cup vinegar | ¼ cup red Burgundy wine |
| 2 cups chopped celery | ½ pint sour cream |
| 2 cups chopped onion | Ac'cent |
| Rosemary | Salt |
| ¼ cup flour | Freshly ground black pepper |

Marinate venison overnight in vinegar, ½ cup of water, Ac'cent, salt and pepper. Drain venison. Place in casserole with celery, onion, a pinch of rosemary and 1 cup of water. Cover and braise in a moderate oven (350°) for 2 hours. Remove venison. Slice it and keep it warm in a chafing dish. Strain stock. Combine flour and butter. Stir until smooth. Add to stock and cook, stirring constantly, until thickened. Stir in wine and sour cream. Pour over venison and serve from chafing dish. Serves 6.

## BEEF BOURGUIGNON: THE MILTON INN

| | |
|---|---|
| 3 pounds beef sirloin, cut in 1-inch cubes | 2 cups quartered mushroom caps |
| | ¼ cup chopped shallots |
| 2 cups red Burgundy wine | 1 tablespoon flour |
| ½ cup butter | |

Melt 6 tablespoons butter in a deep casserole. Add beef cubes, cover and braise in a hot oven (400°) for 20 minutes. Meanwhile sauté mushroom caps and shallots in remaining 2 tablespoons butter. Stir in flour. Add Burgundy and mix well. Pour over beef, cover and return to oven for 30 minutes. Serves 6.

## BASS LIVORNESE: THE MILTON INN

| | |
|---|---|
| 1 four-pound striped bass | ½ cup dry white wine |
| 1 onion, thinly sliced | ½ cup peas |
| 1 garlic clove, minced | ½ cup canned tomatoes |
| ¼ cup olive oil | Italian bread slices, toasted |
| ¼ cup chopped parsley | |

Cut bass into 1½-inch slices. Sauté onion and garlic in olive oil for 10 minutes. Add bass and remaining ingredients, cover and simmer for 20 minutes. Serve on toasted bread. Serves 6.

## FILET OF BEEF: LA CREMAILLERE

| | |
|---|---|
| 1 five-pound beef filet | 1 cup beef gravy |
| 10 small strips larding pork | ½ cup Madeira wine |
| 6 tablespoons Calvados brandy | 1 teaspoon tomato paste |
| ½ cup butter | 1 ounce truffles, chopped |
| 2 carrots, sliced | Celery salt |
| 1 onion, sliced | Salt |
| 1 garlic clove, chopped | White pepper |

Soak pork strips in 3 tablespoons Calvados for 5 minutes. Lard filet of beef with these strips. Rub filet with celery salt, salt and pepper. Roll meat and tie with butcher's twine every 2 inches. Melt butter in roasting pan. Roll filet in butter. Roast it in a very hot oven (500°) for 35 minutes. Turn filet every 10 minutes and baste it frequently with pan juices. Remove filet and keep it hot. Pour fat from pan. Put carrots, onion and garlic into pan and return to oven for 10 minutes or until onion is well browned. Remove pan from oven and place over direct heat. Add remaining 3 tablespoons of Calvados, beef gravy, Madeira and tomato paste. Bring to a boil, reduce heat and simmer for 10 minutes, stirring frequently. Strain, add truffles. Serves 6.

## CHARLOTTE RUSSE: LA CREMAILLERE

| | |
|---|---|
| 9 egg yolks | 1 cup chopped candied fruits |
| 1 cup sugar | ¼ cup kirsch |
| 2 cups milk | 1 tablespoon vanilla extract |
| 3 envelopes | Lady fingers |
| unflavored gelatine | Sweetened whipped cream |
| 2 cups cream, whipped | Chopped toasted almonds |

Combine egg yolks and sugar in the top part of a double boiler and mix thoroughly. Bring milk to a boil and add slowly to egg yolk and sugar mixture, stirring constantly. Set over hot water and cook, stirring constantly, until smooth and thickened. Remove from heat. Soften gelatine in ¾ cup cold water. Add softened gelatine to hot custard mixture and stir until gelatine is dissolved. Cool. Chill until mixture begins to set, stirring occasionally. Fold in whipped cream, fruits, kirsch and vanilla. Pour into dish lined with lady fingers. Chill for 3 hours. Garnish with sweetened whipped cream and almonds. Serves 12.

## FORTY MORE FINE AMERICAN INNS

In these inns country motorists will find congenial surroundings and excellent food. Most are off the beaten path. Not all serve liquor and only about a third provide any lodging.

### NORTHEAST

**SNOWBERRY'S LOBSTER HOUSE,** Pine Point, Me., sits on the shore by the Atlantic. It serves lobsters, clams, other sea food.

**LOVETT'S,** Franconia, N.H., is a 160-year-old farmhouse with Early American decor and American cooking.

**THE SHELBURNE HARBOR INN,** Shelburne, Vt., is a Georgian mansion on Lake Champlain. Menu is mainly French.

**GUNDLACH'S HOFBRAU HOUSE,** Plainville, Mass., is a clapboard farmhouse where guests get German-American cooking.

**THE TOLL HOUSE,** Whitman, Mass., dates from 1709. Its staple is New England food, but it offers one foreign dish each week.

**CHILLINGSWORTH,** East Brewster, Mass., a gray shingle house on the bay side of Cape Cod, serves French food.

**THE WHALE INN,** Goshen, Mass., a farmhouse, serves American food.

**THE FERRY TAVERN,** Old Lyme, Conn., was once a Connecticut River ferry station. Its specialty is sea food.

**SIMSBURY HOUSE,** Simsbury, Conn., is a Victorian mansion. Terrace and carriage house are used for dining. Menu is American.

**THE KREBS,** Skaneateles, N.Y., serves big five-course dinners with American dishes like strawberry shortcake, roast beef, steak.

**THE SILVER HORN,** Millbrook, N.Y., a remodeled old Quaker meetinghouse, serves steaks from its own Angus cattle.

**THE SWISS TAVERN,** Pompton Lakes, N.J., has a Swiss menu featuring *truite au bleu*, veal in white wine.

**THE TOW-PATH HOUSE,** New Hope, Pa., an old canal station, specializes in lobster thermidor. Guests eat on terraces.

**THE PIPERSVILLE INN,** Pipersville, Pa., is an old brick Pennsylvania Dutch inn serving table d'hôte German cooking.

### SOUTH

**THE GRANARY,** built in Georgetown, Md., 140 years ago as a grain depot, specializes in steaks and sea food.

**OLNEY INN,** Olney, Md., is a spacious farmhouse where mint juleps are served on wide lawns. The menu is American.

**THE TIDES INN,** Irvington, Va., on Rappahannock River, has dock for yachts, serves spoon bread and oyster stew.

**THE NU-WRAY INN,** Burnsville, N.C., an inn built around a 125-year-old log house, serves family-style meals at set hours.

**THE SQUIRREL INN,** Summerville, S.C., offers Continental food and good wine in a setting of azaleas and Spanish moss.

**CHALET SUZANNE,** Lake Wales, Fla., has an international cuisine to fit decorations from Spain, Italy, Egypt and Scandinavia.

**OLD TALBOTT TAVERN,** Bardstown, Ky., a white stone inn, serves Kentucky dishes like ham with red-eye gravy.

**SPRING LAKE RESTAURANT,** Bellefonte. Ark., has glassed-in dining room out over trout pond.

### NORTH CENTRAL

**THE GOLDEN LAMB INN,** Lebanon, Ohio, state's oldest inn, is famous for Virginia ham, blackbottom pie, sour cream dishes.

**THE OLD BARN INN,** St. Albans, Mo., formerly a barn, offers an American menu with lavish desserts on patio near a pool.

**THE OLD OLTZ HOUSE,** Creve Coeur, Mo., cooks on order guinea hen, fresh rainbow trout and duckling with wine sauce.

**THE FOX AND HOUNDS,** Hubertus, Wis., is a log house in hills near Milwaukee. A specialty is roast duck with wild rice.

**THE LOWELL INN,** Stillwater, Minn., has an indoor pool from which patrons select their brook trout.

**THE OX YOKE,** Amana, Iowa, is one of four good family-style eating places in the community. Food is German.

### WEST

**THE COUNTRY KITCHEN,** Littleton, Colo., features smorgasbord with choice of 70 Swedish dishes in a chink-log cabin.

**THE COPPER KETTLE,** Aspen, Colo., once a mining post, specializes in international food—a different kind each night.

**ARDOVINO'S,** Anapra, N.M., near El Paso, is isolated white ranch house with windmill, swimming pool. Cooking is Italian.

**LA POSTA,** Mesilla, N.M., an old adobe trading post in desert country, has Mexican food but also serves western dishes.

**PARRY LODGE,** Kanab, Utah, near the Grand Canyon, is a rambling white house serving American dishes.

**OJAI VALLEY INN,** Ojai, Calif., looks out to the Santa Ynez Mountains, offers elaborate luncheon buffets and suppers.

**APPLE VALLEY INN,** Victorville, Calif., is a stone-and-redwood ranch resort with a barbecue pit and a 30-foot-long buffet.

**NEPENTHE,** Big Sur, Calif., has a barbecue pit at the brink of a high cliff over the Pacific, serves steak and hamburger.

**LITTLE RIVER INN,** near Mendocino, Calif., is a farmhouse overlooking the Pacific. Specialties are abalone dishes.

**MON DESIR,** Central Point, Ore., is an old country home with landscaped gardens. Specialty is marinated prime ribs.

**THE CRAB BROILER,** Seaside, Ore., serves local crabs, oysters and razor clams in an English tavern setting.

**THE ALDERBROOK INN,** Union, Wash., is a rambling white lodge on the Hood Canal featuring local salmon and sea food.

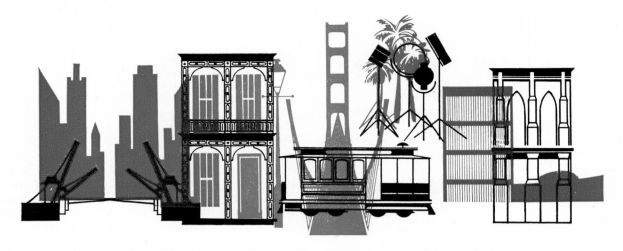

# BIG CITY RESTAURANTS

### NORWEGIAN PANCAKES: SCANDIA

| | |
|---|---|
| 4 eggs, separated | Butter |
| 1 tablespoon sugar | 1 pint vanilla ice cream |
| 1 cup sifted flour | 1 cup sliced strawberries |
| 1½ cups milk | Salt |
| ½ cup beer | Meringue |
| Grated rind of 1 lemon | Flaming sauce |

Combine egg yolks and sugar and stir until sugar is dissolved. Add flour alternately with milk and beer, beating well after each addition. Stir in lemon rind, 2 tablespoons melted butter and a pinch of salt. Beat egg whites until stiff but not dry and fold into batter. Cook pancakes in buttered 8-inch skillet, using about 1 cup batter for each pancake. Makes 6. Stack and keep warm. Spoon ice cream and strawberries onto pancakes. Roll up and place them 2 inches apart on silver platter or ovenproof dish. Cover each pancake with meringue put through pastry tube. Bake in a very hot oven (550°) for 2 minutes or until meringue is lightly browned. Pour flaming sauce around pancakes and serve immediately. Serves 6.

### FLAMING SAUCE

| | |
|---|---|
| 2 jiggers cherry Heering | 6 lemon twists |
| 1 jigger dark rum | |

Combine cherry Heering, rum and lemon twists. Flame sauce and let it burn for 30 seconds.

### VEAL CUTLET CORDON BLEU: PERINO'S

| | |
|---|---|
| 12 thin slices veal | ¾ cup bread crumbs |
| 6 thin slices Swiss cheese | ¾ cup butter |
| 6 thin slices Virginia ham | Salt |
| Flour | Freshly ground black pepper |
| 3 eggs, beaten | 24 cooked asparagus tips |

Flatten the veal slices with a cleaver and sprinkle them with salt and pepper. Put 1 slice of cheese and 1 slice of ham on each of 6 veal slices, cover with remaining veal slices. Pound edges together. Dip in flour, then in eggs, then in crumbs. Fry in butter for about 8 minutes. Serve with hot asparagus tips. Serves 6.

### BEEF BELMONT: CHASEN'S

| | |
|---|---|
| 8 pounds short ribs of beef with bone | 12 pearl onions |
| Bouquet garni (parsley, bay leaf and thyme tied in piece of cheesecloth) | 4 ounces egg noodles |
| | Salt |
| | Freshly ground black pepper |
| 6 celery stalks | 1 cup sour cream |
| 4 carrots, diced | ¼ cup freshly grated horseradish |
| 3 leeks, diced | Pickled green tomatoes |

Place meat in 4 quarts of cold water and bring slowly to a boil. Skim top until clear. Add bouquet garni and simmer for 1½ hours. Remove bouquet garni. Season with salt and pepper to taste. Add celery, carrots, leeks and onions. Simmer for 15 minutes. Add egg noodles and simmer for 10 minutes. Serve the soup with vegetables and noodles in a large soup plate. Then serve the meat separately, accompanied by a sauce of sour cream and horseradish combined, and the pickled green tomatoes. Serves 6.

### CAESAR SALAD: CHASEN'S

| | |
|---|---|
| 9 cups romaine, broken into small pieces | 4 tablespoons lemon juice |
| 1½ cups sourdough bread croutons | 2 tablespoons Worcestershire sauce |
| 3 tablespoons oil | 1 egg, coddled 1 minute |
| 1 garlic clove, cut up | Freshly ground black pepper |
| 9 tablespoons French dressing | 6 tablespoons grated Parmesan cheese |

Combine oil and garlic clove. Let stand for 2 hours. Remove and discard garlic. Arrange romaine and croutons in salad bowl. Combine garlic oil, French dressing, lemon juice, Worcestershire, egg and pepper and stir briskly. Pour over salad and toss well. Sprinkle lightly with Parmesan cheese. Serves 6.

### TOURNEDOS: LA RUE

| | |
|---|---|
| 6 tournedos of beef | 1 cup imported Madeira wine |
| ¾ cup butter | 1½ cups of Madeira sauce |
| 2 shallots, finely chopped | 3 large white truffles, thinly sliced |
| ½ cup brandy | Salt |
| 2 tablespoons chopped tarragon | Freshly ground black pepper |

Tournedos are 2-inch-thick slices of beef tenderloin trimmed of all fat. Sauté tournedos in ½ cup butter as desired—rare, medium, well done. Add shallots and brown just a little, add brandy and flame it. Place tournedos on a platter and keep warm. To sauce remaining in the skillet add tarragon and ½ cup Madeira wine and cook until sauce is reduced two-thirds to its original quantity. Add Madeira sauce and boil for 5 minutes. Season with salt and pepper. Remove from heat and blend in remaining ½ cup Madeira wine and ½ cup butter. Place the sliced truffles on the tournedos and pour the sauce over them. Serves 6.

### ROCHER DE GLACE AUX FRUITES: LA RUE

| | |
|---|---|
| 2 bananas, diced | 2 glasses of Cointreau |
| 3 oranges, diced | Distilled orange blossom water |
| 3 peaches, diced | |
| 1 cup diced fresh pineapple | 36 orange blossoms |
| Fresh strawberries | Fruit sherbets |
| 2 glasses of imported kirsch | 18 Parma candied violets |
| 1 cup vanilla sugar | |

Combine fruit, sugar, Cointreau, kirsch, a few drops of orange blossom water and 12 orange blossoms. Marinate in the refrigerator for 2 hours. Spoon into 6 individual chilled serving dishes. Add alternating spoonfuls of sherbets. Garnish with remaining orange blossoms and candied violets. Serves 6. To make vanilla sugar, cut a 1-inch piece of vanilla bean in half. Scrape out seeds and crush them with 1 cup sugar.

### KAMAAINA: TRADER VIC'S

| | |
|---|---|
| 1 ounce gin | ½ ounce curaçao |
| 1 ounce Lopez coconut cream | 2 ounces 7-Up |
| ½ ounce lemon juice | Fresh mint |

Mix in electric mixer with cracked ice. Serve in ceramic coconut with cracked ice. Decorate with fresh mint. Serves 1.

## SAMOAN FOG CUTTER: TRADER VIC'S

| | |
|---|---|
| 2 ounces light rum | 2 ounces lemon juice |
| 1 ounce brandy | ½ ounce orgeat syrup |
| ½ ounce gin | Sherry wine |
| 1 ounce orange juice | |

Mix all ingredients except sherry in electric blender with a small scoop of shaved ice. Pour into fog cutter mug. Float a small amount of sherry on top. Serve with straws. Serves 1.

## SCORPION: TRADER VIC'S

| | |
|---|---|
| 6 ounces light rum | 1 ounce gin |
| 6 ounces orange juice | 1 ounce brandy |
| 4 ounces lemon juice | 2 ounces orgeat syrup |

Mix all ingredients in electric blender with a scoop of shaved ice. Pour into scorpion bowl filled with cracked ice. Float a gardenia on top and serve with long straws. Serves 4.

## SHRIMP A LA HORCHER: ERNIE'S

| | |
|---|---|
| 1 pound cooked bay shrimp, shelled | 1 tablespoon chopped chives |
| 3 avocados | 1 tablespoon chopped parsley |
| 6 tablespoons cognac | 2 tablespoons chopped shallots |
| ¼ cup wine vinegar | 1 cup olive oil |
| 1½ teaspoons dry mustard | 6 tablespoons chili sauce |
| 3 egg yolks | 2 tablespoons lemon juice |
| 2 tablespoons finely chopped celery | Salt |
| 2 tablespoons horseradish | Freshly ground black pepper |

With a melon baller make small balls of avocados. In 6 *suprême* dishes put a layer of avocado balls, then a layer of bay shrimp. Combine remaining ingredients, mix thoroughly and spoon over shrimp. Serve well chilled. Serves 6. This recipe is named in honor of Otto Horcher, famed Madrid restaurateur.

## VEAL AL PROSCIUTTO: AMELIO'S

| | |
|---|---|
| 24 veal scallops about 3 by 4 inches each | Marsala wine |
| 24 very thin slices of prosciutto | Lemon juice |
| Flour | Chopped parsley |
| Sweet butter | Salt |
| | Freshly ground black pepper |

Dip the veal scallops in flour and sauté them in butter over high heat, allowing a scant 2 minutes for each side. Add a generous splashing of Marsala, enough to deglaze the pan thoroughly. Cover each veal scallop with a slice of prosciutto and season with salt and pepper. Sprinkle with lemon juice and parsley. Pour in ¾ cup of Marsala and simmer uncovered for 10 minutes or until tender. Just before serving, sprinkle the veal and prosciutto very lightly with more of the wine and serve immediately on very hot plates. Serves 6.

## ZUCCHINI FIORENTINA: AMELIO'S

| | |
|---|---|
| 6 small zucchini | ½ cup olive oil |
| 2 eggs, beaten | Salt |
| ½ cup flour | Freshly ground black pepper |

It is very important in this dish to use zucchini that are very young—still in the blossom stage of the plant. Slice the zucchini very thin. Dip the slices in beaten eggs, then in flour lightly seasoned with salt and pepper. Sauté in olive oil about 5 minutes or until golden. Serve immediately. Serves 6.

## BEEHIVE HONEY CAKE: PALACE HOTEL

| | |
|---|---|
| ½ cup milk | 3 tablespoons honey |
| ⅓ cup sugar | 6 tablespoons sugar |
| 1 teaspoon salt | 6 tablespoons cream |
| 2 envelopes granular yeast | 6 tablespoons chopped cashew nuts |
| 2 eggs | |
| ½ cup soft shortening | 6 tablespoons chopped pine nuts |
| 4½ cups sifted flour | |
| 6 tablespoons butter | |

Scald milk, add sugar and salt and stir until sugar is dissolved. Cool to lukewarm. Soften yeast in ½ cup lukewarm water for 5 minutes. Add to milk mixture and stir until yeast is dissolved. Stir in eggs and shortening. Add half the flour and beat well. Add remaining flour and mix thoroughly. Turn out onto floured board and knead until dough is smooth and elastic. Place in greased bowl, turning once to bring greased side up. Cover with damp cloth and let rise in warm place until double in bulk (about 1½ hours). Punch dough down, cover and let rise again until almost double in bulk. Meanwhile combine butter, honey, sugar and cream and bring to a boil, stirring constantly. Boil gently for 10 minutes, stirring. Remove from heat, stir in nuts. Form dough into ball, flatten and fit into greased 10-inch baking pan. Spread honey and nut mixture over dough and let rise 1 inch. Bake in a moderate oven (375°) for 30 minutes. Serves 6.

## ST. HONORE CAKE: PALACE HOTEL

| | |
|---|---|
| ½ recipe pie crust | 1¼ cups flour |
| 1 cup milk | 5 eggs |
| ½ cup butter | Cream filling |

Roll pie crust ⅛ inch thick and with it cover the bottom of a 10-inch pie pan. Bring milk and butter to a boil in saucepan. Add flour all at once and stir briskly with wooden spoon until dough leaves sides of pan and forms a ball in center of saucepan. Remove from heat and add eggs, 1 at a time, beating well after each addition. Continue beating until mixture is smooth and satiny. Put it through pastry bag and form a raised border around the edge of pie crust dough and against sides of pan. Bake in a hot oven (400°) for 30 minutes. Remove carefully from pan. Cool. Fill with cream filling and chill. Serves 12.

## CREAM FILLING

| | |
|---|---|
| 3 cups milk, scalded | 7 eggs, separated |
| 1 cup sugar | ½ teaspoon unflavored gelatine |
| 1 teaspoon cornstarch | |

Combine sugar, cornstarch and egg yolks in top part of double boiler and mix thoroughly. Pour milk slowly over egg yolk mixture, stirring constantly. Set over hot water and cook, stirring constantly, until smooth and thickened. Remove from heat. Soften gelatine in 2 tablespoons water and stir into custard mixture. Cool for 5 minutes. Beat egg whites until stiff but not dry. Fold custard mixture carefully into egg whites. Pour into baked shell. Chill for at least 4 hours. Makes about 6 cups.

## SHASHLIK EN BROCHETTE: PUMP ROOM

| | |
|---|---|
| 2 pounds lamb cut from leg | 1 cup soft bread crumbs |
| 2 cups red Burgundy wine | Oil |
| ½ cup minced onion | 1 teaspoon salt |
| 2 bay leaves | Freshly ground black pepper |
| 1 tablespoon Worcestershire sauce | Hot shashlik sauce |
| 1 garlic clove, crushed | Hot cooked saffron rice |

Cut lamb into 1½-inch cubes. Marinate meat for 48 hours in combined wine, onion, bay leaves, Worcestershire, garlic, salt and pepper. Remove meat from marinade, dip in bread crumbs and thread on skewers. Sprinkle with oil and broil under high heat for 20 minutes or until golden brown, turning frequently. Serve with hot shashlik sauce and saffron rice. Serves. 6

## HOT SHASHLIK SAUCE

| | |
|---|---|
| 2 cups chili sauce | 1 tablespoon honey |
| 1 cup catsup | 1 tablespoon horseradish |
| 1 tablespoon piccalilli | 1 tablespoon chopped chutney |

Combine ingredients in saucepan and mix well. Cook over low heat, stirring constantly, for 10 minutes. Makes about 3 cups.

## SCALLOPS EN BROCHETTE: PUMP ROOM

| | |
|---|---|
| 2 pounds sea scallops | Dried bread crumbs |
| Bacon slices | Salt |
| Oil | Tartar sauce |

Cut each bacon slice into 4 squares. Brush scallops with oil. Dust with bread crumbs. Sprinkle with salt. Thread scallops on skewers alternately with bacon squares. Broil under high heat for about 10 minutes or until bacon is crisp. Serve with tartar sauce. Serves 6.

## CRAB MEAT EN BROCHETTE: PUMP ROOM

| | |
|---|---|
| 3 pounds fresh crab meat | 1 tablespoon dry mustard |
| 3 cups soft bread crumbs | 1 tablespoon chopped chives |
| ½ cup dry sherry | Bacon slices, cut in half |

Combine crab meat, bread crumbs, sherry, mustard and chives. Mix well. Shape into balls the size of walnuts. Wrap each ball in a half-slice of bacon and fasten bacon with toothpick. Thread on skewers and broil under medium heat for 15 minutes or until well browned, turning frequently. Serves 6.

## CHICKEN KIEV: IMPERIAL HOUSE

| | |
|---|---|
| Breasts of 3 three-pound chickens | 4 eggs, beaten |
| 9 tablespoons chilled sweet butter | ½ cup milk |
| | 3 cups sifted fresh bread crumbs |
| 1 cup flour | Vegetable shortening |

Bone chicken breasts, leaving a joint of wing attached. Flatten the breasts with a cleaver, then stuff each one with 3 tablespoons of chilled butter. Carefully seal the edges with toothpicks. Dip the stuffed breasts in flour, then into egg beaten with milk and roll them in bread crumbs. Then re-dip the breasts in flour, in egg and milk mixture and bread crumbs. Fry in 3 inches of hot vegetable shortening (375°) for 8 to 10 minutes or until golden brown. Remove toothpicks, serve immediately. Serves 6.

## FROGS' LEGS PROVENCALE: JACQUES

| | |
|---|---|
| 3 pounds frogs' legs | ¼ cup chopped parsley |
| 1 cup butter | 2 garlic cloves, minced |
| 3 tomatoes, peeled and chopped | 1 cup heavy cream |
| | 1 cup flour |
| 1 cup sliced mushrooms | 1 cup olive oil |

First make tomato sauce—melt butter in skillet, add tomatoes, mushrooms, parsley and garlic and simmer for 10 minutes. Dip frogs' legs in cream, then in flour. Sauté in oil in another skillet for 10 minutes or until brown. Serve with sauce. Serves 6.

## PEPPER STEAK: CLUB BOYAR

| | |
|---|---|
| 3 pounds tenderloin steak, sliced | 1½ cups Espagnole sauce |
| 3 green peppers, sliced | ¾ cup butter |
| 3 onions, sliced | ½ cup flour |
| 9 large mushrooms, sliced | 6 tablespoons red Burgundy |
| 3 tomatoes, quartered | Salt |
| | Freshly ground black pepper |

First make green pepper sauce—sauté green peppers, onions, mushrooms and tomatoes in ½ cup butter for 5 minutes. Add Espagnole sauce and simmer for 10 minutes. Salt and pepper the sliced steak. Dip in flour and sauté in remaining ¼ cup butter for 2 minutes. Add sauce and simmer for 15 minutes, stirring frequently. Add wine and simmer for 3 minutes. Serves 6.

## ESPAGNOLE SAUCE

| | |
|---|---|
| 3 tablespoons butter | 1½ cups beef bouillon |
| 3 tablespoons flour | |

Melt butter, add flour and stir until smooth. Add bouillon gradually and cook, stirring, until thickened. Makes about 1½ cups.

## CLAMS CASINO: CLUB BOYAR

| | |
|---|---|
| 36 cherrystone clams on the half shell | ¼ cup diced green pepper |
| 3 slices bacon, diced | ½ cup diced pimento |
| | 1 teaspoon minced shallots |

Arrange clams in shells on a bed of rock salt. Sprinkle with bacon, green pepper, pimento and shallots. Bake in a hot oven (400°) for 15 minutes or until bacon is brown. Serves 6.

## BAKED REDFISH: BRENNAN'S

| | |
|---|---|
| 1 five-pound redfish (channel bass) | 2 cups canned tomato sauce |
| | Cayenne pepper |
| ½ cup chopped onion | Salt |
| ½ cup chopped celery | Freshly ground black pepper |
| 1 garlic clove, minced | Chopped scallion tops |
| ½ cup oil | Chopped parsley |
| 2½ cups canned tomatoes | 1 lemon, sliced thin |

Sauté onion, celery and garlic in oil in a heavy pot for 10 minutes. Add tomatoes and tomato sauce. Cook uncovered over medium heat for 40 minutes, stirring occasionally. Add 1 cup cold water. Cook for 20 minutes. Meanwhile season fish with salt, black pepper and a few grains of cayenne pepper. Put in baking dish. Pour tomato mixture over the fish. Bake in a slow oven (325°) for 30 minutes, basting several times with the sauce. Garnish with scallion, parsley and lemon slices. Serves 6.

## CRAWFISH BISQUE: BRENNAN'S

| | |
|---|---|
| 20 pounds fresh crawfish | 6 eggs, beaten |
| 1 cup chopped celery | ½ cup chopped scallion tops |
| ½ cup chopped parsley | Cayenne pepper |
| 2 cups chopped onion | 1 tablespoon salt |
| ⅓ cup butter | Freshly ground black pepper |
| 8 stale buns, soaked in water | 1 cup hot cooked rice |
| 4 slices stale bread, crumbled | |

Bring 2 quarts of water to a boil, add crawfish and 2 teaspoons salt. Reduce heat and simmer for 15 minutes. Drain and save stock. Pull out middle tail fin and with it the intestinal vein of each crawfish. Pick fat and meat from tails and heads and save it. Keep head shells for stuffing. Return tail shells to stock, and add ½ cup celery and ¼ cup parsley. Bring to a boil, reduce heat and simmer for 30 minutes. Strain. Chop crawfish meat and add half of it to this bisque. Remove from heat and cover to keep hot. Meanwhile sauté onion and remaining ½ cup celery in crawfish fat and butter in a heavy pot for 10 minutes. Combine drained soaked buns, crumbled bread and eggs and stir into onion mixture. Add remaining chopped crawfish meat, remaining ¼ cup parsley, scallion tops, remaining 1 teaspoon salt, a few grains of cayenne pepper and black pepper. Cook over low heat for 10 minutes, stirring constantly. Stuff crawfish heads with this mixture. To serve, put 5 stuffed crawfish heads and a few spoonfuls of rice in each soup bowl. Pour hot bisque over. Serves 8.

## OYSTERS ROCKEFELLER: ANTOINE'S

| | |
|---|---|
| 36 freshly opened oysters on the half shell | 3 tablespoons minced parsley |
| 6 tablespoons butter | 3 tablespoons minced celery |
| 6 tablespoons finely minced raw spinach | 5 tablespoons bread crumbs |
| | Tabasco sauce |
| 3 tablespoons minced onion | ½ teaspoon Herbsaint |
| | ½ teaspoon salt |

Melt butter in saucepan. Add all the rest of the ingredients except the oysters. Cook, stirring constantly, for 15 minutes or until soft. Press through sieve or food mill. Cool. Place rock salt in pie tins. Set oysters on half shell on top and put a spoonful of sauce on each oyster. Broil under medium heat until sauce begins to brown. Serve immediately in the pie tins. Serves 6. (The exact recipe for Antoine's oysters Rockefeller is a secret of the house. Owner Roy Alciatore gives this as a close facsimile.)

## PIGEONNEAUX ROYALE: ANTOINE'S

| | |
|---|---|
| 6 royal squab | ½ cup chopped onion |
| Butter | Salt |
| 1 cup chopped celery | Freshly ground black pepper |
| 1 cup chopped carrot | Sauce paradis |

Sprinkle squab inside and out with salt and pepper. Rub with butter. Combine celery, carrot and onion and spread on bottom of roasting pan. Place squab on vegetables. Roast in a slow oven 325°) for about 30 minutes. Remove squab. Arrange squab in a deep casserole. Pour sauce paradis over them, cover and bake for 15 minutes. Serve immediately. Serves 6.

## SAUCE PARADIS

| | |
|---|---|
| ¼ cup butter | 2 tablespoons red currant jelly |
| ¼ cup flour | |
| 2 cups double-strength veal stock | 2 cups seedless white grapes |
| | 2 large truffles, sliced |
| ½ cup Madeira wine | |

Melt butter, add flour and stir until smooth. Add veal stock and cook, stirring constantly, until slightly thickened. Add wine and jelly and stir until jelly is melted. Add grapes and truffles. Makes about 4 cups. Chicken stock may be substituted for veal stock.

## POMPANO EN PAPILLOTE: ANTOINE'S

| | |
|---|---|
| 3 medium-sized pompanos, filleted | 2 cups cooked crab meat |
| 1 stalk celery, cut up | 3 shallots, chopped |
| 1 onion, cut up | 1 garlic clove, minced |
| 2 cups dry white wine | 1 bay leaf, crumbled |
| 6 tablespoons butter | Thyme |
| 2 tablespoons flour | Tabasco sauce |
| 2 cups cooked shrimp, chopped | Salt |
| | Freshly ground black pepper |

First make the stock. Combine heads and bones of the pompanos with celery, onion, 1 teaspoon salt and 3 cups of water. Bring to a boil, reduce heat and simmer for 30 minutes. Strain stock. Measure 1 cup of stock and set it aside. Pour remaining stock into skillet and add ½ cup wine. Season fillets with salt and pepper and fold in half. Place in hot stock and simmer for 8 minutes. Remove from heat and allow fillet to cool in stock. Remove fillets and drain. Meanwhile make the fish velouté. Melt 2 tablespoons butter, add flour and stir until smooth. Add 1 cup fish stock and cook until thickened, stirring constantly. Set aside. Sauté shallots in remaining 4 tablespoons butter for 5 minutes. Add shrimp, crab meat, garlic, bay leaf, a pinch of thyme and a dash of Tabasco. Mix well. Add the remaining 1½ cups wine and cook for 15 minutes, stirring frequently. Cool. To make pompano en papillote, cut 6 parchment paper hearts about 8 inches long and 12 inches wide. Brush them with oil. Place a spoonful of sauce on one side of each heart. Put 1 pompano fillet on top and cover with a little sauce. Fold paper hearts over and around to seal in fish and sauce. Arrange them on an oiled baking sheet and brush them with oil. Bake in a hot oven (450°) for 15 minutes or until the paper is browned. Serve pompanos immediately in their paper covers. Rip the paper open at the table. Serves 6.

## SHRIMP ARNAUD: ARNAUD'S

| | |
|---|---|
| 2 pounds cooked shrimp, peeled | ½ cup prepared mustard |
| ¼ cup minced celery | ½ cup vinegar |
| ¼ cup minced shallots | ½ cup olive oil |
| ¼ cup minced parsley | ½ cup crushed red pepper |
| | 1 tablespoon salt |

Combine all ingredients except shrimp and mix well. Pour over shrimp. Marinate for at least 15 minutes. Serves 6.

## CHOCOLATE SOUFFLE: VOISIN

| | |
|---|---|
| 2 ounces sweet chocolate, cut into small pieces | 6 tablespoons flour |
| 1½ cups milk | 2 tablespoons cornstarch |
| Sugar | 9 egg whites, stiffly beaten |
| 6 egg yolks | Butter |
| | Vanilla sauce |

Bring chocolate, milk and 6 tablespoons sugar to a boil, stirring constantly. Mix the egg yolks, flour and cornstarch in a bowl. Add the boiling milk mixture gradually, stirring briskly. Return to the heat and bring to a boil, stirring constantly. Remove from heat and cool. Fold in the egg whites, then pour into a buttered and sugared soufflé dish. Bake in a hot oven (400°) for 25 minutes. Serve with vanilla sauce. Serves 6.

## VANILLA SAUCE

| | |
|---|---|
| 1 cup milk | 1 teaspoon cornstarch |
| 6 tablespoons sugar | 1 teaspoon vanilla extract |
| 3 egg yolks | 2 tablespoons whipped cream |

Bring milk and sugar to a boil. Combine egg yolks and cornstarch. Add milk gradually, stirring briskly. Return to heat and bring to a boil, stirring constantly. Remove from heat. Add vanilla. Cool slightly. Add whipped cream. Makes about 2 cups.

## CHATEAUBRIAND EN PAPILLOTE: BRUSSELS

| | |
|---|---|
| 2 double filets of beef | 3 cups Bordelais sauce |

Broil filets under medium heat for 30 minutes or until medium rare. Cut each filet in half horizontally. Spread the bottom half of each filet with cooled Bordelais sauce, then sew the filets together. Place each filet on a piece of parchment paper brushed with oil. Bring the paper covers up over the filets and roll the edges to form an airtight seal. Put the filets in a shallow pan and roast them in a hot oven (450°) for 3 minutes or until the paper puffs out. Serve filets immediately in their paper bags. Rip the paper open and slice the filets. Serves 6.

## BORDELAIS SAUCE

| | |
|---|---|
| 3 cups dry red wine | ¼ cup butter |
| 1 tablespoon finely chopped shallots | 1 cup cubed beef marrow |
| 5 cups of veal stock | Salt |
| | Freshly ground black pepper |

Simmer shallots in wine until liquid is reduced to about one half. Add veal stock and simmer until sauce is reduced to about 2 cups. Season with salt and pepper. Add butter a little at a time. Remove from heat. Poach marrow cubes in water for 3 minutes to take off the fat and add to sauce. Makes about 3 cups. To make veal stock, combine veal bones, cut up tomatoes, carrots, onion, and celery and sprinkle with a little flour. Brown in a moderate oven (375°) for 1 hour. Put mixture in saucepan with enough liquid to cover—half water and half consommé. Salt and pepper to taste. Simmer for 5 hours. Strain before using.

## ALPINE SNOW HARE: THE FORUM

| | |
|---|---|
| 1 five-pound snow hare, cut in 24 pieces | 1 cup butter |
| 4 cups dry red wine | ½ cup flour |
| 2 cups vinegar | 1 pound pearl onions |
| 2 bay leaves | 1 pound mushrooms, sliced |
| 4 carrots, sliced | 3 ounces beef blood |
| 1 onion, diced | 3 ounces brandy |
| 1 celery stalk, diced | 1 teaspoon salt |
| | 1 tablespoon peppercorns |

Marinate the snow hare for 3 days in combined wine, vinegar, bay leaves, sliced carrot, diced onion, celery, salt and peppercorns. Remove the meat from marinade. Strain and save the marinade. Brown the meat in butter in a skillet until golden. Put the butter and meat into a deep saucepan. Add flour and cook for 1 minute or until the butter and flour mixture is thickened, stirring constantly. Add the marinade, bring to a boil, reduce heat, cover and simmer for 1 hour. Add the pearl onions, mushrooms and 3 carrots, and simmer for 20 minutes. Stir in blood and brandy. Serve immediately. Serves 6. Rabbit may be substituted for snow hare.

## QUENELLES DE BROCHET: LE PAVILLON

| | |
|---|---|
| 1 pound boned pike | Cayenne pepper |
| Ground nutmeg | Salt |
| 2 egg whites | Freshly ground black pepper |
| 3 cups heavy cream | Lobster sauce |

Pound boned pike, adding a dash of nutmeg, a few grains of cayenne, salt and black pepper. Add egg whites gradually. Rub through a fine sieve and place in a saucepan set on ice. Beat with a wooden spoon and gradually work in cream. To form quenelles, heap a tablespoon with mixture and round off the top with the inside of another tablespoon. Carefully scoop quenelle out of first spoon with a spoon which has been dipped in warm water. Invert spoon and slip quenelle into a buttered pan. Form all quenelles this way. Pour a little salted water in pan. Bring water to a boil and poach quenelles over low heat for 10 minutes. Serve with lobster sauce. Serves 6.

## LOBSTER SAUCE

| | |
|---|---|
| 1 two-pound live lobster | ½ cup heavy cream |
| 1 tablespoon butter | 2 tablespoons cream sauce |
| 1 shallot, chopped | 1 teaspoon salt |
| 1 cup dry sherry | Freshly ground black pepper |

Cut the live lobster in 6 or 8 pieces. Sauté cut lobster in butter for 3 or 4 minutes. Add shallot, ½ cup sherry, cream, salt and pepper. Cover tightly and cook for 20 minutes. Remove lobster and save it for another meal. Cook remaining liquid until it is reduced to one half. Add cream sauce and stir until thickened. Season with salt and pepper and add remaining ½ cup of sherry. Strain through a cheesecloth. Makes about 1 cup. This sauce is served with lobster, crab meat or any fish.

# ACKNOWLEDGMENTS

The staffs of many museums, libraries, universities, trade associations, agricultural experiment stations and government offices have helped LIFE gather material for this book. LIFE is grateful to them all. Our special thanks go to Elsa M. Harrington, home economist, who has checked all of the recipes in this book; to James A. Beard, author and food consultant, who has generously advised LIFE on many stories; and to Sam Aaron of Sherry Wine & Spirits Co., Inc. who has been an invaluable wine consultant. This book is also indebted to the following people for their help:

## CHEFS AND RESTAURATEURS IN EUROPE

KARL ARGAUER, *Kahlenberg*, Vienna, Austria
A. DELLA BOSCA, *Rule's*, London, England
PIERRE DESCREUX, *Tour d'Argent*, Paris, France
ALEXANDRE DUMAINE, *Hôtel de la Côte-d'Or*, Saulieu, France
STIG GREEK, *Stallmästaregården*, Stockholm, Sweden
MICHELANGELO MAGISTRINI, *Royal Danieli*, Venice, Italy
PAUL MERCIER, *Pyramide*, Vienne, France
LUDWIG NOACK, *Spatenhaus*, Munich, Germany
UMBERTO PLINI, *Passetto*, Rome, Italy
JOSEF STENZ, *Krone*, Assmannshausen-Rhine, Germany
RAYMOND THUILIER, *Baumanière*, Les Baux, France
ALFRED WALTERSPIEL, *Walterspiel*, Munich, Germany
VITTORIO ZURLA, *Pappagallo*, Bologna, Italy

### IN THE U.S.

ROY ALCIATORE, *Antoine's*, New Orleans, Louisiana
ATTILIO ALLORI, *The Milton Inn*, Cockeysville, Maryland
VICTOR J. BERGERON, *Trader Vic's*, San Francisco, California
SOU CHAN, *House of Chan*, New York City
RENE CHARDAIN, *Newfane Inn*, Newfane, Vermont
DAVE CHASEN, *Chasen's*, Los Angeles, California
ARGANTE CIABATTARI, *Pump Room*, Ambassador East Hotel, Chicago, Illinois
CHARLES DEDMAN, *Beaumont Inn*, Harrodsburg, Kentucky
EDISON DICK, *Jacques*, Chicago, Illinois
E. H. EICHLER, *The Milk Pail*, Dundee, Illinois
ORLANDO FIGINI, *La Rue*, Hollywood, California

ANTOINE GILLY, *La Crémaillère-à-la-Campagne*, Banksville, New York
ROLAND GOTTI, *Ernie's*, San Francisco, California
VICTOR GOTTI, *Ernie's*, San Francisco, California
MAX GUGGIARI, *Imperial House*, Chicago, Illinois
KENNETH HANSEN, *Scandia*, Hollywood, California
LUCIEN HEYRAUD, *Garden Court*, Sheraton-Palace Hotel, San Francisco, California
GEORGE K. JUE, *Lamps of China*, San Francisco, California
GENE LEONE, *Leone's*, New York City
ELLA BRENNAN MARTIN, *Brennan's*, New Orleans, Louisiana
RUTH MULLER, *Voisin*, New York City
INEZ PACINI, *Amelio's*, San Francisco, California
MARGUERITE PAGANI, *Brussels*, New York City
ALEX PERINO, *Perino's*, Los Angeles, California
BRUNO PETOLETTI, *La Rue*, Hollywood, California
PAUL PFOHL, *Club Boyar*, Chicago, Illinois
IVES PLONEIS, *"21,"* New York City
GINNY and HALVOR SMEDSRUD, *Bonanza Inn*, Genoa, Nevada
HENRI SOULE, *Le Pavillon*, New York City
CHARLES STEARNS, *The Bird & Bottle*, Garrison, New York
ALBERT STOCKLI, *The Forum of the Twelve Caesars*, New York City
DION VAN BIBBER, *Stage Coach Inn*, Salado, Texas
GERMAINE CAZENAVE WELLS, *Arnaud's*, New Orleans, Louisiana

## SPECIALISTS AND FOOD AUTHORITIES

CHARLOTTE ADAMS
FLORENCE BROBECK, *Cooking with Curry*
POPPY CANNON
CHARLES CODMAN
FERNANDE GARVIN
MAXWELL KRIENDLER
ALEXIS LICHINE
VIRGINIA PASLEY, *The Holiday Candy Book*
P. P. PIRONE
FRANK SCHOONMAKER
DHARAM JIT SINGH, *Classic Cooking from India*
RUDOLPH STANISH
ANDRE SURMAIN
PATRICIA WINTER

# PICTURE CREDITS

| | | | | | | |
|---|---|---|---|---|---|---|
| END PAPERS | ADOLPH E. BROTMAN | 117–119 | BEN ROSE | | *Floor plan by* JON KONIGSHOFER | |
| 5–7 | TOM YEE | 121–137 | *Illustrations by* ADOLPH E. BROTMAN | 208 | ARNOLD NEWMAN—courtesy WESTINGHOUSE ELECTRIC CORP., BETTER HOMES DEPARTMENT | |
| 9–11 | ELIOT ELISOFON | 141–143 | ELIOT ELISOFON | | | |
| 13–16 | EDGAR DE EVIA | 145–148 | TOM YEE | | | |
| 18–21 | ELIOT ELISOFON | 150–152 | BEN ROSE | | *Floor plan by* HELEN SCHIAVO | |
| 22–23 | EDGAR DE EVIA | 154–157 | ELIOT ELISOFON | 209 | ELIOT ELISOFON | |
| 25–27 | BEN ROSE | 159–163 | *Illustrations by* ADOLPH E. BROTMAN | 210–211 | LESLIE GILL | |
| 29–31 | TOM YEE | 167 | LESLIE GILL | 213–216 | ELIOT ELISOFON | |
| 33–41 | *Illustrations by* ADOLPH E. BROTMAN | 168–169 | *Illustrations by* RENY MARTIN | 218–219 | BEN ROSE | |
| 45–47 | MARY HAMMAN and CHARLES TUDOR | 171–173 | *Illustrations by* RUDOLF FREUND | 221–224 | *Illustrations by* ANTONIO PETRUCCELLI | |
| 49–51 | ELIOT ELISOFON | 175 | FRED LYON from RAPHO-GUILLUMETTE | | | |
| 53 | ELIOT ELISOFON, *background map* C. S. HAMMOND & CO. | 176–177 | J. R. EYERMAN | 226–227 | BEN ROSE except top right PAUL WING | |
| | | 178–179 | FRED LYON from RAPHO-GUILLUMETTE | | | |
| 55–57 | BEN ROSE | 181–184 | *Illustrations by* ADOLPH E. BROTMAN | 229–230 | *Illustrations by* ADOLPH E. BROTMAN | |
| 59–65 | TOM YEE | 187 | EDGAR DE EVIA | 235–247 | ELIOT ELISOFON | |
| 67–75 | *Illustrations by* ADOLPH E. BROTMAN | 189–191 | BEN ROSE | 249 | BEN ROSE | |
| 78–81 | HANS VAN NES | 192–195 | EDGAR DE EVIA | 250–255 | BRADLEY SMITH | |
| 83–86 | BEN ROSE | 197–199 | *Illustrations by* ADOLPH E. BROTMAN | 257–259 | J. R. EYERMAN | |
| 88–91 | TOM YEE | 203 | ELIOT ELISOFON | 260–261 | N. R. FARBMAN | |
| 93–96 | EDGAR DE EVIA | 204–205 | ARNOLD NEWMAN except bottom right courtesy WESTINGHOUSE ELECTRIC CORP., BETTER HOMES DEPARTMENT | 262–263 | LOOMIS DEAN, ELIOT ELISOFON | |
| 98–102 | BEN ROSE | | | 264 | ELIOT ELISOFON | |
| 104–105 | JON BRENNEIS | | | 265 | FRANK SCHERSCHEL | |
| 106–111 | BEN ROSE | | | 266–271 | ELIOT ELISOFON | |
| 113–115 | LESLIE GILL | 206–207 | FRED LYON from RAPHO-GUILLUMETTE | 273–280 | *Illustrations by* ADOLPH E. BROTMAN | |

# INDEX

## INDEX TO PERSONS AND PLACES

PRINTED AND BOUND BY R. R. DONNELLEY & SONS COMPANY,
CHICAGO, ILLINOIS AND CRAWFORDSVILLE, INDIANA

PAPER BY THE MEAD CORPORATION, DAYTON, OHIO

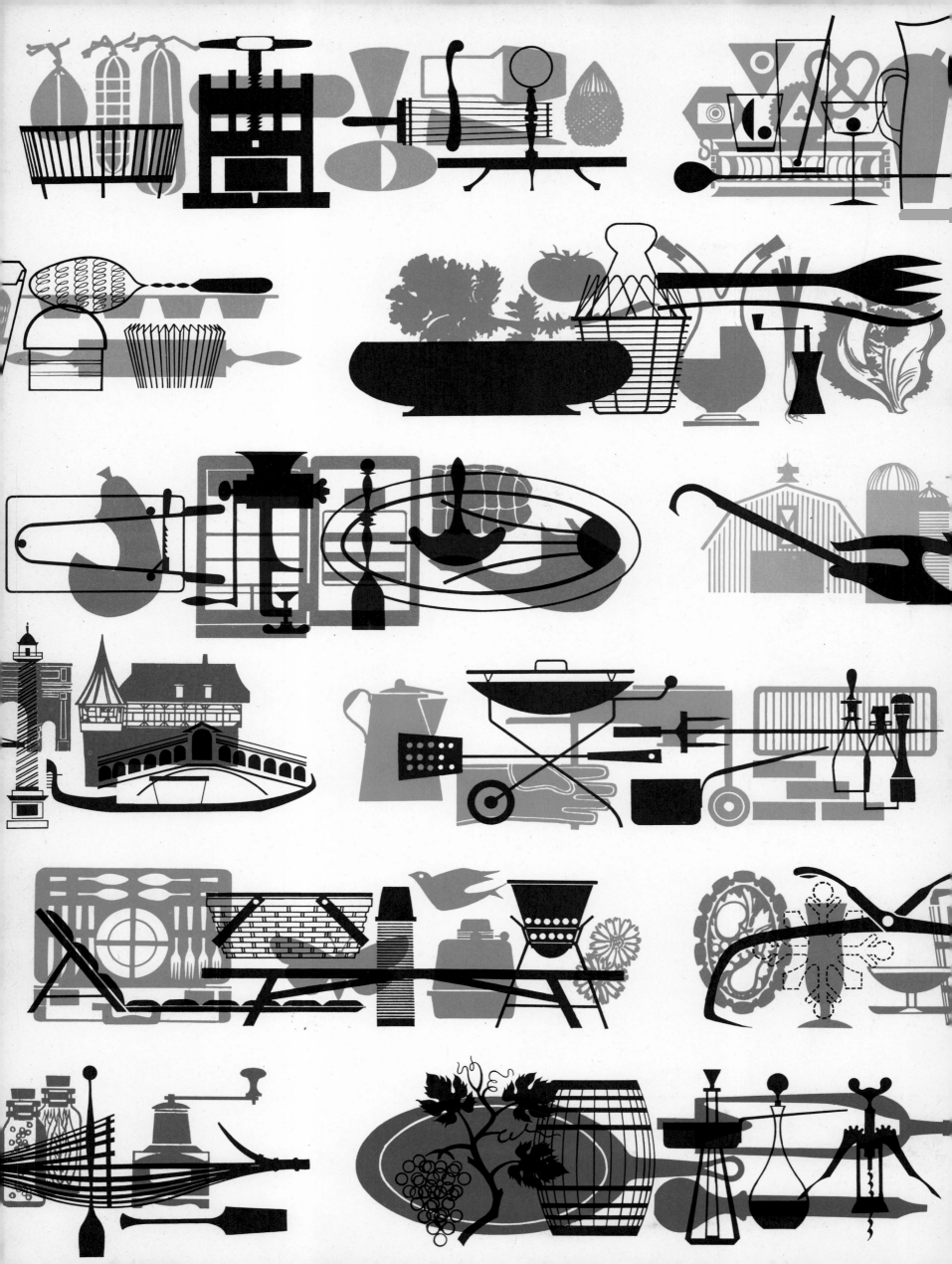